The Making of Samuel Beckett's *Molloy*

BECKETT
DIGITAL
MANUSCRIPT
PROJECT

VOLUME 04

The Making of Samuel Beckett's *Molloy*

ÉDOUARD MAGESSA O'REILLY
DIRK VAN HULLE
PIM VERHULST

UPA
University Press Antwerp

BLOOMSBURY

GPRC
Guaranteed
Peer Reviewed
Content
www.gprc.be

The GPRC label (Guaranteed Peer Review Content) was developed by the Flemish organization Boek.be and is assigned to publications which are in compliance with the academic standards required by the VABB (Vlaams Academisch Bibliografisch Bestand).

The research leading to these results has received funding from the European Research Council under the European Union's Seventh Framework Programme (FP7/2007–2013) / ERC grant agreement n° 313609.

This publication is supported by the Belgian University Foundation.
Uitgegeven met de steun van de Universitaire Stichting van België.

Book design: Stéphane de Schrevel

—

Molloy © Samuel Beckett 1951, 1955 and the Estate of Samuel Beckett

—

The making of Samuel Beckett's *Molloy*
© 2017 Édouard Magessa O'Reilly, Dirk Van Hulle, Pim Verhulst,
Uitgeverij UPA University Press Antwerp
UPA is an imprint of ASP nv
(Academic and Scientific Publishers nv)
Keizerslaan 34 · B-1000 Brussels
T +32 (0)2 289 26 50 · F +32 (0)2 289 26 59
info@aspeditions.be · www.upa-editions.be

—

ISBN of the Bloomsbury edition: 978 1 4725 3256 5
ISBN of the UPA edition: 978 90 5718 536 6
NUR 632
Legal deposit D/2017/11.161/039

Distribution for the Benelux:
ASP/University Press Antwerp
34 Keizerslaan, B-1000 Brussels
www.aspeditions.be
Distribution for the rest of the world:
Bloomsbury
50 Bedford Square, London, WC1B 3DP
www.bloomsbury.com

'c'est un journal intime, ça va bientôt s'arrêter'
(Samuel Beckett, *Molloy*, 1951, 93)

'it's only a diary, it'll soon be over'
(Samuel Beckett, *Molloy*, 2009, 61)

'Cette fois-ci, puis encore une autre je pense'
(Samuel Beckett, manuscript of *Molloy*, FN1, 02r)

'This time, then once more I think, then perhaps a last time'
(Samuel Beckett, typescript of *Molloy*, ET1, 02r)

BECKETT DIGITAL MANUSCRIPT PROJECT

Advisory board
  Charles Krance (series initiator)
  Edward Beckett (honorary member)
  Chris Ackerley
  André Derval
  Daniel Ferrer
  Stan Gontarski
  James Knowlson
  Geert Lernout
  Barry McGovern
  Bernard Meehan
  Rich Oram
  John Pilling
  Jean-Michel Rabaté
  Peter Shillingsburg
  Richard Workman

Editorial board
  Mark Byron
  Vincent Neyt (technical realization)
  Mark Nixon (co-director)
  Magessa O'Reilly
  Dirk Van Hulle (co-director)
  Pim Verhulst
  Shane Weller

Table of Contents

The Beckett Digital Manuscript Project

Series Preface

This volume is part of the Beckett Digital Manuscript Project, a collaboration between the Centre for Manuscript Genetics (University of Antwerp), the Beckett International Foundation (University of Reading) and the Harry Ransom Humanities Research Center (University of Texas at Austin). The development of this project started from two initiatives: (1) the 'inhouse' genetic edition of four works by Samuel Beckett (a cooperation between the Universities of Antwerp and Reading), and (2) the series of Variorum Editions of Samuel Beckett's Bilingual Works, initiated in 1986 by Charles Krance, with the permission and support of Samuel Beckett. With the kind permission of the Estate of Samuel Beckett, these initiatives were developed into the Beckett Digital Manuscript Project, which combines genetic criticism with electronic scholarly editing, applied to the study of Beckett's manuscripts.

The Beckett Digital Manuscript Project consists of two parts:

a   A digital archive of Samuel Beckett's manuscripts (www.beckettarchive.org), organized into 26 research modules. Each of these modules comprises digital facsimiles and transcriptions of all the extant manuscripts pertaining to an individual text, or in the case of shorter texts, a group of texts.
b   A series of 26 volumes, analysing the genesis of the texts contained in the corresponding modules.

The Beckett Digital Manuscript Project aims to contribute to the study of Beckett's works in various ways: by enabling readers to discover new documents and see how the dispersed manuscripts of different holding libraries interrelate within the context of a work's genesis in its entirety; by increasing the accessibility of the manuscripts with searchable transcriptions in an updatable digital archive; and by highlighting the interpretive relevance of intertextual references that can be found in the manuscripts. The Project may also enhance the preservation of the physical documents as users will be able to work with digital facsimiles.

The purpose of the Beckett Digital Manuscript Project is to reunite the manuscripts of Samuel Beckett's works in a digital way, and to facilitate genetic research: the project brings together digital facsimiles of documents that are now preserved in different holding libraries, and adds transcriptions of Beckett's manuscripts, tools for bilingual and genetic version comparison, a search engine, and an analysis of the textual genesis of his works, published in print with a selection of facsimile images, as in the present volume.

Due to an agreement with the Estate of Samuel Beckett and the publishers of Beckett's work, the digital editions only contain draft versions leading up to the publication of the text (the so-called 'avant-texte'), including page proofs. It therefore excludes epigenetic material such as later annotated editions or theatrical notebooks.

Dirk Van Hulle
Mark Nixon

Acknowledgements

First of all, we wish to express our gratitude to Edward Beckett for his unremitting support of the Beckett Digital Manuscript Project.

We also owe a great debt of gratitude to the holding libraries preserving Beckett's drafts, especially Stephen Enniss, Elizabeth L. Garver, Richard Workman and Rich Oram at the Harry Ransom Humanities Research Center, The University of Texas at Austin; the University of Reading's Beckett International Foundation; André Derval (IMEC); Joel Minor and Sarah Schnuriger (Washington University, St Louis); Rick Stapleton and Bridget Whittle (Mills Memorial Library, McMaster University, Hamilton, Ontario); Nicole C. Dittrich and Lucy D. Mulroney (Special Collections Research Center of Syracuse University Library); Amy McCrory, Lisa Iacobellis and Geoffrey D. Smith (Rare Books and Manuscripts Library, Ohio State University); Joel Silver, Breon Mitchell, Zachary Downey and Isabel Planton (Lilly Library, Indiana University); Adrienne Sharpe (Beinecke Rare Book and Manuscript Library); Maria Isabel Molestina and John Vincler (Morgan Library and Museum); Brianna Cregle and AnnaLee Pauls (Rare Books and Special Collections, Princeton University); Elizabeth Harford, Frances Clarke and Aoife Morrissey (Manuscripts Department, National Library of Ireland); Jane Maxwell (Manuscripts and Archives Research Library, Trinity College Dublin); Samantha Blake and Kate O'Brien (BBC Written Archives, Caversham); and Ian Moore (Sound & Vision Reference Team, British Library) for their help with the location and bibliographic description of the documents. To the editorial board of *Samuel Beckett Today/Aujourd'hui* we are grateful for permission to include (in chapter 2.2) a revised version of a section from Dirk Van Hulle's article 'Cognition Enactment: Beckett's *Molloy* Manuscripts and the Reader's Role in Genetic Criticism', *Samuel Beckett Today/Aujourd'hui* 29.1 (2017).

We would also like to thank Vincent Neyt, Wout Dillen, Sarah Fierens, Miche Lemmens, Ellen Vanderstraeten, Nisha Haldar, Eugenie Draelants and Fien Leysen for all their invaluable help with the encoding, proofreading, dating and collation of the textual versions; and especially James Knowlson, John Pilling, Lois More Overbeck, Martha Dow Fehsenfeld, Shane Weller, Mark Nixon, Matthew Feldman, David Tucker, John de St Jorre and Patrick Kearney for their valuable feedback and help with the research.

List of Abbreviations

Holding libraries and archives

BBCWAC — British Broadcasting Corporation Written Archives, Caversham, Reading

BRML — Beinecke Rare Books and Manuscript Library

HRC — Harry Ransom Humanities Research Center, Austin, Texas

IMEC — Institut Mémoires de l'édition contemporaine, Caen, France

IU — The Lilly Library, Indiana University, Bloomington

MU — William Ready Research Collections, McMaster University, Ontario

OSU — Rare Books and Manuscript Library, Ohio State University

SU — Special Collections Research Center, Syracuse University Libraries

TCD — Manuscripts and Archives Research Library, Trinity College Dublin

UoR — Beckett International Foundation, University of Reading

WU — Department of Special Collections, Washington University, Saint Louis

Manuscripts relating to *Molloy*

EM — English autograph manuscript of *Molloy*, fragment in 'Tara MacGowran' notebook, Ohio State University, Rare Books and Manuscripts Library (MS-OSU-RARE-115; see chapter 1.1.2).

EN — English autograph notes on front and back covers of notebook MS 4662, Manuscripts and Archives Research Library, Trinity College Dublin (MS-TCD-4662; see chapter 1.1.2).

ET1 — English partial typescript of *Molloy* (Part I), Olin Library, Washington University, St. Louis, Samuel Beckett papers, Box 3, Folder 49 (MS-WU-MSS008-3-49; see chapter 1.2.2).

ET2 — English complete typescript of *Molloy* (Parts I & II), Olin Library, Washington University, St. Louis, Samuel Beckett papers, Box 3, Folder 50 (MS-WU-MSS008-3-50-1 and MS-WU-MSS008-3-50-2; see chapter 1.2.2).

FN1   French autograph manuscript of *Molloy*, first notebook, Harry Ransom Humanities Research Center, Austin, Texas, Samuel Beckett collection, Box 4, Folder 5 (MS-HRC-SB-4-5; see chapter 1.1.1).

FN2   French autograph manuscript of *Molloy*, second notebook, Harry Ransom Humanities Research Center, Austin, Texas, Samuel Beckett collection, Box 4, Folder 6 (MS-HRC-SB-4-6; see chapter 1.1.1).

FN3   French autograph manuscript of *Molloy*, third notebook, Harry Ransom Humanities Research Center, Austin, Texas, Samuel Beckett collection, Box 4, Folder 7 (MS-HRC-SB-4-7; see chapter 1.1.1).

FN4   French autograph manuscript of *Molloy*, fourth notebook, Harry Ransom Humanities Research Center, Austin, Texas, Samuel Beckett collection, Box 5, Folder 1 (MS-HRC-SB-5-1; see chapter 1.1.1).

FT   French partial typescript (carbon copy) of *Molloy*, Harry Ransom Humanities Research Center, Austin, Texas, Samuel Beckett papers, Carlton Lake Collection, Box 17, Folder 6 (MS-HRC-SB-17-6; see chapter 1.2.1).

NWWT1   English typescript of an extract from *Molloy* first selected but not used by the editors of *New World Writing*, Beinecke Rare Book and Manuscript Library, New Haven, Connecticut, New World Writing Records (YCAL MSS 388), Box 2, Folder 38 (MS-BRML-NWWR-2-38; see chapter 1.3.1).

NWWT2   English typescript of the extract from *Molloy* published in *New World Writing*, Vol. 5 ([April] 1954), Beinecke Rare Book and Manuscript Library, New Haven, Connecticut, New World Writing Records (YCAL MSS 388), Box 22, Folder 546 (MS-BRML-NWWR-22-546; see chapter 1.3.1).

NWWG   English galleys of the extract from *Molloy* published in *New World Writing*, Vol. 5 ([April] 1954), Beinecke Rare Book and Manuscript Library, New Haven, Connecticut, New World Writing Records (YCAL MSS 388), Box 35, Folder 1136 (MS-BRML-NWWR-35-1136; see chapter 1.3.1).

Sp1	English partial typescript specimen of *Molloy*, Olin Library, Washington University, St Louis, Samuel Beckett papers, Box 3, Folder 48 (MS-WU-MSSS008-3-48; see chapter 1.2.2).
Sp2	English partial typescript specimen of *Molloy*, Olin Library, Washington University, St Louis, Samuel Beckett papers, Box 3, Folder 51 (MS-WU-MSSS008-3-51-1; see chapter 1.2.2).
Sp3	English partial typescript specimen (carbon copy) of *Molloy*, Olin Library, Washington University, St Louis, Samuel Beckett papers, Box 3, Folder 51 (MS-WU-MSSS008-3-51-2; see chapter 1.2.2).
TIU	English partial typescript specimens of *Molloy*, related to unpublished *Olympia Reader* by John Calder, Lilly Library, Indiana University, Calder and Boyars papers, LMC 2196, Box 61, Folder 5 (see chapter 1.2.2)

Pre-book publications

MER	Extract from *Molloy*, published under the title 'Extract from Molloy', *Merlin*, Vol. 2, No. 2 (Autumn 1953), 89-103.
NWW	Extract from *Molloy*, published under the title 'Molloy', *New World Writing*, No. 5 (Spring [April] 1954), 316-23.
PR	Extract from *Molloy*, published under the title 'Extract from Molloy', *Paris Review*, No. 5 (Spring [March] 1954), 124-35.
TRA	Extract from *Molloy*, published as 'I' under the title 'Two Fragments', *Transition Fifty*, No. 6 (Winter [October] 1950), 103-5.

References to editions of *Molloy*

1951	*Molloy*. Roman. Paris: Les Éditions de Minuit. 272 pp.
1953	*Molloy*. Roman. Paris: Les Éditions de Minuit. 272 pp.
1955a	*Molloy*. A novel translated from the French by Patrick Bowles in collaboration with the Author. Paris: Olympia Press. 241 pp.
1955b	*Molloy*. A novel translated from the French by Patrick Bowles in collaboration with the Author. New York: Grove Press. 241 pp.
1959a	*Molloy, Malone Dies, The Unnamable: A Trilogy*. No. 71 in the Traveller's Companion series. Paris: Olympia Press. 577 pp.

1959b	*Molloy, Malone Dies, and The Unnamable: Three Novels by Samuel Beckett.* New York: Grove Press. 577 pp.
1959 [1960]	*Molloy / Malone Dies / The Unnamable.* London: John Calder. 418 pp.
1963	*Molloy / L'Expulsé.* No. 81-82 in Collection 10/18. Paris: Union générale d'éditions. 311 pp.
1965	*Three Novels by Samuel Beckett: Molloy / Malone Dies / The Unnamable.* No. 78 in the Evergreen Black Cat series. New York: Grove Press. 414 pp.
1966a	*Molloy / Malone Dies / The Unnamable.* London: Calder and Boyars. 418 pp.
1966b	*Molloy.* Translated from the French by Samuel Beckett and Patrick Bowles. No. 13 in the Jupiter Books series. London: Calder and Boyars. 189 pp.
1971	*Molloy.* Paris: Les Éditions de Minuit. 293 pp.
1982	*Molloy.* No. 7 in Collection 'Double'. Paris: Les Éditions de Minuit. 274 pp.

In the digital edition of the Beckett Digital Manuscript Project, the sentences of all the versions of *Molloy* are numbered (see 'Compare Sentences' in the top banner above the transcription of every page). This numbering system serves as a tool to make the electronic texts citable. The base text that was used for the numbering is the Éditions de Minuit first edition (1951).

Other works by Beckett

BDL	*Beckett Digital Library: a digital genetic edition*, ed. by Dirk Van Hulle, Mark Nixon, Vincent Neyt and Veronica Bălă (Brussels: University Press Antwerp, 2016). The Beckett Digital Manuscript Project, http://www.beckettarchive.org.
BDMP1	*Samuel Beckett's Stirrings Still / Soubresauts and Comment dire / what is the word: a digital genetic edition*, ed. by Dirk Van Hulle and Vincent Neyt (Brussels: University Press Antwerp, 2011). The Beckett Digital Manuscript Project; module 1, http://www.beckettarchive.org.

BDMP2   *Samuel Beckett's L'Innommable | The Unnamable: a digital genetic edition*, ed. by Dirk Van Hulle, Shane Weller and Vincent Neyt (Brussels: University Press Antwerp, 2013). The Beckett Digital Manuscript Project; module 2, http://www.beckettarchive.org.

BDMP3   *Samuel Beckett's Krapp's Last Tape | La Dernière Bande: a digital genetic edition*, ed. by Dirk Van Hulle and Vincent Neyt (Brussels: University Press Antwerp, 2015). The Beckett Digital Manuscript Project; module 3, http://www.beckettarchive.org.

CIWS   *Company | Ill Seen Ill Said | Worstward Ho | Stirrings Still*, ed. by Dirk Van Hulle (London: Faber and Faber, 2009).

CP   *The Collected Poems of Samuel Beckett*, ed. by Seán Lawlor and John Pilling (London: Faber and Faber, 2012).

D   *Dream of Fair to Middling Women*, ed. by Eoin O'Brien and Edith Fournier (Dublin: Black Cat Press, 1992).

Dis   *Disjecta: Miscellaneous Writings and a Dramatic Fragment*, ed. by Ruby Cohn (New York: Grove Press, 1984).

DN   *Beckett's 'Dream' Notebook*, ed. by John Pilling (Reading: Beckett International Foundation, 1999).

E   *Endgame*, preface by Rónán McDonald (London: Faber and Faber, 2009).

ECEF   *The Expelled | The Calmative | The End | First Love*, ed. by Christopher Ricks (London: Faber and Faber, 2009)

KLT   *Krapp's Last Tape and Other Shorter Plays*, preface by S. E. Gontarski (London: Faber and Faber, 2009).

LSB I   *The Letters of Samuel Beckett, vol. I, 1929–1940*, ed. by Martha Dow Fehsenfeld and Lois More Overbeck (Cambridge: Cambridge University Press, 2009).

LSB II   *The Letters of Samuel Beckett, vol. II, 1941–1956*, ed. by George Craig, Martha Dow Fehsenfeld, Dan Gunn and Lois More Overbeck (Cambridge: Cambridge University Press, 2011).

LSB III   *The Letters of Samuel Beckett, vol. III, 1957–1965*, ed. by George Craig, Martha Dow Fehsenfeld, Dan Gunn and Lois More Overbeck (Cambridge: Cambridge University Press, 2014).

LSB IV   *The Letters of Samuel Beckett, vol. IV, 1966–1989*, ed. by George Craig, Martha Dow Fehsenfeld Dan Gunn and Lois More Overbeck (Cambridge: Cambridge University Press, 2016).

M&C	*Mercier and Camier*, ed. by Seán Kennedy (London: Faber and Faber, 2010).
MD	*Malone Dies*, ed. by Peter Boxall (London: Faber and Faber, 2010).
Mo	*Molloy*, ed. by Shane Weller (London: Faber and Faber, 2009).
MPTK	*More Pricks than Kicks*, ed. by Cassandra Nelson (London: Faber and Faber, 2010).
Mu	*Murphy*, ed. by J. C. C. Mays (London: Faber and Faber, 2009).
PTD	*Proust and Three Dialogues with Georges Duthuit* (London: John Calder, 1965).
TFN	*Texts for Nothing and Other Shorter Prose 1950–1976*, ed. by Mark Nixon (London: Faber and Faber, 2010).
TN3	*Krapp's Last Tape: The Theatrical Notebooks of Samuel Beckett 3*, ed. by James Knowlson (London: Faber and Faber, 1992).
Un	*The Unnamable*, ed. by Steven Connor (London: Faber and Faber, 2010).
W	*Watt*, ed. by C. J. Ackerley (London: Faber and Faber, 2009).
WFG	*Waiting for Godot*, preface by Mary Bryden (London: Faber and Faber, 2010)

Note on the Transcriptions

The transcription method applied in this study attempts to represent Beckett's drafts with as few diacritical signs as possible, crossing out deletions and using superscript for additions. No special symbol is used for facing-leaf additions on the verso pages of notebooks, but they are identified as such in the discussion. In the case of open variants, the first alternative is given in subscript, the second in superscript. Uncertain readings are in grey. Bold typeface is used to highlight words in quotations from manuscripts.[1]

Since Beckett does not use the conventions of French punctuation in his typescripts, we do not follow them for passages cited from his manuscripts in that language, only for citations taken from printed sources in French, with the exception of double spaces after full stops and angled quotation marks (« guillemets »), which have been normalized.

[1]   For more detailed information, see the 'Editorial Principles and Practice' guide under 'Documentation' on www.beckettarchive.org.

List of Illustrations

17 After the question 'D'où tirait donc Ballyba ses richesses?' (l. 2-3), Moran starts explaining the economy of Ballyba, based on the excrements of its citizens (FN3, 66r).

18 'du Baume Bengué', deleted on page FN3, 86r.

19 After Moran's famous closing line that it was not raining, despite his earlier claim, Beckett wrote the date 'FIN 1/11/47' (1 November 1947) in large thiumphant capitals, using blue pencil (FN4, 74r).

20 Beckett added the first paragraph of *Molloy* last, on '1.11.47' (1 November 1947), facing the paragraph he had written first in the chronology of the novel, six months earlier (FN1, 01v).

21 The original opening paragraph in the first notebook of *Molloy*, begun on '2.5.47' (2 May 1947) in 'Foxrock' under the heading 'En désespoir de cause' (FN1, 02r).

22 Last page of the English holograph fragment in the 'Tara MacGowran' notebook, with several revisions and marginal doodles (EM, 85v).

23 Draft of a letter concerning the *Molloy* fragment in the 'Tara MacGowran' notebook to an unspecified addressee, probably Alexander Trocchi (EM, 86r).

24 Beckett replaces the quotation from Virgil's *Eclogues* ('quid sit Amor') with a literal translation of the phrase, 'what love was' (ET2, 67r, l. 11).

25 Cappiello's design for the packaging of 'le thermogène' with the demon, as mentioned by Moran.

Introduction: Beckett's Autography

Samuel Beckett wrote *Molloy* near the beginning of an extremely productive period (1946–1950) that saw the creation of his most famous work, *En attendant Godot*, and of the trilogy comprising of *Molloy*, *Malone meurt* and *L'Innommable*, among other works, all written directly in French. It is a period of two turnings, one from his mother tongue to writing in a new language, the other from early work that left him unsatisfied to the prolonged exploration of impoverishment, impotence and ignorance (Knowlson 1997, 351-3).

Though thematically Beckettian, the works of this period are not characterised by the concise, fragmentary form or the sparse, geometric decor that is usually associated with the author. In 'Texte pour rien II', Beckett seemingly refers to the period of *Molloy*'s production as the 'temps de la faconde' (Beckett 1958, 124). Rare in French, *faconde* is usually rendered in English as *glibness* or *wordiness*; Beckett translates his phrase as 'when life was babble' (*TFN* 82). The phrase, in either language, is a thinly veiled denigration of what, to readers, are sentences of flowing symmetry that sing their discomforting poetry with harmony and grace.

Molloy is, as H. Porter Abbott incisively remarked, two novels masquerading as one (Abbott 1973, 99). The novel's two parts, its two travellers, their two quests complement and mirror each other teasingly in a scintillating example of what Marjorie Perloff has called the state of indeterminacy (Perloff 1981). A syzygy of characters, different yet one and the same. This two-part structure is already present in the French manuscript, but to what extent this implies that Beckett had this structure in mind when he started writing is a matter that will be discussed in the present volume of the BDMP.

The genetic analysis of *Molloy* is necessarily based on the material that is still extant. The structure of this book therefore follows the Swiss textual scholar Hans Zeller's basic distinction between '*Befund*' and '*Deutung*' (Zeller 1995), record and interpretation: a description of the available documents (manuscripts, notes, typescripts, pre-book publications, editions) and the analysis of the genesis. The aim of interpreting the record is to understand Beckett's work as both a product and a process. In discussing the genesis of the French *Molloy*, the critical vantage point is the notion of the 'autograph' as coined by H. Porter Abbott. In *Beckett Writing Beckett: The Author in the Autograph*, Abbott encourages his readers to see Beckett's writing in terms of 'continuing incompletion' (Abbott 1996, 20). In the tradition of Augustine's *Confessions* and Wordsworth's *Prelude*, 'replacing storytelling with the radically discontinuous mode of the "spot of time"' (7), Beckett developed the notion of an 'art without end' (20). Although Abbott convincingly argues that Beckett takes the Joycean 'work in progress' to another level, turning his entire œuvre into a 'work forever in progress', a work that 'must go on' (20), Abbott does not study Beckett's autograph manuscripts. In this book, we argue that, in order to further examine Beckett's autography in detail, it may be useful to take his autograph manuscripts into account. This implies the question of the relation between 'autography', the 'autograph' and the 'autographic'.

The notion of autographic art was coined by Nelson Goodman in the chapter 'The Unfakable' in *Languages of Art* (1968): 'Let us speak of a work of art as *autographic* if and only if the distinction between original and forgery of it is significant; or better, if and only if even the most exact duplication of it does not thereby count as genuine. [...] Thus painting is autographic, music nonautographic, or *allographic*' (113). Like music, literature is not autographic.

But if there is only one autograph manuscript of a work of literature, the uniqueness of that document does feature some of the characteristics of autographic art. Thus the French manuscript of *Molloy* can be regarded as 'the unfakable' in Goodman's terms. Unlike its other versions (the Minuit editions, the pre-book publications, the translations by Beckett himself), this particular document shows the traces of the physical writing of the work (*Molloy*) in its entirety, the initial process of putting into words. In that sense it is unique. It is different from all the other versions because it comes much closer to what Abbott calls 'diary fiction'. As Abbott notes, one of the conventions of diary fiction is the situation of the diarist being given paper and asked to fill it while in jail (as in Maxim Gorky's 'Karamora' or Max Frisch's *I'm Not Stiller*) or taking a rest-cure (as in John Updike's *A Month of Sundays*). In Beckett's *Molloy*, the protagonist is given paper and is supposed to fill it, but the convention of the setting is absent, which emphasizes 'the gratuitousness of the text and the mysterious compulsion to write that the author shares with his creature' (Abbott 1984, 20n10). Abbott also points out that *Molloy* is 'technically not diary fiction' (20n10), but if one takes a look at the autograph manuscript, there seems to be more that the author shares with his creature than in the published version. By including the dates and places of the writing sessions, the layers of cancellations and insertions, frequent doodling and changing script, Beckett creates a unique document that approaches the *immediacy effect* of the diary and diary fiction. Of the three main functions of diary fiction as defined by Abbott – the mimetic functions (the illusion of the real), the thematic functions (isolation and self-reflection), and the temporal functions (immediacy, suspense and timelessness) – the manuscript emphasizes the immediacy of the temporal functions: it makes its readers aware of what Gérard Genette has called 'narration intercalée' (Genette 1972, 229), the division of the protagonist into both narrator and narrated, and the division of the narration into two events, the event recorded and the event of recording.

Since 'autography' is 'self-writing', it encompasses the notion of the 'self' without taking it for granted. The 'self' is not a pregiven. It is always in the process of being written. In that sense, we hope to show that a genetic analysis of this writing process can contribute to the study of *Molloy* by adding an autographic dimension.

In chapter 1, we present the physical record. The 'genetic dossier' for *Molloy* is incomplete. We have the autograph French manuscript in four notebooks but only a partial typescript in French, relating to a passage that was cut from a lost typescript, then nothing else until the published novel. The production of the English-language *Molloy* is somewhat better represented in quantity, though nearly all surviving versions are late drafts, lightly revised. There is no complete English-language manuscript because Patrick Bowles, who translated *Molloy* 'in collaboration with the author', lost nearly all the early versions of their work (see chapter 1.2.2). We have an autograph manuscript of only a short portion of the text, partial and complete typescripts, and pre-publication excerpts. In addition, chapter 1 provides detailed information about the publication history of *Molloy* and a broadcast of sections from the novel on the BBC Third Programme.

In spite of the imperfections in the record, the French manuscript is wonderfully rich. The four notebooks, held at the Harry Ransom Center in Austin (Texas), show numerous dates. Beckett dated his writing sessions much more systematically than he did later on, if one compares this document with, for example, the French manuscript of *L'Innommable* (see *BDMP2*). As a result, it is possible – to some extent – to see by how many words the manuscript grew on a particular day. We have tried to map this quantitative development. Beckett himself counted his words (see for instance FN2, 72v, 101v and 124v). The dating is systematic[2] enough to suggest Beckett's resolve to 'produce' a quota of 'words' per day, and there is a logic to the mechanics of creativity as part of 'the obligation to express'. We try to capture these mechanics of creativity. The physical description revealing the circumstances of the writing and the pace of the manuscript's material development is the focus in section 1.1.1. It is an attempt to present the dynamics of the writing process from the perspective of the *'Befund'*, the material as we found it, before moving on to the *'Deutung'*, the interpretation of the French manuscript. Readers can either start at the beginning or jump ahead and follow the cross references leading back to chapter 1, if they so desire.

The autographic dimension, then, is the main subject in chapter 2, structured according to the chronology of the writing process, following the dates and paragraph breaks as indicated in the manuscript. This 'autographic' *Molloy* comes close to what Molloy imagines his readers will think of it: 'c'est un journal intime, ça va bientôt s'arrêter' (1951, 93) – 'Oh it's only a diary, it'll soon be over' (1955, 83; *Mo* 61). The intimacy of the private atmosphere to which this autographic 'journal intime' belongs is contrasted with the first version of the novel after the 'bon à tirer' moment, the moment Beckett decided the text was ready to lead a public life (the 1951 Minuit edition). Step by step, chapter 2 retraces the journey of the writing process, which almost coincides with the narrative sequence. It delineates the text's semantic development, its intra- and intertextual echoes and allusions, its text-generating word play and permutations, and measures the distance that separates it from the published novel.

Finally, chapter 3 retraces the movement from *'Befund'* to *'Deutung'* in the translation of *Molloy*. Based on the documentation described in chapter 1, section 3.1 explores the complicated circumstances of Beckett's collaboration with Patrick Bowles while sections 3.2 and 3.3 study the drafts of the translation, including the pre-book publications in magazines, and the transition from a monolingual to a bilingual work. Unlike for the French original, this part of the genetic analysis is limited by the fact that we generally have late versions for the English text, recording mostly minor and local revisions. However, the notion of autography also extends to the act of

---

2   Of course, we cannot exclude the possibility that he sometimes forgot to date a new writing session.

(self-)translation, which Beckett described to his 'co-author' Patrick Bowles as an attempt to '*write* the book again in another language – that is to say, *write* a new book' (qtd. in Bowles 1994, 27; emphasis added). As such, the act of writing and the act of (self-)translation or re-writing are both part of a larger and bilingual autographic project, in which the public 'product' and the private 'process' intersect in fascinating ways.

1 Documents[3]

3   The documents discussed in this chapter and included in the digital edition of the manuscripts of *Molloy* (BDMP module 4) constitute the genetic dossier as far as it is publicly available to the best of our knowledge. If documents that are now missing (such as the complete typescript and proofs) eventually do surface, they will be incorporated into the online digital edition.

1.1 Autograph Manuscripts

1.1.1 French

French notebooks (FN1, FN2, FN3, FN4)

The autograph French-language manuscript of *Molloy* is held at the Harry Ransom Humanities Research Center of the University of Texas at Austin. It is written in four successive notebooks, referred to hereafter as FN1 through FN4. Carlton Lake describes them as follows:

> This, the original manuscript, was written in four notebooks, three of them cloth-backed, one spiral-bound. With some corrections and additions and occasional doodles and word counts, but giving evidence of having been written rapidly and with fewer hesitations and *repentirs* than *Watt*, for example. Marked at periodic intervals with place and date of composition, from Foxrock, Paris and (mostly) Menton, frequently on a day-to-day basis. The opening passage of *Molloy* was added at the beginning after the rest had been completed.
>
> The second notebook contains diagrams and calculations concerning the celebrated passage about Molloy's manipulation of the sixteen sucking stones from one pocket to another. The last page has biographical notes in Beckett's hand. The previous two pages have diagrams and schemes for crossword puzzles in an unidentified hand. (Lake 1984, 53-4)

All four notebooks are identified by the title 'MOLLOY' and the corresponding roman numeral centered below it (see Fig. 1). They are without brand name or manufacturer's mark other than the patent marking on the back cover of the spiral-bound notebook. Despite the different binding, FN2 and FN3 are of similar dimensions and their covers bear the same pattern in different colours. Both are graph paper notebooks. The cover of FN1 is a heavier paperboard and the title has been carved into it by the pen, leaving ink in the furrows.

Fig. 1: The four notebooks of the French-language autograph manuscript (FN1, FN2, FN3, FN4).

The manuscript appears to be meticulously dated, showing fifty-eight writing sessions, but one cannot exclude the possibility that Beckett did not always date each new writing session. The composition of *Molloy* in French spans six months in 1947 – from the beginning of May to the beginning of November. During this time, Beckett was variously with his mother in Dublin, at home in Paris and at an ill-furnished cottage on the Mediterranean. It was a time of difficult circumstances and slender means as Beckett dealt with his mother's illness, his own ailments and his lack of revenue.

The body of the text is written on the recto side of the folios and facing versos are used for insertions, paralipomena, miscellaneous jottings and occasional doodles.[4] Most datings are on facing versos, apparently at the level on the page that corresponds to the point where the text on the rectos was interrupted and resumed.[5]

4   In textual scholarship, the word 'paralipomenon', from the Greek 'what is left out', denotes jottings, schemes, marginalia, lists or notes that contributed to the work but do not strictly speaking belong to any of its versions. See for instance the definition of 'paralipomenon' by Bodo Plachta in the Lexicon of Scholarly Editing (http://uahost.uantwerpen.be/lse/).

5   There are a few exceptions. For instance, the first dating is on the recto page above the text (FN1, 02r), and another dating is in fact placed at the point of interruption in the main text (FN1, 14r).

First French notebook (FN1)

Survey of Beckett's recorded progress through the first notebook of *Molloy*, 2 May-22 July 1947 (undated days are darkened):

Day	Date	Notebook pages	Approximate word count
	FOXROCK		
Friday	2 May 1947	02r-07r	1300
	66 DAYS		
	PARIS		
Tuesday	8 July	08r-14r	900
Wednesday	9 July	14r-23r	1400
	10 July		
Friday	11 July	23r-32r	1350
Saturday	12 July	32r-41r	1350
	13 July		
Monday	14 July	41r-47r	900
Tuesday	15 July	48r-53r	800
	16 July		
Thursday	17 July	53r-60r	1000
Friday	[18 July]	60r-62r	400
Saturday	19 July	63r-66r	500
Sunday	20 July	66r-71r	800
Monday	21 July	71r-74r	450
Tuesday	22 July	74r-75r	200

Deirdre Bair pithily wrote that Molloy's monologue (Part I of the novel) is organised into two paragraphs, 'the first of five hundred words, the second of about forty thousand' (Bair 1978, 368). The manuscript shows that the novel's first paragraph was composed last of all. The earliest date in the notebook is Friday 2 May 1947 (FN1, 02r), when Beckett was visiting his mother in Foxrock (Dublin). He had been planning to embark on *Molloy* for at least several days, writing to the painter Henri Hayden on 29 April 1947: 'Je ne travaille pas non plus, mais je vais m'y mettre, sans autre nécessité que cela, peu avouable, de me sentir près de moi.' (*LSB IV* 734) ['I'm not doing any work either, but I'm going to set to, without any overriding need except the rather shameful one of feeling close to myself.' (*LSB IV* 735)] Under the apparent title 'En désespoir de cause' ['In desperation; for want of anything better to do'], the text begins by alluding to a possible follow-up story. This is Molloy's second paragraph in the published version, the forty thousand word one, though in the manuscript it is a series of many shorter paragraphs. Beckett then composes the second part of the novel, Moran's account, which he concludes on 1 November 1947 (FN4, 73r) and it is only then that he adds Molloy's first paragraph, about being in his mother's room, on the first two versos of FN1 (see chapter 2.2, Paragraph 1: The Incipit).

The six notebook pages written at Foxrock in May (FN1, 02r-07r – some 1300 words) are moderately revised. The manuscript begins in a broad, ample script, then, on the second page, after some heavy revision around the need to say good-bye to external objects, turns into a somewhat tighter script presenting A and B (A and C in English; see chapter 3.2) approaching each other on the high road. After another reworked sentence, the writing becomes broader again on the next page as we learn why A and B both come to be out on the road as they are. This ample hand continues, nonetheless becoming tighter towards the bottom of each page as space lessens. Overall, the pages bear frequent though minor revisions of word choice, short insertions on facing versos and few interlinear insertions. These pages are close to the Minuit publication. The final version will benefit from stylistic improvements tending towards greater concision. The descriptions of the cud-chewing cows and the hilly countryside will shift from the past (*imparfait*) to the present.

If the approximately 1300 words on pages 02r-07r can be assumed to have been written on the date indicated, 2 May 1947, it seems that only one writing session took place at Foxrock and that Beckett did not return to *Molloy* until July. Beckett biographers indicate that much of his time in Ireland was taken up with doing errands for his ailing mother, drinking with friends and recovering from his binges. Bair and Knowlson also suggest that Beckett may have been devoting time to gathering material for his work as he asked questions and visited sites he had frequented as a youth (Bair 1978, 350, 365-6; Knowlson 1997, 367-8).

The next writing session – six and a half pages (FN1, 08r-14r, roughly 900 words) – was in Paris on Tuesday, 8 July. The script is once again broad and flowing, with relatively light revisions. There is no apparent change of ink, the entire first notebook being in black ink. The flow continues as – judging from the marked dates – Beckett finds ten more occasions to write during the next two weeks. He comes to the end of the first notebook on Tuesday 22 July. Beckett was apparently writing at any free moment, sometimes just one or two pages, at other times nine or ten pages at once. More than two months had elapsed between the first six pages written in Foxrock and the next writing session in Paris. Once home, Beckett filled the more than sixty remaining rectos of the first notebook in a matter of two weeks.

Throughout the first notebook, versos tend to be blank. The text is drafted on the rectos, revisions for the most part are in-line or interlinear though some do appear on the facing verso. In the pages dated 9 July – nine pages (about 1400 words) – Beckett makes a few small doodles on the left versos (FN1, 14v, 15v) as he ruminates on the passage about stray dogs and their role in focussing passing affection. All these pages are close to the Minuit publication, most of the variants resulting from later improvements of concision or clarity.[6]

Beckett either does not write on Thursday 10 July or he simply does not date his manuscript that day.[7] Composition resumes on the 11th (Friday): nine pages, roughly 1350 words. Beckett seems to have some difficulty finishing the A and B episode as evidenced by revisions and doodles (FN1, 27v-28r). He then moves confidently into the first mention of Molloy's mother (the opening paragraph having not yet been written) and of Molloy's need to see her again. Only when Molloy begins describing his method of bicycle riding and his recollection of a treasured bicycle horn (FN1, 30r, 31r) does the page again show effort in composition. The number of variants also rises. On 12 July – nine pages (FN1, 32r-41r) or 1350 words – ideas seem to come more freely as Beckett jots down various paralipomena: the phrase that Molloy's mother did everything she could not to have him, noted on 32v, will be used on page 40r

6   A few, more substantive differences can be noted. Among them, a sentence featuring a scatological image for handwriting (FN1, 20r) will be removed as will a passage where Molloy emphasizes that in speaking of A and B he is speaking of himself (FN1, 20r-21r). For a discussion of these passages, see chapter 2.1.

7   It may also have been a day devoted to rereading and revision. Though in-line revisions can only be immediate, some facing verso insertions, even the occasional interlinear revision may not have been written on the date that pertains to the main text. For the most part, revisions in the first notebook are interlinear.

and a note on the desirability of describing his mother's room written on page 36v will be incorporated in the next day's writing (FN1, 42r). The image of the arctic radiance and the recollection of the cries of the corncrakes (FN1, 33r) appear to have cost Beckett some effort to find the right phrasing and there is moderate revision on the pages concerning the code used to communicate with his deaf, blind mother (FN1, 37r-39r).

Having apparently not worked on *Molloy* on 13 July, Beckett writes some 900 words on Bastille day (FN1, 41r-47r), composing the end of this particular consideration of Molloy's mother and the beginning of the scene at the town gates, where Molloy is accosted by a policeman. A small doodle appears on page 41v. Otherwise, versos continue to be blank and the composition advances with only moderate revisions. Variants continue to be frequent but generally stylistic, favouring concision, more idiomatic French as well as greater clarity (and some downplaying of Molloy's subjectivity), pointing to a continuation of the work already evident in many of the manuscript revisions. About 800 words are added the next day, as the composition advances with light revision. Molloy's lament upon being prodded by the policeman's club is added (FN1, 49r) and a brief mention of Molloy's father is removed (FN1, 53r). Some of these revisions are discussed in chapter 2.1.

After a one-day break (always with the caveat that Beckett may not have dated each writing session), 17 July might be Beckett's most productive day so far in *Molloy* but for an apparent brake on page 60r. The day yields some 1000 words covering roughly 7 folio rectos (FN1, 53r-60r). Picking up Molloy's session with the *commissaire*. A paralipomenon on page 57v about social workers is cancelled and incorporated on page 58v, the first long facing verso insertion in the manuscript (the first paragraph having not yet been written). Otherwise, the versos are blank except for a small doodle (FN1, 59v) facing the sentences recording Molloy's release. At the bottom of page 59r and at the top of page 60r, Beckett carefully retraces words faintly written with a failing pen. This likely marks an occasion when he interrupted his writing but neglected to note the date when he resumed the next day (18 July). Beckett adds about 400 words (FN1, 60r-62r) recounting Molloy's release and the reasons to which it might be attributed.

Saturday 19 July marks the apparent beginning of a five-day writing spree. The writing sessions are nonetheless shorter, never yielding more than five pages. On the first day, Beckett continues Molloy's ruminations on good citizenry (FN1, 63r-66r – roughly 500 words). These pages include two short facing insertions (FN1, 63v, 65v). The date on page 65v reads '30.7.47', probably a lapse for 20 July, coming as it does between '19.7.' (FN1, 62v) and '21.7.' (FN1, 70v). The five pages thus misdated (some 800 words) begin with Molloy's shadow play on the police station wall and continue until his sudden recollection that he was on the way to see his mother. They feature a short insertion on page 58v and otherwise blank versos. We note roughly the same rate of linear and interlinear revisions and few substantive variants. The following day produces about 450 words (FN1, 71r-74r) with one facing verso insertion. On Tuesday 22 July, Beckett fills the last page and a half of the first notebook and straight away continues in the second, inscribing the same date on the front flyleaf verso of the second notebook. There is a small doodle on page 73v (FN1) facing the change of scene as Molloy's night in a ditch begins. The lined inside back cover of the first notebook is blank (FN1, 76r).

The first notebook shows confident progress through the material. There are few facing insertions, only small, simple doodles unrelated to the story and no massive deletions. Most revisions are in-line or interlinear and reflect hesitations as to formulation. Variants show a tendency toward greater concision, a more natural (literary) French as well as greater clarity. With some variation, all of this holds true for the following three notebooks.

Second French notebook (FN2)

Survey of Beckett's recorded progress through the second notebook of *Molloy*, 22 July-4 September 1947 (undated days are darkened):

Day	Date	Notebook pages	Approximate word count
Tuesday	22 July	01r-03r	700
Wednesday	23 July	03r-05r	500
	24 July		
	25 July		
	26 July		
	MENTON		
Sunday	27 July	05r-07r	750
Monday	28 July	08r-14r	1800

	29 July		
Wednesday	30 July	14r-15r	350
Thursday	31 July	15r-19r	1100
Friday	1 August	19r-22r	650
Saturday	2 August	22r-24r	750
	4 days		
Thursday	7 August	25r-33r	2300
	5 days		
Wednesday	13 August	33r-36r	900
Thursday	14 August	36r-37r	350
Friday	15 August	37r-40r	800
Saturday	16 August	40r-45r	1350
Saturday (bis)	16 August (bis)	45r-55r	2700
	17 August		
	18 August		
Tuesday	19 August	55r-59r	1200
Wednesday	20 August	60r-64r	1200
Thursday	21 August	64r-67r	600
Friday	22 August	67r-71r	1100
Saturday	23 August	71r-75r	1000
Sunday	24 August	75r-77r	550
Monday	25 August	77r-97r	5300
	26 August		
	27 August		
	28 August		
Friday	29 August	97r-101r	1200
Saturday	30 August	102r-105r	1150
Sunday	31 August	105r-111r	1600
Monday	1 September	111r-117r	1700
Tuesday	2 September	117r-125r	2000
Wednesday	3 September	126r-134r	2450
Thursday	4 September	135r-143r	2400

On 22 July, Beckett fills the last two rectos of the first notebook and moves on to the second. The total output for Tuesday the 22nd is about 1000 words. It is the fourth day of five consecutive days of writing. The front flyleaf verso bears the date '22.7.47' in black ink and, below it, in blue ink, 'Paris'. The text on page 1r, in black ink, continues the sentence begun in the first notebook as Molloy lies in a ditch, under the gaze of a flea-bitten dog. The script in the second notebook is smaller and tighter. In FN1, each page bears 100 to 120 words. In the second, there is some variation in the size of the script but most pages hold more than 200 words. Otherwise, Beckett continues with a rhythm similar to the one he had in the first notebook. There are relatively few hesitations in the composition though a few time-consuming doodles begin to appear. The paralipomenon noted on page 01v about the pastoral scenery is promptly put to use on page 03r and a short insertion appears on page 02v. This last verso also bears the enigmatic, framed notation 'Fin du Sténo.' ['End of steno.'] in blue ink at the same level as an asterisk, in the same blue ink, in the bottom right margin of the facing page 03r (see Fig. 11 in chapter 2.1).[8] On Wednesday 23 July, the last day of the five-day writing spree, Beckett produces about 500 words (FN2, 03r-05r). This contribution features Molloy's calculation of his farts. Beckett made calculations (FN2, 04v) to arrive at the figures he uses (see Fig. 12 in chapter 2.1). There are also apparently unrelated calculations on page 03v. According to John Pilling's chronology for 1947, this is the very day Beckett and his companion, Suzanne Déchevaux-Dumesnil, left Paris for colourful Menton on the Côte d'Azur (Pilling 2006, 101; see also *LSB II* 53). Beckett would spend some ten weeks in a sparsely furnished cottage lent him by 'a distant relative' (Cohn 2005, 161), where the bulk of *Molloy* would be written.

Four days later, on Sunday 27 July, Beckett sits down to continue his work in Menton and notes the change of location along with the date (FN2, 04v). The work is unusually arduous as Beckett endeavours to have Molloy explain the dissociation he feels between words and objects (see chapter 2.1). He produces little more than two pages (FN2, 05r-07r). The next day (28 July)

---

8   Although no additional manuscript material of the French *Molloy* has been found apart from the four notebooks discussed in this section, the note 'Fin du Sténo' (FN2, 02v) may suggest that Beckett had drafted a fragment of the text on a separate steno pad, which he then copied into the manuscript of his novel. Such a smaller notepad would have been easier to carry around than the larger notebooks.

is apparently the most productive day to date (FN2, 08r-14r, more than 1800 words), unless Beckett wrote part of the 1800 words on 29 July and simply forgot to date this writing session. Versos are generally blank but for a few short facing insertions and one long one (FN2, 10v) where Beckett reworks Molloy's second encounter with the police, after running over Lousse's dog Teddy.

During the next dated session (30 July), Beckett produces only about 350 words (FN2, 14r-15r). On Thursday 31 July, he writes four pages (FN2, 15r-19r – 1100 words) recounting Teddy's burial under a tree. August 1st and 2nd are once again days of meagre production: fewer than 650 words, then a bit more than 750 words (two to three pages each day). While composing Molloy's description of the moon as seen through the window bars of Lousse's house, Beckett draws circles divided by vertical lines to test proportions (FN2, 21v; see Fig. 2). The uppermost of these two doodles of the moon has bled through to the recto and onto page 20v.

A paralipomenon on page 21v about the difficulty of talking about the moon without losing one's head (see Fig. 2) will be integrated at the top of page 23r. The session of 2 August shows heavy revision in the passage where Molloy attempts to describe the uncertainty and unknowability of all things, a passage Beckett wrote and crossed out twice (FN2, 23v, 24r) then rewrote again after a four-day hiatus (see chapter 2.1).

On Thursday 7 August, Beckett starts by writing the third version of this difficult passage – Molloy's comments on 'un monde figé en perte d'équilibre' (FN2, 25r) ['a world collapsing endlessly' (1955, 53; *Mo* 38)], which is remarkably close to the final text. Molloy continues his considerations on the moon he sees upon awakening. Then comes his comical tantrum, dressed in a woman's nighty, demanding that the butler fetch his clothes (FN2, 25r-33r). Facing this tantrum, Beckett has doodled small but ornate abstractions (FN2, 29v) that have bled through to page 28v. Page 30v features a long facing insertion as part of the scene with the butler. Revisions are nonetheless light. An inkblot on page 30v has bled through to page 29r.

The writing session on Wednesday 13 August (FN2, 33r-36r, close to 900 words) is particularly untroubled with almost no crossing out, though there are facing insertions. Even the variant rate (compared to the published text) drops, particularly on page 35r, which features Molloy's ruminations about the place his knife will hold in the planned inventory of his possessions.

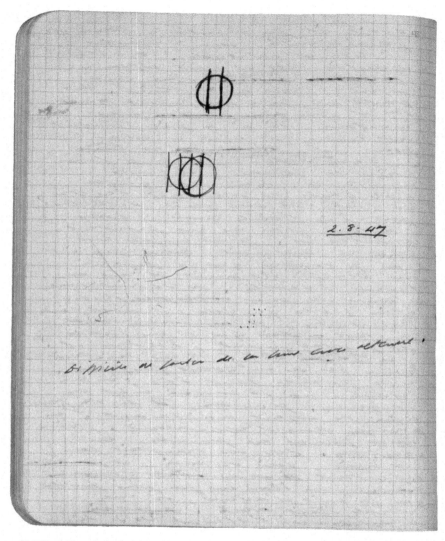

Fig. 2: Drawing of Molloy's description of the moon divided in three parts by the vertical bars, as seen through the windows of Lousse's house, with a date and a paralipomenon underneath (FN2, 21v).

The next day produces fewer than 350 words (FN2, 36r-37r), the one after that a little more than twice that amount (FN2, 37r-40r). The pages show little effort, few strikethroughs, only a few neat insertions on facing versos and, overall, stylistic variants. The low production in these days may be a function of other demands on Beckett's time rather than difficulty in composition. On 15 August, Beckett writes to George Reavey that he has been suffering from 'an abscess in the jaw and tooth trouble'. In the same letter he reveals that the book he is writing will probably be entitled *Molloy* (*LSB II* 60). On page 39v we read the date '16.8' and five folios later the date '16.8.47' (FN2, 44v). Whether this was an error on Beckett's part or whether he sat down and dated his work twice on the same day, we cannot know. Even taken separately, these sessions had a high yield. Taken together they represent a production of more than 4000 words. Versos are getting more use as facing insertions become more frequent. Though no more heavily revised than any other pages, the text of page 43r – Molloy's ruminations about his time in Lousse's garden – will be completely rewritten before publication (see chapter 2.1). A doodle on page 47v faces the conclusion of Molloy's reflections on the many windows in Lousse's house and his decision not to dwell upon the episode. Another doodle (FN2, 53v) faces Molloy's considerations concerning his falls. The date on page 54v is framed to separate it from a long insertion subsequently written all around it – Molloy's disclaimer about *preferring* and *regretting* with regards to whether or not he took his meals during his stay with Lousse.

The next writing session is dated 19 August, the first of seven consecutive days of writing. There are insertions, now, on most facing versos. On page 56v Beckett made pen scratchings to test a new nib and a simple looped doodle facing Molloy's presentation of Ruth. The date on page 59v ('20.8') seems to be awkwardly poked in just below a paralipomenon related to Molloy's sexual intercourse with Edith/Ruth – 'on ~~doit~~ être aut ~~autrement~~ ~~ete~~' – which may have been jotted down the previous day. It is struck through and put to use immediately upon beginning the day's writing: ~~Je pense~~ Entre pouce et index on ~~est~~ autrement mieux' (FN2, 60r) ['Twixt finger and thumb 'tis heaven in comparison' (1955, 77; *Mo* 57)]. On the same page, across from the account of Ruth's death, there is a small diamond-shaped doodle, meticulously filled with vertical lines and a small curved doodle facing Molloy's departure from Lousse's house (FN2, 62v). A paralipomenon on page 63v – 'se tailler une une [sic] veine / vaincu par la douleur / dus résister' – is incorporated on page 66r, when Molloy contemplates suicide: 'Je pris dans ma poche le couteau à légumes, l'ouvrit et m'appliquai à m'en ouvrir le poignet, mais ~~je n'avais pas~~ je n'en avais pas entamé l'épiderme que la douleur me vaincait [sic] déjà, de sorte que je refermai le couteau et le remis dans ma poche' (FN2, 66r) ['I took the vegetable knife from my pocket and set about opening my wrist. But pain soon got the better of me [...] then I gave up, closed the knife and put it back in my pocket' (1955, 82; *Mo* 61)].

Beckett produces almost four pages on 21 August (FN2, 64r-67r – 600 words). On 22 August he changes to blue ink (which allows us to know where the writing was interrupted) and we see him continue in mid-sentence. The date is framed by horizontal lines above and below (FN2, 66v). Directly beneath is an illegible scrawl – possibly a place name (perhaps 'Menton') or a squiggle to test the pen nib and ink flow. The nib may in fact have been damaged or of poor quality as the letters become thicker and even less differentiated than is customary for Beckett, most noticeably on pages 68v and 69r. Some words are but a blue blur on the page.

Beckett draws X figures and an inverted V on page 69v across from Molloy's description of a mysterious object he has taken from Lousse's house, then he draws the joined X's of the knife rest on page 70v (see Fig. 3).

The pages dated 23 August (FN2, 71r-75r) are among the most difficult to read as Beckett continues to use the same blue fountain pen. In a mathematical moment he also writes 22 over 7 on page 70v – Molloy's example of 'la vraie division' (FN2, 71r) ['true division' (1955, 86; *Mo* 64)] – but performs no calculation. On page 72v, we see the notation 'p. 53', the number is circled then crossed out and, underneath, '72' is written. This number corresponds to the number of recto pages Beckett has filled in FN2. On Sunday 24 August, Beckett resumes Molloy's meditations upon the extent of his region. The point where the writing resumes is heavily reworked and the difficulty of this section may have prompted the interruption of work on the previous day. Beckett cancels text and retries on the facing verso before finding the words he will use.

According to Beckett's own dating, in the week from Tuesday 19 until Monday 25 August he fills more than forty pages in FN2 (well above ten thousand words). The last date accounts for roughly half of this production. On 25 August, it seems as if some twenty pages of text are written, the equivalent of four days at Beckett's usual rate of production. The next date is four days later (29 August). Whether that Monday was a particularly

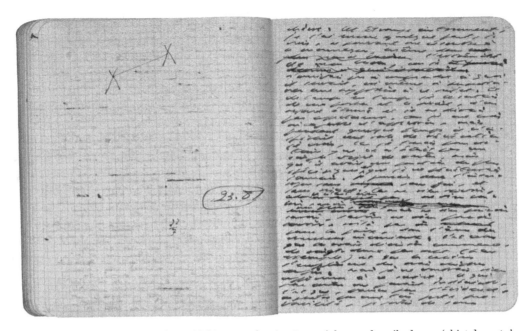

Fig. 3: The knife rest Molloy takes with him upon leaving Lousse's house, described as an 'objet de vertu' on the facing page (FN2, 70v-71r).

productive day or whether Beckett neglected to note the date of his following session or sessions, there is no way of knowing. Small differences here and there, in writing rhythm or in the way the ink is applied (for instance, 81r, 86r, 89r, 90r, 91r) allow one to think he may have interrupted and resumed his work without dating. By the same token, a twenty-page day is not impossible. These pages recount Molloy's first night after leaving the town where his mother lives, then his time at the seaside and the famous sucking-stone permutations (see cover). On page 85v, Beckett jots a five-point programme (see chapter 2.1). The meticulous description of the systematic transfers of sucking stones (FN2, 82r-85r), then the programmatic development sketched in these paralipomena (FN2, 85v-93r) can account for an output of more than twenty pages in one day. There is also evidence of quick writing in hard to read passages such as on page 82r. Meanwhile, Beckett took time to visualise and graph the movements of the sucking stones (FN2, 81v, 82v) and page 86v features a simple doodle, a question mark and the word 'Kabbala' underscored with a wavy line (see chapter 2.1). About half of the versos in this session feature facing insertions, which may not all have been written on the same day.

After an apparent break of four days, Friday 29 August is the start of ten consecutive writing days, even though on 5 September Beckett produces less than a page. This writing spree will bring him to the end of the second notebook and well into the third. Once again, the last day of the series represents the greatest output, almost half of the total. The dating of 7 September is followed by 43 pages and a hiatus of almost two weeks in the recorded dates. It is unlikely that Beckett wrote these 43 pages in one day. More likely, he neglected to note all the dates of his working sessions.

29 and 30 August together represent an output of about four pages each day. Coincidentally, the starting point of the text of the 29th happens to be the same as that of the only manuscript draft of the English translation (EM). On that day, Beckett has some trouble with Molloy's comparative study of his leg pains (FN2, 100r). On page 101v, there is an apparent page count: '102' is in fact the number of rectos Beckett has so far written in this notebook, but it does not include the 75 pages of the first notebook.[9] Page counts such as these indicate that Beckett was keeping track of his progress. Especially in the second part of the novel they can be interpreted as evidence that Beckett was pacing himself and that he was aiming for some degree of symmetry or balance between the novel's two parts.[10] On page 102v there is a simple squiggle in black ink amidst pages written and revised in blue ink.[11] Paralipomena are noted on page 113v, the first recalls the seaside episode just recounted and the second notes a phrase about the forest that is immediately put to use on the facing recto. A time-saving technique is illustrated on page 113r. When Beckett is unable to recall a word, or he does

---

9   Page 124v features the number '125' (circled), representing a similar page count. Apparently, Beckett did not start counting until after *Molloy* had grown into a novel of some length.

10   That Beckett was gradually trying to shape his novel into two symmetrical parts does not necessarily contradict what Charles Juliet reports about Beckett's declaration to the effect that he 'hadn't planned it, or thought it all out' with respect to the details of Molloy's and Moran's respective accounts (Juliet 1995, 140). For a discussion of this compositional and structural matter, see chapter 2.2 (the introduction to the discussion of Moran's part).

11   An inkblot that appears to originate on page 104v or 104r bleeds through to page 103r.

not know it, he often leaves a space in which he inscribes a question mark. The word 'caroubes' ('carobs') will be filled in later. This seems to indicate a flow of writing that he did not want to interrupt for the sake of finding one word. He did not write the word in English either, apparently preferring not to interrupt the French discourse.

The date '2.9' (FN2, 116v) is baroquely framed with a doodle. On the facing recto, perhaps the place where the eve's work had been interrupted, the words 'le tenter' (FN2, 117r) are retraced as though Beckett were 'feeling his way back into' his *Molloy* state of mind (Bowles 1994, 27). Despite this seemingly ponderous start, it is a productive day (FN2, 117r-125r) and will bring Beckett to the end of Part I. The writing progresses apace, with less than the usual rate of deletions and revisions on the rectos and few facing insertions. Beckett finishes with a horizontal stroke to end Part I (FN2, 124r; see Fig. 15 in chapter 2.1), under which he later writes a word count, '40.000 app.', underlined then framed. This points to a desire for symmetry and comparable length of the novel's two parts.

On 3 September, with no more of a break than a night's sleep, but after taking time to neatly frame the date, Beckett launches into Part II, Moran's report (FN2, 125v-126r). Composition appears to continue as it has been going in the preceding sessions. The rate of revisions and of variants is comparable throughout. The handwriting is brisk and compact, the story progresses with apparent ease. Some versos are blank, some bear long insertions, but most only brief ones. On this day, the longer insertions bring details on Gaber's and Moran's respective personalities (FN2, 130v, 131v). There are black pen scratchings on page 124v as on page 133v (Beckett may have been rereading with another pen at a later date) but everything else is in the same blue ink. On 4 September, Beckett writes the eight and a half pages that bring him to the end of the second notebook. There is some evidence of difficulty on page 142r where Moran tells of his misgivings about taking communion on a lager and his discomfort in making small talk with Father Ambrose (see chapter 2.2). Though most of this work is done in the same ink, this page bears a small revision in black ink. The next recto (FN2, 143r), the last of the notebook, begins 17 lines down as the upper part of the page is marked by ink bleeding through from the verso.

Pages 143v and 144r, written in darker blue ink, are devoted to the design of a crossword puzzle, apparently in another hand, possibly that of Suzanne. The next verso is written upside down in black ink and crossed out several times in blue. It includes a brief autobiographical note on Beckett and the draft of a letter requesting, on the owner's behalf, an estimate for work to be done at the Villa Irlanda in Menton, where Beckett is staying (see chapter 2.2). In the undated draft, Beckett mentions that he expects to be leaving in two to three weeks. The inside back cover includes calculations of debts to various friends who had helped out Beckett and Suzanne. Further calculations appear on the back cover.

Third French notebook (FN3)

Survey of Beckett's recorded progress through the third notebook of *Molloy*, 5 September-14 October 1947 (undated days are darkened):

Day	Date	Notebook pages	Approximate word count
	MENTON		
Friday	5 September	01r	150
Saturday	6 September	01r-03r	500
Sunday	7 September	03r-46r	11400
	11 days		
Friday	19 September	46r-53r	1950
	20 September		
	21 September		
Monday	22 September	53r-68r	3800
	23 September		
	24 September		
Thursday	25 September	68r-72r	900
	13 days		
	PARIS		
Thursday	9 October	72r-78r	1600
	10 October		
Saturday	11 October	78r-85r	1600
Sunday	12 October	85r-89r	1200
	13 October		
Tuesday	14 October	89r-96r	1700

FN3 is spiral-bound but otherwise similar to FN2. Beckett continues the sentence from the previous notebook next to the date '5.9.47', neatly framed inside the front cover. He is still in Menton, as the note on the inside of the front cover indicates. This is Beckett's eighth consecutive day of writing, but today he is just christening the new notebook, writing only about 150 words. Three quarters of the way down the inside front cover, across from Moran's judgement of the stew Martha has served, we see a second date, '6.9'. The first verso (FN3, 01v) features a small funnel-shaped doodle and paralipomena. This second session is also short, yielding only two pages (FN3, 01r-03r – 500 words). Sunday 7 September is Beckett's tenth consecutive day of writing. There is no new date until page 45v, between 7 and 19 September, and yet Beckett produced 43 pages of text (FN3, 03r-46r) in this period, something in the neighbourhood of 11,400 words.

Among the 43 pages following the date of 7 September there are some lightly revised pages but also some that are heavily revised, such as page 11r, where finalising the distinction between agents such as Moran and messengers such as Gaber required considerable work (see chapter 2.2). A long facing insertion (FN3, 20v) shows Moran wondering whence comes his foreknowledge of Molloy. As he ponders the name, he is unsure if the ending is *ose, ote, one* or *oc* (FN3, 22r). This foreshadowing of *Malone* will disappear from the French text (1951, 174) but return in the English-language version in the place of *ote* (1955, 153; *Mo* 117). Moran's single sentence about tucking his son into bed (FN3, 39r) is augmented by a long insertion about their relationship that stretches across two versos (FN3, 38v-39v), one of the rare substantive changes made in the course of composition. There is only one time-consuming doodle, a meticulously patterned and coloured half snail, half butterfly on page 8v (with a small geometric tracing and paralipomena beneath it – the paralipomena are cancelled, having been incorporated on the facing page 9r). Otherwise, Beckett's energies were channelled into the many revisions throughout these pages. Page 13r is a rare recto to feature doodling, a small geometric pattern at the top of the page, and some letters are retraced on the third and sixth lines. There are black pen scratchings on pages 4v and 30v and blue pen scratchings on page 43v. Otherwise the notebook is written in blue ink throughout.

It seems plausible that the 43 pages were in fact produced over several days, only the first of which was noted, but it would be difficult to say where the breaks are. There are no obvious disruptions or juncture points though they might be masked by revisions. In an insertion on page 37v, Beckett again uses a question mark rather than lose time searching for a word, as he characterises the way in which Moran usually takes leave of Martha. (The word 'désinvolture' will appear in the published text (1951, 186), the word 'off-handedly' will render it in English (1955, 165; *Mo*, 125)).

According to the dates in the notebook, there was an eleven-day break in writing. Still in Menton, Beckett dated three more sessions in September: Friday the 19th (FN3, 46r-53r, 1,950 words), Monday the 22nd (FN3, 53r-68r, 3800 words) and Thursday the 25th (FN3, 68r-72r, 900 words).

Beckett writes smoothly on 19 September. There are some facing insertions, the longer ones being on page 50v about Moran's reluctance to prune his trees and about his despondent grey hen.[12] Writing on 22 September seems to have been a bit more arduous. A long insertion on page 55v describes young Jacques' gift for remembering dates. There are simple doodles on pages 62v and 63v across from the pages where Moran begins his consideration of Molloy's country, Ballyba.

At this point, we come across the long portion of text devoted to a detailed description of Ballyba's exploitation of its citizens' faeces for agricultural purposes (66r-78r) – all of which was cut from the novel (see chapter 1.2.1, chapter 2.2 and the Appendix). On page 64v of the third notebook, just before the deleted passage begins, we read '(II) 83'. We take this to be another page count that includes the 18 pages at the end of the second notebook that belong to Part II, Moran's report, and the 65 pages of the current third notebook. The ink and penmanship are different from the surrounding pages, so this notation seems to have been made at a later date.[13]

We read the circled and partially scratched out '25.' (FN3, 67v) as a date (25 September), marking the beginning of the last writing session in Menton. Page 67v is a busy verso, besides four insertions (one long) there is a paralipomenon on the mode of election ('mode d'élection', crossed out,

---

12   The same page also features black pen scratchings. On page 54r there is an apparently meaningless interlinear black squiggle and coffee or tea spills that have bled through from page 54v. Two sketches on page 53v resemble floor plans.

13   This page count might indicate that Beckett was at some point in the composition (perhaps upon typing it up) considering to cut the topic and counting to determine if the novel's two parts would still be of comparable length.

incorporated on page 70r) of an official who is first called the 'Odibil' and then the 'Obidil' (see chapter 2.2). Numerous paralipomena appear on page 70v that nourish the composition through to page 78r.

The top line on page 72r is the last line Beckett writes in Menton. His time by the Mediterranean was productive. Over 210 notebook pages, more than 50,000 words, including the episode at Lousse's house, Molloy's relationship with Ruth, the episode by the beach and later wanderings as well as half of Moran's report, from his dominical habits and Gaber's visit, through his consultation with father Ambrose, to his long preparations and detailed survey of what he knows about his quarry. All in all, more than half the novel was written in the Mediterranean air, during the months of August and September.

In the days following, he and Suzanne return to Paris (*LSB II* 53). On 9 October, Beckett sits down and continues in black ink. The date ('PARIS 9.10.47') is framed and next to it, in blue ink, Beckett has written an upper case 'N' (FN3, 71v). Further down the verso, a small doodle is followed by an insertion. The facing text up to the end of the writing session concludes the deleted portion about Ballyba's fecal economy (see chapter 1.2.1, chapter 2.2 and the Appendix). The first five paralipomena on page 70v (written in Menton in blue ink) are crossed out in black ink upon being incorporated and the last two paralipomena are added in black ink. The versos of this first session in Paris hold occasional insertions, two more small doodles (FN3, 74v, 77v) and paralipomena (FN3, 76v).

After a one-day hiatus, Beckett resumes on Saturday 11 October, near the bottom of page 78r, with the words: 'Voilà donc une partie de ce que je croyais savoir sur Ballyba' ['That then is a part of what I thought I knew about Ballyba' (1955, 184; *Mo* 140)]. Most of page 79r is a commentary on what precedes and was also cut from the novel (see chapter 1.2.1, chapter 2.2 and the Appendix). There is a flower-like doodle on page 81v facing text with several heavily retraced words where Moran, having just set out on his quest, wonders what he is looking for. The change of writing venue has not inhibited the composition. Beckett finished off the third notebook with consecutive sessions of 1200 to 1700 words per day.

On Sunday 12 October, Beckett writes five pages with relative ease (FN3, 85r-89r). There are pen scratchings and an insertion on page 88v, otherwise the versos are blank. No writing was done on the 13th. On Tuesday 14 October, Beckett fills the remaining seven rectos of the third notebook ending in mid-sentence where the writing space was exhausted (FN3, 89r-96r). Versos continue to be mostly blank. There is a calculation in graphite pencil on page 94v, as well as blue inkblots and black ink scratchings on page 93v and a blue inkblot on page 94r, which – like the rest of these pages – is written in black ink.

The back cover bears the patent graphic for the spiral binding, the only commercial mark on any of the four notebooks. There are also black pen scratchings near the graphic at the bottom and the inscription '4 – 13' at the top, but its purpose is unclear.

Fourth French notebook (FN4)

Survey of Beckett's recorded progress through the fourth notebook of Molloy, 16 October – 1 November 1947 (days without writing are darkened). The novel's first paragraph is added to FN1 on 1 November:

Day	Date	Notebook pages	Approximate word count
Thursday	16 October	01r	100
Friday	17 October	01r-24r	3850
	18 October		
	19 October		
	20 October		
Tuesday	21 October	24r-38r	3050
	22 October		
	23 October		
Friday	24 October	38r-47r	2050
	25 October		
Sunday	26 October	48r-61r	2900
	27 October		
	28 October		
	29 October		
Thursday	30 October	61r-74r	3050
	31 October		
Saturday	1 November	FN1, 01v-02v	300

FN4 is clothbound like FN1 and FN2. The cover is dark green. The visual aspect of its pages recalls that of FN1, where there are fewer words per page. The inside front cover bears the paralipomenon 'Lampe !' though the topic, as 'lanterne', has already been mentioned on the previous page (FN3, 96r). The first line of the notebook (FN4, 01r) is the continuation of a sentence interrupted by the end of the third notebook and may or may not be included by the date '16.10.47' inscribed on the facing inside front cover. As with FN3, this first entry is barely a christening, amounting to less than a page.

The next day, Beckett inscribes the date '17.10.47' on the same inside front cover and proceeds to fill the next twenty-four recto pages (FN4, 01r-24r). The pages of the notebook have twenty-two printed lines. Beckett begins by writing on each line, resulting in a load of about 110 words per page for the first thirteen pages. Starting on page 14r, apparently frustrated with the notebook's format, Beckett began squeezing in more lines of text without regard for the printed lines, fitting in 36 to 39 lines per page. These pages average about 180 words per page. The date of 17 October is followed by more than 3,800 words (FN3, 01r-24r) before the next date (four days later). This session was more arduous than most. Doodles appear on pages 03v and 14v, opposite text where Moran finds the time long without his son and on pages 08v and 21v facing Moran's descriptions of the vagabonds he meets in the forest while waiting for his son.

The next date (Tuesday 21 October) is framed with quick strokes and Beckett composes some fourteen pages (more than 3,000 words) – including the series of questions Moran asks himself (FN4, 29r-30r)[14] to pass the time on his third day waiting for his son – before inscribing the next date, three days later, on Friday 24 October (FN4, 38r-47r; 2,050 words). On page 40v there is a doodle possibly inspired by the scene opposite describing the 'belle ligne droite et sombre de l'horizon' ['sharp dark sweep of the horizon' (1955, 218; Mo 167)]. The last lines of the session (FN4, 47r) are struck through with a blue pencil, rewritten in black ink on the facing verso, again struck through with blue pencil and then rewritten below in black ink. These are likely later emendations to the description of the far-off lights of Bally.[15]

The same blue pencil is used for an insertion (FN4, 47v) dated 26 October. An elaborate globular doodle on page 52v and several retraced words on the

14   Versos feature a few long insertions.
15   Page 60r features an inkblot that is also visible on pages 59v and 60v.

facing recto indicate that Beckett may have spent some time meditating the scene in which Gaber frees Moran of his mission (see chapter 2.2). Otherwise, the writing is freer, though moderately revised. The last pages of Moran's report seem to flow easily in the manuscript. The writing is legible and though facing verso insertions are not infrequent there seem to be few trouble spots. The rate of variants in relation to the published text is relatively low.

Even the date '30.10.' (FN4, 60v) seems to have been written quickly as Beckett speeds towards the end of Moran's report (the return home). The use of different writing implements in these final pages shows two layers of work. The session of Thursday 30 October progressed much as the previous ones had. There are a few facing insertions and several cancellations and rewritings, all in black ink. A relatively elaborate but small doodle appears on page 71v opposite Moran's description of the desiccated beehives (see Fig. 4). Later, a blue colouring pencil is used to apply a second layer of revision. Returning to the writing session of 26 October, lines at the bottom of page 47r, already crossed out in black ink, are once again cancelled in blue pencil. A facing revision in black ink is cancelled in blue pencil and a new revision written in black ink beneath it. The same blue pencil is used to emend pages written on 30 October (61r, 62v-63r, 64v, 67r). A paralipomenon on page 64v shows three layers of inscription: what appears to be 'voix' ['voice'] in pale black ink is overwritten with a large blue pencil notation of 'voix qui commence' ['voice that begins'] then cancelled with broad strokes in the same blue pencil. The same pencil is used to write in large triumphant underlined capitals: 'FIN 1/11/47' (FN4, 74r; see Fig. 19 in chapter 2.2). Pages 73v and 74r have been yellowed by the sun as can be seen from the outline on 73v of a rectangular object that rested on the open page. The remaining folios in the notebook are blank.

As seen on page 46v, Beckett's habitual black ink appears to have been used in conjunction with the blue pencil and it is this black ink that is used to compose Molloy's first paragraph, also dated 1.11.47 (FN1, 01v-02v). The paragraph reads as an 'autographic' recollection of hours spent in his mother's room the previous spring when Beckett began writing the novel (see chapter 2.2).

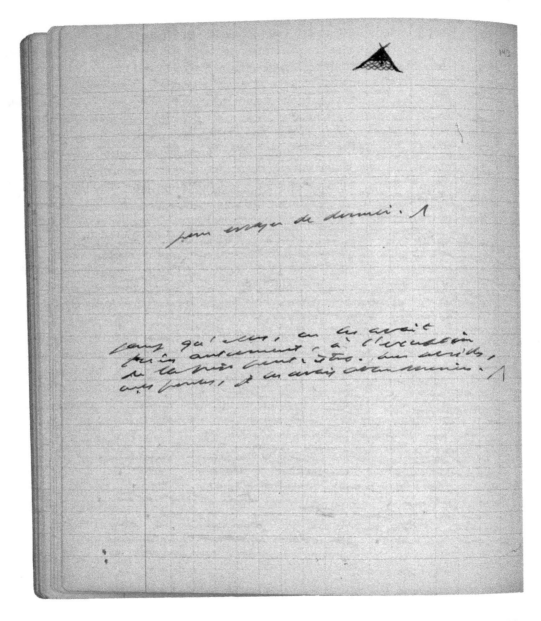

Fig. 4: Doodle of Moran's desiccated beehives, which he describes as having a little roof with a sharp ridge and steep overhanging slopes on the facing page (FN4, 71v).

1.1.2 English

English manuscript fragment (EM)

The only manuscript pages of *Molloy* in English are in the Tara MacGowran notebook held in the Thompson Library Rare Books Collection at Ohio State University at Columbus (call number SPEC.RARE.115). The notebook is in a glass wool-lined, red leather protective case, ornamented with the initials 'TMG'. It is inscribed as follows on the front cover: 'for / Tara MacGowran / with love from Sam / Paris June 1965'. Tara MacGowran, born the previous November, was the infant daughter of Beckett's good friend, the actor Jack MacGowran (see Fig. 5).

Above this inscription, Beckett made a list of the items contained within, again in blue ink: 'Early version <u>Fin de Partie</u> / <u>From an Abandoned Work</u> / <u>Fragment of translation from Molloy</u> / Other fragments'. Below the inscription to Tara MacGowran is a draft of a French letter to an unspecified addressee, written upside down in black ink. There is another scrap of a letter at the bottom of the back cover, again upside down and in black ink, but it is unclear whether this belongs to a different letter or still to the one begun at the bottom of the front cover. Three quarters of the back cover are taken up by four blue ink drawings of rectangles with a St. Andrew's cross in the middle, so that they look like envelopes on their sides. The purpose of these drawings is unclear. A piece of blotting paper, heavily stained with black ink, has been inserted between the inside cover and the front flyleaf.

The notebook was at various times used in both orientations so that many pages are upside down, whichever cover we take as the front. There are as many as six separate works represented in the notebook, including a draft of an unpublished French story that begins 'Ici personne ne vient jamais' (01r-17r; black ink), a partial draft of *Fin de partie* (18r-48r; blue ink), *From an Abandoned Work* (70v-48v, upside down; black ink), the *Foirade* 'il est tête nue' (76v-70v, upside down; black ink), and seven lines of French dialogue between 'E'[stragon] and 'V'[ladimir] under the title 'Godot' (97v; black ink). The *Molloy* fragment covers pages 77v-86r (blue ink) and is followed by eleven blank folios (86v-97r). EM also contains miscellaneous jottings and is rich in doodles, recalling the elaborately-doodled notebooks of *Watt*.

The only date in the notebook is on the opening page: '15.3.52' (EM, 01r). Other than assuming that this is the day the notebook was first put to use and

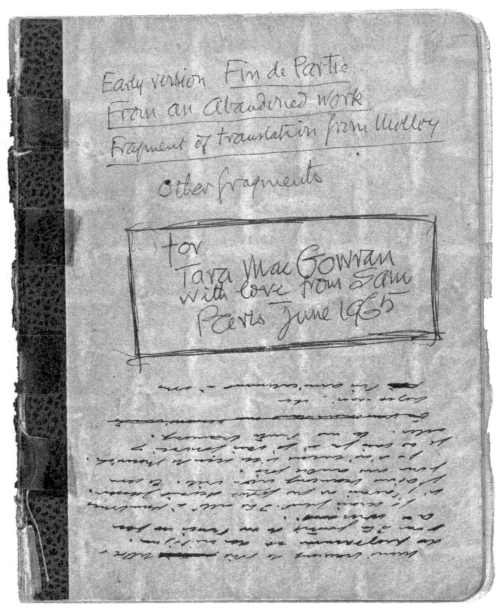

Fig. 5: The 'Tara MacGowran' notebook (OSU) was used in both orientations and contains partial drafts of up to six separate works (EM, front cover).

that it is prior to the writing of the *Molloy* excerpt, which begins deep in the notebook's interior, there is no clear indication when this draft translation was made. However, the succession of the fragments in the notebook, as well as the direction in which they were written, allow us to reconstruct the chronology of the document and establish an approximate dating for the *Molloy* draft.

The story 'Ici personne ne vient jamais' was clearly interrupted on page 15r. The last sixteen lines are crossed out, the fifteen preceding ones heavily revised, and halfway down the left-hand folio there is a figurative doodle. Just below this drawing, Beckett has written the note 'Paris, beaucoup plus tard' (14v). At this point, he resumed the story on the right-hand side, in a more stable hand with little revision, until the bottom of page 15r, but stopping well before the end of the page. Two additional rectos were added, in a frenzied scrawl with more revision, possibly at a later date again, but this has not been recorded. The story breaks off at the bottom of 17r, not filling the page, and the many doodles on the verso page (16v) suggest yet another bout of writer's block. Exactly how much later the story was resumed and when it was eventually abandoned is impossible to say, but it seems that Beckett intended to make it much longer, as the next folio he used in the normal writing direction is 77v – sixty pages later – for the *Molloy* fragment. Beckett's correspondence with Alexander Trocchi and Jérome Lindon situate the draft in late 1952 or early 1953 (see chapter 3.1), and the seven lines from *En attendant Godot* on page 97v, which follow the eleven blank folios (87r-96r) after *Molloy*, can be related either to the French première of the play at the Théâtre de Babylone in early January 1953, or its *reprise* in late September 1953 (Knowlson 1997, 386, 398).

It seems that Beckett now turned the notebook around to begin drafting the *Foirade* 'il est tête nue' (76v-70v) and *From an Abandoned Work* (70r-48v), as they appear upside down and back to front. This is confirmed by the *Fin de partie* fragments (18r-48r), which were written in the standard direction again, Beckett turning the notebook around a second and last time to write from the front towards the back. Since he first filled the rectos – using the versos for additions in his customary way – but then continued writing text on the versos – at times around the earlier additions – he probably optimized what little space was left at this point in the notebook, cramming the text of *Fin de partie* in between the other material already there. The only other available writing space was at the far back of the notebook, roughly forty pages later, i.e. the eleven blank folios (87r-96r) after the *Molloy* fragment (77v-86r), but this may have dislocated the material too much.

The *Molloy* draft begins with 'And now my progress [...]'. It corresponds to (1955, 103-11; *Mo* 77-83) and, coincidentally, to the words where Beckett resumed the writing in French on 29 August (FN2, 96v).[16] The text is written on the verso pages, using the rectos for additions. Apart from the first four folios of *From an Abandoned Work*, *Molloy* is the only draft in the notebook for which Beckett adopts this pattern consistently. Such a deviation from his usual working habit may be explained by the fact that he was revising a translation by Richard Seaver (see chapter 3.1). Being right-handed, it would have been most practical for Beckett to place Seaver's version on his left-hand side, write on the verso sides of the notebook, and use the rectos for additions. This would allow him to place the original and the revision right next to each other, without an intermediate page separating the two versions. Many paratextual decorations testify to the difficulties and hesitations his revision of the translation occasioned for Beckett (see chapter 3.1). From the first page, the manuscript is accompanied by elaborately filled-in doodles, not on the facing recto, but in the top and left margins of the writing page.[17]

The last facing rectos are blank until page 86r where Beckett drafted, in similar ink, a few lines of a letter about the translation, probably intended for Alexander Trocchi, chief editor of *Merlin* (see Fig. 23 in chapter 3.1). The *Molloy* fragment in EM was planned to appear in the literary magazine, but eventually a different passage was chosen (see chapter 3.1).

These pages are, in any event, the earliest surviving draft of the novel in English. If Beckett and Bowles referred to this fragment during their

16   This passage appears to be a remarkably coherent textual unit. In his letter of 18 November 1953 to Barney Rosset, Patrick Bowles suggested it as one of the passages from *Molloy* that might be used for pre-publication in a literary magazine: 'The following are suggested points of beginning and ending for any other extracts you may decide to send out: [...] page 90: And now my progress, ... TO END' (SU, Grove Press Records, box 98). And when the BBC Third Programme broadcast a passage from *Molloy* on 10 December 1957, this was also the passage that Beckett singled out from the novel (see Feldman 2014).

17   One doodle develops from a cancellation in the text (EM, 77v). A thick vertical bar in the left margin of page 78v might have been the germ of another doodle. The next page bears a fully decorated web doodle in the same position. The facing recto (EM, 80r) has another elaborate geometrical decoration. Heavy vertical bars again appear on page 81v. Page 82v bears a boat-like figure in the top margin.

collaboration, it is a good indication of how thoroughly the translation was revised. The rate of variants is higher than in the corresponding pages of ET1 (90r-97r) and whereas the variants in ET1 are generally localized stylistic revisions, EM contains several sentence-length variants (see chapter 3.2).

English notes (EN)

The only other surviving holograph material for the English *Molloy* consists of jottings on the covers of a notebook held at Trinity College Dublin (TCD-MS-4662). Frost and Maxwell describe the item as follows:

> Soft covered 'l'Aigle' exercise book with black spine, stitched. The covers have a woven design and an illustration of an eagle. Folios ruled in small rectangles with a left hand margin in red. Pages removed from between fols 5 and 6 and fols 13 and 14 without obvious loss of text. The volume has been conserved. 217 × 172 mm[,] i-iii, 30 fols, ms. (Frost and Maxwell 2006, 184)

The front cover of this notebook has one partial sentence from *Molloy* with a false start at the top, just above the illustration of an eagle, and one complete sentence written upside down at the bottom – both in blue ink:

> ~~xxx~~
> To ~~reply~~ couch a reply in terms
> To give me an explicit answer, though / in terms if necessary veiled, was not
>
> [To give me an explicit reply, though in terms if necessary veiled, was not beyond his powers. (ET2, 55r; 1955, 189; *Mo* 144 – Sentence 3563)]
>
> But even if it had always ~~been part of my~~ figured in my / extruction, except on one single occasion, / then that single occasion would have been enough / to tie my hands, I was so scrupulous.

[But even if it had always figured in my instructions, except on one single occasion, then that single occasion would have been enough to tie my hands, I was so scrupulous. (ET2, 55r; 1955, 188; *Mo* 144 – Sentence 3559)]

The back cover has two additional sentences in black ink, at the bottom, below a series of squiggles where Beckett tested his pen:

save insofar as such a son might / bear ~~her stamp~~ like a scurf of / placenta, her stamp.

[After all perhaps I knew nothing of mother Molloy, or Mollose, save in so far as such a son might bear, like a scurf of placenta, her stamp. (ET2, 26r; 1955, 153; *Mo* 116 – Sentence 2742)]

~~Some~~

~~Much of what~~

Much of what they had it takes away, much they never / had it foists upon them.

[Much of what they had it takes away, much they never had it foists upon them. (ET2, 28r; 1955, 156; *Mo* 118 – Sentence 2796)]

The four sentences are from Moran's story. As the survey above illustrates, variants from the published text are minor, but the jottings predate ET2, the only surviving typescript of *Molloy* Part II (see 1.2.2).

They were probably made in Dublin, between late May and early September 1954, when Beckett stayed with his ailing brother, Frank, and revised batches of *Molloy* typescript as Patrick Bowles sent them to him (see 3.1). None of these early corrected typescripts have survived – only the versions retyped by Bowles incorporating Beckett's annotations – so the notes on the front and back covers of TCD-MS-4662 are the only material traces left of this stage in the translation process. It seems they are alternative phrasings that Beckett tried out before correcting Bowles's text. It is no coincidence that this particular notebook was used to draft them, as Beckett had also started translating *Malone meurt* in it while staying in Ireland.

In addition to a fragment of *Malone Dies*, TCD-MS-4662 also features an unfinished dramatic dialogue in French between two characters called X and F (related to *Fin de partie*), a geographical description of Germany, an abandoned prose fragment in French, and various draft letters in both French and English.[18]

18   It is peculiar that *Molloy* material only occurs on the front and back covers of this notebook, but some of the removed pages may have served this purpose as well. For a more detailed description of the contents of this notebook, see Dirk Van Hulle and Pim Verhulst, *The Making of Samuel Beckett's Malone meurt / Malone Dies*, Brussels and London: University Press Antwerp and Bloomsbury (forthcoming).

1.2 Typescripts

1.2.1 French

French typescript fragment (FT)

In a separate collection (the Carlton Lake collection), the Harry Ransom Center holds a partial typescript of the French text of *Molloy*. It consists of only fourteen leaves, pages 211-224 of a now lost but presumably once complete typescript, starting with the passage where Moran announces that he is going to say what little he knows about Molloy's country (corresponding with the text at the bottom of page FN3, 61r) and writes a digression, suggesting with a nod to Camus that he does not think even Sisyphus – 'à en croire une doctrine en vogue' ['as the fashion is now'] – is required to scratch himself always at the same appointed places and that hope is hellish, 'la disposition infernale par excellence' ['hellish hope'] (FN3, 62r; FT, 211r; *Mo* 139).

The paragraph starting with 'Par le pays de Molloy j'entends la région fort restreinte [...]' (FN3, 62r) ['By the Molloy country I mean that narrow region...' (1955, 182; *Mo* 139)] starts on the first page of this partial typescript (FT, 211r, third line from the bottom; see Fig. 6).

The typescript is annotated with various writing implements (grey pencil, blue pencil, black ink, purplish-red ballpoint). In *Samuel Beckett and the Problem of Irishness* (2009), Emilie Morin suggests that some of the handwritten comments that are not Beckett's are Mania Péron's; that Mania Péron 'disapproved of Beckett's explicit attacks upon Irish political conservatism'; and that she may have supressed 'Beckett's aggressive tone due to the likely bewilderment that such directionless hostility might have caused a French audience' (89).[19] According to Morin, Mania Péron recommended

19   Maya 'Mania' Péron, was the wife of Alfred Péron, a close friend of Beckett's in Paris. Before the Second World War, Beckett had translated parts of his novel *Murphy* into French together with Alfred, who died on his way home after being liberated from a concentration camp. Beckett continued his friendship with Mania Péron after the war and regularly called on her to help him with his French writing. Russian by birth, she was a native speaker of French, having lived in France since the age of five, and she also held an English teaching

that Beckett remove the long passage on Ballyba's economy, changing Moran's question 'D'où Ballyba tirait-il donc ~~ses rie~~ **sa richesse**. Je vais vous le dire.' ['What then was the source of Ballyba's prosperity? I'll tell you.'] into 'D'où Ballyba tirait-il donc **son opulence**? Non, je ne dirai rien.' ['What then was the source of Ballyba's prosperity? No, I'll tell you nothing.'] (FT, 214r; *Mo* 140)

It is certainly plausible that some of the annotations on this typescript are Mania Péron's. The annotations in blue pencil and (some of the ones in) grey pencil are in a round handwriting and might be hers.

For instance, on the first page, Moran refers to the moment he clung to the wicket in the lane. In the manuscript and the typewritten layer of inscription on the typescript this passage reads: 'la nuit où je me pendais à mon guichet' (FN3, 62r; FT, 211r) ['the night I clung to the wicket' (1955, 182; *Mo* 139)]. The word '**pendais**' is underlined in grey pencil and the marginal annotation in grey pencil suggests that it be replaced by '**m'accrochais**'. Beckett eventually did not use this verb, but he did replace 'pendais' by '**m'agrippais**' (1951, 206).

As for the annotations in blue pencil: when Moran explains the nomenclature for the subdivisions of the territory, he says the system is 'd'une beauté et simplicité remarquables' (FN3, 63r; FT, 212r) ['of singular beauty and simplicity' (1955, 183; *Mo* 139)]. An annotation in blue pencil suggests adding an extra indefinite article before 'simplicité': 'd'une beauté et ^d'une^ simplicité remarquables' (FT, 212r). Beckett, however, did not take this recommendation into account; the published version reads: 'd'une beauté et simplicité remarquables' (1951, 207). The blue pencil may be the same as the one with which the revisions at the end of FN4 were made (see chapter 1.1.1). In that case, the blue-pencil annotations on the typescript may be Suzanne Déchevaux-Dumesnil's (using the same writing tool as her partner).

The more extensive and radical annotations in purplish-red (fuchsia) ballpoint, however, appear to be Beckett's. The purplish-red colour is the same as that of Beckett's annotations in his working copy of *Krapp's Last Tape* for the London production of 1973 (UoR MS 1227/7/10/1). One of the annotations in purplish-red is the change from '**En France**' to '**Dans les pays évolués**' (FT, 212r). On the same page, the word 'huguenote', to designate the

degree, allowing her to 'spot an Anglicism when she saw one', as James Knowlson observes (1997, 342, 361).

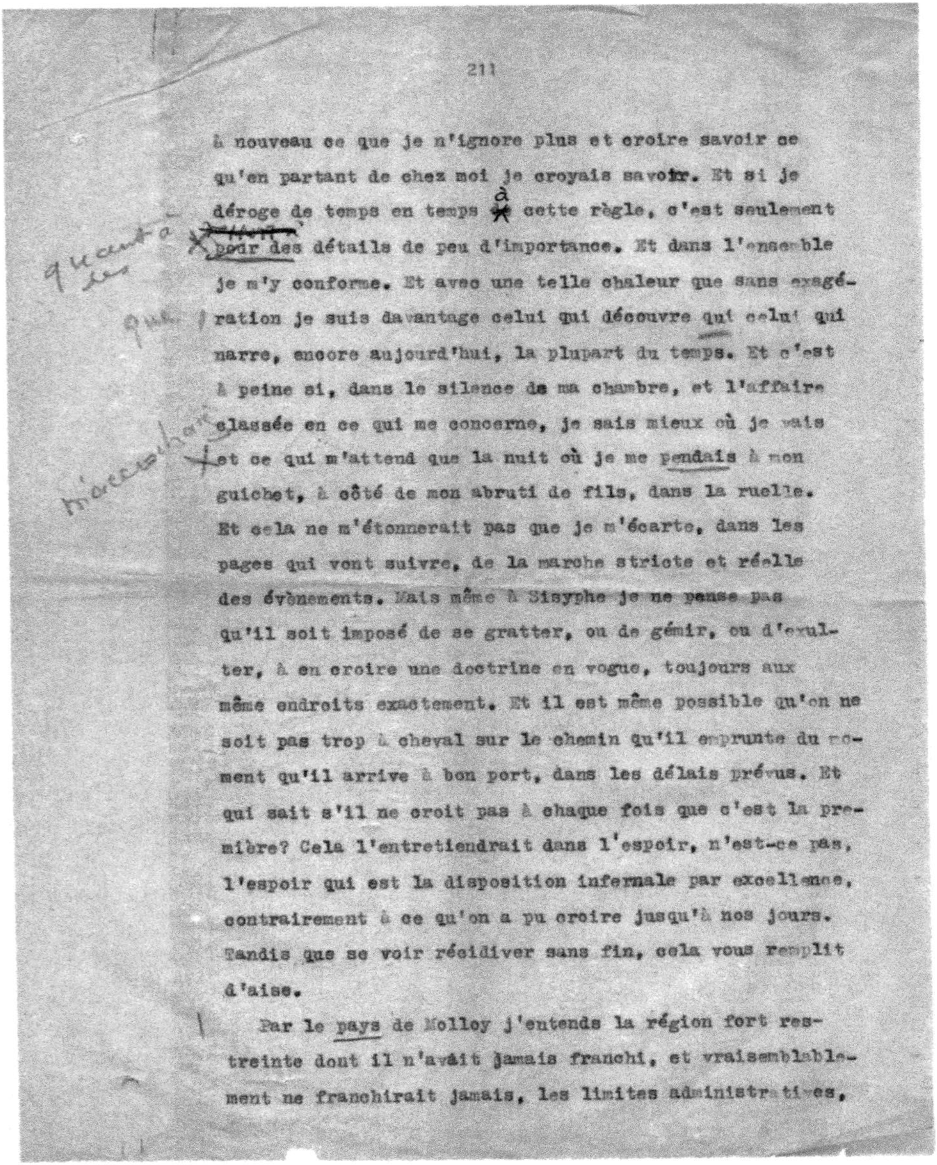

à nouveau ce que je n'ignore plus et croire savoir ce
qu'en partant de chez moi je croyais savoir. Et si je
déroge de temps en temps à cette règle, c'est seulement
pour des détails de peu d'importance. Et dans l'ensemble
je m'y conforme. Et avec une telle chaleur que sans exagé-
ration je suis davantage celui qui découvre que celui qui
narre, encore aujourd'hui, la plupart du temps. Et c'est
à peine si, dans le silence de ma chambre, et l'affaire
classée en ce qui me concerne, je sais mieux où je vais
et ce qui m'attend que la nuit où je me pendais à mon
guichet, à côté de mon abruti de fils, dans la ruelle.
Et cela ne m'étonnerait pas que je m'écarte, dans les
pages qui vont suivre, de la marche stricte et réelle
des évènements. Mais même à Sisyphe je ne pense pas
qu'il soit imposé de se gratter, ou de gémir, ou d'exul-
ter, à en croire une doctrine en vogue, toujours aux
même endroits exactement. Et il est même possible qu'on ne
soit pas trop à cheval sur le chemin qu'il emprunte du moment qu'il arrive à bon port, dans les délais prévus. Et
qui sait s'il ne croit pas à chaque fois que c'est la première? Cela l'entretiendrait dans l'espoir, n'est-ce pas,
l'espoir qui est la disposition infernale par excellence,
contrairement à ce qu'on a pu croire jusqu'à nos jours.
Tandis que se voir récidiver sans fin, cela vous remplit
d'aise.

Par le pays de Molloy j'entends la région fort restreinte dont il n'avait jamais franchi, et vraisemblable-
ment ne franchirait jamais, les limites administratives,

Fig. 6: First page of the partial French typescript, featuring the start of the paragraph 'Par le pays de Molloy j'entends [...]' (FT, 211r, l. 3 from the bottom).

priest who invented the nomenclature Bally and Ballyba, was first changed into 'calviniste', and subsequently the whole passage was cut (see chapter 2.1):

> Ce fut un prêtre, au seizième siècle, en pleine persécution **huguenote** calviniste, qui imagina cette nomenclature. Et elle fut reprise, abandonnée, reprise et abandonnée, selon les fortunes des théories de présence, jusqu'au triomphe définitif, se confondant avec le sien, de la vraie croyance. (FT, 212r)

Whereas Emilie Morin (2009) and Adam Winstanley (2014, referring to Morin) suggest that these changes were made by Mania Péron, we are inclined to assume that the fuchsia annotations and some of the ones in grey pencil may be Beckett's own emendations. We therefore do not exclude the possibility that the line 'Non, je ne dirai rien.' pencilled above 'Je vais vous le dire' (FT, 214r; see Fig. 7) may be Beckett's and that the omission of the passage on Ballyba's economy was Beckett's own idea.

The end of the cut passage is also marked, by means of an asterisk in grey pencil on the typescript (FT, 224r; see Fig. 8).

1.2.2 English

The surviving English typescripts of *Molloy* are all the product of Beckett's collaboration with Patrick Bowles, who had been selected to translate the novel. In an unpublished 1990 interview with Martha Dow Fehsenfeld, Bowles explained why so little material remains:

> I've lost nearly all the manuscripts and so on that I ever had because they were stored in the studio of a friend of mine, whom all the people in the Merlin group knew, her name was Shirley Wales. I believe that she is now deceased. But she kindly agreed to look after something like 14 suitcases of books and manuscripts, you see. And she stored them in her basement in her cellar and one winter in Paris there was a tremendous storm that lasted several weeks and the basement was flooded, completely, and she rescued some of my books and put them upstairs, but most of it I'm afraid she just had to

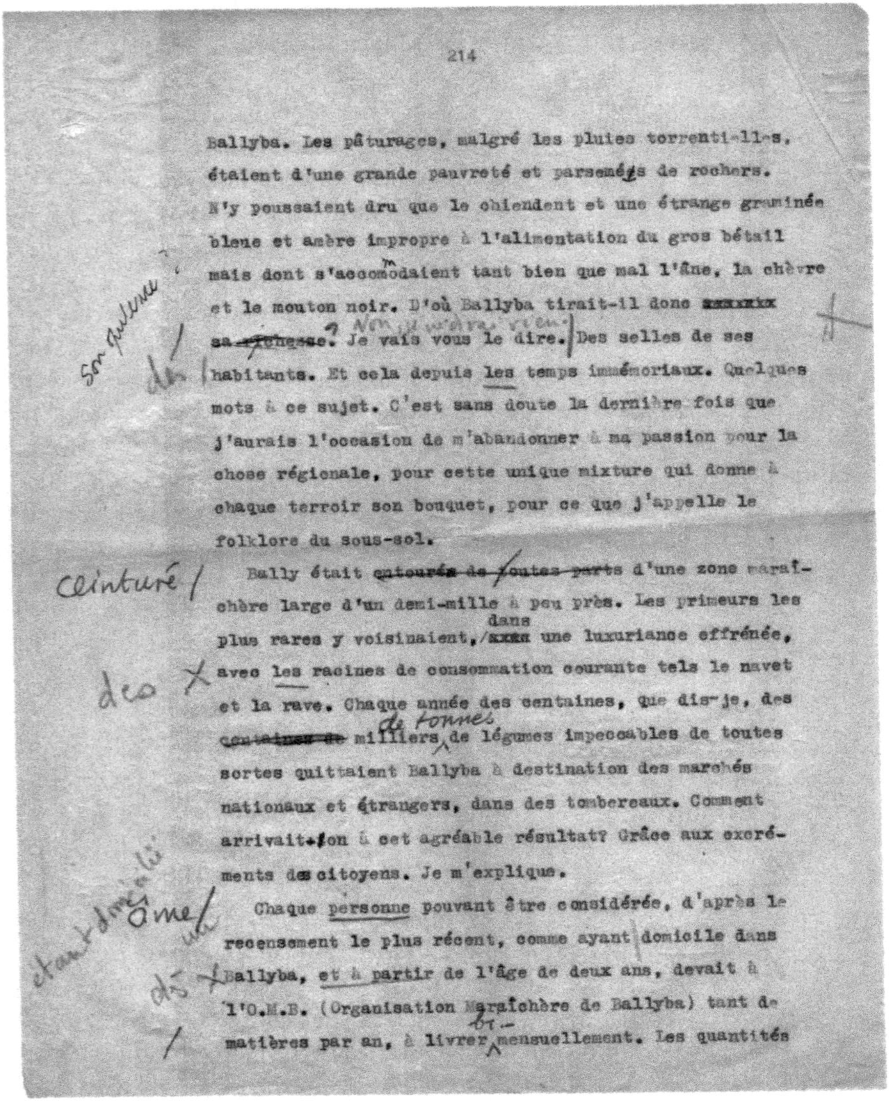

Ballyba. Les pâturages, malgré les pluies torrenti-lles,
étaient d'une grande pauvreté et parsemées de rochers.
N'y poussaient dru que le chiendent et une étrange graminée
bleue et ambre impropre à l'alimentation du gros bétail
mais dont s'accomodaient tant bien que mal l'âne, la chèvre
et le mouton noir. D'où Ballyba tirait-il donc xxxxxxx
sa richesse. Je vais vous le dire. Des selles de ses
habitants. Et cela depuis les temps immémoriaux. Quelques
mots à ce sujet. C'est sans doute la dernière fois que
j'aurais l'occasion de m'abandonner à ma passion pour la
chose régionale, pour cette unique mixture qui donne à
chaque terroir son bouquet, pour ce que j'appelle le
folklore du sous-sol.

Bally était entouré de toutes parts d'une zone maraîchère large d'un demi-mille à peu près. Les primeurs les
plus rares y voisinaient, dans une luxuriance effrénée,
avec les racines de consommation courante tels le navet
et la rave. Chaque année des centaines, que dis-je, des
centaines de milliers, de tonnes de légumes impeccables de toutes
sortes quittaient Ballyba à destination des marchés
nationaux et étrangers, dans des tombereaux. Comment
arrivait-on à cet agréable résultat? Grâce aux excréments des citoyens. Je m'explique.

Chaque personne pouvant être considérée, d'après le
recensement le plus récent, comme ayant domicile dans
Ballyba, et à partir de l'âge de deux ans, devait à
l'O.M.B. (Organisation Maraîchère de Ballyba) tant de
matières par an, à livrer mensuellement. Les quantités

Fig. 7: 'Non, je ne dirai rien.' pencilled above 'Je vais vous le dire', marking the omission of the passage on Ballyba's economy (FT, 214r, l. 7).

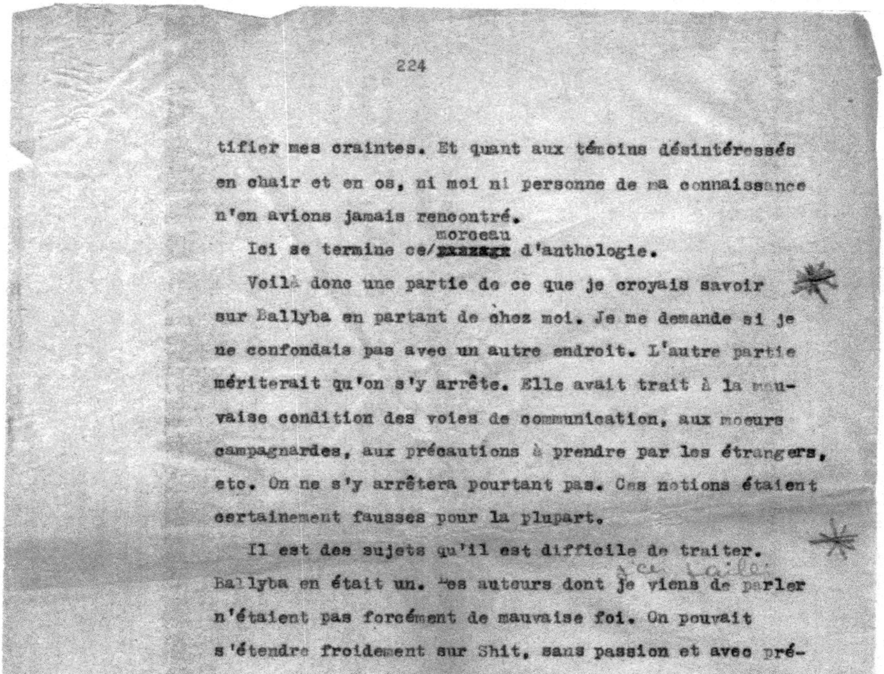

tifier mes craintes. Et quant aux témoins désintéressés
en chair et en os, ni moi ni personne de ma connaissance
n'en avions jamais rencontré.

    morceau
Ici se termine ce/~~passage~~ d'anthologie.

Voilà donc une partie de ce que je croyais savoir
sur Ballyba en partant de chez moi. Je me demande si je
ne confondais pas avec un autre endroit. L'autre partie
mériterait qu'on s'y arrête. Elle avait trait à la mauvaise condition des voies de communication, aux moeurs
campagnardes, aux précautions à prendre par les étrangers,
etc. On ne s'y arrêtera pourtant pas. Ces notions étaient
certainement fausses pour la plupart.

Il est des sujets qu'il est difficile de traiter.
Ballyba en était un. Les auteurs dont je viens de parler
n'étaient pas forcément de mauvaise foi. On pouvait
s'étendre froidement sur Shit, sans passion et avec précision. Pas sur Ballyba. Y être viciait le jugement, ne
plus y ~~xxx~~ être ne rendait pas le calme. N'y avoir
jamais été semblait sa meilleure chance, à condition
de ne pas faire attention aux racontars. C'est là une
chose que je ne savais pas en partant de chez moi. Je
croyais que j'allais tout voir de mes propres yeux, me
faire une opinion ne devant rien à personne, ajouter
Ballyba aux endroits où j'étais passé. Serait-ce à qui
ne l'a jamais ~~connu~~ que l'amour livre le mieux ses secrets?

A quelques vingtaines de pas de mon guichet la ruelle
se met à longer le mur du cimetière. La ruelle descend, le
mur s'élève de plus de plus. Passé un certain point on

Fig. 8: The end of the omitted passage on Ballyba's economy is marked by means of the first asterisk in grey pencil in the right margin (FT, 224r).

throw away, it was – perhaps if she had known that the Beckett manuscripts were there – because that was where I kept the original manuscripts of the translation of <u>Molloy</u> with Beckett's corrections on it, you see. And that was all – in both our handwriting. (Bowles 1990)[20]

It would have been interesting to study these documents, as they would have offered more insight into the translation process and the nature of the collaboration between Beckett and Bowles than is the case now, but that is forever out of the question.

The only surviving typescripts of the English *Molloy* (three near identical specimens of the novel's opening, a typescript of Part I, and a complete typescript of Parts I and II) are intermediate versions sent to Barney Rosset of Grove Press in New York, to keep him up to date about the translation's progress. According to Patrick Bowles, translating *Molloy* was a meticulous fifteen-month process (Bowles 1994, 25). Given the nature of their working method (see chapter 3.1), it is safe to conclude that all of the typescripts we have were produced by Bowles and that most of the manuscript annotations on the typescripts are in Beckett's hand – sometimes traced in a different colour of ink, possibly by Bowles. Because they are relatively late drafts – apart from the earlier but short specimens – they deviate only slightly from the published text, which puts considerable limitations on the genetic study undertaken in chapter 3. Part I of *Molloy* is the only section of the novel for which we have two typescripts and consequently their comparison reveals the most about the collaboration between Beckett and Bowles, as well as the evolution of their co-translated text.

There is one more partial typescript at the Lilly Library of Indiana University (IU), consisting of three excerpts – the first paragraph and two other short excerpts from Part I – but these appear to be later extracts taken from a published version of the novel (see TIU below).

20   We thank Lois More Overbeck and Martha Dow Fehsenfeld for giving us access to the material, and Martha Dow Fehsenfeld in particular for allowing us to quote from it in this volume (e-mail to Pim Verhulst, 10 October 2012). For a study of how this loss of material sheds a different light on the 'Notes' about his collaboration with Beckett that Bowles published in the *P.N. Review 96*, Vol. 20, No. 1 (March-April 1994), see Verhulst and Dillen 2014.

Three English specimens (Sp1, Sp2, Sp3)

The earliest surviving drafts of the Beckett-Bowles collaboration are at the Olin Library of Washington University, St. Louis, in box 3 of the Samuel Beckett Papers (MSS008).

There are two early specimens, a nine-page typescript (Sp1) and a seven-page typescript (Sp2), each with a title page. The second of these is accompanied by its carbon copy (Sp3). The text of the specimens is identical with a few exceptions. Sp2 appears to be a clean copy of Sp1, though it too is flawed. Sp1 has fewer words per line and therefore the text occupies more pages. Sp1 bears a few manuscript corrections by Beckett in blue pen. Sp2 and its carbon copy are free of manuscript annotations, though the carbon copy (Sp3) is smudged in several places.

Sp1 bears a total of four corrections in pen on pages 01r, 05r, and 08r, all of which are incorporated in Sp2. A misspelling is corrected (Sp1, 05r) and a missing question mark is inserted (Sp1, 01r), but the other two revisions are substantive: a comma is inserted after 'solace' (Sp1, 05r) and 'more' is revised to 'less' (Sp1, 08r). This last revision departs from the French original (see chapter 3.2).[21] Conversely, the words 'to fear, there was nothing' are missed in Sp2 (04r) but present in Sp1 (06r), an obvious typographical oversight. Elsewhere, the comma after 'animals' (Sp1, 07r) disappears (Sp2, 05r). This comma reappears and is maintained in all subsequent versions of the translation.

Sp1 was an early – though already much reworked – sample of the *Molloy* translation that Beckett and Bowles sent to Barney Rosset on 28 July 1953. In his letter to Rosset of 25 August 1953, Bowles explained that the specimen was already the eighth draft of the novel's opening few pages (see chapter 3.1). Sp1 is typed on different paper with a dragonlike watermark absent from both Sp2 and Sp3. This flawed duplicate and its carbon copy were probably made by someone at Grove Press. At the bottom of its title page, Sp2 also has a small yellow sticker with red lettering of Beckett's American agent: 'MARION SAUNDERS / 104 East 40th STREET / NEW YORK 16 / Murray Hill 5-4667'. Across the sticker is written in blue ink: 'property of Grove Press

---

21 'Oui, c'était un poméranien orangé, plus j'y songe plus j'en ai la conviction.' (1951, 15) becomes 'Yes, it was an orange pomeranian, the ~~more~~ less I think of it the more certain I am.' (Sp1, 08r)

795 Broadway / N. Y. 3'. This marks it as the typescript that was sent to *New World Writing* by Georges Borchardt of the Marion Saunders agency on 6 August 1953, before it was replaced with the more advanced thirty-seven-page typescript of Part I from which the editors of the magazine could choose an extract (see ET1 below and NWW in chapter 1.3.1).

First English typescript (ET1)

This yellowed typescript in the Samuel Beckett papers (MS008) at the Olin Library of Washington University, St. Louis (box 3, folder 49) only includes Part I of *Molloy*. It has handwritten labeling in grey pencil on the first page – likely added in the offices of Grove Press – that identifies the text as 'Molloy / by Samuel Beckett / (First 37 pages) / English translation / by Patrick Bowles / All American rights to / this translation owned / by Grove Press.' The crossed out reference to the first thirty-seven pages of this partial typescript is due to the fact that the document was conveyed to Grove Press in two batches, a first of thirty-seven pages in mid-October 1953, followed by a second one of 101 pages on 18 November 1953 (see chapter 3.1). The typescript is comprised of 108 pages in total, with no title page. The note '3 copies' is also written in grey pencil at the top left corner of the first page. There is evidence of at least one carbon copy, as part of ET2 (see below). If not lost with Bowles's destroyed papers, the third copy was possibly given to Maurice Girodias, who had agreed to publish the English *Molloy* in Paris as part of 'Collection Merlin' under the Olympia Press imprint. Unfortunately, his business files have not survived either (see chapter 1.4.1), so it seems unlikely that the third copy of *Molloy*, Part I still exists.

Bowles's description of their working method for Part I (see chapter 3.1), as well as the nature of the handwriting itself, suggests that the majority of the manuscript revisions are in Beckett's hand. It is an uncharacteristically clear hand, probably because this document was – at one point – intended as a (temporary) clean copy for Grove, so Beckett had to ensure the handwriting was legible. Some manuscript annotations may not actually be Beckett's – more likely Bowles's, writing under Beckett's direction – but it is safe to assume that the majority of corrections were authorized. Since Bowles reports having lost a considerable amount of his papers, ET1 is to be read as the result of an undocumented number of meetings and revisions, so that it is impossible to tell exactly how many versions preceded it.

ET1 includes some x'ing out, overtyping and interlinear typed insertions. Minor typing errors (such as a wrong letter) are often corrected by overtyping the correct letter. For mistakes involving several letters, the mistake is covered over by exes (less frequently by slashes) and the word is retyped cleanly on the line. Some typing practices do mark this as a document not compiled by Beckett. To cancel a word, Bowles usually overtypes it with the letter 'm' first before x'ing it out, and some mistyped letters are scratched out with a sharp object, which Beckett never does in his own typescripts. Finally, the letter 'a' is so often mistyped as a 'q' that it seems someone unaccustomed to the azerty key arrangement of a French typewriter – like the South African expatriate Bowles – was operating it. Other features are less aberrant. For example, on some occasions, a typed insertion is interlinear (usually with a typed slash on the line to serve as insertion point).

As the result of preceding undocumented work, compiled by Bowles, these typed corrections are usually not revisions properly speaking but hesitations as he transcribed what had already been agreed upon. Interlinear typed insertions can have been added later by re-inserting an already typed page in the typewriter but are more likely to be immediate and part of the typing process. The integrity of the right margin is compromised on many pages, some lines stretching to the edge of the paper so that a typed final stop had to be partially overtyped on the last letter (e.g. ET1, 67r, l. 16; 94r, l. 9). Likewise, an inserted comma (e.g. ET1, 106, l. 8 from the bottom) is cramped into a non-existent space. The final two pages are heavily creased along their left margin.

Manuscript revisions are almost all interlinear. A few margins bear an insertion point, a deletion mark or a single letter to correct a typographical error. Most margins are bare. The earliest manuscript correction is on page 07r where 'A or B' is revised to 'A or C', but another occurrence of 'A or B' five lines lower is left unrevised (see chapter 3.2). Otherwise, there are no revisions before page 10r. By the time this typescript was produced, the opening pages had already been revised separately, as evidenced by Sp1, Sp2 and Sp3 (see above). The bulk of the manuscript revisions are on pages 11r-37r. They are almost all in black ink. Cancelled words are normally heavily blacked out rather than simply struck through. It is worth noting the almost complete absence of emendations in the remaining seventy pages of the typescript. A good number of the rare manuscript emendations are mere spelling corrections and many pages are without any changes at all. Beckett would revise Part I more thoroughly later, as part of ET2 (see below).

Besides the revisions in black ink, and a unique correction in blue ink of 'knifes' to 'knives' (ET1, 52r), there are occasional pencil marks (ET1, 14r, 16r, 22r, 24r, 25r, 27r, 72r and 85r). On page 24r two small pencil underscores are accompanied by a question mark in the left margin, possibly made by Rosset or someone else at Grove. Another possibility is that this pencil marking was made by the editors of *New World Writing*, who used the first thirty-seven pages of this typescript to select an extract for their magazine (see NWW in chapter 1.3.1). The clearest remnant of this is a pencil mark in the right margin near the top of page 13r, which signals the end of the extract that appeared in *New World Writing*. Other traces left by the editors are harder to discern because they were erased. Halfway down the page 'having' was capitalized and underlined in grey pencil, so that an extract could begin with the sentence 'Having waked between eleven o'clock and midday' (ET1, 13r). In the left margin next to this line the editors had written what appears to be 'Start / here' (ET1, 13r). The hardest erasure to decipher on this page occurs in the top margin: 'Original / to be returned / to agent' in the top left corner extending to the middle, and 'Molloy / Samuel Beckett' in the top right corner (ET1, 13r).[22] More pencil annotations were erased on page 14r. The word 'shit' had been encircled (ET1, 14r), an obscenity which the editors of *New World Writing* marked for censorship on their own copies of the pre-book publication extracts (see NWW in chapter 1.3.1). Finally, on page 23r, an arrow in the left margin was erased, pointing to the passage beginning 'And suddenly I remembered my name, Molloy', which was also bracketed with grey pencil, probably for use in the extract as well.

Second English typescript (ET2)

The final typescript in the Samuel Beckett papers (MSS008) at Washington University, St. Louis's Olin Library (box 2, folder 50) is the only complete version of *Molloy* in the English genetic dossier. The typescript includes a title page identifying the manuscript as: 'MOLLOY / by / SAMUEL BECKETT / Translated from the French by / PATRICK BOWLES / in

22   These erased grey pencil annotations were made partially visible by manipulating the colour balance of the digital facsimiles.

collaboration with the author'. Patrick Bowles sent Beckett's corrected version of Part II to Barney Rosset on 20 January 1955, together with a second and more heavily revised copy of Part I to replace ET1, as he explained in his cover letter:

> Here is the complete manuscript of Molloy. It was slightly delayed by Beckett's recent illness. He gave it to me last week and I have inserted his corrections, where he has not inserted them himself. I am sending you a second copy of Part I. Of this, the first 30 pages have been retyped and the corrections on the rest have been inked in. If you are able sooner or later to return one of these copies of Part I to me I should be grateful since I now have no check copy with which to correct proofs. (SU, Grove Press Records, box 98)

Luckily for our genetic study of the translation process, Rosset held on to both copies of Part I, possibly because Bowles could check the *Molloy* proofs using the lost typescript(s) he had given to Maurice Girodias of Olympia Press to set the novel from (see chapter 1.4.1).

Part I counts 108 numbered pages, 30r-108r being a carbon copy of ET1. In both the freshly-typed and the carbon copy portions, there is some x'ing out and overtyping as well as the occasional interlinear typed insertion. The freshly-typed pages (ET2 Part I, 01r-29r) are almost completely without manuscript annotations of any kind.[23] They incorporate nearly all of the fifty or so manuscript revisions in ET1. In seven cases, however, ET2 goes beyond what is indicated in ET1 to bring the text to its published form, reminding us that the few documents we have of the Bowles-Beckett collaboration represent isolated snapshots of a long process with many undocumented intermediary stages.

At the bottom of 29r there is an arrow pointing right, followed by the handwritten note 'p. 30' in black ink, indicating the place where the retyped text should connect with the remainder of Part I (see Fig. 9). This consists of the – notably more yellowed – carbon copies of 30r-108r of ET1. It is here

---

23 A missing question mark is added on page 23r; on page 28r, a comma is added and an insertion point is drawn under a typed interlinear emendation; page 29r bears a spelling correction and two deletions.

that the majority of holograph revisions begin. The manuscript emendations made to pages 30-108 of ET1 had to be copied to ET2 by hand. Unlike ET1, cancellations are not blacked out but struck through – keeping the cancelled text legible. There are also occasional manuscript additions to the ends of lines where, presumably, the carbon copy did not transfer well (ET2 Part I, 43r, 45r, 52r). As we have seen, there are few manuscript revisions beyond 37r of ET1, most of them being typographical corrections.

Many new revisions were also made to Part I of ET2, in multiple sessions, judging from the three inks that were used, in addition to grey pencil. A fuchsia-coloured ballpoint pen and a black fountain pen are adopted throughout ET2 Part I, 30r-108r. Revisions in blue ballpoint start on 57r and continue to appear sparsely as far as 99r. This writing implement is least often used but for a few marks in grey pencil (ET2 Part I, 36r, 78r, 79r, 81r, 83r, 88r, 90r, 92r). Revisions in black alone are by far the most numerous and many of the revisions in fuchsia are overwritten – as though to confirm them – in either black or blue ink. This suggests that the pink revision campaign was first, followed by one in black and one in blue, but the relationship between the latter two is more difficult to establish, due to the sometimes faded hues of the inks.

The pagination of Part II restarts at 1. It is composed of 102 pages numbered 2 to 101 – the first page has no number. There are two pages mistakenly numbered 36, which have been differentiated by the addition of (a) and (b) in black ink. Pages 37r-101r are typed with a fresh typewriter ribbon, the previous pages of Part I having become progressively fainter. On 100r of Part II, an incomplete typed line is finished off by hand. The last page bears deep creases and the top right corner has been torn away and reaffixed with transparent plastic tape, now yellowed. Revisions made to Part II are all in black ink. Though some may be in Bowles's hand – as he explains in his letter quoted above – Beckett authorized all changes. The opening pages of Part II are the more substantially revised, but considerable energy was invested in reworking later pages as well, such as 49r, 53r, and 56r. Many other pages have only one or two revisions and some are free of any manuscript emendations. All in all, Part II is less heavily revised than Part I, at least on this typescript, which we must keep in mind is a very late document in the genesis of the translation. The typescript of Part I was almost a year older and therefore had more time to gradually accumulate revisions (see chapter 3.1).

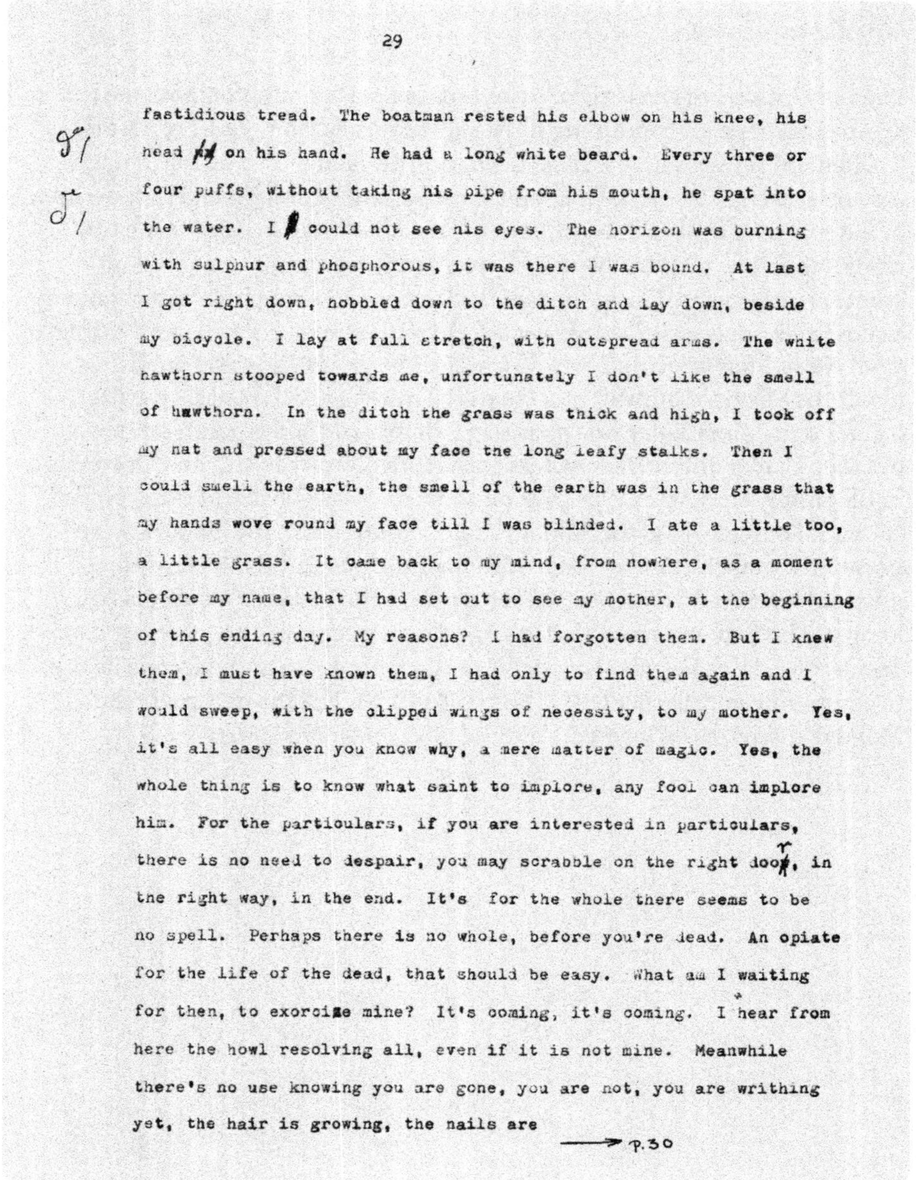

fastidious tread. The boatman rested his elbow on his knee, his
head on his hand. He had a long white beard. Every three or
four puffs, without taking his pipe from his mouth, he spat into
the water. I could not see his eyes. The horizon was burning
with sulphur and phosphorous, it was there I was bound. At last
I got right down, hobbled down to the ditch and lay down, beside
my bicycle. I lay at full stretch, with outspread arms. The white
hawthorn stooped towards me, unfortunately I don't like the smell
of hawthorn. In the ditch the grass was thick and high, I took off
my hat and pressed about my face the long leafy stalks. Then I
could smell the earth, the smell of the earth was in the grass that
my hands wove round my face till I was blinded. I ate a little too,
a little grass. It came back to my mind, from nowhere, as a moment
before my name, that I had set out to see my mother, at the beginning
of this ending day. My reasons? I had forgotten them. But I knew
them, I must have known them, I had only to find them again and I
would sweep, with the clipped wings of necessity, to my mother. Yes,
it's all easy when you know why, a mere matter of magic. Yes, the
whole thing is to know what saint to implore, any fool can implore
him. For the particulars, if you are interested in particulars,
there is no need to despair, you may scrabble on the right door, in
the right way, in the end. It's for the whole there seems to be
no spell. Perhaps there is no whole, before you're dead. An opiate
for the life of the dead, that should be easy. What am I waiting
for then, to exorcise mine? It's coming, it's coming. I hear from
here the howl resolving all, even if it is not mine. Meanwhile
there's no use knowing you are gone, you are not, you are writhing
yet, the hair is growing, the nails are ⟶ p. 30

Fig. 9: An arrow with a handwritten note 'p. 30' in black ink indicates where the retyped text of ET2 Part I should reconnect with the carbon copy of ET1, in the bottom right corner (ET2, 29r).

Lilly Library extracts (TIU)

The Lilly Library of the University of Indiana at Bloomington holds a five-page typescript containing three short extracts from Part I of *Molloy* (Calder and Boyars papers, LMC 2196, Box 61, Folder 5). The typed upper case title 'MOLLOY' in the top left corner is struck through and handwritten in the centre of the top margin. There is a note in the top right corner that reads: 'To follow p. 220'. There is some x'ing out and overtyping but no manuscript revision. Given the fact that the extracts conclude with a note by Maurice Girodias – the founder of the Olympia Press – as well as an extract from Alexander Trocchi's novel *Helen and Desire* (1954) – also published under the Olympia imprint – the material may be related to an *Olympia Reader* that John Calder was planning to publish at some point, but never did. The Calder and Boyars papers at the Lilly Library of Indiana University in Bloomington (LMC 2196) contain some information about these plans (Box 78, Folder 29). As this folder is dated '1966–1969', the extracts were presumably taken from a Calder edition of the novel and thus represent post-publication documents. Beckett's role in the matter – if any – is not known. The first extract is Molloy's opening paragraph (1955, 7-8; *Mo* 3-4). The second describes his visits to his mother, her room and the code he uses to communicate with her (1955, 20-4; *Mo* 13-6). The third extract relates Molloy's discovery of 'love' with Edith (1955, 74-9; *Mo* 55-8).

1.3 Pre-Book Publications

1.3.1 English

Prior to the appearance in March 1955 of the first Olympia Press edition of *Molloy*, four extracts from the translation were published in literary magazines:[24]

1. 'Two Fragments', *Transition Fifty*, No. 6 (Winter [October] 1950), 103-5; corresponding to pp. 86-9 of the 1955 Olympia Press edition. (The fragment from *Molloy* is numbered 'I')
2. 'Extract from Molloy', *Merlin*, Vol. 2, No. 2 (Autumn 1953), 89-103; corresponding to pp. 7-34 of the 1955 Olympia Press edition.
3. 'Extract from Molloy', *Paris Review* No. 5 (Spring [March] 1954), 124-35; corresponding to pp. 92-106 of the 1955 Olympia Press edition.
4. 'Molloy', *New World Writing*, No. 5 (Spring [April] 1954), 316-23; corresponding to pp. 7-18 of the 1955 Olympia Press edition.

Only one of these extracts – in *Transition* – was translated by Beckett alone, the others being the fruits of his collaboration with Patrick Bowles. The documents relating to these four pre-book publication extracts, the texts of which differ slightly from the corresponding passages in the Olympia Press first edition of the novel published in 1955, are as follows:

1 *Transition* extract ('Two Fragments') – (*TRA*)

Georges Duthuit's *Transition* was a revival and renewal of Eugene Jolas' pre-war *transition*. Along with capitalisation came a sharper focus on art and literature. The issue featuring the extract from *Molloy* also includes English translations of works by Julien Gracq, Pierre Reverdy, Francis Ponge, Lautréamont, Alfred Jarry and – in Beckett's (unsigned) translation – the

---

24 The text of these extracts is reproduced in the 'Appendix' to the 2009 Faber and Faber edition of *Molloy*, edited by Shane Weller (*Mo* 185-224).

last chapter of Emmanuel Bove's *Armand* and Guillaume Apollinaire's poem 'Zone'. The thousand-word extract from *Molloy* (TRA, 103-5) is followed by a 600-word extract from *Malone Dies* (TRA, 105-6), respectively numbered 'I' and 'II' without reference to the novels. The extracts are credited as 'Translated by Samuel Beckett' (TRA, 106), a fact he confirms in a letter to Rosica Colin on 19 May 1953 (*LSB II* 381). What prompted Beckett to render the passages into English is unclear and no draft material has been preserved.[25]

TRA is the first extant version of the passage that recounts, after Molloy's departure from Lousse's house, his difficulty in reaching his mother and his reflections upon the extent of his region (1955, 86-9; *Mo* 64-6). Published in October 1950, it pre-dates the collaboration with Patrick Bowles that was to produce the full-length published translation of the novel. It also pre-dates the manuscript pages of EM, which were not written before late 1952 or early 1953. Being the earliest sample, the passage differs considerably from the published novel – though in form rather than content – and it also had an autobiographical significance for Beckett (see chapter 3.1).

2 *Merlin* extract ('Extract from Molloy') – (*MER*)

Merlin was an English-language literary quarterly founded by the Scottish writer Alexander Trocchi in Paris in 1952. Richard Seaver served for a time as an editor (Seaver 1991, xv). Almost every issue included a work of Beckett's and considerable advertising space was devoted to promoting Olympia Press editions of *Watt* and *Molloy*. According to Seaver, *Merlin*'s zeal in promoting Beckett's work was the reason it never succeeded in securing magazine rate privileges from French postal authorities (Seaver 1991, xviii-xix).

The *Merlin* extract is a long excerpt corresponding to the first twenty-five pages of the novel (1955, 7-34; *Mo* 3-24). Originally, Trocchi and Seaver wanted to use a different excerpt from *Molloy*, starting with 'And now my progress', all through to the end of Part I (1955, 103-24; *Mo* 77-93). But after Beckett's failed attempt to revise Seaver's translation of the short passage

25   John Pilling, who has researched the papers of Georges Duthuit in the private possession of his son Claude, assured us he has not come across material in the collection, or in Beckett's correspondence with Duthuit, which sheds any light on these fragments (e-mail to Pim Verhulst, 24 July 2015). We are grateful to John Pilling for his kind assistance and for sharing his knowledge with us.

in the Tara MacGowran notebook (see chapters 1.1.2 and 3.1), he decided to drop the plan momentarily. The passage eventually published in *Merlin* was a result of his collaboration with Patrick Bowles. The first page of the extract (MER, 88) shows an illustration by Robert Culff. The text goes past the episode about the characters A and B to cover Molloy's visit to his mother, and then his apprehension and release by the police. It ends with Molloy by the canal, where he meets the boatman and his donkeys.

No page proofs for this extract have been found, though given Beckett's close affinity with *Merlin* at this time through Patrick Bowles, he is likely to have received a set. Based on ET1, this text of *Molloy* is slightly more advanced and most of the revisions were picked up in ET2 and the published novel.

3 *Paris Review* extract ('Extract from Molloy') – (*PR*)

The extract published in *The Paris Review* is credited as 'Translated by Patrick Bowles in collaboration with the author' (PR, 124). It was later anthologised in *Best Short Stories from the Paris Review* (1959) with the title 'Stones'. Despite its new title, the text covers more than just the famous episode of Molloy's sucking stones but continues some pages on to cover Molloy's brief interaction with the women who see him at the seaside and his great pain as he hobbles on legs of different lengths (1955, 92-105; *Mo* 68-79).

The Paris Review was established shortly after *Merlin*. At first, Alexander Trocchi, Richard Seaver and their colleagues viewed its appearance with a mixture of suspicion, anxiety and scorn but, as fellow Merlinite Christopher Logue notes in his memoirs: 'The rivalry between the magazines did not last; some of us were published in both, their editors became friends' (Logue 1999, 162). So much is clear from Patrick Bowles's letter to Barney Rosset of 28 October 1953, which is the first mention of an extract from *Molloy* in *The Paris Review*:

> As to Molloy, we are working on it again, it is going on steadily. Something cropped up concerning it today, which you should know of: The Paris Review want to print an extract of it, in the issue they are preparing, the next-but-one. They have quite a large circulation, about 8000: it might be a useful advertisement for the book, apart from anything else: but the questions

involved are the following: they sell a large number in the U.S. Would this interfere with your plans? Beckett is in agreement, provided you are. Next, the choice of extract: this must wait for about two weeks until the sequence we are on now is finished and everyone concerned has a copy of it, to decide which is to be printed where, in serial. (SU, Grove Press Records, box 98)

In *The Paris Review* Bowles saw an opportunity to attract more attention to the novel, and Olympia's 'Collection Merlin' series in which it was to appear, than *Merlin* could with its smaller print run and audience. On 10 November, Rosset answered he was 'all for using a section of the translation there' (SU, Grove Press Records, box 98). Having brooded on the idea for two weeks, he contacted Bowles on 10 November 1953 with a counterproposal:

> There is one thing which I would like to do with Paris Review if they print a section – and that is to make a reprint of just that Beckett selection which I would send around to my mailing list. It would be good advertising for Paris Review (full credit being given to them) and a good preview here to stir up more interest for the eventual publication of the book. If Paris Review would supply me with the reprints it would be very nice – but if that were not possible I suppose I could print them myself. If they would print them for me that would certainly suffice as payment for us. (SU, Grove Press Records, box 98)

Though the idea was discussed somewhat further in correspondence with George Plimpton, one of *The Paris Review* editors, it was eventually deemed too costly because of the extract's length (SU, Grove Press Records, box 98). On 18 November 1953, Bowles informed Rosset that '[t]he Paris Review have chosen an extract which begins on page 78 at "You'd think that once well clear of the town…" [*Mo* 66] and ends on page 92 at "To hang myself from a bough, with a liane" [*Mo* 79] (SU, Grove Press Records, box 98). Bowles is referring to the pagination of ET1, but eventually the passage would be shortened by two pages, starting with 'There are people the sea doesn't suit' (ET1, 80r; *Mo* 68).

By 5 December 1953, the proofs of the extract had been corrected, as appears from Bowles's letter to Rosset:

The extract appearing in Paris Review has also been altered, here and there, but not drastically: it can rest as you have it and the little minor changes of a word from time to time or a phrase can rest until the book is translated entire. However if it is possible to have a look at any proofs of whatever extracts may be printed that would ensure a more final version in the magazines etc. Of course it depends on whether the said magazines have the time to send out proofs. (SU, Grove Press Records, box 98)

The Paris Review proofs have not been located, but a comparison with ET1 reveals that the extract in the magazine is virtually identical to the relevant passage in the typescript of Part I.[26] In about a dozen places it is more advanced than ET1, and almost all of these differences are reflected in manuscript revisions made to ET2.

4 *New World Writing* extract ('Molloy') – (*NWW*)

New World Writing was the fifth Mentor Selection, a series begun in 1952 by the New American Library of World Literature with the aim of acquainting American readers with 'a genuine cross-section of the best' (NWW, 2-3) avant-garde writing of the time, including fiction, non-fiction and verse. The extract from *Molloy* is in the company of work by Sean O'Faolain, Kenneth Rexroth, William Carlos Williams, Ralph Ellison, Wallace Stevens and Dylan Thomas, as well as translations of three modern Arabic poets. It is followed by Niall Montgomery's essay on Beckett's work, 'No Symbols Where None Intended'.

The *New World Writing* extract is a short excerpt, adding just a page or two to the text of the specimens, and its end corresponds to the location of

---

26   *The Paris Review* Archives (MA 5040) at the Morgan Library & Museum do not contain any draft material, proofs or correspondence relating to the extract from *Molloy*. There is only a permission request for its inclusion in *The Paris Review Anthology* (1989), signed by Beckett (box 1). We are grateful to Reader Services Librarian, Maria Isabel Molestina, and Head of Reader Services, John Vincler, for their kind help with the Morgan Library collection. Contacting Editorial Assistant Caitlin Youngquist at *The Paris Review* itself did not yield any further results.

a pencil mark four lines down 13r of ET1 (see 1.2.2). However, this extract was not the editors' first choice.

As mentioned before, this pre-book publication was handled by Beckett's American agent, Marion Saunders, through Barney Rosset and Grove Press. Georges Borchardt of the firm sent a seven-page specimen – probably Sp2, since it has a Marion Saunders sticker (see chapter 1.2.2) – to Arabel J. Porter, an editor of *New World Writing*, on 6 August 1953.[27] Her Associate Editor, Marc Jaffe, wrote to Borchardt twice, on 3 and 26 September 1953, to apologize for the long delay in the magazine's response, due to the summer holidays. Still no decision had been made by 19 October 1953, when Marion Saunders personally sent Jaffe the first thirty-seven pages of *Molloy*, adding that it was 'the only manuscript of their translation that Grove Press have and they would like it back within a week'. At the top of Saunders' letter, Victor Weybright, the founder of the New American Library, noted in grey pencil: 'I find this pretty / hard going. / We might / start on / p 23 – / to p 37', a suggestion which Arabel J. Porter approved. This is the place on ET1 where a grey pencil arrow was erased in the left margin, pointing to the passage starting 'And suddenly I remembered my name, Molloy' (ET1, 23r; see chapter 1.2.2). Weybright and Porter then forwarded the typescript to Jaffe on 19 October 1953, who pencilled a short but clear note at the bottom of the cover letter: 'Just so you get Beckett / in no. 5 without fail'.

On 26 October 1953, Weybright contacted Jaffe again, suggesting a different starting point for the extract: 'I think it would be quite a coup to publish the MOLLOY translation commencing on page 13 midway down the page: "..having waked between eleven o'clock and midday (I heard the angelus, ..." to the end of the section'. Again, this is exactly the place on ET1 (13r; see chapter 1.2.2) where several notes by the *New World Writing* editors have been erased, including a marking that highlights the beginning of the passage mentioned in Weybright's letter. Three days later, on 29 October 1953, Barney Rosset informed Beckett of the news he had received from Marion Saunders regarding the *Molloy* extract in *New World Writing*, namely that they 'want definitely to use it – from page 13 to the end I believe' (SU, Grove Press Records, box 84). Beckett was 'glad N.W.W.

---

27   Unless noted otherwise, all the archival material referred to in this section is part of the *New World Writing* Records preserved at the Beinecke Rare Book & Manuscript Library (BRML) of Yale University (YCAL MSS 388, box 2, folder 38).

are taking the Molloy extract', but he wondered 'why they don't want the first 13 pages?' in his letter to Rosset of 4 November 1953 (SU, Grove Press Records, box 84). Two days earlier, on 2 November 1953, Pamela Cottrell of *New World Writing*'s Editorial Department had returned the thirty-seven-page typescript – together with the seven-page specimen – to the Marion Saunders agency, as Grove wanted to have it back as soon as possible. So, in order to prepare their extract for publication, the magazine had its own copy made of the original typescript, in two separate stages, a twenty-four-page, and a thirteen-page document.

First New World Writing *typescript (NWWT1)*

The first typescript in the *New World Writing* Records (BRML, YCAL MSS 388, box 2, folder 38) is twenty-four numbered pages long and runs from the middle of 13r to the end of ET1 (37r), opening with the sentence: 'Having waked between eleven o'clock and midday (I heard the angelus, recalling the incarnation, shortly after) I resolved to go and see my mother' (NWWT1, 01r). There are line counts in grey pencil at the bottom of almost every page, in addition to a note in the top margin of the first page: 'NWW / COPY not used Molloy / Samuel Beckett' (NWWT1, 01r). There are two important reasons why this extract was eventually 'not used' in the magazine.

First of all, it was not continuous. Four long sections are singled out with blue square brackets from the *Molloy* extract on this twenty-four-page typescript, dropping a total of '155 lines' from the text, as an anonymous internal memo to Arabel J. Porter of 3 December 1953 calculates. On the same day, Marc Jaffe sent Marion Saunders their chosen extract, stating the urgency of the matter:

> The deadline is close upon us and I would appreciate word from Beckett through you as soon as humanly possible. As a matter of fact, if you feel that his approval will be forthcoming, we can put the material in the works before the formal word comes through. Please advise.

What Saunders advised about the extract is unknown, but when she contacted Beckett, he did not approve, as a letter from Barney Rosset to Patrick Bowles of 7 December 1953 explains:

Now – as to New American Writing – it appears from what came to us this morning from Marian Saunders [sic] that Beckett says the excerpt should be all or nothing. I am not clear as to just what that means, but I take it that at least he wants them not to cut anything out of the excerpt from the place in the manuscript where they start until the place they stop. (SU, Grove Press Records, box 85)

Writing to Rosset personally on 14 December 1953, Beckett clarified what he meant: 'I was annoyed by NWW's horrible montage. The excerpt is always unsatisfactory, but let it at least be continuous. I don't mind how short it is, or how little beginning or end, but I refuse to be short-circuited like an ulcerous gut' (*LSB II* 432). What Beckett did not fully grasp – because it was never stated explicitly – is that *New World Writing* cut the extract short for reasons of indecency.

Patrick Bowles, on the other hand, understood immediately what Rosset meant when he told the translator that the magazine wanted to 'jump around' in the *Molloy* extract. In his letter of 5 December 1953 to Beckett's American publisher he wrote:

> I assume you mean New World Writing wants to censor their section. In what way? If they want to do it Beckett would have to see the proofs and agree to them, and considering as you point out, that you are printing the book complete, he will probably be willing for the extracts to be jumped around, but I expect it depends to some extent what jumping around really means, after all if the extract is one long hop I don't suppose he'll be overjoyed. So far as I'm concerned it seems inevitable and not too much to be lamented so long as the book is there. I'm eager to see. (SU, Grove Press Records, box 85)

Rosset, however, was not willing to be pragmatic, as he pointed out to Patrick Bowles on 7 December 1953:

While I think we would get some good out of having a section in the magazine I also see Beckett's point of view, and it does seem to me that they ought to have the guts to go ahead with it or quit calling themselves New World Writing and change it to Non-objectionable New World Writing. Do let me know the exact situation so that I can make sense when I talk to the editors at the New American Library, and present the situation as it actually is. (SU, Grove Press Records, box 85)

The only way to really understand the situation as it was is to look at the typescript edited for publication by the *New World Writing* editors. NWWT1 has over twenty instances where a word, a phrase or an entire sentence is circled with red ballpoint and question-marked because it was considered indecent. While some of these cases still fall within the passages selected, it is clear that the editors had done their best to avoid the cruder ones:

1 'balls' (NWWT1, 01r) – **not in extract**
2 'the hole in the arse' (NWWT1, 02r) – **not in extract**
3 'shit' (NWWT1, 02r) – **not in extract**
4 'peeing' (NWWT1, 02r) – **not in extract**
5 'faeces' (NWWT1, 03r)
6 'In any case it can't have amounted to much, a few niggardly wetted goat-droppings every two or three days' (NWWT1, 03r)
7 'unstuck' (NWWT1, 05r)
8 'my prick in my rectum' (NWWT1, 06r) – **not in extract**
9 'to wipe myself' (NWWT1, 07r)
10 'have a stool' (NWWT1, 07r)
11 'Oh I don't say I wipe myself every time I have a stool, no, but I like to be in a position to do so' (NWWT1, 07r)
12 'the scratching of the balls, digital emunction and the peripatetic pee' (NWWT1, 13r)
13 'To break wind' (NWWT1, 20r) – **not in extract**
14 'gas escapes from my fundament' (NWWT1, 20r) – **not in extract**
15 'break winds' (NWWT1, 20r) – **not in extract**
16 'break winds' (NWWT1, 20r) – **not in extract**
17 'break winds' (NWWT1, 20r) – **not in extract**

18 'break wind' (NWWT1, 20r) – **not in extract**
19 'break wind' (NWWT1, 20r) – **not in extract**[28]
20 'shit' (NWWT1, 23r) – **not in extract**
21 'shitting' (NWWT1, 23r) – **not in extract**

The zealousness of the *New World Writing* editors did not end there, as
they also emended – using the same red ink – the punctuation, the spelling
and even the word order of *Molloy* in over a hundred and fifty places
on their twenty-four-page typescript. Because Beckett had rejected the
selection, an alternative needed to be found, and very quickly so because
the magazine wanted to have a piece by him in issue no. 5. It is possible that
the editors asked Marion Saunders to have another look at the thirty-seven-
page typescript of *Molloy* so they could make another selection, as Saunders
herself did not return the original typescript to Barney Rosset until 7 May
1954 (SU, Grove Press Records, box 98).

Second New World Writing *typescript (NWWT2)*

The text of the second typescript in the *New World Writing* Records (BRML,
YCAL MSS 388, box 2, folder 546) is thirteen pages long and corresponds to
the extract eventually published in the magazine. It begins with the opening
of the novel and ends at the top of 13r on ET1, where a pencilled line still
marks its end in the original typescript on which NWWT2 was based (see
chapter 1.2.2). A sheet with bio- and bibliographical information about
Beckett precedes the extract. Every page has a typed number top center
and the upper right corner contains word counts in blue crayon. Printer's
markings in red pencil and crayon, as well as galley breaks in grey pencil,
occur throughout the text. This time, five words are circled or question-
marked in red – 'piss' and 'shit' on 02r, and 'farting', 'suck' and 'suckle' on
08r – but only the first two were considered harmful, as an undated memo

---

28 The expression 'break wind(s)' had already been pre-censored by *New World
Writing* staff when they copied the original typescript of *Molloy*. There, the
term read 'fart(s)' (ET1, 33r-34r). Because of this substitution, the syntax is
wrong in sentences like 'Four break winds every fifteen minutes.' (NWWT1,
20r) – instead of 'Four farts every fifteen minutes.' – so that an editor at *New
World Writing* pencilled 'please / check' in the margin next to this windy
passage (NWWT1, 20r).

by Arabel J. Porter indicates: 'Can use pp 1-13 / (on my mark). / Two bad words / on p. 2 – but / that's all'. No cuts are made from the text but, again, the spelling and punctuation of *Molloy* is tampered with in roughly forty places. Most of these editorial emendations were retained for the printed text because Beckett either did not receive the galleys, or too late to correct them.

New World Writing *galleys (NWWG)*

The *New World Writing* Records (BRML, YCAL MSS 388, box 35, folder 1136) contain galleys for the *Molloy* extract, which consist of one long continuous scroll, folded several times, and a shorter snippet with the closing lines. The proofs are uncorrected, apart from three small editorial notes in grey pencil: 'par. V', which appears to be a confirmation that a new paragraph does indeed start with 'This time, then once more I think, then perhaps a last time, then I think it'll be over' (NWW, 317) in the original text; another 'V' next to the faded words 'divines from' and 'escarpment' (NWW, 318), probably to check their legibility in the final copy; and 'ital. (?)' in the right margin next to the underlined (also in grey pencil) 'a fortiori' (NWW, 319), which is not italicized in the published text. At the start of the scroll, 'M. Saunders / (agent) / proof' is written in dark red crayon, underneath what appears to be 'O.K. / M. Saunders' in a fainter shade of red crayon. These red annotations are connected to Arabel J. Porter's letter to Marion Saunders of 18 January 1954, for Beckett's attention, to which she attached the galleys for the extract:

> I take pleasure in sending you these (uncorrected) galley proofs of the section of your novel, MOLLOY, which we shall print in our next NEW WORLD WRITING.
> As usual, we are on a tight schedule, and must return corrected proofs to the printer by January 26th. If you have any corrections to make, do please return them to us.

A week was not enough to mail the extract across and back over the Atlantic, while allowing Beckett time to read and correct the galleys, so it seems that Marion Saunders approved the text in his stead. On 21 April 1954, Beckett informed Barney Rosset: 'Received New World Writing with Niall Montgomery. Witty specification' (*LSB II* 480), referring to the title of Montgomery's essay ('No Symbols where None Intended', taken from *Watt*). He does not comment on the extract's many typographical errors and editorial interventions, possibly because it was a *fait accompli* anyway.

Beckett clearly identified the *New World Writing* extract as the work of Bowles and himself, writing to his friend Pamela Mitchell on 25 November 1953: 'Bowles is pleasant to work with and we finished translating the first half of *Molloy*, of which an extract is to appear in next issue of *New World Writing* I think' (*LSB II* 421). However, Bowles was not credited as the (co-) translator of the extract from the novel, which was not even introduced as a work originally written in French. It was Beckett that pointed out the oversight to Bowles, who sent a disappointed letter about the incident to Barney Rosset on 17 May 1954, shortly after the magazine's appearance:

> Samuel Beckett [...] has showed me the new copy of NEW WORLD WRITING 5, just arrived, with the extract from MOLLOY. He pointed out to me it wasn't listed either as my translation, or even as a translation at all.
>
> Did the editors of NEW WORLD WRITING not know of this, that it was a translation, and that I translated it, from the original book in French? I suppose the magazine will be on the stands by now, and it is probably too late to do anything in this issue. However; can this misunderstanding be rectified? I attach some importance to it. Would you be good enough to ask them to do something about it for their next edition? [...]
>
> I should like to hear from you, when you are able; and I do hope you will be kind enough to see about this NEW WORLD WRITING confusion. (SU, Grove Press Records, box 98)

Rosset did not take any blame – nor did he actually apologize – in his answer to Bowles of 26 May 1954, telling him to take the matter up with Beckett's American agent instead:

> We were as surprised as you to find that New World Writing did not mention a translator for the section of MOLLOY. What was even more disconcerting – they did not even say that MOLLOY was originally written in French.

Although we submitted the manuscript to them we had
nothing to do with the selling of it. That was all up to Marian
Saunders [sic], an agent not directly concerned with us, and I
would think it her responsibility to see to it that credits were
properly placed. (SU, Grove Press Records, box 98)

Rosset is partly right in stating that it is the duty of the literary agent to see to
the proper acknowledgement of all parties involved, but he is not being very
polite by saying that the unmentioned French origin of the text was more
disconcerting than the oversight of the translator's name. While Rosset did
add in his letter about the *New World Writing* mishap that he and Marion
Saunders 'also asked them to make a correction and give your name as the
translator', he also said that 'whether they will or not is another matter'.
Rosset had had an earlier opportunity to think of Bowles's interests, but he
was only acting in those of his author – and his own. On 16 December 1953,
Marc Jaffe sent him the biographical sketch of Beckett that the magazine
wanted to print, asking Rosset to phone in any corrections he would like to
make, but he only asked to have the publication date '1954' removed, not
feeling confident the novel would appear in time (SU, Grove Press Records,
box 98). Bowles is not mentioned at this point. It cannot have been a pleasant
feeling for him that both Rosset and Saunders were only representing
Beckett, especially not for a translator with literary ambitions of his own (see
chapter 3.1). Perhaps due to a sense of guilt, Rosset did press *New World
Writing* about the translator's fee, sending Bowles a cheque for $60 on
8 June 1954 (SU, Grove Press Records, box 98).

1.4 Editions

1.4.1 French

James Knowlson (1996, 377-8) and Shane Weller (2011, 111-4) recount how *Molloy* was eventually accepted – in a 'last ditch effort' – by the 'young, débutant publisher' Jérôme Lindon of Les Éditions de Minuit, after dozens of houses, including Éditions K, Gallimard and Seuil, had previously turned it down. Supported by the praise of prominent literary figures such as Tristan Tzara and Max-Pol Fouchet, Beckett's future wife, Suzanne Déchevaux-Dumesnil, brought the novel to the attention of Robert Carlier, the literary director of the Club Français du Livre, who recommended the work to Georges Lambrichs, the chief commissioning editor of Minuit. Suzanne first supplied him with typescripts of *Malone meurt* and *L'Innommable*, explaining in her letters of 4 and 5 October 1950 that she did not have a presentable copy of *Molloy* at the moment, but that Carlier would bring one round to the office on Friday 6 October in the afternoon (*LSB II* 205-6). In the meantime, Lambrichs had started on *Malone meurt* – deciding to publish an extract from the novel in the Minuit journal *Nouvelle revue littéraire 84* – but it was Lindon who first read *Molloy* on arrival, liking it so much that he immediately accepted the book for publication.[29] Contracts for *Molloy*, *Malone meurt* and *L'Innommable* were signed by Beckett and returned to Minuit by Suzanne on 15 November 1950, the proofs of *Molloy* following on 22 January 1951.[30] As Weller explains, publication was delayed since 'the printer, a catholic from Alsace [...] did not wish to be identified in the book

29   In an interview with Knowlson, Lindon describes the copy as unstapled and unbound, typed on separate sheets, which conforms to FT (see chapter 1.2.1) but several copies of *Molloy* circulated at the time, so it is not necessarily the same (Knowlson 1997, 377).

30   Beckett was asked to include a typescript with his corrected proofs, but it is not known if he did (letter from Philippe Hautefeuille to SB, 22 January 1951, IMEC, Fonds Samuel Beckett, Boîte 1, Correspondance 1946–1953). Unfortunately, there is no draft material for *Molloy* in the Fonds Samuel Beckett at IMEC. In reply to our request if the archives of Les Éditions de Minuit contain any manuscripts, typescripts, proofs or annotated editions related to the novel, Irène Lindon wrote: 'Je regrette de ne pouvoir vous aider dans votre recherche mais les manuscrits comme les épreuves sont toujours renvoyés aux auteurs.' ['I regret not being able to help you in your research

because he considered it obscene', which Minuit cleverly solved by referring to him as 'The special printers of Les Éditions de Minuit' (2011, 114).

The first edition of *Molloy* appeared in Paris on 10 March 1951.

1951   *Molloy. Roman.* Paris: Les Éditions de Minuit. 272 pp.

The original run of 3000 included fifty numbered deluxe copies, and an additional 500 copies were printed and numbered on special paper for friends of Minuit, according to the text on the back flyleaf of the book:

L'EDITION ORIGINALE DE CET OUVRAGE
COMPORTE CINQUANTE EXEMPLAIRES SUR
VELIN SUPERIEUR ALBELIO DES PAPETERIES
DE CONDAT, NUMEROTES DE 1 A 50 ET
COMPORTANT LA MENTION
"EDITION ORIGINALE"
IL A ETE TIRE EN OUTRE, POUR LE COMPTE
DES AMIS DES EDITIONS DE MINUIT
CINQ CENTS EXEMPLAIRES SUR ALFA
DES PAPETERIES NAVARRE, NUMEROTES
DE 1 A 500 ET COMPORTANT LA MENTION
"LES AMIS DES EDITIONS DE MINUIT"

On the back of the front flyleaf facing the title page, the following works 'DU MEME AUTEUR' are mentioned:

A paraître chez le même éditeur :
MALONE MEURT (roman)
L'INNOMMABLE (roman)
ELEUTHERIA (pièce en 3 actes)
EN ATTENDANT GODOT (pièce en 2 actes)

Aux Editions Bordas :

but manuscripts and proofs alike are always returned to the authors.']
(e-mail to Dirk Van Hulle, 10 November 2016).

MURPHY (roman) 1947

This first edition was followed by a second one in May 1953.

1953   *Molloy. Roman.* Paris: Les Éditions de Minuit. 272 pp.

By this time 'MALONE MEURT (roman)' and 'EN ATTENDANT GODOT (pièce en 2 actes)' were available, but 'L'INNOMMABLE (roman)' and 'ELEUTHERIA (pièce en 3 actes)' were still '*A paraître*'. However, Beckett would soon change his mind about *Eleutheria* and the play would not appear with Minuit until 1995, six years after his death. The reference to the French translation of *Murphy,* published by Bordas, was also dropped. According to Federman and Fletcher, the second edition was '[r]eprinted photographically' from the first (1970, 53), but a letter from Beckett to Jérôme Lindon of 2 March 1952 reveals that he asked for a few small corrections to be made to the text of *Molloy*: 'Je vous renvoie aujourd'hui Molloy et Godot. Molloy: une dizaine de petites corrections qui n'affectent pas la composition.' (*LSB II* 325) ['I am today returning *Molloy* and *Godot*. *Molloy*: ten or so small corrections that do not affect the composition.' (*LSB II* 325)] While it seems that Beckett made the changes to a copy of the text, the editors of his letters note that 'the corrections to *Molloy* have not been documented' (*LSB II* 326n1). A collation of the 1951 and 1953 editions reveals the following minor corrections:

Segment	Minuit 1951	Page	Minuit 1953	Page
524	**mes** disposaient à mettre	36	**me** disposaient à mettre	36
966	dans **ces** vêtements à lui	65	dans **ses** vêtements à lui	65
1616	Quoi ? La plier **?**	118	Quoi ? La plier**.**	118
1867	je serai obligé **de** rester	134	je serai obligé **d'y** rester	134
1950	des **allouettes** peut-être	140	des **alouettes** peut-être	140
3090	Avec **ces** petits camarades	188	Avec **ses** petits camarades	188
4483	et le **retint** par la manche	254	et le **retins** par la manche	254
4671	d'être sans **ambiguité**	263	d'être sans **ambiguïté**	263
4773	il n'y **existât** point de madone	268	il n'y **existait** point de madone	268

In 1963 *Molloy* was reissued, together with the story 'L'Expulsé' ('The Expelled'), by the Union générale d'éditions (an imprint of Plon) as No. 81/82 in the collection 'Le Monde en 10 x 18'. On 4 October 1962 Lindon asked Beckett if he had any objections to *Molloy* appearing in this series alongside other Minuit titles such as *Les gommes* (Alain Robbe-Grillet), *La modification* (Michel Butor), *Moderato Cantabile* (Marguerite Duras) and *La Route des Flandres* (Claude Simon). Since all books in the series reproduced a detail from a modern painting on the cover, Lindon suggested a work by Bram van Velde might be suitable (IMEC, Fonds Samuel Beckett, Boîte 4, Correspondance 1962–1964). Eventually, an abstract etching by Avigdor Arikha was used, resembling his illustrations for the limited edition of *L'Issue*, published by Georges Visat in 1968. The text of *Molloy* is followed by a 'Dossier de presse' and Bernard Pingaud's essay 'Beckett le précurseur', which the author had asked Beckett to look at and correct (letter from Jérôme Lindon to SB, 28 November 1962, IMEC, Fonds Samuel Beckett, Boîte 4, Correspondance 1962–1964). The Minuit files contain an annotated copy of Pingaud's afterword, but the handwriting is not Beckett's, and there is no indication that he was involved in other aspects of the edition. The punctuation of *Molloy* is altered in many places and some words are omitted, but no substitutions occur and several errors were overlooked, which suggests that Beckett did not receive proofs.

The first complete resetting of the novel by Minuit occurred on 27 June 1971.

1971   *Molloy*. Paris: Les Éditions de Minuit. 293 pp.

After Beckett won the Nobel Prize for Literature in 1969, Lindon made plans for a hardback edition of his complete works. *Molloy* was the first book to appear in the series, followed by *Malone meurt*, *L'Innommable* and *Théâtre I* – consisting of the plays *En attendant Godot*, *Fin de partie*, *Acte sans paroles I & II* – after which no other volumes came out (Weller 2011, 128). Minor errors – though not all of them – were corrected on this occasion but no major revisions undertaken, as opposed to the reset 1971 edition of *L'Innommable* (Van Hulle and Weller 2014, 76), and new mistakes were introduced as well, for example '**mes-ger**' (1971, 178) instead of '**messager**' (1953, 166). The substitution of certain verbs and nouns, like '**s'avéra**' (1953, 67) with '**se révéla**' (1971, 72), '**fut**' (1953, 112) with 'était' (1971, 121), and '**exertions**' (1953, 195) with '**contorsions**' (1971, 210), or entire phrases such as '**Ce qui me permit de**' (1953, 94) with '**Si bien que je pus**' (1971, 101), suggests that Beckett was involved in the process:[31]

Segment	Minuit 1953	Page	Minuit 1971	Page
0029	**Etait**-elle déjà morte	7	**Était**-elle déjà morte	8
0116	**au delà** des champs	11	**au-delà** des champs	11
0119	gravi jusqu'à la **plateforme**	11	gravi jusqu'à la **plate-forme**	11
0144	je le **regardais** s'éloigner	13	je le **regardai** s'éloigner	14
0148	la ville **dont** il vient de sortir	14	la ville **d'où** il vient de sortir	15
0151	de paresse **flanante** qui à	14	de paresse **flânante** qui à	15
0248	en vain **qu'on** vienne	20	en vain **pour qu'on** vienne	21
0272	et la gardai **par devers** moi	21	et la gardai **par-devers** moi	23
0282	et de **tièdeurs**, je m'en	22	et de **tièdeurs**, je m'en	24
0316	compter **au delà** de deux	25	compter **au-delà** de deux	26
0320	**Eclairé** par ces raisonnements	25	**Éclairé** par ces raisonnements	27
0390	l'une pour les **bien-portants**	28	l'une pour les **bien portants**	30
0411	**Ecoutez**, dis-je.	29	**Écoutez**, dis-je.	31
0482	leur **rendre**, puisqu'ils	33	leur **rendre** puisqu'ils	35
0490-1	on a beau **reculer. Elles** vous	33	on a beau **reculer, elles** vous	36
0636	**L'Egéen**, assoiffé de chaleur	43	**L'Égéen**, assoiffé de chaleur	46
0666	Pardon, **Monsieur**, c'est bien X	45	Pardon, **monsieur**, c'est bien X	49
0681	le sourire, Pardon, **Monsieur**	46	le sourire, Pardon, **monsieur**	50
0681	excusez-moi, **Monsieur**, quel	46	excusez-moi, **monsieur**, quel	50
0706	écrasé votre chien, **Madame**	48	écrasé votre chien, **madame**	52
0712	une **Madame** Loy, autant le	49	une **madame** Loy, autant le	52
0712	première, **Monsieur**, j'ai besoin	49	première, **monsieur**, j'ai besoin	53
0759	**ballotant** à mi-cuisse au bout	52	**ballottant** à mi-cuisse au bout	56
0760	Car **s'ils** m'accusaient de les	52	Car **ils** m'accusaient de les	56
0851	**Etrange** impression	56	**Étrange** impression	60
0930	me renvoyant à **d'autre** nuits	62	me renvoyant à **d'autres** nuits	67
0987	qui **s'avéra** bientôt impuissant	67	qui **se révéla** bientôt impuissant	72
1003	que **j'avais**, que je m'y	68	que **j'avais** que je m'y	74

31 No proofs or letters related to this edition have been found in the Minuit files at IMEC.

1020	ma bicyclette, **appuyee** contre	69	ma bicyclette, **appuyée** contre	75
1040	**au delà** de toutes les autres	71	**au-delà** de toutes les autres	77
1111	changements **dûs** au cycle	78	changements **dus** au cycle	84
1161	de ces **affaissements**, mais	82	de ces **affaiblissements**, mais	88
1191	Elle avait le **facies** légèrement	84	Elle avait le **faciès** légèrement	91
1209	me suppliât **de** désister.	85	me suppliât **de me** désister.	92
1237	Pauvre **Edith**, je hâtai sa fin	87	Pauvre **Édith**, je hâtai sa fin	94
1341	**Ce qui me permit de** reprendre	94	**Si bien que je pus** reprendre	101
1394	percer **ça** et là	98	percer **çà** et là	106
1412	dans une **Egypte** sans bornes	100	dans une **Égypte** sans bornes	108
1432	**Evidemment** vers les quatre ou	101	**Évidemment** vers les quatre ou	109
1441	et **rengaîner** le criss.	102	et **rengainer** le criss.	110
1468	confectionné une **pagaïe**.	104	confectionné une **pagaie**.	113
1507	comme un verset **d'Esaïe**, ou	108	comme un verset **d'Ésaïe**, ou	117
1540	toute imparfaite qu'elle **fut**	112	toute imparfaite qu'elle **était**	121
1648	par-ci, **par-là** qui eux	121	par-ci, **par-là**, qui eux	131
1656	ne soit rejeté **sur le champ**	122	ne soit rejeté **sur-le-champ**	132
1697	**non** pas un mot	124	**non**, pas un mot	134
1742	**Qand** il s'agissait de mon	127	**Quand** il s'agissait de mon	137
1782	et lui en **assénai** un bon	129	et lui en **assenai** un bon	139
1819	et villages, **relies** entre eux	131	et villages, **reliés** entre eux	141
1822	l'étrange **lumiere** de la	131	l'étrange **lumière** de la	141
1859	**pour** ridiculiser par la suite	134	**pour la** ridiculiser par la suite	144
1869	Et **quand** je dis	134	Et **quand,** je dis	145
1888	branches noir **dont** il tombait	137	branches noir **d'où** il tombait	147
1907	et raides, **ou** aurait dit	137	et raides, **on** aurait dit	148
1922	dans les yeux à **demi-clos**	138	dans les yeux à **demi clos**	149
1928	comme je l'avais **prévu**	139	comme je l'avais **prévue**	150
1929	tremblant **au delà** des troncs	139	tremblant **au-delà** des troncs	150
2113	la plus **métieuleuse** n'a	147	la plus **métieuleuse** n'a	159
2121	le bedeau **sur le champ** s'il	148	le bedeau **sur-le-champ** s'il	160
2123	les choses se **passaient** à la	148	les choses se **passsaient** à la	160
2125	**Etrange** paroisse dont les	148	**Étrange** paroisse dont les	160
2140	**Etes**-vous à jeun, mon fils ?	149	**Êtes**-vous à jeun, mon fils ?	161
2146	l'enseignement de l'**Eglise**	150	l'enseignement de l'**Église**	161
2176	Un voisin **libre-penseur** vint à	151	Un voison **libre penseur** vint à	162

A woefully imperfect text appeared in 1982 in Minuit's pocketbook collection 'Double', followed by a long essay (*'Molloy'*: un événement littéraire, une oeuvre') in which Jean-Jacques Mayoux emphasizes the continuity of Beckett's œuvre.

1982   *Molloy*. No. 7 in Collection 'Double'. Paris: Les Éditions de Minuit. 274 pp.

Though it corrects some of the errors that crept into the 1971 edition, egregious typographical mistakes such as typos, skipped words and lines mar the text in several places, suggesting that Beckett did not correct proofs for it.[32] However, in addition to small adjustments of punctuation, a few words also differ, hinting at some form of authorial involvement. For example, 'à **souhaiter**, à mon idée' (1971, 32) was changed to 'à **désirer**, à mon idée' (1982, 27), '**grande sensibilité**' (1971, 108) to '**grande simplicité**' (1982, 88) and '**tantôt à plat ventre**' (1971, 136) to '**tantôt sur le ventre**' (1982, 111), all unique variants. It is possible that Beckett made these adjustments to a copy of the text, which was used as a template for the 'Double' edition, but that he did not correct proofs for it, hence the many mistakes. Most of these errors have been corrected in the current 'Double' print and e-book versions, which conform well to the most recent paperback edition by Minuit (2009).

1.4.2 English (Paris)

The first appearance of the English *Molloy* as a stand-alone book was in Paris with Olympia Press, the publishing house of Maurice Girodias – the son of Jack Kahane, founder of the Obelisk Press.

---

32   The Minuit files in the Fonds Samuel Beckett at IMEC contain no material relating to this edition.

1955a   *Molloy*. A novel translated from the French by Patrick Bowles in collaboration with the Author. Paris: Olympia Press. 241 pp.

According to the 'achevé d'imprimer' at the back of the book, it was 'PRINTED MARCH 1955 BY / IMPRIMERIE MAZARINE'. On the title page, *Molloy* is described as 'a novel / *translated from the French / by Patrick Bowles / in collaboration with the Author*'. In the bottom right corner, the book is listed as being part of 'COLLECTION MERLIN', actually run by the editors of the Paris-based, English-language magazine *Merlin*, but published by Maurice Girodias under his Olympia imprint (see chapter 3.1). As Federman and Fletcher describe the cover, it is characterised by a 'design in yellow, blue, and black running over back and spine to front' (1970, 79), but the artist is not credited. In his Olympia Press bibliography, Patrick Kearney attributes the cover to Shinkichi Tajiri, who 'recalled doing a design for Girodias, who used it without informing the artist' (2007, 72). The top inside flap of the rear dustwrapper gives the French price as 'FRS 1.200'. Kearney points out that some copies are known to have 'SPECIAL PRINTING FOR SALE / IN THE U.K. & COMMONWEALTH' in place of the French price, which is substituted with '12/6' (2007, 72). Still other copies were overstamped 'FRANCE FEATURES' and 'FRANCE FEATURES / 15, NEW ROW, ST. MARTIN'S LANE, / LONDON, W.C.2' on the cover (Federman and Fletcher 1970, 79). Both variations were intended for distribution in Great Britain, where Beckett had not yet found a publisher for his prose, but the typesetting is identical.

Beckett and Bowles certainly proofread this edition (see chapter 3.1), but neither proofs nor galleys have been located.[33] Differences from ET2 are few, mostly corrections of errors and minor adjustments (see chapters 3.2 and 3.3).

33   In his detailed bibliography of the publishing house, Patrick Kearney notes 'there are no known printing records for Olympia Press' (2007, 18). The 'Patrick J. Kearney Collection on the Olympia Press' at Princeton University (C1262) does not contain any *Molloy*-related material either – with special thanks to Brianna Cregle and AnnaLee Pauls for their help with the archive. John de St Jorre, author of *The Good Ship Venus: The Erotic Voyage of Maurice Girodias and the Olympia Press*, also confirms that Girodias 'didn't keep any records or pay any attention to contracts, agreements, etc' (2009, 65). Mr de St Jorre, who kindly consulted Patrick Kearney on our behalf, stated that he was 'simply ignorant of Beckett's material' (e-mail to Pim Verhulst, 28 November 2015).

Patrick Kearney also mentions 'a tradition of an Olympia Press edition of *Molloy* in paper boards', which 'seems to have started with advertisements in similarly bound editions of *The Ginger Man* [1958], *I hear Voices* [1957] and *Watt* [1958]', but in fact 'it does not appear that such an edition was actually published' (2007, 72).

The only reissue of *Molloy* by Olympia was in a collection together with *Malone Dies* and *The Unnamable*.

1959a   *Molloy, Malone Dies, The Unnamable: A Trilogy.* No. 71 in the Traveller's Companion series. Paris: Olympia Press. 577 pp. [*Molloy*: pp. 1-240]

According to the colophon, the book appeard in October 1959. The dustjacket boasts the legendary olive-green colour with black lettering for which the series is famous and, while similar editions appeared in the USA (Grove Press, 1959) and the UK (John Calder, 1960), this was the only one to present the collection prominently and explicitly as a 'A Trilogy' on the cover (see chapters 1.4.3 and 1.4.4).

The idea to publish the three novels as one book had actually first been suggested by John Calder, who contacted Beckett about the matter on 8 November 1956 (IU, Calder and Boyars papers, box 40, folder 42). When he heard the news, Beckett wrote enthusiastically to Jérôme Lindon on 11 November 1956: 'Ils proposent de publier M., M.M., et L'I. en un seul volume. Le rêve pour mes rheumatismes.' (*LSB II* 671) ['They are proposing to publish *M.*, *M.M.*, and *L'I.* in a single volume. A dream for my rheumatics.' (*LSB II* 672)]. According to Calder, 'Girodias made difficulties' at first, because he owned the English language rights to *Molloy*, but an agreement was reached whereby Olympia would subcontract *Molloy* to Calder in exchange for shared rights to *Malone Dies* and *The Unnamable*, for which he had obtained the English language rights directly from Lindon (Calder 2014, 210-1). In order to share costs, Barney Rosset and Grove Press became part of the deal as well, so that three simultaneous editions of the 'trilogy' came to be marketed in France, the UK, the USA and related territories. This is not to say, however, that the 'collaboration' was perfectly coordinated.

After the third instalment of the 'trilogy', *The Unnamable*, had appeared as a separate book in 1958, Rosset renewed contact with John Calder to discuss their plans for a collected edition. On 10 April 1959, he was told the following by Lesley Macdonald at Calder:

> You will have received our reply to your cable re the BECKETT TRILOGY, that this is now set, and we are are getting proofs of it next Monday, 13th instant.
> Would you like to see these, and if acceptable to you we can supply repro pulls before machining our own edition. It is set in 10pt and 2 pts leaded to a 24 pica em measure, 37 lines to a page, in Times Roman. (SU, Grove Press Records, box 102)

Surprised by the news that Calder had already set their edition, Rosset immediately contacted Girodias for more information. He replied on 15 April 1959:

> I received your letter regarding the Beckett trilogy. John is supposed to send me two thousand copies of this, to be sold here under our imprint; I have not yet been able to get a definite price for this from him. This edition should already be on the market but he recently informed me that he had not yet found a printer, his usual printers objecting to a few words in MOLLOY. I would appreciate having detailed news from you on this subject. I am, in any case, willing to buy 2,000 copies either from you or from John. Will you please take note of this and act in accordance with your arrangements with John. (SU, Grove Press Records, box 102)

Baffled by this lack of communication, as well as the idea that now two different versions of the 'trilogy' would circulate, Rosset seemed nevertheless determined to proceed with his own edition in his answer to Girodias of 23 April 1959:

> Apparently both Calder and I have reset the Beckett trilogy. John says that he is sending on page proofs of his to us when it is ready. In the meantime, we have set ours and are waiting for galleys. It is, of course, possible that we would refrain from going all the way through into page proofs, but I doubt it. As our type

face is slightly bigger than his, I imagine that our book will be of slightly greater length. I suggest that you wait a bit longer before making a decision and let me tell you how long our book is going to be and let you see a sample page. Actually, the first two volumes will follow the style that we used in the third volume. Also, I will tell you what 2,000 copies would cost. Actually, I have no feeling about your taking the copies from John, if that is more convenient for you. However, do wait a brief time. (SU, Grove Press Records, box 102)

Girodias waited two months before contacting Rosset again, on 18 June 1959, regarding the possibility of using the American edition:

As you know I was supposed to reproduce John Calder's type for the Beckett trilogy and we were to share the expense of the typesetting of his edition. Indeed, I would very much have preferred that he print 2,000 copies for us as it would have reduced the cost price but this proved impossible because the book has to be incorporated in the Travellers series, the format of which is much smaller than your usual one and his.

Now the printers in England have started a strike which may be a long one and which makes it impossible for Calder to know exactly when he will be able to let me have proofs on art paper of his type. I should, therefore, like to know the position of your edition; is the typesetting finished and would it be possible for us to make the arrangement I wanted to make with John? We must work out a solution to the problem very soon as all our printers are closing down for the whole month of August and it is essential for us to print the book before then. Could you, therefore, please answer by return and, if possible, send me a specimen page showing the size of type, etc. (SU, Grove Press Records, box 102)

On 22 June 1959, Richard Seaver replied that Grove would be modelling *Three Novels* after their edition of *The Unnamable* – which they were using as a template for the reset texts of *Molloy* and *Malone Dies* – so Girodias could look at that for a specimen. Having received the Calder proofs by 25 June 1959, Girodias confirmed to Rosset that indeed 'it would involve too great a reduction which would make my edition illegible' and he decided to use Grove's text instead, without additional alterations.

In the same letter, Girodias made a good suggestion for a more coordinated approach to their endeavour:

> As Beckett seems to have revised Calder's proofs, don't you think it would be easier to have the galley proofs of your edition corrected by one of your proof readers, working from Calder's final proofs? It seems a little hard to impose on an author a revision of two different sets of galley proofs of the same book. (SU, Grove Press Records, box 102)

But in his reply of 30 June 1959, Seaver showed no intention to follow this advice:

> Unfortunately our communication with Calder in England is not always extraordinary, and I did not know – nor do I think anyone here knew – that Beckett had already revised Calder's proofs. Had we known of course, it would have been easier and saved considerable time to work directly from them. However, since Beckett has now corrected our proofs, and assuming we receive them by the 7th, we will rush them through and could hope to air mail you repro proofs within ten days of our receipt of the galleys. (SU, Grove Press Records, box 102)

To make matters even more complicated, it is unclear whether Beckett did actually correct Calder's proofs (see chapter 1.4.4) and – even though he did vet galleys for Grove – it is not certain that his corrections made it to New York in time for publication, if at all (see chapter 1.4.3). The possibility therefore exists that no first edition of the three novels was checked by him.

1.4.3 English (US)

The first American edition of *Molloy* as a separate book appeared with Grove Press, New York in August 1955.

1955b   *Molloy*. A novel translated from the French by Patrick Bowles in collaboration with the Author. New York: Grove Press. 241 pp.

The cover, designed by Roy Kuhlman, features a horizontal black banner at the top, with the title 'MOLLOY' printed inside a white rectangular box. The bottom shows three vertical banners – white, black and dark green – with 'A NOVEL' printed vertically in white against the black background of the middle banner. The centre of the cover is taken up by a horizontal white banner with an abstract design, under which 'SAMUEL BECKETT' is printed in black. The back cover shows a large photograph of the author in profile. The inside front flap provides bio- and bibliographical information about Beckett, which is followed by a long excerpt from Jean Blanzat's review in *Le Figaro Littéraire* that continues on the inside back flap. According to the colophon, the book was 'MANUFACTURED IN THE UNITED STATES OF AMERICA', but this is not completely true, as the sheets were imported from France.

From the moment Rosset got in contact with *Merlin* for an English translation of *Molloy* (see chapter 3.1), plans were made for a simultaneous edition in Europe and the US, in order to share costs. It was not until the Beckett-Bowles collaboration neared its final stages that Grove began to make concrete plans for the edition with *Merlin* and Girodias. On 28 September 1954, Rosset suggested to Alexander Trocchi: 'For example, we might print books here, and sell them to you at cost, or try some procedure which would reverse that idea' (SU, Grove Press Records, box 98). After consulting with Girodias, Collection Merlin's then Chairman, Christopher Logue, replied the following to Rosset on 11 October 1954:

> The cost of importing sheets into France from America is excessive because of the dollar-franc balance. Therefore, unless you had intended to produce the book by photo-offset or a similar method, in which case we could import the cellulose stencils, he suggests that we do the printing here and export to you the number of sheets you desire. Naturally, the title page of

the sheets you ordered would be altered to carry the GROVE PRESS imprint. If you are agreeable to these means we would of course make every effort to produce the book in accordance with your ideas of its appearance and size. The binding would be your own affair. (SU, Grove Press Records, box 98)

Preferring not to work with a middleman, Rosset wrote directly to Girodias from this point on, suggesting to him on 27 October 1954:

Rather than go into an involved discussion of the possibilities of our importing sheets from you or vice versa I would like to start with the idea of our photo-offsetting the book and printing here, using page proofs to be furnished by you. If we were to do that we would naturally pay you a fee. This is a much simpler way of doing things, especially as paper prices, etc. do not seem to be much cheaper in France than here. (SU, Grove Press Records, box 98)

Rosset included a sample page that pleased him of a book on the Grove Press list and he asked Girodias to do the same from his end, using copy from the *Molloy* manuscript itself, to decide who would be photo-offsetting whose edition. On 28 January 1955, Girodias proposed that Olympia could provide Grove with 'good proofs on printed paper, or transparent paper' and offered to send a specimen from Sade's *Justine*, in Baskerville type, which would also be used for *Molloy* (SU, Grove Press Records, box 98). Negotiations having stalled somewhat by 16 February 1955, Rosset informed Girodias that he would pay him $200 for his proof sheets of *Molloy*. Even though he had calculated that photo-offsetting the edition would cost Grove Press as much as setting their own edition from type, he found it worth paying the amount because it saved him the trouble of proofreading and airmailing manuscripts back and forth to the author and translator (SU, Grove Press Records, box 98). On 21 February 1955, Girodias promised he would send Rosset the corrected proofs by early March, which is when he expected Bowles and Beckett to be finished with them (SU, Grove Press Records, box 98). Rosset received a set on 2 March 1955, but he was not happy with it:

The page itself looks fine, but – and I cannot emphasize this too strongly – many of the pages are completely unsuitable for reproduction purposes. Entire words and sentences are indistinct. Perhaps the paper is too hard or the printing was not done correctly. We must have a better set than the one you have provided us with. Many of the pages are perfectly all right, but then some are completely impossible. For example, just going through the book at random I opened to page 116. Here the page number and the title at the top are very blurred and the bottom line is completely blurred.

I trust you will quickly go over a set similar to ours and see for yourself the impossibility of using it for photographic purposes. If we were to go over every word and ink in the faded spots it would be simpler for us to start all over again and set the type. As I already implied above, perhaps if you use a soft paper you would be able to get a better imprint from the press. (SU, Grove Press Records, box 98)

On 5 March 1955, Girodias explained to Rosset that these were merely 'first proofs […] yet to be corrected' by Beckett and Bowles, and that the final proofs would go to press within the next ten days, as soon as author and translator were finished with them (SU, Grove Press Records, box 98). While it relieved him to have news from Paris, Rosset did not hear from Girodias again until 13 April:

I am very sorry the proofs of 'Molloy' have been so delayed. In fact, our printers have given us proofs which were not satisfactory at first, and they have had to reprint them. Four sets of proofs have been sent to you yesterday, 1 by air mail, and 3 by ordinary mail.

I am very much afraid that the job is not really satisfactory in spite of the fact that this is the second trial. I feel that our printers should have done better and I suggest that, if you think that these proofs are not good enough for reproduction, we start all over again. As soon as you receive the set we have airmailed, please let us know if you need further proofs or not; perhaps you will need further proofs of a few pages only: this, of course, would be quicker. (SU, Grove Press Records, box 98)

Rosset again asked for new proofs, but they still had not arrived by 14 May 1955, when he cabled to Paris: 'PLEASE INFORM US IMMEDIATELY CONCERNING NEW MOLLOY REPRODUCTION PROOFS NOT YET RECEIVED HERE NEEDED MOST URGENTLY' (SU, Grove Press Records, box 98). Girodias replied on the same day, explaining:

We have sent to you two days ago, by air mail, several sets of a new printing of 32 pages of proofs of "Molloy".

We have really had no luck with this affair. Our printers, who are usually very dependable, have had to admit finally that their type was defective. They had been trying to remedy this defect, first, by printing proofs in a special manner, and afterwards by replacing the damaged or blurred letters. They have done so only on 32 pages so far in order to avoid unnecessary expenses in the event you would not accept new proofs.

If, however, you do accept them, please cable us once more, and we will undertake to send you proofs of at least the same quality for the remainder of the book, within a few days. (SU, Grove Press Records, box 98)

By 17 May the proofs had arrived in New York and Rosset cabled Girodias to do the same with the remainder of the book and airmal it urgently (SU, Grove Press Records, box 98). On 16 June, Girodias wrote to Rosset, hoping that he had 'received by now the complete proofs of "Molloy"' and that he 'found them satisfactory', adding: 'it has cost us more to obtain those proofs than it would have to reset the type!' (SU, Grove Press Records, box 98) Rosset confirmed he had received the pages on 27 June 1955, in a remarkably understanding letter – unless a note of sarcasm is to be detected:

We did receive complete set of proofs of MOLLOY and we have sent them on to the printer, who accepted them with great reluctance. I want to thank you for your excellent cooperation in getting them to us, and I know that it is through no fault of yours that the quality is so poor. The printer is extremely dubious as to the acceptability of the book which we will be forced to put on sale in this country, but we are going ahead anyway and hoping for the best. In this connection I would very much appreciate receiving two copies of your edition of MOLLOY, one to be sent by air mail and the other by surface mail. Enclosed you will find a check for $200 as per our agreement. (SU, Grove Press Records, box 98)

At this point, the correspondence between Girodias and Rosset about *Molloy* abruptly ends. Because the Grove Press edition took another two months to appear, and the typeface looks as good as that of the Olympia Press edition, it is possible that Rosset eventually decided to break up the Olympia book and actually photo-offset from the Paris edition, rather than the unsatisfactory page proofs Girodias sent him. At first sight, the text of *Molloy* in the Grove edition looks exactly identical to that of the Olympia Press, apart from the title page, which reads 'GROVE PRESS / NEW YORK' in the bottom right corner instead of 'COLLECTION MERLIN' (see chapter 1.4.2). The only noticeable difference is that the Grove page is not cut off so closely to the text as the Olympia page, making it a slightly larger book, though equal in bulk. However, a collation of the Olympia and Grove editions reveals minor variants:

Segment	Olympia 1955	Page	Grove 1955	Page
0106	was **sharp,** for they	10	was **sharp** for they	10
0123	What shall I **do?** What	11	What shall I **do ?** What	11
0444	in that **connexion** namely that	28	in that **connexion,** namely that	28
0796	destroy the brute **on** the	49	destroy the brute **of** the	49
0880	were leaves, **then** that	52	were leaves, **hen** that	52
0881	**How** difficult	52	**How,** difficult	52
0888	what he is **not.**	52	what he is **not,**	52

0893	in **ruins,** I don't know	52	in **ruins.** I don't know	52
0992	no longer **know**	60	no longer **kouw**	60
1001	**And** the things	61	**Anp** the things	61
1005	my **ha,** and my boots	61	my **hat** and my boots	61
1171	slab of **bread.**	73	slab of **bread**	73
1172	my **hands,**	73	my **thand**s,	73
1172	bottle were **brought**	73	bottle were **brough**	73
1175	**Itwas** likely to have been	74	**I was** likely to have been	74
1275	of **here,** and	80	of **here** and	80
1495	eight of my **sitxeen** stones	95	eight of my **sixteen** stones	95
1497	an extraordinary **hasard.**	95	an extraordinary **hazard.**	95
1558	**But** when they saw	100	**dut** when they saw	100
1572	one had to look **away.**	101	one had to look **aawy.**	101
1807	awkward **assaillant**	114	awkward **assailant**	114
1938	the air and **hun red** miles	123	the air and **hundred** miles	123
2392	I could not **understand**	139	I could not **understan**	139
3073	It was green **and** showed	166	It was green **an** showed	166
3098	through **to** the bitter end	166	through the bitter end	166
4402	right or **left,** as	221	right or **left** as	221
4495	words of **sollicitude**	225	words of **solicitude**	225
4594	crucified himself.	229	crucified himself**?**	229

As the survey suggests, Grove used the two-month window between their own edition and Olympia's to peruse the text and correct unspotted misprints – though not all of them. Since Rosset did not have the original type for the text, the only way Grove could have corrected these mistakes was by reprinting bits of word on similar paper using the same typeface as the edition (Baskerville), cut them out and paste them onto the original proof sheets sent from Paris, before offsetting the book. Close inspection of the altered passages in the Grove text reveals that some letters do appear slightly more askew or further apart than normal, which may be the result of this cut-and-paste method.

Some errors unique to the Grove text are puzzling in this respect. Where the Olympia text correctly reads 'on', 'ruins,', 'But', 'understand' and 'away',

Grove has 'of', 'ruins.', 'dut', 'understan' and 'aawy' (1955, 49, 100, 101, 139), which are clearly mistakes.[34]

There were plans to release hardback and softcover versions of *Molloy* at the same time, but the reason for the paperback's later publication in 1956, for which the remaining sheets were bound, is explained by Rosset in his letter to Beckett of 31 August 1955:

> We altered our original plan to bring the book out simultaneously in hard and soft bound edition, and we are now publishing the hardbound edition only, at least for the moment. My attorney here in New York felt that that was much the wiser course to pursue because he felt that we might run into censorship problems and by steering clear of the paperbound book for awhile [sic] at least we might avoid a lot of unnecessary trouble. (Rosset 2016, 91)

The next reprinting of *Molloy* by Grove was part of a collected edition, together with *Malone Dies* and *The Unnamable* (see chapter 1.4.2).

1959b   *Molloy, Malone Dies, and The Unnamable: Three Novels by Samuel Beckett.* New York: Grove Press. 577 pp. [*Molloy*: pp. 1-240]

---

34   The explanation for why this happened, even though Grove used the Olympia edition – or even the corrected proofs – to offset their edition may lie in the poor quality as well as the multitude of proofs that Rosset received from Paris. As mentioned above, Girodias sent Grove a first batch of uncorrected proofs, followed by different sets that were allegedly vetted by Beckett and Bowles. Because no single set was entirely satisfactory, Rosset may have assembled a text from the best pages in every state, possibly using the Olympia edition for pages lacking an acceptable specimen in one of the batches. In this process, Rosset may have (inadvertently) used pages from the proofs uncorrected by Bowles and Beckett, which would explain why the Grove edition has some errors not present in the Olympia text. The eclectic nature of this approach would also explain why Grove found it necessary to correct – inconsistently – a text already passed for press by the author and his translator.

The front cover is a photograph of Beckett looking straight at the reader, taken by Brassaï (Gyula Halász). 'Three Novels by / SAMUEL BECKETT' appears in the bottom left corner, opposite 'MOLLOY / MALONE DIES / THE UNNAMABLE' in the bottom right, both in yellow. The back cover gives information 'ABOUT SAMUEL BECKETT', followed by two excerpts from reviews by Harold Hobson (*The Saturday Review*) and Stephen Spender. Critical appraisal of all three novels continues on the inside front and back flaps – including Horace Gregory (*The Commonweal*), Kenneth Rexroth, the *Oregon Journal*, the *N. Y. Times Book Review*, Hugh Kenner and Wallace Fowlie – but Rexroth's description of *Molloy* stands out: 'A major modern classic . . . . It is a grim revery of empty progress through time and space, punctuated with dog-like sex and paretic battle'. The excerpts are preceded by a brief introduction to 'Beckett's three French postwar novels', described as 'a trilogy' despite his explicit wish not to do so, as expressed in a letter to Barney Rosset of 5 May 1959:

> Delighted to hear you are doing the 3 in 1 soon. Simply can't think, as I told Calder, of a general title and can't bear the thought of word trilogy appearing anywhere, what a hopeless unsatisfactory bastard I am. If it's possible to present the thing without either I'd be grateful. If not I'll cudgel my fused synopses for a word or two to cover it all. (*LSB III* 230)

But on 22 June 1959 Beckett wrote to Grove: 'can find no general title for the three works in one volume and can only suggest MOLLOY MALONE & UNNAMABLE' (SU, Grove Press Records, box 82). At the bottom of this letter, a Grove staff member pencilled: 'MOLLOY, MALONE DIES / and THE UNNAMABLE / Three Novels by Samuel Beckett', which is exactly how it appeared on the title page.

As Beckett's correspondence with his American publisher further reveals, not only was the text of *Molloy* reset and carefully pre-proofed for this edition, he also received a set of galleys and a setting copy with queries, from Jeanne Unger, on 26 May 1959:

> Under separate cover we are sending you the new galleys of MOLLOY and MALONE DIES, which have been set for inclusion in the one-volume trilogy with THE UNNAMABLE.

The galleys were set from the volumes we had already published (offset from Olympia Press editions), which had typographical errors in them. The proofreaders have corrected the obviously typographical errors, but have queried other things.

With the galleys sent to you are lists of these queries and copies of the volumes MOLLOY and MALONE DIES from which the galleys were set. The questions are indicated on the galleys and on the book pages.

We will appreciate it if you will resolve as many of these as possible, making the corrections on the galley sheets (preferably in ink of a different color from that used by the proofreaders), and making any other changes you find necessary, and return the galleys to us by sea mail. We will not need the bound copies of the books if your corrections are on the galleys. (SU, Grove Press Records, box 82)

A week later, on 22 June 1959, Richard Seaver expressed his worries about the approaching deadline to Maurice Girodias: 'Corrected galleys have been forwarded to Beckett, but just when he will return them is unclear at this point. Since we're publishing in October we must have them back fairly soon' (SU, Grove Press Records, box 102). On the same day, Beckett notified Judith Schmidt that he was 'returning to Grove Press today by registered surface mail the proofs of MOLLOY and MALONE DIES with my answers to queries' (SU, Grove Press Records, box 82). Beckett's corrections had still not arrived by 9 July 1959, two weeks later, when Richard Seaver wrote another worried letter to Maurice Girodias (SU, Grove Press Records, box 102).

Again, the correspondence between Grove and Olympia suddenly breaks off at this point. While it is clear that Girodias offset his own version of the 'trilogy' in the Traveller's Companion series from the American edition – the two being completely identical – it is less clear whether Beckett's corrections ever made it to New York, as neither galleys nor queries have been preserved in the Grove Press Records. If Beckett's corrections were used for the edition, he – and Grove's proofreaders – missed a good few mistakes, as the following survey of variants illustrates:

Segment	Grove 1955	Page	Grove 1959	Page
0007	I got **here** thanks to him	7	I got **there** thanks to him	3
0013	say my **good-byes**	7	say my **goodbyes**	3
0140	crouched like **Belacqua**	12	crouched like **Belaqua**	8
0154	a **pomeranien** I think	13	a **pomeranian** I think	10
0209	at all **seasons,** by a long lace	16	at all **seasons** by a long lace	13
0251	be able to **recognise** them?	19	be able to **recognize** them?	15
0399	position to do so, **if** I have to	26	position to do so, **If** I have to	22
0427	in his **shirt-sleeves,**	27	in his **shirtsleeves,**	23
0437	a little **gentle,** I mean refrain	28	a little **gentle.** I mean refrain	24
0675	I say, **this** or that or any	41	I say, **this, this** or that or any	38
0690	and fell to **the ground, an ineptness all the more unpardonable as the dog, duly leashed, was not out on the road, but in on** the pavement	42	and fell to the pavement	39
0698	in **defence** of a country	43	in **defense** of a country	39
0712	**Mrs** Loy	44	**Mrs.** Loy	40
0880	were leaves, **hen** that too	52	were leaves, **then** that too	48
0881	**How,** difficult	52	**How** difficult	48
0888	what he is **not,**	52	what he is **not.**	48
0951	my **crutch** and	57	my **crtuch** and	53
0952	pretending **be to** angry	57	pretending **to be** angry	53
0963	**waistcoat**	58	**waist-coat**	54
0967	Whereas the **room**	58	Whereas the **moon**	55
0992	no longer **kouw**	60	no longer **know**	57
1001	**Anp** the things	61	**And** the things	58
1038	the benefits **for** both	63	the benefits **for for** both	60
1062	yet it **mean.** nothing to me	66	yet it **means** nothing to me	62
1064	I did not dare **stopt**	66	I did not dare **stop.**	62
1076	said to **me,** but	67	said to **me** but	63
1084	I would have **beeen** I think	67	I would have **been** I think	64
1171	slab of **bread**	73	slab of **bread.**	70
1172	my **thands,**	73	my **hands,**	70
1172	bottle were **brough**	73	bottle were **brought**	70
1302	some dry and **odourless**	81	some dry and **odorless**	78
1308	I crossed the **alley**	82	I crossed the **ally**	79

| 113 |

1332	**these** are things that do not	83	**there** are things that do not	80
1337	See how **all things**	83	See how **things**	80
1338	which quarter of the **heavens**	83	which quarter of the **heaven**	80
1361	two **crosses** joined,	85	two **crosses,** joined,	82
1361	right and **the left** respectively.	85	right and **left** respectively.	82
1371	rather, I **left** the shelter	86	rather, I **felt** the shelter	83
1377	with renewed **vigour**	86	with renewed **vigor**	83
1385	I had **never** succeeded in	87	I had **not** succeeded in doing	84
1395	the **livid tongues** of fire	87	the **living tongue** of fire	85
1402	I would have **felt** it changing	88	I would have **left** it changing	85
1437	**preferring** their warm beds	90	**perferring** their warm beds	88
1438	especially the morning	90	especially **in** the morning	88
1474	**between** my four pockets	93	**among** my four pockets	90
1488	pocket of my **greatcoat**	94	pocket of my **great coat**	91
1498	if at a **pinch** I could	95	if at a **pitch** I could	92
1504	stiff leg **and my stiffening leg,**	95	stiff leg,	93
1514	All (**all !**) that	96	All (**all!**) that	94
1524	a similar **redestribution**	98	a similar **redistribution**	95
1571	at the **seaside !**	101	at the **seaside!**	99
1572	one too had to look **aawy.**	101	one too had to look **away.**	99
1575	why **not ?**	101	why **not?**	99
1602	nurse the former, **and reduce its sufferings to the minimum, to the maximum, by using the former** exclusively,	104	nurse the former exclusively,	101
1603	this **resource !**	104	this **resource!**	101
1606	I **still had** one bad	104	I **had still** one bad	101
1609	But **I couldn't !**	104	But **I couldn't!**	102
1610	**What ?**	104	**What?**	102
1612	to all intents and purposes, **intents and purposes,** I'm lost	104	to all intents and purposes, I'm lost	102
1649	had **increased,** since	107	had **increased** since	104
1653	the eyesore **here** called by its	107	the eyesore **he** called by its	105
1691	rid me of her, in **the** end?	109	rid me of her, in end?	107
1709	it's in my **dribble** as well	109	it's in my **drible** as well	107
1712	for **fear** of its	110	for **the fear** of its	107

1721	throw away, or give **away.**	110	throw away, or give **way.**	108
1724	better **off,** or any worse	110	better **off** or any worse	108
1735	at this **stage,** was	111	at this **stage** was	109
1763	**oh** not with true love, no	113	**or** not with true love, no	110
1763	you see who I **mean,**	113	you see who I **means,**	110
1774	the **neccessary** words	113	the **necessary** words	111
1813	educate myself, or amuse	115	educate myself,(or amuse	113
1830	in the **forest,** a place	116	in the **forest** a place	114
1867	happen to **be,** unless	118	happen to **be** unless	116
1870	I said this, **or,** I said	118	I said this, **or** I said	116
1929	**beyong** the harsh trunks	122	**beyond** the harsh trunks	120
2022	**Contentedly** I inhaled	127	**Certentedly** I inhaled	123
2026	in, on a **Sunday,** to	127	in, on a **Sunday** to	123
2069	leave his **finger in it** as	128	leave his **finger** as	125
2072	scenting **flattery,** for	129	scenting **flattery** for	125
2089	**When it came to the point we said no more.**	129	*	126
2099	To buck me up!	129	To buck me up.	126
2120	of these **manœuvres,** yes	130	of these **maneuvers,** yes	127
2127	**a** such **at** time	131	**at** such **a** time	128
2204	I made **a first** attempt	133	I made **my first** attempt	130
2250	liked **plants,** in all	135	liked **plants** in all	132
2331	**Mrs** Clement,	138	**Mrs.** Clement,	135
2383	I arrived **home**	139	I arrived **hime**	136
2401	before my **cheval-glass.**	140	before my **cheval glass.**	137
2414	The **liliaceae,** papa	140	The **lilaceae,** papa	137
2549	accepted **it,** I	144	accepted **it.** I	141
2593	each messenger **had** his own	146	each messenger **has** his own	143
2621	lager must be **left** to settle	148	lager must be **let** to settle	145
2625	**three quarters** empty	148	**threequarters** empty	145
2640	at my **stamps,** he said.	148	at my **stamps** he said.	145
2642	he **said,** with unimaginable	148	he **said** with unimaginable	145
2912	a **temperature?** I said	160	a **temperature** I said	157
2940	May I **go** up?	162	May I **got** up?	159
3041	**I** was for her to decide	164	**It** was for her to decide	161
3069	his **favourite** stamps	165	his **favorite** stamps	163

3083	the last **crumb,** had	166	the last **crumb** had	163
3093	the fatuous **clamour**	166	the fatuous **clamor**	164
3099	have I to **apologise**	166-7	have I to **apologize**	164
3117	what **I should** do	167	what **should I** do	165
3118	a **neighbour's** light	168	a **neighbor's** light	165
3121	**humour** this weakness	168	**humor** this weakness	165
3139	one **neighbour** in this way	168	one **neighbor** in this way	166
3164	in **favour** of a heavy	170	in **favor** of a heavy	167
3196	**whinging** for food	172	**whining** for food	169
3196	**whinging** for sleep	172	**whining** for sleep	169
3200	in the **right-hand** pocket	172	in the **righthand** pocket	169
3202	on the **bunch,** in my pocket	172	on the **bunch** in my pocket	169
3213	out of **bed,** pulling	172	out of **bed** pulling	170
3225	the benches **creaking**	173	the benches **cracking**	171
3228	**dishevelled,** her clothes	173	**disheveled,** her clothes	171
3248	The night was **fine,** in my	174	The night was **fine** in my	171
3272	do it at **all,** I got	175	do it at **all.** I got	172
3283	**music. I could** just hear	175	**music. could** just hear	172
3290	to the **grocer's,** or to Mrs **Clement's,**	175	to the **grocer's** or to Mrs **Clement's**	173
3297	we had got **into** the habit	176	we had got **in** the habit	173
3300	thank **God** for his goodness	176	thank **Good** for his goodness	174
3311	**imagining** myself in a world	177	**imaging** myself in a world	174
3312-4	**I could have solved it at a pinch. But already I was called elsewhere by the image of my son no longer behind me, but before me. Thus in the rear I** could keep my eye on him	177	I could keep my eye on him	174
3338	school he **attended,** were	178	school he **attended** were	176
3359	till **the** day he could	179	till **the the** day he could	177
3426	other **knick-knacks.** Martha's	184	other **knick-knacks,** Martha's	182
3429	fatal to cows and **horses**	184	fatal to cows and **horse**	182
3470	drank the water **to** the streams	185	drank the **of** the streams	183
3483	**I'd** give you	186	**I'l** give you	183
3530	allowed considerable **licence**	187	allowed considerable **license**	185
3536	I told him she **had** been	188	I told him she **has** been	185
3566	**peaceably** pursued	189	**peaceably** pursued	187

3587	of my two **knees** I had	190	of my two **knees,** I had	188
3638	the sky **sinking**	192	the sky **shining**	190
3639	insufficiently **observed**	192	insufficiently **abserved**	190
3657	Condom **is** on the Baise	193	Condom **in** on the Baise	190
3687-90	And if you can't find one second-hand? **I said. You told me second-hand, he said. I remained silent for some time. And if you can't find one second-hand,** I said at last, what will you do?	193-4	And if you can't find one second-hand, I said at last, what will you do?	191
3774	trying to **understand, I** said	195	trying to **understand. I** said	193
3784	Take **your** face away,	196	Take **you** face away,	193
3802	people asking **him** how he	196	people asking how he	194
3803	give his **name** and	196	give his **name,** and	194
3806	you've **enough** and	196	you've **enough,** and	194
3850	time **enough,** later on	198	time **enough** later on	196
3909	look at your **stick? I** said	201	look at your **stick. I** said	198
3917	threw me **a** last look	201	threw me **al** last look	199
3927	I **said,** Why of course	201	I **said** Why of course	199
3951	panting **and I** saw	203	panting **and** saw	200
3975	It was evening I had	205	It was evening. I had	203
4020	It was his turn **no** laugh.	207	It was his turn **to** laugh.	205
4107-8	as **possible** I got rid of	210	as **possible,** I got rid of	208
4112	without **incident** And	210	without **incident.** And	208
4140	it **has** been for a long time	212	it **had** been for a long time	210
4161	**His** eyes were staring	213	**He** eyes were staring	211
4306	spy out the **lie** of the land	216	spy out the **life** of the land	215
4386	**my** breath no longer mingling	220	**by** breath no longer mingling	218
4387	**tha** fact of his having	220	**the** fact of his having	218
4414	of **whom** I have refrained	222	of **whim** I have refrained	220
4566	into the **dust-pan**	228	into the **dustpan**	226
4569	I am sorry, **it** would	228	I am sorry, **It** would	226
4574	**I if** I once made up my mind	228	**If** I once made up my mind	226
4583	Did the serpent **crawl or,** as	228	Did the serpent **crawl, or** as	227
4610	Same **questions** for my son.	230	Same **question** for my son.	228
4630	more often than **of** my hens	231	more often than my hens	229

4631	not as men **dance,** to amuse	231	not as men **dance** to amuse	229
4635	These **evolutions** I finally	231	These **evolution** I finally	229
4637	I understand, **or,** Don't worry	231	I understand, **or** Don't worry	229
4642	a hum **peculliar** to it	231	a hum **peculiar** to it	230
4659	near my **sundrenched** hives,	232	near my **sun-drenched** hives,	231
4706	so **accustomed,** on	235	so **accustomed** on	233
4709	the rain **descended,** and	235	the rain **descended** and	233
4727	No, I spent **two.** This	236	No, I spent **two,** This	235
4745	Not only his **face.** He held	237	Not only his **face,** He held	235
4767	**It** must have impressed	237	**I** must have impressed	236
4789	gives **but** a feeble idea	238	gives a feeble idea	236
4807	Of **course** I would have	238	Of **course,** I would have	237
4925	**I** tried to understand	241	**It** tried to understand	240
4934	**I understand** it,	241	**I understood** it,	240

Apart from the normalization to American spelling, some though not all obvious mistakes in the 1955 text were righted, but new ones were introduced as well, the worst being omitted text and several cases of *saut du même au même*, when two lines begin similarly and the intermediate passage has been overlooked by the typesetter. Beckett, however, seems not to have noticed anything when he received his copy, writing to Judith Schmidt on 5 November 1959: 'I am delighted with the book. I always wanted to see the three together and I am very grateful to Grove for doing me so proud' (SU, Grove Press Records, box 82). In his letter to Barbara Bray, written on the same day, Beckett made an amusing variation on the '3 in 1' epithet he was so fond of using: 'It is a handsome volume once you get rid of the jacket and I am pleased to have the 3 between 2 boards at last.' (*LSB III* 250)

Corrected copy of Grove Press *Three Novels* (1959)

No proof material has been found for the American 1959 edition of *Three Novels*, but the Grove Press records at Syracuse University do hold a dissembled and disarranged, loose-sheet copy of the 1959 edition with annotations. It is scattered across four folders: *Molloy* is in 'Production, Setting copy' (box 103, folders 1 and 2) – missing the first two pages of the novel (pp. 3-4) – and it is followed by *Malone Dies* and a fragment of

The Unnamable (box 103, folder 3). The rest of *The Unnamable* has been filed under 'Production, Working copy' in the same box. The majority of the grey pencil corrections – not in Beckett's hand – were made to the text of *Molloy*, with *Malone Dies* and *The Unnamable* being almost clean. Since galley breaks (#1-121) are indicated throughout the book in red or black ballpoint and grey pencil, this annotated copy was probably used to set the 1965 Evergreen Black Cat (BC-78) paperback reprint of *Three Novels*, for which a draft title page is included in the folders.

1965   *Three Novels by Samuel Beckett: Molloy / Malone Dies / The Unnamable.* No. 78 in the Evergreen Black Cat series. New York: Grove Press. 414 pp. [*Molloy*: pp. 6-176]

A comparison of this 1965 Black Cat edition with the 1959 Grove Press version of *Three Novels* shows that most of the marked or annotated passages were adjusted for this reprint:

Segment	Grove 1959	Page	Grove 1965	Page
0399	position to do so, **If** I have to	22	position to do so, **if** I have to	20
0796	destroy the brute **of** the	45	destroy the brute **on** the	37
1763	you see who I **means,**	110	you see who I **mean,**	83
1813	educate myself,**(** or amuse	113	educate myself, or amuse	85
2022	**Certentedly** I inhaled	123	**Contentedly** I inhaled	93
2383	I arrived **hime**	136	I arrived **home**	102
2392	I could not **understan**	136	I could not **understand**	102
2412	The **lilaceae,** papa	137	The **lilaceae,** papa	103
2493	each messenger **has** his own	143	each messenger **had** his own	107
2940	May I **got** up?	145	May I **get** up?	118
3283	**music. could** just hear	172	**music. I could** just hear	128
3300	thank **Good** for his goodness	174	thank **God** for his goodness	129
3311	**imaging** myself in a world	174	**imagining** myself in a world	129
3426	turf or scraps of **bogoak**	182	turf or scraps of **bog oak**	134
3429	fatal to cows and **horse**	182	fatal to cows and **horses**	134
3451	in the **ashtray**	182	in the **ash-tray**	135
3536	I told him she **has** been	185	I told him she **had** been	137

3639	insufficiently **absorbed**	190	insufficiently **observed**	140
4585	waiting for the **antechrist**	227	waiting for the **antichrist**	166

On two occasions, a correction deviates from Beckett's text: the 1959 misprint 'May I **got** up' (1959, 145) is changed to 'May I **get** up' (1965, 118) instead of 'May I **go** up' (1955, 162), and '**bogoak**' (1959, 182) is spelled as '**bog oak**' (1965, 134).

1.4.4 English (UK)

Unlike its French and American counterparts, *Molloy*'s first appearance in the UK was not as a stand-alone book but as part of *Three Novels* in an edition printed by John Calder.

1959 [1960] *Molloy / Malone Dies / The Unnamable*. London: John Calder. 418 pp. [*Molloy*: pp. 5-176]

The front cover shows an abstract design by John Sewell, a constellation of circles, squares, rectangles and triangles in various shades of pink, white and black. The back cover is also entirely pink and carries advertisements for 'Calder Novels' (Alain Robbe-Grillet, Marguerite Duras, Nathalie Sarraute) and 'Calder Plays' (Ionesco, Adamov), situating Beckett in the company of predominantly French writers. The inside front flap introduces him as a bilingual author, as well as 'the true literary successor of James Joyce':

> Beckett writes with equal facility in English and French. This volume contains what is probably his most powerful work, the trilogy of novels written in French since the war, now appearing for the first time under one cover, as the author had always planned. *Molloy* has previously been available in Great Britain in the Olympia Press translation of Patrick Bowles, which is used in this volume. [...] The English reader is now able to read these three novels as one work, a masterpiece considered by many the finest work of imaginative fiction since *Ulysses*.

Despite Beckett's objection to the term (see chapters 1.4.2 and 1.4.3), Calder – like Rosset – described *Molloy*, *Malone Dies* and *The Unnamable* as a 'trilogy' in the blurb. When the British publisher asked Beckett for a title, he replied on 19 December 1958: 'I can think of no general title. TRINITY would not do. It seems to me the three separate titles should be enough. If anything better occurs to me I'll let you know' (*LSB III* 187). Because no other suggestion was forthcoming, Calder renewed his request on 29 December 1958: 'May we just use a general title "Trilogy" on the jacket with the three books listed underneath?' (*LSB III* 191n1). But Beckett was firm in his reply of 6 January 1959: 'Not "Trilogy", I beseech you, just the three titles and nothing else' (*LSB III* 191). When he informed Barbara Bray that the British publication of *Three Novels* was imminent on 26 March 1959, again referring to the collection as '3 in 1', Beckett expressed more anxiety about Calder's choice of title: 'Please God he doesn't call it a trilogy' (*LSB III* 222). Possibly following Rosset's example, Calder used the phrase '3 novels by Samuel Beckett' on the spine of the book and 'three novels by Samuel Beckett' on the front cover, under which the separate titles appear. They are repeated on the title page, without the blanket term, but the colophon sneaks in the dreaded word 'trilogy' again: 'THIS TRILOGY PUBLISHED IN ONE VOLUME IN 1959 BY JOHN CALDER (PUBLISHERS) LTD., 17 SACKVILLE STREET, LONDON, W.I'.

Though the title page gives 1959 as the date of publication, Federman and Fletcher note that the book was not released until late March 1960 (1970, 84). So, while Calder's edition was indeed the first to unite the three novels under one cover in the UK, it had been globally preceded by the Olympia and Grove editions. This is ironic, since it was Calder who originally proposed the idea of publishing them together in 1956 (see chapter 1.4.2). The main reason for the delay was that Calder's usual printers, Taylor Garnett Evans & Co., had objected to the passage in which Molloy vividly describes his sexual intercourse with Ruth/Edith (1955, 76-7; *Mo* 56-7). They had contacted a firm of solicitors, who advised them not to proceed with the printing unless certain alterations were made (letter from Noel B. Ranns to Lesley Macdonald, 13 February 1959; IU, Calder and Boyars papers, box 61, folder 10). Calder refused to change the text and decided to work with Wodderspoons & Co. instead. While the Calder and Boyars papers at IU contain several references to corrected proofs in the correspondence with the printers (box 61, folder 10), it is unclear if and to what extent Beckett was involved in this process. The corrected prelims for the edition carry a note in an unidentified hand – certainly not Beckett's – suggesting that his corrections did not arrive in time: 'Proof received back / too late $^{Dec.\ '59}$ to / incorporate in book' (IU, Calder and Boyars papers, box 61, folder 9).[35]

A comparison of the Calder *Three Novels* to the 1955 Olympia Press edition on which it was based does reveal that the English version corrects many of the errors in the Olympia text, while introducing relatively few mistakes – the most flagrant one being two switched lines in sentences 1363-4. However, as the survey below also shows, the edition emends the text in several places, and these changes may not have been authorized by Beckett. He would, in fact, revert some of them in a later, separate Calder edition of *Molloy* (1966) for which he is certainly known to have vetted proofs (see 1966b below).

Segment	Olympia 1955	Page	Calder 1959 [1960]	Page
0141	**because.** I mean if by some	12	**because,** I mean if by some	11
0146	I mean **of course** the fields,	13	I mean, **of course,** the fields,	11
0154	a **pomerenien** I think	13	a **pomeranian** I think	12
0198	I **am, I** will not say alone	16	I **am, I** will not say alone	13
0198	**means** but it's the word	16	**means,** but it's the word	13
0266	**generation, I** don't know why	19	**generation.** I don't know why	16
0298	you say **mag** you say ma	21	you say **mag,** you say ma	17
0302	**goat-droppings** every two	22	**goat-droppings,** every two	18
0305	**shrunken** hairy old face	22	**shrunken,** hairy old face	18
0332	**deaf blind impotent** mad	24	**deaf, blind, impotent,** mad	19
0333	That is to **say** I could say it	24	That is to **say,** I could say it	19
0333	I could say **it** but I won't say	24	I could say **it,** but I won't say	19
0372	into and **of course** out of this	25	into and, **of course,** out of this	20
0389	**Modestly** I pointed to my	26	**Modestly,** I pointed to my	20
0441	not of the **pastures** but of the	28	not of the **pastures,** but of the	22
0444	in that **connexion** namely	28	in that **connection,** namely	22
0520	good-will of the **overanxious**	32	good-will of the **over-anxious**	25
0566	I got **down. I** put my foot	34	I got **down, I** put my foot	26
0641	a **neverfailing** toughness	39	a **never failing** toughness	30

35 No author's proofs were found in the Calder and Boyars papers at IU for this edition, nor in the Fonds John Calder at IMEC. We are grateful to André Derval for his assistance with the unprocessed Calder files at IMEC.

0666	this *is* X, is it not**?, X being	40	this *is* X, is it not**? X being	31
0682	the right **word** the one	41	the right **word,** the one	32
0694	almost **angelfaces**	43	almost **angel faces**	33
0699	the lady in her stride	43	the lady **was** in her stride	33
0721	on **reflexion**, in the long run	45	on **reflection**, in the long run	34
0737	**Mrs**—the house where	46	the **Mrs.**—the house where	35
0785	It was a larch.	48	It was a larch **tree.**	37
0848	sat down in the **latter** and	50	sat down in the **latter,** and	38
0863	finally **realized** I was wearing	51	finally **realised** I was wearing	38
0908	or **not,** I shall hear it always	54	or **not** I shall hear it always	41
0915	but I **confine** myself to	54	but I **confined** myself to	41
0964	I take **cognizance** so clearly	58	I take **cognisance** so clearly	44
0997	the same **principle,** I can't	61	the same **principle.** I can't	46
1005	my **great coat**, my **ha,**	61	my **greatcoat**, my **hat**	46
1062	it **mean.** nothing to me	66	it **meant** nothing to me	49
1084	would have **beeen** I think	67	would have **been** I think	50
1158	ground at least, **at least,** I who	72	ground at least, I who	54
1175	**Itwas** likely to have been	74	**it was** likely to have been	55
1186	its **connexion** with my	75	its **connection** with my	56
1190	of **an** extraordinary flatness	75	of extraordinary flatness	56
1239	her stick **between** my legs	77	her stick **betweens** my legs	57
1247	in this **connexion**	78	in this **connection**	58
1248	in this **connexion**	78	in this **connection**	58
1271	**herbacious** plants	80	**herbaceous** plants	59
1278	my course **is** not yet fully run	80	my course **it** not yet fully run	60
1314	after a few **throes** came to rest	82	after a few **throws** came to rest	61
1334	half-**standing** half-lying	83	half-**standing,** half-lying	62
1347	the air **I hoped** of one who	84	the air, **I hoped,** of one who	62
1351	I **apologize** for these details	84	I **apologise** for these details	63
1363-4	For this little object did not seem to have any base properly so-called, but stood with equal stability on any one of its **four bases, and without any change of appearance, which is not true of the sawing-horse. This strange instrument I think I still** have somewhere,	85	For this little object did not seem to have any base properly so-called, but stood with equal stability on any one of its **true of the sawing-horse. This strange instrument I think I still four bases, and without any change of appearance, which is not** have somewhere,	63

4381	I have had so many	219	I **must** have had so many	160	
4384	I **realized** my mistake	220	I **realised** my mistake	161	
4433	You **recognize** me?	223	You **recognise** me?	163	
4441	I did not **recognize** this	224	I did not **recognise** this	163-4	
4458	Do you **recognize** me?	224	Do you **recognise** me?	164	
4459	Do I **recognize** you?	224	Do I **recognise** you?	164	
4490	he did not **realize** the state	225	he did not **realise** the state	165	
4492	I let a roar.	225	I let **out** a roar.	165	
4495	words of **sollicitude**	225	words of **solicitude**	165	
4524	the second I **realized**	226	the second I **realised**	165	
4542	It was **Spring** when I got there	227	It was **spring** when I got there	166	
4572	I let a roar, of triumph	228	I let **out** a roar, of triumph	167	
4582	fat of his leg (arse?)**?**	228	fat of his leg (arse?).	167	
4610	Same **questions** for my son.	230	Same **question** for my son.	168	
4645	not to **emphasize** the dance	232	not to **emphasise** the dance	169	
4652	to **jeopardize** my credit	232	to **jeopardise** my credit	170	
4654	the pains I **had** lavished	232	the pains I **have** lavished	170	
4664	repidly **unrecognizable**	233	rapidly **unrecognisable**	170	
4712	**stock still**, under my umbrella	235	**stock-still**, under my umbrella	172	
4722	not **rubberized** as a rule	236	not **rubberised** as a rule	172	
4922	I **recognized** them and	241	I **recognised** them and	176	
4922	they seemed to **recognize** me	241	they seemed to **recognise** me	176	

As the survey shows, many commas and full stops were introduced, and
Beckett's original spelling was adjusted to UK norms, including his
preference for '**connexion**' and '**reflexion**', which became '**connection**' and
'**reflection**'. Grammar and syntax, too, were normalized, especially in the
case of elliptical sentences, and verbs or tenses were freely adapted. Some
corrections of errors in the Olympia edition also led to new mistakes, for
example: 'Then I searched high and low, often with success, being fairly
familiar with the places where **Itwas** likely to have been' (1955, 74), which is
changed to '**it was**' in the Calder edition (1959 [1960], 55) instead of '**I was**'.
In some cases, the Calder text wrongly assumes a word in the Olympia text to
be incorrect, such as when Molloy refers to his hat on a lace: 'I threw it from
me with a careless lavish gesture and back it came, at the end of its string or
lace, and after a few **throws** came to rest against my side' (1959 [1960], 61),

which should be '**throes**' (1955, 82; see 1966b below). Another example is 'the dog **unheeded**' (1959 [1960], 160) instead of '**unneeded**' (1955, 219).

Especially this latter type of intervention suggests that Beckett did not proofread the edition – or that his proofs arrived too late to be used – and that Calder was responsible for introducing these changes. As he was already lagging behind Olympia and Grove with his edition of the *Three Novels*, it may have been rushed into production at the very last stage – an impression that is generally confirmed by the business files of Calder and Boyars at IU.[36] Again, Beckett did not seem to have noticed anything out of the ordinary when his copies of the book arrived on 4 May 1960, merely commenting to John Calder: 'I like appearance very much' (IU, Calder and Boyars papers, box 40, folder 43).

While Calder preferred not to delay the publication of the book any further, he did make immediate plans for a later reprint that would include Beckett's corrections. On 11 April 1960, Lesley Macdonald sent Wodderspoons a list of changes to be made to the type before it could be dissembled or 'dissed' (IU, Calder and Boyars papers, box 61, folder 10). Two options for reproduction were considered – stereotypes (a plaster copy of the original type) and repro pulls (glossy proofs suitable for photo-offsetting) – but since the former (£350-400) was considerably more expensive than the latter (£100), the choice fell on two sets of repros (letter from Lesley Macdonald to John Calder, 25 April 1960; IU, Calder and Boyars papers, box 61, folder 10). The proofs of the corrected pages were carefully checked and returned to Wodderspoons on 20 June 1960, when the 'OK' to pull the two sets was given (IU, Calder and Boyars papers, box 61, folder 10).[37] Unfortunately, neither repros nor corrections have been retrieved. In any case, later reprints of *Three Novels* were not set from the repros, since Lesley Macdonald posted a corrected copy of the first edition to Lowe & Brydone, the new printers, for the second edition of *Three Novels* (see 1966a below).

36   On 25 September 1959, Calder's production manager Lesley Macdonald wrote the following to the printer Wodderspoons about *Three Novels*: 'This job is very very urgent in view of all the hold-ups, so please do your best to get it off the machines as quickly as possible' (IU, Calder and Boyars papers, box 61, folder 10).

37   Dated notes containing this information, in grey pencil and black ballpoint, were added in the bottom margin of a Wodderspoons letter to Calder of 25 May 1960.

Corrected copy of John Calder *Three Novels* (1959 [1960])

While no galleys or page proofs have been found for the 1960 version of *Three Novels*, the Calder and Boyars papers at IU do contain an annotated copy of this first UK edition (box 61, folder 8). Thirty-one corrections, not in Beckett's handwriting, were made in blue biro to the text of *Molloy* and most of them were incorporated in the second printing of Calder's *Three Novels*.[38]

1966a   *Molloy / Malone Dies / The Unnamable*. London: Calder and Boyars. 418 pp. [*Molloy*: pp. 5-176]

For this edition, the text of *Molloy* was not entirely reset but the type simply adjusted in a few places, resulting in the following variants from the 1960 first edition:[39]

---

38   A letter from editor Dulan Barber to Lesley Macdonald dated 18 November 1965 suggests that he was responsible for making the corrections on the 1959 copy of Calder's *Three Novels*: 'Herewith a copy of the Beckett Trilogy. I have made the corrections to MOLLOY as requested by JMC [John Mackenzie Calder]'. The copy was then sent to the printer on 24 November 1965 with the following note: 'There are some corrections to the prelims as marked in the enclosed copy, and also some minor corrections to the text of the first novel MOLLOY' (IU, Calder and Boyars papers, box 61, folder 10).

39   Many of the typos in the first edition were also corrected for this reprint. Patrick Bowles may have been partly responsible for this, as he told Beckett on 9 March 1960 that he had found about 40 misprints in the *Trilogy*, which he listed and gave to Calder. Bowles also included a 'transcript' with his letter to Beckett, regarding what he called 'a couple of minor suggestions and one apparent misreading miscorrected' in the *Molloy* text of *Three Novels*. While the enclosure itself has not been found, Beckett briefly answered Bowles's queries: 'Your page numbers don't correspond with the numbers in edition so I comment out of context on the points raised:

1.   I prefer "let out"
2.   to be titillated is probably all right. Certainly not "to titillation"
3.   "deserve of" is not a Gallicism: xxx sound English, but suppression of "of" perhaps an improvement.
4.   "gives to reflect" correct.
5.   "prey of" compressed to "prey to" probably xxx for emphasis reasons.
6.   "rending" is correct. French "délivrant" I think.'

Segment	Calder 1959 [1960]	Page	Calder 1966a	Page
0141	**because,** I mean if by some	11	**because.** I mean if by some	11
0146	I mean, **of course,** the fields	11	I mean **of course** the fields	11
0511	If it is unlawful to be without papers, why did they not insist on my getting them.	24	If it is unlawful to be without papers, why did they not insist on my getting them**?**	24
0623	dog bustling about the **herd,**	29	dog bustling about the **flock,**	29
0714	having killed her dog I was morally obliged to help her carry **it** home and bury **it**	34	having killed her dog I was morally obliged to help her carry **him** home and bury **him**	34
0762	with a knife or **secateurs,**	36	with a knife or **secateur,**	36
0901	nothing stirs, has **never** stirred, will **never** stir	40	nothing stirs, has **ever** stirred, will **ever** stir	40
0908	or **not** I shall hear it always	41	or **not,** I shall hear it always	41
1909	the cloth **in** my pocket	89	the cloth **of** my pocket	89
2374	cordial, he **said,** I declined	102	cordial, he **said.** I declined	102
2714	or, **it's** a touch of neuralgia	111	or, **It's** a touch of neuralgia	111
2943	the providential **hinderance**	119	the providential **hindrance**	119
3292	breathing even and	129	**his** breathing even and	129
3361	a pocket **Monte Cristo**	131	a pocket **Monte-Cristo**	131
3470	drank the water **to** the streams	136	drank the water **of** the streams	136
3595	despaired at first ever	139	despaired at first **of** ever	139
3621	that when the innumerable	140	that when **of** the innumerable	140
3628	great classical **paralysis** were	140	great classical **paralyses** were	140
3948	the tree life	148	the tree **of** life	148
3954	**the** vigils and imaginings	148	**these** vigils and imaginings	148
3970	pushing each **other** as far as	149	pushing each **one** as far as	149

It is difficult to place these comments without context, but the first point raised may pertain to the the change of the expression **'let a roar'** in the Olympia text (1955, 225, 228) to **'let out a roar'** in *Three Novels* (1959 [1960], 165, 167), Bowles having compared the two. These letters are preserved in the James and Elizabeth Knowlson archive at the University of Reading (UoR, JEK A/2/37) but neither the 'transcript' nor the 'list' for Calder has been found.

Most of these changes revert the text of *Molloy* to the 1955 Olympia/Grove first edition, but some introduce new variants, such as the '**herd**' of sheep (1959 [1960], 29) that becomes a '**flock**' (1966, 29), or the less objectified description of Lousse's dead dog Teddy, referred to as '**him**' (1966, 34) rather than '**it**' (1959 [1960], 34).

Corrected galleys of Calder and Boyars Jupiter Books *Molloy* (1966)

While the annotations on a copy of the 1960 edition of Calder's *Three Novels* were not made in Beckett's hand, they were certainly authorized. They also occur on a set of galleys in the Calder and Boyars papers at IU (box 61, folders 6-7) which was corrected by the author. The galleys consist of sixty-one oversized sheets, each holding three pages of text, and the back of the final sheet has a note in blue ballpoint: 'Molloy. / Marked Set.' Marion Boyars mailed the galleys to Beckett on 27 September 1965 with the following note:

> We have just had the galleys of Molloy and I am enclosing a copy herewith. We are of course reading the book very thoroughly, and John tells me that he has a few notes on corrections that you discussed with him some time ago. But nevertheless, I thought that you might like to have a look at this. If you have any comments, I hope very much that you will write to me. (IU, Calder and Boyars papers, box 40, folder 45)

Beckett reacted somewhat confused on 7 October 1965:

> I am not quite sure as to why the fresh proofs of Molloy. However I am correcting them and you will have them back next week by the latest. There are quite a few mistakes. I do not know what John meant by author's changes. It was never my intention to make any. (IU, Calder and Boyars papers, box 40, folder 45)

John Calder himself confirmed the receipt of Beckett's corrected galleys on 18 October 1965, explaining what he meant:

Sorry about sending you fresh proofs of <u>Molloy</u>, but if you can bear to go through them again I would appreciate it. I had made notes of errors in our original edition, but the volume seems to have slipped through my fingers. As you will no doubt find further mistakes, perhaps it is just as well this way, although I hate to put any further burden on you. Marion's remark about authors [sic] changes was, I think a mistake – she meant corrections. (IU, Calder and Boyars papers, box 40, folder 45)

There are two sets of annotations on the *Molloy* galleys. The first set was made by someone at Calder in blue ballpoint. These fifty-three corrections mostly remedy misprints or obvious mistakes and normalize spelling to UK standards, in particular the suffix '-ize', which is consistently rendered as '-ise'. Occasionally, unclear type is marked with an 'X'. The second set of annotations was made in the fuchsia shade of ballpoint that Beckett frequently used. Most of the 142 corrections simply fix typos or restore omitted text, but in two cases Beckett also corrected what seem to be instances of censorship by the printers, for example in the episode with Lousse's parrot: 'He exclaimed from time to time, ~~damn~~ ^{Fuck} the son of a bitch, ~~damn~~ ^{fuck} the son of a bitch' (p. 39; *Mo* 35). The second occurs in the sucking stones episode: 'Pausing then, and concentrating, so as not to make a ~~mess~~ ^{balls} of it' (p. 77; *Mo* 72). The remaining corrections either revert the text of *Molloy* to the 1955 first edition or introduce minor new variants. While it is not clearly stated on the galleys which purpose they served, the pagination exactly matches that of the 1966 Calder and Boyars reprint of *Molloy* as a stand-alone text in the Jupiter Books series.

1966b   *Molloy*. Translated from the French by Samuel Beckett and Patrick Bowles. No. 13 in the Jupiter Books series. London: Calder and Boyars. 189 pp.

All of the changes that Beckett made on the galleys were implemented in the published text, leading to the following variants from the 1960 version of *Molloy* in *Three Novels*:

Segment	Calder 1959 [1960]	Page	Calder 1966b	Page
0141	**because,** I mean if by some	11	**because.** I mean if by some	11
0146	I mean, **of course,** the fields,	11	I mean **of course** the fields,	11
0266	**generation.** I don't know why	16	**generation,** I don't know why	16
0372	and, **of course,** out of this	20	and **of course** out of this	20
0389	**Modestly,** I pointed to my	21	**Modestly** I pointed to my	21
0511	If it is unlawful to be without papers, why did they not insist on my getting them.	24	If it is unlawful to be without papers, why did they not insist on my getting them**?**	25
0623	dog bustling about the **herd,**	29	dog bustling about the **flock,**	30
0714	having killed her dog I was morally obliged to help her carry **it** home and bury **it**	34	having killed her dog I was morally obliged to help her carry **him** home and bury **him**	35
0762	with a knife or **secateurs,**	36	with a knife or **secateur,**	38
0901	nothing stirs, has **never** stirred, will **never** stir	40	nothing stirs, has **ever** stirred, will **ever** stir	42
0908	or **not** I shall hear it always	41	or **not,** I shall hear it always	43
1314	after a few **throws** came to rest	61	after a few **throes** came to rest	65
1430	a few **survivors,** but	67	a few **survivors** but	71
1637	apart, **of course,** from the	79	apart **of course** from the	84
1909	the cloth **in** my pocket	89	the cloth **of** my pocket	95
2374	cordial, he **said,** I declined	102	cordial, he **said.** I declined	109
2714	or, **it's** a touch of neuralgia	111	or, **It's** a touch of neuralgia	119
2943	the providential **hinderance**	119	the providential **hindrance**	127
3041	it was **worthwhile** going to	120	it was **worth while** going to	129
3047	worse than old, **ageing**	121	worse than old, **aging**	129
3184	in **child-bed** as likely as not	125	in **childbed** as likely as not	134
3292	breathing even and	129	**his** breathing even and	138
3311	a world less **ill contrived**	129	a world less **ill-contrived**	139
3361	a pocket **Monte Cristo**	131	a pocket **Monte-Cristo**	141
3470	drank the water **to** the streams	136	drank the water **of** the streams	145
3565	**peaceably** pursued our way	138	**peacably** pursued our way	148
3595	despaired at first ever	139	despaired at first **of** ever	149
3621	that when the innumerable	140	that when **of** the innumerable	150
3628	great classical **paralysis** were	140	great classical **paralyses** were	150
3801	Come back **here,** and ask me,	143	Come back **here** and ask me,	154

3948	the tree life	148	the tree **of** life	158
3954	**the** vigils and imaginings	148	**these** vigils and imaginings	159
3958	I seemed to see myself **ageing**	149	I seemed to see myself **aging**	159
3959	the idea of **ageing** was not	149	the idea of **aging** was not	159
3970	pushing each **other** as far as	149	pushing each **one** as far as	160
4585	waiting for the **antechrist**	167	waiting for the **Antichrist**	179

It seems that Calder used Beckett's proofreading of this new *Molloy* edition as an opportunity to make small corrections to the reprint of *Three Novels* that would appear in the same year, as they share several variants. Why not all changes that Beckett indicated on the galleys of the Calder Jupiter *Molloy* were transferred to the 1966 reprint of *Three Novels* is unclear. As a result, the two Calder editions differed slightly – for example with respect to '**throws**' (1966a, 61) and '**throes**' (1966b, 65) or '**antechrist**' (1966a, 167) and '**Antichrist**' (1966b, 179) – with the Jupiter Books edition being the most authoritative and reliable.

1.5 Broadcasting Scripts

1.5.1 English

An extract from *Molloy* Part I, produced by Donald McWhinnie and read by Patrick Magee, with musical intermezzos by Beckett's cousin John, was aired by the BBC Third Programme on 10 December 1957, with a repeat broadcast following on 13 December 1957. The original recording of *Molloy* is available in the BBC Sound Archive at the British Library (T5564R C1) and several different versions of the broadcasting script have survived.

BBC script

The so-called 'Play Library' of the BBC Written Archives in Caversham, Reading, contains a copy of the broadcasting script.[40] The title page listing cast, rehearsal and recording dates is missing, but the second page, with the transmission dates as well as the opening and closing announcements, is present. The document shows some markings, in ink and in pencil, but there is no clear relation to the broadcast, and the hand is unidentified. 'MUSIC' is added before the first paragraph of text, indicating that the broadcast begins with a musical prelude, which is not clear from the typewritten script. Parts of the text are placed between brackets and some words are encircled, underlined or boxed, but to what purpose is unclear.

McMaster script

A second copy of the BBC broadcasting script is located in The Samuel Beckett Collection of McMaster University, Ontario (box 1, item 12). This is a complete script, including the two preliminary pages with broadcast details. The text is identical to that of the BBC script, but the annotations – in blue ballpoint – are different.

---

40   We would like to thank Samantha Blake of the BBC Written Archives in Caversham, Reading for her help with retrieving the script, and Matthew Feldman for his additional advice on the different versions.

The title page has the number '24374' in the upper right corner and the transmission dates are corrected:

     TRANSMISSION:
     ~~Sunday,~~ ^{TUES} ~~8~~¹⁰th December; ~~6.20 — 7.20~~ ^{9.45 – 10.45} p.m. THIRD
     PROGRAMME
     RECORDED REPEAT:
     ~~Tuesday~~ ^{FRIDAY} ~~10~~¹³th December; ~~9.15 — 10.15~~ ^{8.15 – 9.15} p.m. THIRD
     PROGRAMME

The total duration of the recording ('59'42"') is noted in the middle of the page on the right-hand side. There is no official stamp of the BBC Play Library.

The text itself shows just four annotations, three of which coincide with a longer pause in the broadcast, marked by the symbol 'e/o' or 'l/o' in the script. The first is inserted between 'No, I shall never draw it up, // yes, perhaps I shall' (p. 7; 1955, 109; *Mo* 81); the second comes after 'The dirty <u>old brute.</u>' (p. 13; 1955, 113; *Mo* 85); and the third delays the onset of 'But I think not.', which negates the previous sentence: 'And so I shall perhaps some day when I have less horror of trouble than <u>today.</u>' (p. 20; 1955, 119; *Mo*, 90). In this case, the symbol 'e/o' or 'l/o' is connected to a marginal annotation by means of a straight line: '+ breath'. An 'X' has also been added after the sentence 'And yet it might have been better for me to try and stay.' (p. 19; 1955, 118; *Mo* 89), but this does not coincide with a longer pause in the broadcast. It is unclear who was responsible for these annotations, but they do not appear to have been written in Beckett's hand.

McMaster photocopy

The most important copy of the BBC broadcasting script is a xerox preserved in the Samuel Beckett Collection of McMaster University, Ontario (box 1, folder 12). The annotations – also photocopied – do not correspond to any of the previously discussed scripts but they are closest to the text as broadcast. In the top right corner, an unidentified hand – possibly that of producer Donald McWhinnie – has written 'AS RECORDED', and there is a stamp at the bottom of the first page:

     | 135 |

This suggests that the McMaster photocopy was the script actually used for the production.

The first page, entitled "An extract from / 'MOLLOY'" lists the names of the main parties involved in the production. Berthold Goldschmidt, the conductor, goes uncredited, but his name is mentioned in the closing announcement, and so is Patrick Bowles, with whose aid Beckett translated *Molloy*. Also mentioned are the dates and times of the rehearsals (Saturday 30 November, 10.30 a.m. – 5.30 p.m.; Sunday 1 December, 10.30 a.m. – 5.00 p.m.; Monday 2 December, 10.30 a.m. – 5.00 p.m.), which all took place at Langham studio. The rehearsals of Sunday and Monday were each followed by a ninety-minute recording session from 5.00 – 6.30 p.m. They are designated as TLO 42849 and TLO 42849a, the former referring to the text, the latter to the music. The original transmission and the repeat broadcast are listed for Sunday 8 December from 6.20 – 7.20 p.m. and Tuesday 10 December from 9.15 – 10.15 p.m. but they would eventually be moved until Tuesday 10 December from 9.45 – 10.45 p.m. and Friday 13 December from 8.15 – 9.15 p.m. (see McMaster script above).

The second page of the script, also entitled 'An Extract from 'MOLLOY' gives the correct dates. It also includes the opening and closing announcements of the broadcast as well as the beginning and the ending of the extract:

TLO 42849   Opening Cue: 'And now my progress, slow and painful at all times...'
Closing Cue: 'Molloy could stay, where he happened to be' (MUSIC)

This is indeed the passage that Beckett singled out in his letter of 30 June 1957 to Donald McWhinnie, referring to the page numbers in the first Grove/Olympia edition of *Molloy*: 'from p. 103, line 11, "And now my progress..", to end of Part I, with a cut, p. 107, line 25, "Perhaps it is less to be thought...", to p. 108, line 5, "Time will tell."' (BBCWAC; *LSB II* 47).[41] The passage that Beckett wanted to have cut referred to Molloy's arse-hole:

> Perhaps it is less to be thought of as the eyesore here called by its name than as the symbol of those passed over in silence, a distinction due perhaps to its centrality and its air of being a link between me and the other excrement. We underestimate this little hole, it seems to me, we call it the arse-hole and affect to despise it. But is it not rather the true portal of our being and the celebrated mouth no more than the kitchen-door. Nothing goes in, or so little, that is not rejected on the spot, or very nearly. Almost everything revolts it that comes from without and what comes from within does not seem to receive a very warm welcome either. Are not these significant facts. Time will tell. (1955, 107-8; *Mo* 80-1).

It does not feature in the the typed text of the BBC broadcasting script, but the passage was further cut down to remove Molloy's reference to the 'portal of our being' altogether. The following lines are crossed out in pencil on the broadcasting script:

> ~~So that I would have hesitated to exclaim, with my finger up my arse-hole for example, Jesus-Christ, it's much worse than yesterday, I can hardly believe it is the same hole. I apologize for having to revert to this lewd orifice, 'tis my muse will have it so.~~

<hr/>

41   This passage corresponds to (1955, 103-24; *Mo* 77-93). It is also the same extract as the one singled out for translation by Richard Seaver in the Tara MacGowran notebook (see chapter 1.2.1). Matthew Feldman (2014) helpfully reproduces the outline of the BBC broadcasting script, with the corresponding page numbers of the 2009 Faber edition of *Molloy*, indicating at which point the text was interrupted by a musical intermezzo. However, as the following survey illustrates, the actual recording deviated from the script in several important respects.

[*already cut passage cited above*] ~~But I shall do my utmost none the less to keep it in the background, in the future. And that will be easy, for the future is by no means uncertain, the unspeakable future. And when it comes to neglecting fundamentals, I think I have nothing to learn, and indeed I confuse them with accidentals. But to return to my weak points,~~ (p. 6; 1955, 107-8; *Mo* 80-1)

As a result, the text of the BBC broadcast jumps from p. 107, l. 20 (*Mo* 80, l. 28) to p. 108, l. 11 (*Mo* 81, l. 12), so that Molloy's story about the effect of the seaside on his weaknesses runs on uninterrupted by the arse-hole aside: 'For as long as I had remained at the seaside my weak points, while admittedly increasing in weakness, as was only to be expected, only increased imperceptibly, in weakness I mean. // let me say again that at the seaside they had developed normally' (p. 6).

Another passage crossed out on the broadcasting script is: '~~What's all this, I thought I had lost the sense of smell. Can one speak of pissing, under these conditions? Rubbish!~~' (p. 8; 1955, 109; *Mo* 82). The preceding sentence, however, was retained: 'I give you my word, I cannot piss, my word of honour, as a gentleman. But my prepuce, sat verbum, oozes urine, it smells of kidney' (1955, 109; *Mo* 82).

The third and last substantial cut occurs at the end of the broadcasting script, when Molloy hears a voice telling him not to fret: '~~These words struck it is not too much to say as clearly on my ear, and on my understanding, as the urchin's thanks I suppose when I stooped and picked up his marble~~' (pp. 24-5; 1955, 123; *Mo* 93). This sentence was possibly removed because it refers back to an earlier passage in the novel that was not part of the broadcasting excerpt:

> Thanks I suppose, as the urchin said when I picked up his marble, I don't know why, I didn't have to, and I suppose he would have preferred to pick it up himself. Or perhaps it wasn't to be picked up. And the effort it cost me, with my stiff leg. The words engraved themselves for ever on my memory, perhaps because I understood them at once, a thing I didn't often do. (1955, 66; *Mo* 48)

Whether these changes were decided in the recording studio or cleared by Beckett in advance during the meetings with his cousin John or Donald McWhinnie is unknown.[42] Since the production had been allotted 60 minutes in the Third Programme broadcast schedule, it is not unthinkable that ad-hoc adjustments had to be made in order to keep the recording within its appointed timeframe. This explanation is less tenable, however, when a single word is crossed out, as in the following example:

> And it was these little adjustments, as between Galileo's vessels, that I can only express by saying, I feared that, or, I hoped that, or, Is that your mother's name? said the sergeant, for example, and that I might ~~doubtless~~ have expressed otherwise and better, if I had gone to the trouble. (p. 20; 1955, 119; *Mo* 90)

Instead of an attempt to skimp on broadcast time, this alteration comes across as a deliberate attempt to undermine the certainty and self-confidence of Molloy, which is reinforced by the faltering tone in which Magee delivers the lines. The second deletion of a word in the script was ignored in the broadcast, which does include 'fortunately': 'For my wrists were still quite strong, ~~fortunately,~~ in spite of my decrepitude, though all swollen and racked by a kind of chronic arthritis probably' (p. 22; 1955, 121; *Mo* 91).

The script also contains two minor additions, which mostly serve to gear the text of *Molloy* to recitation. In the first instance, a phrase is repeated a third time to create a rapport between form and content, as Magee is audibly lost when talking confusedly about his leg:

---

42   The script deviates from the published text on two more occasions. In the first, it adds a comma after 'shall' in the following example, but this is inaudible in the broadcast: 'And though it is no part of my tottering intentions to treat here in full, as they deserve, these brief moments of the immemorial expiation, I **shall** nevertheless, deal with them' (1955, 105; *Mo* 79). In the second, it corrects a typo ('beyond') in: 'trembling **beyong** the harsh trunks' (1955, 122; *Mo* 92). For more information about Beckett's role in the broadcast, see Feldman 2014.

But I couldn't! What? Lean on it! For it was shortening, don't forget, whereas the other, though stiffening, was not yet shortening, or so far behind its fellow that to all intents and purposes, intents and purposes, ^{intents & purposes.} I'm lost, no matter. (p. 2; 1955, 104; *Mo* 78).

In the actual recording the sense of confusion is even more acute, as Magee starts to mutter almost inaudibly towards the end of the sentence. The second addition also emphasizes the spoken nature of the text by means of repetition: 'Come come ^{come}. Fate is rancorous, but not to that extent' (p. 8; 1955, 109; *Mo* 82). Many other small deviations from the published text of *Molloy* occur in the broadcast – additions, deletions, substitutions – likely to have arisen in the heat of recitation, as they do not appear as annotations on the script:

Page	Molloy 1955	BBC broadcast
104	the **help** of my crutches	the **aid** of my crutches
104	And **the worse**, to my mind	And **worst of it**, to my mind
104	the old bad leg **that** I often longed to	the old bad leg I often longed to
109	(dangerous to scream)	(**no, no, no, no,** dangerous to scream)
109	no, not a word on that subject	no, **no, no,** not a word on that subject
110	I **shall** never draw up	I **will** never draw up
110	I **shall** perhaps	I **will** perhaps
110	I may get **poorer,** or **richer**	I may get **richer,** or **poorer**
111	I **knew no longer**	I **no longer knew**
113	**I've lost** her name **again**, Rose	**what's** her name **uhm**, Rose
113	That's something **that** never escapes me	That's something never escapes me
113	and **had** spent his whole life there	and spent his whole life there
115	how difficult it **was** not to do again	how difficult it **is** not to do again
116	**But** it was a day I dreaded too.	**But, but** it was a day I dreaded too.
116	I considered **that** the forest	I considered the forest
116	in this **sense**, that I was there	in this **way**, that I was there
118	Molloy, **and** then a fine phrase	Molloy, **ah, ah** then a fine phrase
119	but **I** heard a murmur	but **I, I, I** heard a murmur
119	and so I shall perhaps **some** day	and so I shall perhaps **one** day
119	**and** I won't be able to move	I won't be able to move

120	bring myself to do **a thing like** that.	bring myself to do that
120	out of this forest **with all possible speed**	out of this forest **as soon as possible**
120	**Perhaps** it was only autumn.	**But perhaps** it was only autumn.
121	racked **by** a kind of chronic arthritis	racked **with** a kind of chronic arthritis
122	such violence **that** I couldn't get it off	such violence I couldn't get it off
122	**the forest ended and** I saw the light	I saw the light
122	exactly as **I had foreseen**	exactly as **I'd seen**
123	faintly outlined **against** the horizon	faintly outlined **on** the horizon
123	ludicrously idle questions **for** a man	ludicrously idle questions **to** a man
123	lapsed down **to the bottom of** the ditch	lapsed down **into** the ditch

Magee also uses contractions where the text of *Molloy* does not, again moving the text away from the written to the spoken word. Forms affected by this are: 'had not' (hadn't), 'it is' (it's), 'do not' (don't), 'what is' (what's), 'there is' (there's), 'would not' (wouldn't), 'could not' (couldn't), 'you have' (you've), 'you are' (you're), 'I would' (I'd), 'he is' (he's), 'I had' (I'd), 'did not' (didn't), 'that is' (that's), 'was not' (wasn't), 'I have' (I've) and 'does not' (doesn't). On one occasion, near the end of Part I, a contraction is lengthened: 'Don't fret Molloy, we're coming' (1955, 123; *Mo* 93) becomes 'we are coming'.

The last two annotations that remain to be discussed affect the musical arrangement of the production. According to the script, there should be an interlude both before and after the sentence 'The heart beats, and what a beat' (p. 8; 1955, 109; *Mo* 82), in order to isolate it, but the second instance of (~~MUSIC~~) is crossed out, so that the sentence is preceded by music in the broadcast, but not followed, causing the text to run on. In the second case, the musical intervention separating the sentences 'For I was there' // 'And being there I did not have to go there' (p. 16; 1955, 116; *Mo* 87) is crossed out on the script, but in the recording it is merely delayed to come after 'That is all I wished to say, and if I did not say it at the outset it is simply that something was against it', which thus becomes separated from the next sentence: 'But I could not, stay in the forest I mean, I was not free to.' (1955, 116; *Mo* 87)

1.6 Genetic Map

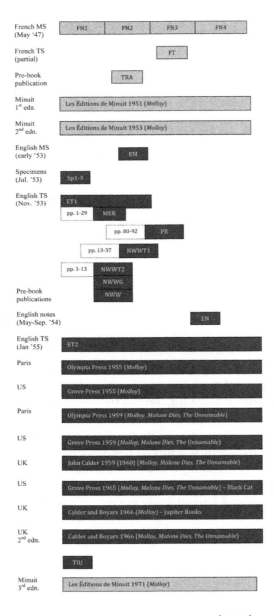

2 Genesis of *Molloy* (French)

In June 1969, Samuel Beckett received a visitor from Egypt at his apartment in Paris. Nadia Kamel was a PhD student and her first question to Beckett was whether his work was the result of several versions and revisions. His answer was that, in the period of the interview, the writing was difficult, with many cancellations, but that until 1952, he wrote fast, without cancellations.[42]

Entirely 'without cancellations' is probably an overstatement, but – judging from the pre-1952 manuscripts – it is true that the writing seems to have proceeded extremely fluently. In this respect, the French manuscript of *Molloy* is no exception. As explained in the introduction this autograph is unusual in that, with its relatively consistent indication of dates, it is also 'autographic' in Nelson Goodman's sense (1968, 113). Like any literary text, *Molloy* is of course 'allographic' – it can be replicated. But the French manuscript is unique. The immediacy of the writing itself, combined with the mimetic function of the pages Molloy is supposed to 'blacken' (1955, 15; *Mo* 68), creates the equivalent of being in front of an 'unfakable' painting (Goodman 1968, 112), that is, of dealing with autographic art.

The immediacy of the writing is part of what H. Porter Abbott (1984) called the 'temporal function' of diary fiction, and although *Molloy* is technically not diary fiction, its autograph manuscript approximates it to an uncanny degree. Moreover, Molloy himself imagines an audience that will call his writings a 'journal intime' (FN2, 67r; 1951, 93), a 'diary' (1955, 83; *Mo* 61). Not unlike the French manuscript of *L'Innommable*, the diachrony of the genesis almost coincides with the synchronic structure of the narrative. Every day, the text goes on or digresses, and it is as if neither Molloy nor Beckett himself is entirely sure what he will write the next day. As a result, the text creates the impression (perhaps the illusion) that Beckett proceeded as gropingly as Molloy did. That is why this chapter examines the genesis of this autograph manuscript as if it were a sort of diary, not an autobiographical diary, but 'a species of autography (self-writing)' in the sense suggested by

42   'NK. Votre œuvre est-elle le fruit de plusieurs ébauches ?
      SB. Jusqu'à 1952, j'écrivais très vite, sans ratures, maintenant c'est plus difficile,
      j'ai beaucoup de peine, je fais des ratures et ce que j'écris est très court comme
      Bing qui vient de paraître et *Sans* qui doit paraître aux Éditions de Minuit.'
      (Samuel Beckett, interview with Nadia Kamel, qtd. in Kamel 2016, 142)

H. Porter Abbott (see Introduction).[43] The chapter will follow the chronology of the writing as indicated in the manuscript.

43   Abbott's 'working distinction between autography and autobiography is that autography is the larger field comprehending all self-writing and that autobiography is a subset of autography comprehending narrative self-writing and more specifically that most common narrative, the story of one's life' (1996, 2).

2.1 PART I

The beginning of the genesis, not the incipit

Beckett may well have been in his mother's room when he wrote the first sentences of *Molloy*, but those first sentences were not 'I am in my mother's room'.[44] The place and date indicated on the first recto of notebook FN1 is '2.5.47 FOXROCK' (FN1, 02r). Under the apparently provisional title 'En désespoir de cause'[45] (see chapter 1.1.1 and chapter 2.1, writing session '31.8[.47]'), Beckett started writing what – in the published version of *Molloy* – is the novel's massive second paragraph. This monolithic text, ending where the novel's first part ends, was originally divided into paragraphs (at least until page 29r of the second notebook). Often, the start of a new paragraph coincides with the start of a new writing session. This

---

44 Because the first paragraph was added last (after Beckett had written the closing sentence of the novel), it will be discussed at the end of chapter 2.2.

45 Beckett used the same phrase on 8 November 1969 in a letter to Barbara Bray, apparently recalling that he had used it as a provisional title for *Molloy* more than twenty years earlier: 'Wrote first sentence this morning désespoir de cause again of God knows what and who cared. Feels like beginning <u>Molloy</u> only 1/4 century worse' (*LSB IV* 192). The text he had begun was a forerunner of the *Foirade/Fizzle* 'Pour finir encore'/'For to end yet again' (Pilling 2006, 182), the drafts of which are contained in a notebook at Boston College (box 11, folder 6). Beckett gave it to Calvin Israel in May 1976 and the cover bears the inscription 'Nabeul / December / 1969', underneath which Beckett added: '1st 2 pages given to Oxfam / for sale'. J. C. C. Mays consulted this fragment before it was auctioned by Sotheby's on 4 and 5 December 1972, noting that it was dated '8.11.69.' and '10.8.69.' and began with the words: 'mais que même dans ces lieux extrêmes donc' (1980). Since 8 November 1969 is the same date as Beckett's letter to Bray, this must be the sentence he wrote that day. Mays discloses that the manuscript was purchased for £240 by the bookseller Larry Wallrich, but his papers in the Stuart A. Rose Manuscript, Archives, and Rare Book Library at Emory University do not contain the document (with thanks to Kathy Shoemaker for her kind help). Beckett did type up the fragment and gave it to Geneviève Asse, who made engravings for it and eventually published the text separately as *Abandonné* – Beckett's choice of title – in a deluxe edition by Georges Visat (Knowlson 1996, 578-9). Eight years later, on 23 May 1977, the phrase 'désespoir de cause' recurred in another letter to Bray (*LSB IV* 462), this time when Beckett embarked on *Company*, so that it came to mark the beginning of new prose writing with uncertain outcome. As a translation for the expression, the editors of Beckett's letters propose: 'for want of anything better to do' (*LSB IV* 193n2).

paragraph structure served as a sort of scaffolding that was eventually taken away, but it did help in shaping the novel during the writing process. For that reason, the original paragraphs of the manuscript will also be marked in the following account of the genesis, in the chronological order of their composition.

Paragraph 2 (FN1, 02r)

> **'2.5.47. FOXROCK.**
> **En désespoir de cause'**
> (FN1, 02r)

The first sentence, in which Molloy states that he may write one more story after this one, is heavily crossed out:

> Cette fois-ci, puis encore une autre je pense, puis ~~le silence je pense, quelque chose me le dit, encore une fois~~ ~~bientôt~~ ~~et puis le silence, non pas qu'on veuille~~ **se taire**, ~~non, mais on devient~~ **muet**, ~~la tête est~~ **muette**, ~~le monde est~~ **muet**. ~~Tout devient~~ **muet**, ~~la tête et le reste celui du~~ **muet** – ~~c'est~~ ᶜᵉ ˢᵉʳᵃ fini je pense, avec ce monde-ci aussi. (FN1, 02r)

The repeated references to all-enveloping silence and muteness are deleted. And instead of the muteness, the next few lines suggest blindness:

> C'est mieux, le sens de l'avant-dernier. Tout s'estompe, s'éclipse. Un peu plus et on sera comme aveugle. (FN1, 02r)

The idea of the end – **'c'est fini'** – is changed into the future tense, **'ᶜᵉ ˢᵉʳᵃ fini'**, thus prefiguring Clov's opening words in *Fin de partie*: 'Finished, it's finished, nearly finished, it must be nearly finished' (*E* 6). The sense of the penultimate or 'le sens de l'avant-dernier' will become the 'premonition of the last but one but one' (1955, 8; *Mo* 4) in the published English version, with variants in the drafts (see chapter 3.2).

Molloy sees A and B going slowly towards each other. Here and there, the French text shows small traces of Beckett's mother tongue, for instance when Molloy notes that the air must have been sharp because they wore overcoats, 'car ils portaient **leurs manteaux**' (FN1, 04r), the plural 'manteaux' is changed into the more idiomatic singular ('car ils avaient **leur manteau**', 1951, 10) in the first edition. The section written in Foxrock ends at the bottom of page 07r with the description of B's 'grand bâton' ['stout stick' (1955, 11; *Mo* 6)], and the notion that Molloy had nothing to fear but that he went in fear nonetheless.

'**Paris 8.7.47**'
(FN1, 08r)

On the next page, Beckett picks up the narrative thread where he left it two months earlier. He marks the place and date in the top right corner and starts writing: 'Mais ça il l'ignorait sans doute.' (FN1, 08r) In other words, in Foxrock, the narrative had reached the point where the text says there was nothing they could do to him, or very little, and in Paris it continued: 'But he can't have known it' (1955, 12; *Mo* 6).

The writing session of 8 July ended with the description of the Pomeranian (following A), which allows for an autographic reading: the little dog follows wretchedly ('suivait mal'), stops, turns in circles ('de longues girations'), gives up, and starts again – 'comme font les poméraniens quand ils veulent chier (la constipation chez les poméraniens est signe de bonne santé)' (FN1, 14r) ['Constipation is a sign of good health in pomeranians' (1955, 14; *Mo* 8)]. The French original contains a scatological pun that is lost in the English version: whereas the dog is said to give up in English, the manuscript reads: '~~faisait~~ **laissait tomber**, je veux dire abandonnait' (FN1, 14r). The idiomatic expression 'laisser tomber' still retains the idea of dropping something. The suggestion of droppings may not be the most sophisticated pun in the direct context of the constipated dog, but there is a psychological dimension that makes the whole scene more relevant to the genesis in that it thematizes the act of writing. Among his excerpts from Ernest Jones's *Treatment of Neurosis*, Beckett wrote the line 'Les constipés se promènent' and noted that the 'Aim of psychoanalysis' was 'to release pent-up energy & make it available for normal sublimation' (TCD 10971/8/22r). The notes from Jones's *Papers on Psycho-Analysis* also mention several actions considered to be symbols for defecation, such as 'writing up [a] diary' (TCD 10971/8/18r) and the 'inability over a long period to write a letter & then producing an epistle' (TCD 10971/8/19r). This analogy between scatology and autography will be further elaborated in the second part of *Molloy* and in other works such as *Malone Dies* (Saposcat) and *Krapp's Last Tape*. Here, the theme is only briefly mentioned, but at an interesting place: the closing of the first dated writing session after a two-month period of creative 'constipation'. The notions of turning in circles like a constipated Pomeranian that wants to defecate, giving up and starting again ('laisser tomber', 'abandonner' and 'recommencer') invite a reading in terms of autography at the beginning of the novel. Since 'writing up [a] diary' is considered one of the symbols of defecation, according to Beckett's psychology notes, the rather systematic dating of the writing sessions in the manuscript of Molloy's narrative reinforces the impression of an autographic project.

'9.7.47'

(FN1, 14r)

This moment is marked with a date, in the middle left of the page, and it is literally marked *as* a moment, a 'given moment' (1955, 14; *Mo* 8), since the new writing session starts with the words: 'A un moment donné, pré-établi si vous y tenez, **moi je n'y tiens pas** ^ni j'y tiens ni je n'y tiens^' (FN1, 14r). Whether this moment is pre-established or not does not matter to Molloy in the *Merlin* and *New World Writing* prepublications ('I don't mind', MER, 92; NWW, 320) and only a little bit in the published version ('I don't much mind', 1955, 14; *Mo* 8), but this relative indifference is complicated in the manuscript by the double negative; he neither minds nor doesn't mind. Apart from the reference to Leibniz's pre-established order, the notion of the pre-established nature of the moment also has an autographic dimension: the moment is 'given' ('9.7.47') in the sense that the author happens to start writing again on this day, which inadvertently informs the narrator's narrative. The foil between the actual writing process and Molloy's narration is extremely thin and at times permeable. The text constantly thematizes this autographic situation, notably in this paragraph, when Molloy says: 'Dire que je fais tout mon possible pour ne pas parler de moi.' (FN1, 18r-19r) ['And to think I try my best not to talk about myself.' (1955, 15; *Mo* 9)]

The scatology/autography analogy is more explicit in the manuscript. In the published text, Molloy suggests that 'you would do better, at least no worse, to obliterate texts than to blacken margins, to fill in the holes of words till all is blank' (1955, 16; *Mo* 9). In the manuscript, these texts are described with fecal imagery, as thin droppings or diluted oozings which resemble an arse's soot: 'on ferait mieux, enfin, aussi bien, d'effacer les textes que de noircir les marges, **ces** ~~petits textes~~ **qui de leur** ~~minces~~ **chutes maigres suintements qui font penser à la suie d'un cul,** de les boucher jusqu'à ce que tout soit blanc' (FN1, 19r-20r).

And next to the scatological passages, the focus on the 'self' was also more explicit in the manuscript. Whereas the published text simply reads 'Ramener le silence, c'est le rôle des objets' (1951, 17) ['To restore silence is the role of objects' (1955, 16; *Mo* 10)], the manuscript was quite a bit longer: 'c'est là le rôle des objets, ramener le silence dans les bas-fonds, **je parle de moi, je ne parlerai jamais que de moi, quand je parle d'A ou de B ou des vaches je parle de moi, je suis payé pour le savoir'** (FN1, 20r-21r). Both the scatological image for handwriting (FN1, 20r) and the passage where Molloy emphasizes that in speaking of A and B he is speaking of himself (FN1, 20r-21r) will be removed.

After Molloy mentions his hat (fastened to his buttonhole) and his greatcoat, he concludes that it would be 'premature' (1955, 17; *Mo* 10) to speak of his possessions at present. Thus (the very first draft of) this novel already prefigures the content of the next, in which Malone will draw up his inventory: 'Mais j'en parlerai plus tard, quand il s'agira de **faire l'inventaire de mes possessions,** à moins que je ne les perde d'ici là' (FN1, 22r-23r).

Paragraph 3 (FN1, 23r-25r)

'11.7[.1947]'
(FN1, 22v)

On 11 July Beckett started a new paragraph with Molloy's observation that he must have been on the top or the slopes of 'une éminence peu ordinaire' (FN1, 23r) ['some considerable eminence' (1955, 17; *Mo* 10)], for otherwise he could not have seen so many things.

Paragraph 4 (FN1, 25r-27r)

During the same writing session, Beckett wrote several short paragraphs. Paragraph 4 opens with a rare statement of certainty, about B not having passed this way again – although Beckett was uncertain about what term to use for this character: 'Ce qui est certain c'est que mon bonhomme (**le pèlerin (?**)) ne repassa pas par là' (FN1, 25r). The 'pilgrim' became 'l'homme au bâton' in the Minuit edition (1951, 19) ['the man with the stick' (1955, 18; *Mo* 11)]. Of all the noises Molloy heard that night, not one was of the heavy 'uncertain' footsteps of B (in the French version, C in the English; see chapter 3.2), nor of his club.

Paragraph 5 (FN1, 27r)

Molloy feels divided between, on the one hand, the murmurs of 'mon être perplexe' and, on the other hand, those of the outside world (FN1, 27r). In the English version, this 'être perplexe' is translated with a reference to *Murphy*: 'my little world' (1955, 18; *Mo* 11).

Paragraph 6 (FN1, 28r)

Molloy then closes the topic of A and B: 'A et B, jamais je ne les revis.' (FN1, 28r) ['A and C I never saw again.' (1955, 18; *Mo* 12)] But he immediately starts doubting his own statement: 'suis-je sûr de ne jamais les avoir revus? Et qu'est-ce que j'appelle voir et revoir?' (FN1, 28r) ['And am I sure I never saw them again? And what do I mean by seeing and seeing again?' (1955, 19; *Mo* 12)] Before the next topic is introduced, Molloy inserts a moment of silence, as when the conductor taps on his stand before the beginning of a concert. The theme is announced as the 'désir d'un frère' (FN1, 28r) ['the craving for a fellow' (1955, 19; *Mo* 12)].

Paragraph 7 (FN1, 28r-32r)

The craving for a fellow leads him to the decision to go and see his mother: 'Mais puisque nous en sommes au désir d'un frère, je ~~vous~~ dirai que [...] je ~~pris la décision~~ ᵣésolus d'aller voir ma mère' (FN1, 28r-29r; 1955, 19; *Mo* 12). He adjusts his crutches and finds his bicycle, adding the parenthesis '(tiens! je ne m'attendais pas à cela)' (FN, 29r) ['(I didn't know I had one)' (1955, 19; *Mo* 12)]. Again, the 'pre-established order' of the narrative is both suggested and undermined by a clearly unreliable narrator who simply tells his tale as he goes along, questioning the principle which Beckett dubbed the 'snowball act' during his lectures on 'Racine and the Modern Novel' at TCD. According to Rachel Burrows' notes, this 'snowball act' releases a purely mechanical chain of circumstances ('enchaînement mécanique fatale [sic] de circonstances'): 'Arbitrary direction given to material by artist – constant acceleration to crisis. Irreversible – final valid statement of personality' (TCD MIC 60, 40). Later, Beckett told Charles Juliet about the composition of *Molloy* that he 'hadn't planned it, or thought it all out' (Juliet 1995, 140; see chapter 1.1.1, note 10). This approach corresponds to what the French genetic critic Louis Hay has dubbed 'écriture à processus' (Hay 1986-7). The opposite, 'écriture à programme', is the approach Beckett disliked in writers such as Balzac, whose characters are explained in terms of chains of causes that make their actions seem perfectly consistent. He studied several of Balzac's novels during his Honors (*Père Goriot, Le Cabinet des antiques, Louis Lambert, Les Proscrits, Eugénie Grandet, Un ménage de garçon* and *Ursule Mirouët*),[46] which allowed him to use Balzac as a contrastive background to present his poetics of the modern novel in his lectures and to put the following analysis in the mouth of one of his characters[47] in *Dream of Fair to Middling Women*:

46 Beckett's interest in Balzac – mainly per negativum – is also noticeable indirectly, for instance in one of the excerpts he took from Jules Renard's *Journal* in his *Dream Notebook*, notably a comment from the diary dated 3 October 1895 to the effect that 'Balzac is truthful as a whole, but not in detail' (*DN* 33, entry 226).

47 Interestingly, this comment is not made by Beckett's alter ego Belacqua, but by his friend Lucien, modeled after Jean Beaufret, Beckett's friend at the École Normale Supérieure (Knowlson 1997, 152). If Lucien can be seen as a Racinian 'confidant', Beckett not only makes his character criticize Balzac, but simultaneously puts his critique into practice by favouring and applying Racine's technique of using 'confidants' to depict the complexity of the main character's mind.

To read Balzac is to receive the impression of a chloroformed world. He is absolute master of his material, he can do what he likes with it, he can *foresee and calculate* its least vicissitude, *he can write the end of his book before he has finished the first paragraph*, because he has turned all his creatures into *clockwork cabbages* and can rely on their staying put wherever needed or staying going at whatever speed in whatever direction he chooses. The whole thing, from beginning to end, takes place in a spellbound backwash. (*D* 119; emphasis added)

In the case of *Molloy*, especially the first part, Beckett did the opposite: instead of being able to write the end of his book before he had finished the first paragraph, he had to write the whole book before being able to write the first paragraph. The end cannot be foreseen or calculated and the characters are not clockwork cabbages. Nonetheless, one could argue that Moran (in the second part) may have been conceived as a (parody of a) character of the Balzacian type (see chapter 2.2), but then again, Moran's initial composure eventually turns into decomposition.

In this context of characterization, the treatment of background as a means to create atmosphere was a technique Beckett appreciated in Racine, again as opposed to Balzac. In his lecture on Racine's *Andromaque*, Beckett zooms in on the example of Racine's image of Troy in flames as observed from the sea, and emphasizes that this is 'not explicating background' as in Balzac:

> All to create atmosphere, not explicating background of Balzac. Artistic not psychological value. Doesn't want to guarantee characters by it. Situating them in facts that will explain them. Character – victim of fatality – can't be explained. Troy etc. give substance and harmonies to living character: worth more than their face value. Depth to character as overtone is to note. (TCD MIC 60, 69)[48]

48   The interplay between the background and the protagonist was presented by Beckett in visual terms, comparing it to 'clair-obscur' (TCD MIC 60, 53). In an interview taken by S. E. Gontarski, Martha Fehsenfeld and Dougald McMillan, Rachel Burrows explained this more extensively than in her notes on Beckett's lectures: 'So in the light of his own work, it's interesting to remember his likes and dislikes in those early days. He loved the "clair-obscur," the light comes in

In his manuscript of *Molloy*, Beckett does not use the background to explain his character à la Balzac. Molloy happens to find his bicycle, which leads him to the consideration that this is perhaps the moment to mention that he is no mean cyclist (1955, 19; *Mo* 12). Originally, Beckett wrote 'Il est peut-être temps que', before turning this into an 'obligation to express': ~~'Il est peut-être temps que~~ Cela me ~~mett~~ met dans **l'obligation de remarquer** que, tout ~~inf~~ estropié que j'étais, je ~~faisais de la~~ ^{montais à} bicyclette ~~à cett~~ avec un certain bonheur, à cette époque' – adding **'Ce n'est pas le cas aujourd'hui'** (FN1, 30r). The latter remark, that he no longer mounts his bicycle with pleasure, is left out in the subsequent versions, possibly because it would have suggested too much foreshadowing and 'foreseeing' à la Balzac. Then again, some lines further, the manuscript lacks a few short passages that do feature in the published texts: the meta-remark 'Il faudrait récrire tout cela au plus-que-parfait.' (1951, 22) ['This should all be rewritten in the pluperfect.' (1955, 20; *Mo* 13)] and the passage where the bicycle is addressed directly: 'Chère bicyclette, je ne t'appellerai pas vélo' (1951, 21) ['Dear bicycle, I shall not call you bike' (1955, 19; *Mo* 12)].

Describing his bicycle would be a pleasure to Molloy. He refrains from doing so ('Je me retiens de la détailler', FN1, 30r), but cannot help mentioning the little horn it had instead of a bell ('je dirai seulement qu'elle avait une petite corne', FN1, 30r). Unfortunately, however, he has to speak of another subject: 'de ~~ma mère. celle qui m'a donné~~ ^{me donna} le jour' (FN1, 31v, 32r). The direct reference to his mother is first deleted in the text on the right-hand side and replaced on the opposite page by the description of her as the one who brought him into the world, 'par le trou du cul, si j'ai bonne mémoire' (FN1, 31v) ['through the hole in her arse if my memory is correct' (1955, 20; *Mo* 13)]. Again, the psychology notes are not far away. From Ernest Jones's *Papers on Psycho-Analysis* Beckett took excerpts on the 'Infantile cloacal theory of birth,' that is, the child's idea that 'babies [are] made of faeces (cp. flowers from dung)' (TCD 109771/8/19r). Molloy's

at one moment to leave the rest in shadow. He quoted Gide as saying "Balzac paints like David, Dostoevski like Rembrandt." He saw Gide and Proust as the successors to Dostoevski because they dared to preserve the complexity of the real, the inexplicable, unforeseeable quality of the human being. He rejected the naturalistic novels of writers like Balzac, which only depict the surface which he said had been peeled off by Proust.' (qtd. in Gontarski, Fehsenfeld and McMillan 1989, n.p.)

description of his mother is immediately followed by his laconic scatological appreciation of being born: 'Premier emmerdement.' (FN1, 31v) ['First taste of the shit.' (1955, 20; *Mo* 13)]

Paragraph 8 (FN1, 32r-33r)

'12.7[.47]'
(FN1, 31v)

The next day, Beckett starts with a short paragraph about the setting of Molloy's story. Both the place and the time are equally vague. The 'where' is 'ce pays ~~désolé~~ ^{damné}' (FN1, 32r) ['this accursed country' (1955, 20; *Mo* 13)] and the 'when' of the start of his penultimate journey is 'la 2me ou la 3me semaine de juin' (FN1, 33r) ['the second or third week of June' (1955, 21; *Mo* 13)], when the sun is at its 'pitilessmost'.

Given Beckett's proclaimed dislike of compositional calculation, foreseeing and other forms of Balzacian 'écriture à programme' – at least in the early days of his career – it should be mentioned that during Beckett's 'écriture à processus' there are nonetheless moments when he thinks of something that he should not forget to include in the narrative. Typically, these moments are marked by paralipomena on the left-hand side (short jottings, usually not full sentences, announcing a theme that occurs a few pages further in the body of the text). In traditional scholarly editing, paralipomena were not included in an edition because, strictly speaking, they do not belong to a version of the text. But from the vantage point of genetic criticism, they are among the most interesting aspects of the genesis because they are an important catalyst of the writing process. In the dynamics of Beckett's 'écriture à processus', the paralipomena serve as the 'on and on' of the obligation to express. In this particular case, Beckett writes on the facing verso: 'Fait son possible pour ne pas m'avoir / je le sais pertinemment' (FN1, 32v). This is a precursor of a sentence on page 40r in the next (long) paragraph on Molloy's mother – who, due to a *lapsus calami*, is remarkably referred to with a male personal pronoun: 'Je ne lui en veux pas trop, à ma mère, je sais pertinemment qu'**il** [sic] a tout fait pour ne pas m'avoir.' (FN1, 40r) ['My mother. I don't think too harshly of her. I know she did all she could not to have me.' (1955, 23; *Mo* 15)] The suggestion that his mother might be male reinforces the idea of mental motherhood, echoed in the opening paragraph, where Molloy says that he has replaced his mother and, in his turn, might 'mother' a son: 'I have taken her place. I must resemble her more and more. All I need now is a son' (1955, 8; *Mo* 3).

Paragraph 9 (FN1, 34r-42r)

'Ma mère' are the first words of a new paragraph on a new page: 'Ma mère me voyait volontiers' (FN1, 34r) ['My mother never refused to see me' (1955, 21; *Mo* 13)]. When Molloy notes that he calls her 'Mag', his explanation is slightly more elaborate in the manuscript, admitting that he sometimes felt the urge to call her 'mother' or 'ma': 'Moi je l'appelais Mag, quand je devais lui donner un nom. ~~Sans doute avais-je envie de~~ J'avais sans doute envie au fond de l'appeler maman ou ma, alors je l'appelais Mag' (FN1, 35r). He calls it an 'épithèse' by means of the letter g, which for him 'abolished the syllable Ma, and as it were spat on it' (1955, 21; *Mo* 14). The manuscript reads: 'la lettre g abolissait la syllabe ma, et l'idée ma, et **en quelque sorte** crachait dessus' (FN1, 35r), which was changed into '**pour ainsi dire**' ['so to speak'] in the Minuit edition (1951, 23), emphasizing the self-conscious nature of Molloy's language. He admits that this habit of his simultaneously 'satisfied a deep and doubtless unacknowledged need, the need to have a Ma, that is a mother, and to proclaim it, audibly' (1955, 21; *Mo* 14). The formulation of this need took a few attempts: 'Et en même [temps] je ~~réalisais mon bes un profond besoin de mon être,~~ satisfaisait⁵ à un besoin profond, et sans doute inavoué, celui d'avoir une ma, c'est à dire une maman, et de l'annoncer, à haute voix, **vous me comprenez**.' (FN1, 35r) In the subsequent version, Molloy no longer counts so explicitly on his audience's understanding. When he explains that in his part of the world 'da' means father, this part of the world was called 'ma **putain de patrie**' (FN1, 36r) ['my fucking country'] in the manuscript, before it was changed into the more neutral expression 'ma **région**' (1951, 23).

In a paralipomenon, Molloy wonders whether he should describe the room, but decides he won't as he will undoubtedly have the opportunity to do so later on, when he will have found refuge in it: 'Décrirai-je la chambre? Non. J'en aurai sans doute plus tard l'occasion. Quand j'y chercherai asile, à bout d'expédients, qui sait?' (FN1, 36v) In the body of the text the same question is raised (and deleted again), but without the explanation: '~~Décrirai-je la chambre? Non.~~' (FN1, 37r) Beckett probably judged it was too soon to introduce this passage here; he eventually introduced it five pages further on (FN1, 42r). The manuscript also contains a rare exclamation mark: 'elle était contente de me sentir!' (FN1, 37r) ['she was happy to smell me.' (1955, 22; *Mo* 14)] – which was removed in the Minuit edition (1951, 24).

After Molloy has explained the code by means of which he communicated with his mother ('Un coup signifiait oui, deux non, trois je ne sais pas, quatre argent, cinq adieu' ['One knock meant yes, two no, three I don't know, four money, five goodbye' (1955, 22; *Mo* 14)]), he adds that he did not care whether she confused 1, 2, 3 and 5, again addressing an audience: '**Entendons-nous:** qu'elle confondît oui, non, je ne sais pas et adieu, cela m'était indifférent' (FN1, 38r) – and yet again this appeal to the audience was removed in the Minuit edition (1951, 24). The cruel treatment is slightly softened in the manuscript when he refers to his mother as 'poor woman', who understood but little of his code, in a fragment that was cut: '**la pauvre femme**, ~~qu à supposer~~ pour peu qu'elle eût saisi les grandes lignes de mon système, ce qui ~~est~~ est fort peu probable', FN1, 39r).

In *L'Innommable / The Unnamable*, there is a tendency in the genesis (including the translation) toward more negative expressions (Van Hulle and Weller 2014, 209-15). In the genesis of *Molloy*, there are examples of this phenomenon, but also several examples of the opposite. For instance, when Molloy finds 'a more effective means of putting the idea of money into her head' (1955, 23; *Mo* 15), the manuscript speaks of 'un moyen **moins aléatoire**' (FN1, 39r), which was changed into 'un moyen **plus efficace**' in the Minuit edition (1951, 25).

In the first writing layer of the manuscript, as soon as Molloy has introduced his more effective method (thumps of the fist instead of knocks of his index-knuckle), he immediately attenuates his attitude by adding that he does not think too harshly of his mother: '[...] coups de poing, sur le crâne. **Je ne lui en veux pas trop**, à ma mère' (FN1, 39r). In the subsequent versions this attenuation is delayed. First of all, Beckett added 'ça elle comprenait, tout de suite' to the manuscript (FN1, 39r) ['That she understood' (1955, 23; *Mo* 15)], and then further additions in the Minuit edition (and the English versions): 'D'ailleurs je ne venais pas pour l'argent. Je lui en prenais, mais je ne venais pas pour cela.' (1951, 25) ['In any case I didn't come for money. I took her money, but I didn't come for that.' (1955, 23; *Mo* 15)] The reason why Molloy does not think too harshly of his mother is that she had done all she could not to have him. In the manuscript, this sentence (FN1, 40r) – which was announced by a paralipomenon (see paragraph 8) – did not yet contain the remark 'sauf évidemment le principal' (1951, 25) ['except of course the one thing, and if she never succeeded in getting me unstuck, it was that fate had earmarked me for less compassionate sewers' (1955, 23; *Mo* 15)].

Her good intentions ('it was well-meant', 1955, 23; *Mo* 15) were good enough for Molloy. But after this affirmation he immediately proceeds by negating it or – as the narrator of *The Unnamable* calls it – by invalidating it as uttered (*Un* 1): 'cela me suffit. **Non, cela ne me suffit pas**' (FN1, 40r). Not unlike the (deleted) passage where he considers describing the room but immediately decides against it, this moment is one of the first instances of epanorthosis, a figure of speech that will become more prominent in *L'Innommable* / *The Unnamable*. Molloy often immediately corrects himself, and sometimes just interrupts himself, to negate what he has just uttered. On the next page, he suggests that it was only with his mother that he – and then he suddenly interrupts himself: 'avec cette vieille femme [...] et avec elle seule, **j'ai – non, je ne peux pas le dire**' (FN1, 41r). The manuscript does not reveal what is left unsaid; the only word it gives away is the verb ('**j'ai –**'; the Minuit edition only mentions the personal pronoun '**je –**', 1951, 26) ['I – no, I can't say it' (1955, 20; *Mo* 16)].

'**14 juillet [1947]**'
(FN1, 40v)

Just after this self-interruption in the narrative, Beckett interrupted the writing session. He continued on Bastille Day, but he did not provide any specifics on what Molloy has or has done ('j'ai –'; see above) with his mother. That is for the reader to imagine. The previous sentence in the manuscript speaks of a '**race**' ('moi dernier de ma **race**'), which is changed to 'mon **engeance**' (1951, 25) ['my foul brood' (1955, 23; *Mo* 15)] – suggesting that Molloy is the last (so far) of the first-person narrator's self-engendered and self-engendering literary offspring. And this is where Beckett introduced Molloy's question about describing the room (prepared in the paralipomenon on page 37r), but with the addition 'my prick in my rectum' (1955, 24; *Mo* 16) to indicate the circular structure: 'Décrirai-je la chambre? Non. J'en aurai sans doute plus tard l'occasion. Quand j'y chercherai asile, à bout d'expédients, la queue dans le rectum, qui sait' (FN1, 42r).

Paragraph 10 (FN1, 43r)

A very brief paragraph, starting with the word 'Bon' (FN1, 43r), concludes the passage about Molloy's mother and reads as a sort of *'programme'* included in the 'écriture à processus': 'Now that we know where we're going, let's go there.' (1955, 24; *Mo* 16) But this 'programme' is immediately followed by an ironic statement, suggesting that it is so nice to know where one is going in the early stages that it almost rids one of the wish to go there – which can be read as a way of ridiculing the Balzacian type of 'écriture à programme'.

Paragraph 11 (FN1, 43r-47r)

The new paragraph starts with Molloy's speculations about the reasons why he seems distraught: the night must have tired him and the sun poisoned him (1955, 24; *Mo* 16). Although Beckett's first draft is very close to the published version, he did make a few stylistic revisions, such as the change from a rising sun ('le soleil, **se levant**', FN1, 43r) to a sun that is hoisting itself higher and higher ('le soleil, **se hissant**', 1951, 27). When he says he confuses east and west, 'et les autres **points cardinaux**', adding 'Tant pis, tant pis' (FN1, 43r), these cardinal points are replaced by the poles ('les pôles', 1951, 27) and the interjection is left out. The first draft is slightly more loquacious. In the manuscript version, Molloy implies that the reasons he comes up with are quite speculative and could just as well be others ('Enfin, que ce fût à cause de cela ou d'autre chose, **je n'**étais pas dans mon assiette', FN1, 43r). While he is talking about his being out of sorts, he actually does seem to be quite 'dans son assiette', for the expression 'pas dans mon assiette' ['out of sorts' (1955, 25; *Mo* 16); literally 'not in my plate'] leads him to make a pun: 'Elle est profonde, mon assiette, une assiette à soupe, et il est rare que je n'y sois pas.' (FN1, 44r) ['They are deep, my sorts, a deep ditch, and I am not often out of them.' (1955, 25; *Mo* 16)]

In spite of being distraught, he covers several miles and finds himself under the ramparts. The manuscript speaks of '**plusieurs kilomètres**' (FN1, 44r), which Beckett changed to '**quelques milles**' in the Minuit edition (1951, 27), thus emphasizing the Irish setting (see chapter 2.2, paragraph 34 and chapter 3.2). The town is called '**notre ville**' in the manuscript, whereas the

Minuit edition 'vaguens' this to 'la ville' (1951, 27).[49] Molloy dismounts and pushes his bicycle on his crutches. Again, the manuscript is more loquacious. Molloy starts explaining how he went about, extending one crutch to support himself and using the bicycle as a second crutch: **'Voici comme je m'y prenais: je ne détachait⁵ du cadre qu'une seule béquille, la bicyclette elle-même me tenait lieu de l'autre'** (FN1, 45r). In the published version, this explanation is reduced to the comment **'Je m'arrangeais. Il fallait y penser.'** (1951, 27) ['I managed somehow. Being ingenious.' (1955, 25; *Mo* 17)]. Some two hundred metres further, he is hailed by a policeman. Again, the reference to the metric system is omitted and the details are 'vaguened' in the published version: **'quelques 2 cents mètres** plus loin' (FN1, 45r) ['some 200 metres further'] becomes **'un peu** plus loin' (1951, 27) ['a little further on' (1955, 25; *Mo* 17)]. If the published version occasionally becomes more elaborate than the manuscript, it is often to stress uncertainty rather than to add more details. When Molloy says he saw a policeman, he immediately adds the self-conscious reflection that this was an elliptic way of speaking because it was only later that he realized what it was. This realization was simply a matter of deduction in the manuscript, leading to certainty: 'car ce ne fut que plus tard que, **par déduction**, je **pus en avoir la certitude'** (FN1, 45r). The Minuit edition undermines this certainty by adding an uncertainty: 'car ce ne fut que plus tard, **par voie d'induction, ou de déduction, je ne sais plus**, que je **sus ce que c'était.'** (1951, 27) ['Eliptically speaking, for it was only later, by way of induction, or deduction, I forget which, that I knew what it was.' (1955, 25; *Mo* 17)] When the policeman asks Molloy what he is doing there, the published version adds a sentence that stresses not just the fact that Molloy was used to this question, but indirectly also that he apparently never really manages to answer it adequately:

Que faites-vous là? dit-il.
Je me repose, **répondis**-je.
Vous vous reposez? dit-il.

Que faites-vous là ? dit-il.
J'ai l'habitude de cette question, je la compris aussitôt.
Je me repose, **dis**-je.

---

49 Rosemary Pountney's concept of 'vaguening', to describe Beckett's tendency in the later drafts of his plays to remove specific details, was inspired by a note he made to himself ('vaguen') on a typescript of *Happy Days* (Pountney 1998, 149). The same tendency can be identified in the drafts of his prose.

Oui, dis-je.	Vous vous reposez, dit-il.
Voulez-vous répondre	**Je me repose**, dis-je.
à ma question? **dit**-il.	Voulez-vous répondre
(FN1, 45r-46r)	à ma question ? **s'écria**-t-il.
	(1951, 28)

Beckett made quite a few revisions in this short exchange. Instead of answering ('répondis-je'), Molloy just 'says' that he is resting. Whereas the policeman repeats Molloy's words with a question mark, he simply affirms them (without question mark) in the published version. In the manuscript, Molloy answers the question ('Oui'), which does not satisfy the policeman. In the Minuit edition, Molloy simply repeats his statement ('Je me repose'), which now infuriates the policeman ('s'écria-t-il'). Molloy explains that this is a general phenomenon: whenever he thinks he answers a question, in reality he does nothing of the kind. That is what happens when he is obliged to speak: the relatively straightforward expression 'quand je suis **obligé de converser**' (FN1, 46r) is changed to a higher register in the Minuit edition: 'quand je suis **acculé à la confabulation**' (1951, 28) ['reduced to confabulation' (1955, 25; *Mo* 17)].

Molloy understands that it is his attitude when at rest that bothers the policeman. Again, the manuscript is more specific in the description of this attitude, mentioning that Molloy places his feet asymetrically on the ground ('**pieds asymétriquement par terre**', FN1, 46r). The published version stresses the policeman's eloquence ('**C'était un beau parleur**', 1951, 28), when he explains that the law is the same for everyone, rich and poor, young and old, happy and sad. When Molloy replies that he is not sad, the policeman becomes angry in the manuscript ('**Il s'emporta**', FN1, 47), while the published text suggests that Molloy immediately understood that his reply was a mistake: '**Qu'est-ce que j'avais dit là !**' (1951, 28).

When the policeman asks for his papers, Molloy gives him the only paper he has, a bit of newspaper to wipe himself (or to be in a position to do so if he has to). While the register in the manuscript is rather vulgar ('pour **me torcher**', FN1, 47r), the choice of words in the Minuit edition is more neutral ('pour **m'essuyer**', 1951, 28). Molloy's story builds up the policeman's anger and at the very moment one expects him to explode (when Molloy thrusts the piece of news/toiletpaper under his nose), the narrative switches to the weather, comically truncating what was a frustrating conversation for both participants.

Paragraph 12 (FN1, 48r-50r)

'15.7[.47]'
(FN1, 47v)

This sudden switch coincides with the beginning of a new writing session. The last line of the previous session ('je sortis ce papier de ma poche et le lui ~~montrai.~~ ^{mis sous le nez}', FN1, 47r), in which Molloy specifies that he did not just show the policeman the paper but thrust it under his nose, ends at the bottom of the page (and at the end of the line). Not unlike the closing lines of *L'Innommable*, written on the last page of the last notebook (Van Hulle and Weller 2014, 206), Beckett here seems to have set himself the 'pensum' to fill the page (FN1, 47r) and simply stopped when he arrived at the finish line. The next day, 15 July 1947, he started with a completely new paragraph: 'Le temps était au beau.' (FN1, 48r) ['The weather was fine.' (1955, 26; *Mo* 17)]

Molloy's remark that he was not – or rather did not feel – unhappy is marked by a hesitation that seems partially the result of creative undoing in the manuscript, where a deletion precedes the interruption: 'Je **n'étai n'é** – je ne me sentais pas malheureux' (FN1, 48r); in the Minuit edition Molloy interrupts himself after 'Je **ne** –' (1951, 29). Here and there, Beckett has added a few words between the stage of the first draft and the Minuit edition, such as '**la tête dans les mains**' (1951, 29) ['their heads in their hands' (1955, 27; *Mo* 18)] – which was to become a recurring image in Beckett's later works.

Paragraph 13 (FN1, 50r-60r)

At the police-station, Molloy is introduced to a strange official, 'sprawling' in an arm-chair (1955, 27; *Mo* 18). The neutral expression '**assis** dans un fauteuil' (FN1, 50r) was changed to '**vautré** dans un fauteuil' in the Minuit edition (1951, 30). Apart from the questions about Molloy's mother, the official also asks questions about his father in the manuscript version, to which Molloy replies he is completely ignorant about the man: '**Aux questions qu'il me posa relatives à mon père je répondis que je n'avais jamais connu ce monsieur ni entendu parler de lui**' (FN1, 53r). This passage about Molloy's father did not make it into the published version. The revision process thus effectively helped obliterate 'ce monsieur' from Molloy's storyworld.

'17.7.47'

(FN1, 52v)

When Beckett did not immediately find the right word, he sometimes left a blank space, for instance in Molloy's reply to the question in which district his mother lives – '**Le quartier?**' (FN1, 53r). These are the first words of a new writing session, dated 17 July 1947. When Molloy deduces from the sound of the bellowing cattle that his mother lives by the shambles, he adds that the bellowing was often louder than his mother's chatter, but he does not immediately find the French word and just leaves open a blank space, in order not to interrupt the flow of the writing: 'plus fort que **ses**   ' (FN1, 53; see Fig. 10). By the time the text was published, Beckett found the word he was looking for: 'plus fort que **son babil**' (1951, 31) ['stilling her chatter' (1955, 28; *Mo* 19)].

Suddenly Molloy remembers his name and cries that it is Molloy. To which the sergeant asks whether that is his mother's name. Between Molloy's statement and the sergeant's question, the deliberately distracting comment that they let him keep his hat on was not yet part of the manuscript. It was interjected at a later stage: '**On me laissait garder mon chapeau, je me demande pourquoi**' (1951, 32). Similarly, between Molloy's 'Let me think!' and the sergeant's 'Take your time' (1955, 29; *Mo* 20) the interrogation is interrupted at a later stage by Molloy's self-conscious reflection that at least he imagined that this was how it was: '**Enfin je m'imagine que cela devait se passer ainsi**' (1951, 32).

On the other hand, the manuscript contains several descriptions of the actions that were cut. For instance, after Molloy has finally managed to say that his mother's name must be Molloy too, the sergeant reaches for his telephone and gives the instruction to take Molloy away: '**Il tendit la main vers son téléphone. Emmène-le, dit-il**' (FN1, 57r). When they take Molloy away and tell him to sit down, he tries to reply but is too slow: '~~**Quand j'eus compris [...] mes lenteurs à répondre**~~' (FN1, 57r), after which Beckett decided to cut things short. He deleted the passage and made Molloy summarize instead: '**On s'expliqua. J'abrège**' (FN1, 57r).

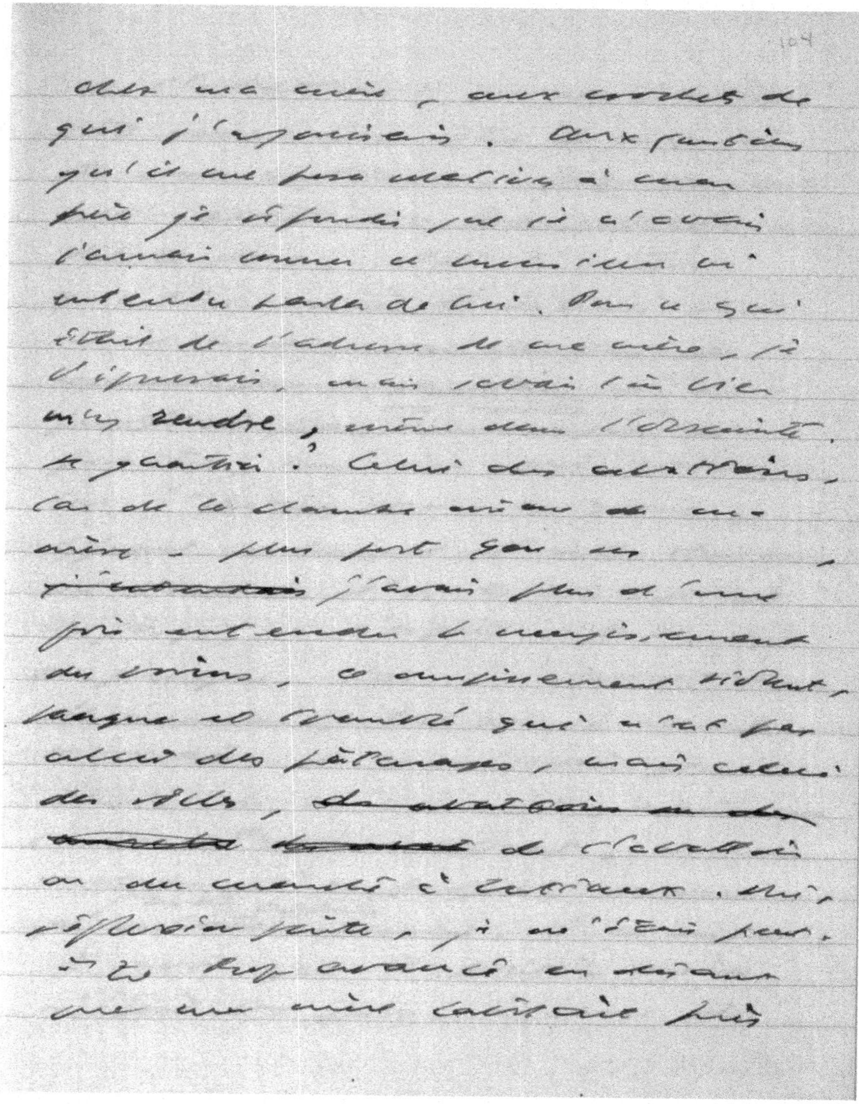

Fig. 10: 'plus fort que **ses**   ': blank space for a word Beckett did not immediately find, which later became '**son babil**' (FN1, 53r, l. 12).

Then again, when – a few lines further – the manuscript is *shorter* than the published version, it is due to a metanarrative reflection. The manuscript just mentions that they paid no attention to him and that he repaid the compliment. In the Minuit edition, this is followed by a comment that disrupts the narrative flow:

> Alors comment pouvais-je savoir qu'ils ne faisaient pas attention à moi et comment pouvais-je le leur rendre ? Je ne sais pas. Je le savais et le leur rendais, un point c'est tout. (1951, 33)

> [Then how could I know they were paying no attention to me, and how could I repay the compliment, since they were paying no attention to me? I don't know. I knew it and I did it, that's all I know. (1955, 30; *Mo* 20)]

In the manuscript, Molloy is not yet bothered by this afterthought. He suddenly sees a large woman rising up before him, dressed in black (FN1, 58r). The published versions deliberately add more information to confuse the narrative: 'une grande et grosse femme vêtue de noir, **de mauve plutôt**' (1951, 33) ['or rather in mauve' (1955, 30; *Mo* 20)]. This process of confusing and disrupting the narrative is only the continuation of a tendency that is already noticeable in the manuscript. For instance, after having noted that the 'big fat woman' is dressed in black, Molloy continues (in the first writing layer) to say that she is holding something out to him: '~~Elle me tenda~~', but Beckett stops in the middle of the word and makes Molloy wonder if it was perhaps a social worker: 'Je me demande encore aujourd'hui si ce n'était pas une assistante sociale' (FN1, 58r). Only then does he continue with the story he was telling: 'Elle me **tendait** un bol rempli ~~de thé probablement~~' (FN1, 58r). The neutral reference to the bowl of tea is cancelled and replaced by an addition on the facing verso, describing the liquid in more repellent terms: '**d'un jus grisâtre qui devait être du thé vert saccharin[é] lacté à la poudre**' (FN1, 57v; 1951, 33)[50] ['a mug full of a greyish concoction which

---

50 Beckett forgot to add the acute accent to 'saccharine' in the manuscript (FN1, 57v). This was corrected in the Minuit text (1951, 33), but because the typescript and the proofs preceding the edition have not been found, it is impossible to know if Beckett himself or an editor at Minuit was responsible for the correction.

must have been green tea with saccharine and powdered milk' (1955, 30; *Mo* 20)]. The aside 'Je vais vous dire une chose: quand les assistante[s] sociales vous offrent de quoi casser la croûte, à titre gracieux [...] on a beau reculer' (FN1, 58v)[51] ['Let me tell you this, when social workers offer you, free, gratis and for nothing, something to hinder you from swooning [...] it is useless to recoil' (1955, 30; *Mo* 21)] was literally an aside, written on the verso (FN1, 58v) facing the body of the text, and prepared in a paralipomenon on the previous verso: '~~je vais vous dire une chose, quand les assistantes sociales~~' (FN1, 57v) – jotted down as soon as the woman in black entered the scene. After the caustic sentence 'Lorsqu'on n'a rien, il est honteux de ne pas aimer la merde' (FN1, 58v)[52] ['To him who has nothing it is forbidden not to relish filth' (1955, 30; *Mo* 21)], Molloy concludes his aside with the intention to resume his narrative: '**Je reprends**' (FN1, 58v). These two words concluding the aside are left out in the subsequent versions. In the manuscript they physically indicate the point where the aside on the verso ends and the narrator picks up the narrative thread on the recto.

The manuscript contains more parentheses than the published version. The content of these parentheses is not omitted, but the brackets are left out. One of these parentheses is Molloy's comment upon hearing the mug rocking with a noise of chattering teeth: '**(où [sic] ~~éta~~ étaient-ce effectivement mes dents que j'entendais? Non, car je n'avais déjà plus de dents, à ce moment-là)**' (FN1, 59r). In the published version this becomes: 'le bol vacillait avec un bruit de dents qui claquent, **ce n'était pas les miennes, je n'en avais pas,** et le pain ruisselant se penchait de plus en plus' (1951, 34) ['not mine, I had none' (1955, 30; *Mo* 21)]. By leaving out the brackets, Beckett made the interruption more disturbing. The afterthought is not clearly separated from the narrative, but is allowed to disrupt it without warning.

Molloy suddenly flings everything far from him. The first writing layer states that he threw it to the ground. In a subsequent revision campaign Beckett again complicated the simple statement by adding more uncertainty (in an addition between the lines): '**ou contre le mur, je n'en sais rien**' (FN1, 59r) ['or

---

51 The expression 'de quoi casser la croûte' (FN1, 58v) was revised for the published text to 'de quoi ne pas tourner de l'œil' (1951, 33), and also the 's' missing in 'assistante[s] sociales' (FN1, 58v) was added (1951, 33).
52 The Minuit version is slightly different: '**A qui** n'a rien il est **interdit** de ne pas aimer la merde' (1951, 34).

against the wall' (1955, 31; *Mo* 21)]. The physical place of the page break is another interesting moment. The page ends with Molloy's remark that he will not tell what followed because it is too humiliating or tiresome: '**Je ne dirai pas la suite, humiliante** pour moi, ~~enfin pénible~~ plutôt pénible plutôt' (FN1, 59r); and the next page starts with the continuation of the sentence, announcing the wish to go elsewhere out of weariness: 'car je suis las de cet endroit et je veux aller ailleurs' (FN1, 60r). The grey pencil of the first writing layer is retraced, and the deletion and supralinear addition are also made during this delayed revision, which suggests that this retracing may indicate a transition from one writing session to the next.

Paragraph 14 (FN1, 60r-66r)

[**18.7.1947**]

The date of 18 July 1947 is not marked (see chapter 1.1.1), but this seems a plausible place in the text for a break. Following this hypothesis, Beckett stopped here on 17 July 1947, started again on 18 July by retracing the last sentence he wrote the previous day, and then opened a new paragraph. Beckett indeed fulfils his character's wish and releases him in the very first sentence of the new paragraph, thus playing the role of the French 'on' – 'they' in the English version: 'on me dit que je pouvais disposer' (FN1, 60r) ['they told me I could go' (1955, 31; *Mo* 21)]. The narrative is again more loquacious in the manuscript, Molloy adding that he was released after 3 or 4 hours' detention: 'On me relaxait en somme, après 3 ou 4 heures de détention' (FN1, 60r). While this relatively precise information is left out in the published version, another note is added in the next sentence. The same pattern seems to be confirmed: whereas the extra information in the manuscript furthers the narrative's progress, the extra text that is added at later stages tends to disrupt the narrative. When Molloy mentions that he found himself at freedom again ('en liberté'), the published version adds: '**si c'était bien elle**' (1951, 34) ['if that is what it was' (1955, 31; *Mo* 21)].

The writing seems to proceed smoothly. As if Beckett's pen has difficulty following Molloy's train of thought, it jumps a few letters, shortening 'protecteur' to 'procteur': 'Avais-je, sans le savoir, **un procteur** en haut lieu?' (FN1, 60r).[53]

Molloy's analysis of the possible reasons why they don't punish him takes recourse to common sense – **'le bon sens'** (FN1, 61r) – in the manuscript, but **'la sagesse'** (1951, 34) ['reason' (1955, 31; *Mo* 21)] in the Minuit edition: it is simply not worthwhile. But even as he discusses this act of reason, he keeps dwelling unreasonably long on it, so long that even Beckett eventually thought it was better to cut part of it. The manuscript explains that culprits were treated rudely to prevent them from reoffending: **'Ce que fait la loi alors, par l'intermédiaire de ses agents les plus humbles, c'est de faire subir au délinquant** ~~un mauvais traitement~~ des rudesses **rapide**s **et pour ainsi dire extemporané**es**,** ~~afin~~ de sorte **qu'il prenne peur et se garde de récidiver.'** (FN1, 61r) The published text is much shorter: **'Il est préférable de s'en remettre aux** agents' (1951, 34) ['It is better to leave things to the police' (1955, 31; *Mo* 21)].

> **'19.7[.47]'**
> (FN1, 62v)

On 19 July 1947, the beginning of a new writing session was marked by a difficult start: '~~Qu'on m'apprenne~~ ~~seulement~~ ~~en quoi consiste la bonne conduite et~~ On n'a qu'à ~~m'app~~ m'apprendre en quoi consiste la bonne conduite pour que je me conduise bien' (FN1, 63r) ['I have only to be told what good behaviour is and I am well-behaved' (1955, 32; *Mo* 22)].

It is noteworthy that Beckett complicates the narrative with a small revision when Molloy says he is intelligent and quick: **'je suis** intelligent et vif' (FN1, 63r). Beckett not only changed the present into a past tense, but he also translated this change of mind into a moment of hesitation: **'car je – j'étais** intelligent et vif' (1951, 35).

In terms of temporal setting, a significant change between the manuscript and the published version is the revision that indicates that Molloy's last step was taken, not the other day as the draft suggests – 'depuis mes premiers

---

53 It is also possible that 'procteur' is a multi-layered pun. In English, the word 'proctor' is roughly synonymous with 'prosecutor' and in Greek 'prôctos' means 'anus', relating to a recurrent theme in the novel.

^{pas} jusqu'à mes derniers, exécutés **l'autre jour**' (FN1, 63r) – but longer ago: '**l'année dernière**' (1951, 35).

Stylistically, the manuscript version is more formal and learned in its description of the 'peripatetic piss' (1955, 32; *Mo* 22) than the Minuit edition: '**la micturition en pleine marche**' (FN1, 64r) became '**la pissade ambulante**' (1951, 36).

The allusion to Wordsworth's definition of poetry – 'Poetry is the spontaneous overflow of powerful feelings: it takes its origin from emotion recollected in tranquillity' (Wordsworth 1936, 740) – was present from the very first draft in French. Beckett only hesitated about the word 'émotion'. He briefly considered replacing it by 'commotion', which would have obscured the allusion to the preface of the *Lyrical Ballads*: 'c'est dans la tranquillité de la décomposition que je me rappelle cette longue ~~émotion~~ ~~commotion~~ émotion confuse que fut **mon existence**' (FN1, 65r). At a later stage, he also replaced the overly dramatic 'mon existence' (perhaps too reminiscent of existentialism) by 'ma vie' (1951, 36) ['my life' (1955, 32; *Mo* 22)]. This 'tranquility of decomposition' also relates to Beckett's reading of Gide's essay *Dostoïevsky*, in which Dostoevsky's 'quietism' is contrasted with Balzac's composure (see chapter 2.2).

The paragraph ends with the elaboration on 'crying': 'Alors crions. C'est censé faire du bien. Oui, cette fois-ci, puis encore une autre, peut-être.' (FN1, 66r; 1951, 36) ['Let me cry out then, it's said to be good for you. Yes, let me cry out, this time, then another time perhaps, **then perhaps a last time.**' (1955, 33; *Mo* 23)] The addition of 'then perhaps a last time' echoes the meta-reflection in the first line of the manuscript (the opening line of the second paragraph in the published text), announcing the next novel and even a third one after that (see chapter 3.2). In the manuscript, this is a clear end of the paragraph.

Paragraph 15 (FN1, 66r-73r)

'[2]0.7.47'
(FN1, 65v)

The new paragraph coincides with a new writing session, inadvertently dated '30.7.47' (FN1, 65v) – which clearly should be '20.7.47', for the next writing session is dated '21.7' (FN1, 70v). The paragraph opens with 'Le soleil déclinant donnait en plein sur ~~le mur la façade~~ la blanche façade du poste' (FN1, 66r). When Beckett eliminated the paragraph breaks (between the manuscript and the version published by Minuit in 1951), he made a smooth transition in a most economical way, by simply adding two words that link the sentence to the crying at the end of the previous paragraph: **'Crions que** le soleil [...]' (1951, 36) ['Cry out that the declining sun fell full on the white wall of the barracks' (1955, 33; *Mo* 23)].

The 'complex' shadow of Molloy and his bicycle is turned into different shapes by Molloy's gesticulations, causing the policeman on guard at the door to tell him to go away. In the manuscript, the verb is **'déguerpir'** (FN1, 66r); the Minuit version is more colloquial: **'filer'** (1951, 37). The next sentence shows the same modulation of the register: **'Peu à peu mes excentricités prirent fin'** (FN1, 66r) becomes **'Je me serais calmé tout seul'** (1951, 37) ['I was calm again' (1955, 33; *Mo* 23)]. The policeman does not understand Molloy's request for help, so Molloy manages on his own: **'Je me débrouillai seul. ~~J'avais envie~~'** (FN1, 67r). This was left out in subsequent versions. The 'envie' in the unfinished sentence probably related to food, for Molloy is hungry and he regrets having refused the social worker's snack ('le casse-croûte de l'assistante sociale', FN1, 67r). So, he starts sucking a pebble to forget his hunger and thirst. The tendency to modulate the register works the other way round here: the simple expression **'fait passer'** in 'ça rafraîchit, **fait passer** la faim, trompe la soif' (FN1, 67r) becomes **'déjoue** la faim' in the Minuit edition (1951, 37) [appeases, soothes, makes you forget your hunger, forget your thirst' (1955, 33; *Mo* 23)]. The next sentence shows a similar construction with 'faire': 'L'agent ~~me~~ **faisait entendre des objurgations'** (FN1, 67r). The rather contrived expression relating to the agent's harsh rebukes is simply replaced by 'L'agent **venait vers moi'** (1951, 37) ['The man came towards me' (1955, 33; *Mo* 23)]. The interval between the writing of the manuscript and the publication of the text was apparently used to find a balance in the register.

Molloy's comment about his difficulty to tear himself away from this prison ('**Décidément j'ai du mal à m'arracher à cette prison**', FN1, 67r) was omitted in the published text. He notes that somewhere someone laughed, and not only outside, but even 'inside'. While the draft suggests that inside Molloy some*thing* was laughing ('En moi aussi il y avait **quelque chose** qui riait', FN1, 67r), this became some*one* ('**quelqu'un**') in the published text (1951, 37). This is quite a substantial variant, suggesting the Chinese boxes structure of what Daniel C. Dennett dubbed the 'Cartesian theatre' – the idea that incoming sensory data are processed by a little 'quelqu'un', a 'homunculus' inside our brain. In the manuscript of *L'Innommable*, Beckett even drew a doodle of a creature with a 'homunculus' inside its head (see Van Hulle and Weller 2014, 117; Bernini 2014).

Molloy concludes that, finally, everything was ready to go ('**Enfin tout fut prêt**', FN1, 67r), thus providing explicit closure to the preceding scene. This formula was omitted in the published text, possibly because clearly not everything was ready since three sentences later, shortly after he sets off, he realizes he has forgotten where he was going.

Although metareflections are often added only after the first draft, Molloy's comment about his use of the 'présent mythologique' (FN1, 68r; 1951, 37) ['mythological present' (1955, 34; *Mo* 23)] when speaking of the past was already part of the manuscript. And whereas the manuscript is typically slightly more detailed in terms of descriptions of the setting, it only mentions one canal ('me voilà [...] aux bords du canal', FN1, 69r), whereas the published version adds: '**il y en a même deux**' (1951, 38) – which buttresses the suggestion that the setting is Dublin with its two – Royal and Grand – canals. The canal 'goes through the town' (1955, 34; *Mo* 24); if that is the case, Molloy wonders why he sees hedges and fields. But he decides not to fret. In the manuscript, the first writing layer reads 'Ne **me** tourmente pas' – addressing some unnamed 'other'. The 'm' was subsequently overwritten, and Molloy addresses himself, taking a different perspective: 'Ne **m'e** tourmente pas, Molloy' (FN1, 69r) ['Don't torment yourself, Molloy' (1955, 34; *Mo* 24)].

Although the general pattern seems to be that the revision tends to add more uncertainty to the narrative, there are also counterexamples. When Molloy sees a barge on the canal, he supposes it is a cargo of nails and timber on its way to some carpenter – to which the manuscript adds '**si je pouvais**

m'en croire les yeux' (FN1, 69r).[54] In this case, Molloy's questioning the reliability of his own eyesight was left out in the published text.

Again, the text conjures the image of a man resting his elbow on his knee, his head on his hand – 'le coude sur son genou et la tête sur la main' (FN1, 70r) – recalling Walter von der Vogelweide's poem 'Ich saz ûf eime steine':

> Ich saz ûf eime steine / und dahte bein mit beine, / dar ûf satzt ich den ellenbogen; / ich hete in mîne hant gesmogen / daz kinne und ein mîn wange. / dô dâhte ich mir vil ange, / wie man zer welte solte leben. (von der Vogelweide 1994, 72)

> [I sat upon a stone / And crossed one leg over the other / On which I placed my elbow / On my hand I rested / My chin and one cheek / Then I thought hard / About how one should live in the world][55]

But the existential *sérieux* is undermined by the subsequent observation: the image of the man spitting into the water every three or four puffs, without taking his pipe from his mouth.

Molloy dismounts and lies down, beside his bicycle, in the ditch, where the white hawthorn stoops towards him: 'La blanche aubépine se penchait vers moi' (FN1, 70r). The reference to Proust was present from the very first draft onwards. The hawthorn triggers one of the involuntary memories in Proust's *À la recherche du temps perdu*, which Beckett marked as 'Rev. 5' or revelation 5 in the margin of his copy of the third volume of *À l'ombre des jeunes filles en fleurs*:

---

54 This image recalls the 'dying barge / carrying a cargo of nails and timber' from the poem 'Enueg I' (*CP* 6).

55 'Walther v.d. Vogelweide: Gedichte' is one of the items on the list of '<u>Books sent home</u>' from Germany in Beckett's 'Whoroscope' Notebook (UoR MS 3000, 17v), and the volume is still in his personal library (*BDL*, http://www.beckettarchive. org/library/VOG-ALT.html). While the poem is unmarked in this book, Beckett did copy the opening lines in his earlier student notes from the Middle High German Period (TCD MS 10971/1, 8r). It would remain a constant source of reference in his work, occuring as late as the short prose text *Stirrings Still*, the narrator regretting 'the want of a stone on which to sit like Walther and cross his legs' (*CIWS* 112).

> Tout d'un coup dans le petit chemin creux, je m'arrêtai touché au cœur par un doux souvenir d'enfance, je venais de reconnaître aux feuilles découpées et brillantes qui s'avançaient sur le seuil, un buisson d'aubépines défleuries, hélas, depuis la fin du printemps. (Proust 1929, 215)

Beckett had studied this particular revelation quite carefully, since in his copy of the *Recherche*'s first volume (*Du Côté de chez Swann*) he marked two passages with the marginalia 'Rev. 5 prepared'.[56] The exuberance of these passages requires a quotation in full to preserve their Proustian flavour:

> La haie formait comme une suite de chapelles qui disparaissaient sous la jonchée de leurs fleurs amoncelées en reposoir ; au-dessous d'elles, le soleil posait à terre un quadrillage de clarté, comme s'il venait de traverser une verrière ; leur parfum s'étendait aussi onctueux, aussi délimité en sa forme que si j'eusse été devant l'autel de la Vierge, et les fleurs, aussi parées, tenaient chacune d'un air distrait son étincelant bouquet d'étamines, fines et rayonnantes nervures de style flamboyant comme celles qui à l'église ajouraient la rampe du jubé ou les meneaux du vitrail et qui s'épanouissaient en blanche chair de fleur de fraisier. Combien naïves et paysannes en comparaison sembleraient les églantines qui, dans quelques semaines, monteraient elles aussi en plein soleil le même chemin rustique, en la soie unie de leur corsage rougissant qu'un souffle défait.
>
> Mais j'avais beau rester devant les aubépines à respirer, à porter devant ma pensée qui ne savait ce qu'elle devait en faire, à perdre, à retrouver leur invisible et fixe odeur, à m'unir au rythme qui jetait leurs fleurs, ici et là, avec une allégresse juvénile et à des intervalles inattendus comme certains intervalles musicaux, elles m'offraient indéfiniment le même charme avec une profusion inépuisable, mais sans me le laisser approfondir davantage, comme ces mélodies qu'on rejoue cent fois de suite sans descendre plus avant dans leur secret. (Proust 1928, 200)

56   See the *BDL*, http://www.beckettarchive.org/library/PRO-ALA-1.html.

Puis je revenais devant les aubépines comme devant ces chefs-
d'œuvre dont on croit qu'on saura mieux les voir quand on a
cessé un moment de les regarder, mais j'avais beau me faire
un écran de mes mains pour n'avoir qu'elles sous les yeux, le
sentiment qu'elles éveillaient en moi restait obscur et vague,
cherchant en vain à se dégager, à venir adhérer à leurs fleurs.
Elles ne m'aidaient pas à l'éclaircir, et je ne pouvais demander à
d'autres fleurs de le satisfaire. Alors me donnant cette joie que
nous éprouvons quand nous voyons de notre peintre préféré une
œuvre qui diffère de celles que nous connaissions, ou bien si l'on
nous mène devant un tableau dont nous n'avions vu jusque-là
qu'une esquisse au crayon, si un morceau entendu seulement au
piano nous apparaît ensuite revêtu des couleurs de l'orchestre,
mon grand-père m'appelant et me désignant la haie de
Tansonville, me dit : 'Toi qui aimes les aubépines, regarde un peu
cette épine rose; est-elle jolie !' En effet c'était une épine, mais
rose, plus belle encore que les blanches. (Proust 1928, 201)

These passages about the white and the pink hawthorn prepare not only
revelation 5, which Beckett marked in his copy, but also the narrator's
important aesthetic experience relating to the composer Vinteuil's works,
the white hawthorn relating to his sonata, the pink hawthorn to the septet:
knowing the sonata and discovering the septet cause the same 'new joy' as
the discovery of the pink hawthorn after having enjoyed the white variety.
The elaborate analogy serves as a complex background, and its very elabo-
rateness contrasts sharply with the shortness of Beckett's one-sentence
reference: in the first half of the sentence Molloy first evokes the hawthorn
scene, only to smother any possibility of an aesthetic experience in the
sentence's second half: 'malheureusement je n'aime pas l'odeur de l'aubépine'
(FN1, 70r).

While Molloy is lying in the ditch he remembers that, 'at the beginning of
this ending day' (1955, 35; *Mo* 24), he had set out to see his mother: 'au matin
de ~~ce jour qui finissait~~ cette journée finissante' (FN1, 71r). Again, Beckett seems to
deliberately make the foil between fiction and reality as thin as possible:
Molloy's ending day corresponds with the end of Beckett's working day. He
finished his writing session with the word 'finissante'.

The next day, '21.7' (marked on the facing verso), starts with a question: 'L̶e̶s̶ ᵐᵉˢ raisons?' (FN1, 71r). Molloy does not remember his reasons for going to his mother, but he is confident that he only needs to invoke them again – '**invoquer**' in the manuscript (FN1, 71r), '**retrouver**' in the published text (1951, 39) – to fly to his mother with the wings of necessity. It was only in a second writing phase that Beckett turned the wings into clipped wings: 'sur les ailes ᵈᵉ ᵖᵒᵘˡᵉ de la nécessité' (FN1, 71r). Molloy seems to feel dead, but he realises there is no use 'knowing' he is dead, since he is not: 'On a beau se savoir **mort**, on ne l'est pas' (FN1, 72r). The word 'mort' was changed to 'ᵈᵉ́ᶠᵘⁿᵗ' in an overlay addition, thus recalling the word 'defunctus' and the idea of finishing a 'pensum' in the closing paragraph of Beckett's essay *Proust*, which evokes the relationship between the sonata and the septet ('Septuor') of Vinteuil:

> The narrator [...] sees in the red phrase of the Septuor [...] the ideal and immaterial statement of the essence of a unique beauty, a unique world, the invariable world and beauty of Vinteuil, expressed timidly, as a prayer, in the Sonata, imploringly, as an inspiration, in the Septuor, the 'invisible reality' that damns the life of the body on earth as a *pensum* and reveals the meaning of the word: '*defunctus*'. (*PTD* 93; emphasis added)

Molloy's pensum is not yet defunctus; he is still 'writhing' ('On se tortille encore', FN1, 72r), but all the morticians are dead ('tous les croque-morts sont morts'): 'Quelqu'un a tiré les rideaux, soi-même **probablement**' (FN1, 72r-73r). The idea that Molloy himself has drawn the blinds is made slightly less probable in the published version, where 'probablement' is replaced by Beckett's favourite word '**peut-être**' (1951, 39) ['you perhaps' (1955, 35; *Mo* 25)]. So, the man who 'knows' he is dead but isn't gets up and goes to his mother who thinks she is alive. With this impression ('Voilà mon impression', FN1, 73r) Molloy closes the paragraph.

Paragraph 16 (FN1, 73r-74r)

In order to go to his mother, Molloy first needs to get out of the ditch, no matter how happy he would be to vanish there. The Proustian allusions in the previous paragraph and the last part of Beckett's *Proust* suggest a Schopenhauerian *basso continuo*. This last part of the essay focuses on the significance of Proust's botanical images and on the importance of music in his work: 'The influence of Schopenhauer on this [musical] aspect of the Proustian demonstration is unquestionable' (*PTD* 91), but his influence with regard to the botanical images is equally strong. Schopenhauer uses plant life to illustrate his point about the will-to-live: 'just because the plant is without knowledge, it ostentatiously displays its organs of generation in complete innocence' (Schopenhauer 1969, vol. 2, 295). Beckett's paraphrase in *Proust* reads: 'Flower and plant have no conscious will. They are shameless, exposing their genitals' (*PTD* 89). So if flowers evoke the will-to-live, Molloy's mention of the white hawthorn while lying in the ditch and his statement that he dislikes the smell of hawthorn are equally significant. Elsewhere in *Die Welt als Wille und Vorstellung*, Schopenhauer links this will-to-live to *'fuga mortis'*: 'it is not really th[e] *knowing* part of our *ego* that fears death, but *fuga mortis* comes simply and solely from the blind *will*, with which every living thing is filled' (vol. 2, 468; original emphasis). If the episode in the ditch where Molloy would 'joyfully [...] vanish' (1955, 35; *Mo* 25) can be read as a moment he considers giving up, the moment he decides to get out of the ditch seems to be inspired by Schopenhauer as well, notably by the notion of the 'denial of the will'. As Schopenhauer stresses, this 'denial' has nothing to do with suicide:

> Suicide, the arbitrary doing away with the individual phenomenon, differs most widely from the denial of the will-to-live, which is the only act of its freedom to appear in the phenomenon [...] The vehemence with which it wills life and revolts against what hinders it, namely suffering, brings it to the point of destroying itself, so that the individual will *by an act of will* eliminates the body that is merely the will's own becoming visible, rather than that suffering should break the will.

Just because the suicide cannot cease willing, he ceases to live; and the will affirms itself here even through the cessation of its own phenomenon. (Schopenhauer 1969, vol. 1, 398-9)

Instead of giving in to his urge to vanish in the ditch, Molloy decides to get up, confident that he will come back one day: 'un jour **(l'ai-je dit à sa place? Je ne sais pas)** je retrouverai le commissaire et ses ~~assistants~~ aides' (FN1, 73r). The metanarrative parenthesis was left out in the published version. But the text continues on this metanarrative level, although Molloy soon arrives at an impasse in the middle of his sentence: 'Car camper un être, un endroit, j'allais dire une heure, mais je ne veux offenser personne, [...] pour ensuite ne plus s'en servir, ce serait, **comment ~~dirais-je,~~** dire, **non, je ~~n'ose rien affirmer~~** n'affirmerai rien à ce sujet' (FN1, 74r) ['For to contrive a being, a place, I nearly said an hour, but I would not hurt anyone's feelings, and then to use them no more, that would be, how shall I say, I don't know' (1955, 36; *Mo* 25)]. The change from 'comment dirais-je' to 'comment dire' foreshadows Beckett's last work, *Comment dire*. In the manuscript, Molloy deliberately interrupts himself ('non'), first because he does not dare affirm what he is on the verge of saying, then because he simply decides not to affirm anything on this subject. But in the published text, the 'non' was omitted and the last part of the sentence was replaced by a statement of ignorance and impotence: 'comment dire, **je ne sais pas**' (1951, 40). The writing session of 21 July 1947 ended here, in this cul-de-sac.

'**22.[07.47]**'
(FN1, 73v)

The next day, Beckett started with the notable aesthetic statement 'Ne pas vouloir dire, ne pas savoir ce ~~que l'on~~ qu'on veut dire, ne pas pouvoir ~~dire~~ ce qu'on **sait**[57] qu'on veut dire, et toujours dire ou presque, voilà ce qu'il importe de ne pas perdre de vue, dans la chaleur de la **composition**' (FN1, 74r). John Fletcher (1964, 137) and many other critics have pointed out the correspondence to the famous lines from the *Three Dialogues with Georges Duthuit*: 'The expression that there is nothing to express, nothing with which to express, nothing from which to express, no power to express, no desire

---

57   For '**sait**' the published text reads '**croit**' (1951, 40).

to express, together with the obligation to express' (*PTD* 103). Molloy's statement came first, though. It was written 'in the heat of composition' (1955, 36; *Mo* 25) on 22 July 1947 ('22.' is marked on the facing verso, FN1, 73v), whereas Beckett started to work on writing up the *Three Dialogues* with the help of notes supplied by Duthuit in March 1949 (Pilling 2006, 106). In the manuscript of *Molloy*, the aesthetic statement ends with the word '**composition**', which is replaced by '**rédaction**' in the published text (1951, 40). Thus, the text in each of these two stages – composition (in the manuscript) and revision (in the subsequent versions) – reflects the autography's 'continuing incompletion' (Abbott 1996, 20) or 'mere gress', which Beckett preferred over 'progress' because of its 'purity from destination and hence from schedule' (*LSB I* 186). With this statement Beckett closed the paragraph.

Paragraph 17 (FN1, 74r-FN2, 03r)

Molloy did decide that he would get up and leave the ditch, but he has not left it yet. In the ditch, on the canal-bank, he spends the night, but when – with hindsight – he thinks of that night he finds nothing. In the manuscript, Molloy's 'pensée' is specified as '**ma pensée rieuse gémissante**' (FN1, 74r), which might be a reference to the Presocratic pair of 'laughing' and 'weeping' philosophers, Democritus and Heraclitus (TCD MS 10967/24r) – whom Beckett would later refer to as 'Hemocritus et Deraclitus, / philosophes muets' (*TN3* 247), interchanging their initials on the inside of the back cover of the production notebook for *Krapp's Last Tape*. The manuscript mentions only one night; the published version adds the possibility that there was more than one, thus again decomposing the composition: '**Je dis cette nuit, mais il y en eut plusieurs peut-être**' (1951, 40).

Molloy does remember the morning, the shepherd and his dog watching him wake up. The last lines of the notebook ('A ses côtés un chien haletant, qui me regardait aussi, mais moins fixement que son maître,' FN1, 75r) end with a comma, in the middle of the sentence.

The next day, Beckett marked the date ('22.7.47 / Paris') on the verso of
the front flyleaf and continued in the second notebook: 'car à de temps en
temps il s'arrêtait de me regarder pour se mordiller furieusement les chairs'
(FN2, 01r) ['for from time to time he stopped watching me to gnaw at his
flesh' (1955, 36; *Mo* 25)]. The temporal setting is again slightly more specific
in the manuscript, according to which the scene with the shepherd and
his dog when Molloy wakes up takes '**5 ou 6 minutes**' (FN2, 01r). Beckett
makes Molloy wonder if the dog took him for a sheep, adding the word
'black' above the line: 'Me prenait-il pour un mouton ^noir^' (FN2, 01r). Molloy
recognizes the anxious bleating of the sheep without the least hesitation
('sans **la moindre hésitation**', FN2, 01r) – which eventually became 'sans
peine' (1951, 41) ['without any trouble' (1955, 37; *Mo* 26)]. But after five or
six minutes Molloy's visual and intellectual acuity vanishes when in his eyes
and 'in his head' ('dans ma tête', FN2, 01r) a fine rain begins to fall (1955, 37;
Mo 26), which he later refers to as a mist[59] that rises in him every day and
'veils' not just the world, but even himself from himself ('me voile à moi', FN2,
02r). The metaphor of the veil has a long history in Beckett's works, which
goes back at least to his reading of Schopenhauer, who refers to the Indian
notion of the veil of Maya to suggest that phenomena are only an illusory
appearance. One of the most famous occurrences of the veil is the July 1937
letter to Axel Kaun (*LSB I* 512-21), where Beckett applies it to language, but
the link to the eyes is more prominent in the short text in German which
Beckett wrote in the 'Clare Street' Notebook in August 1936, just before he
went to Germany:

---

58   'Paris' is written in blue ink; the date in black ink.
59   The manuscript reads '**pluie**' (FN1, 02r), the Minuit edition '**bruine**' (1951, 42).

There are moments when the veil of hope is finally torn apart and the suddenly liberated eyes see *their* world, as it is, as it must be. Alas, it does not last long, the revelation quickly passes, the eyes can only bear such pitiless light for a short while, the membrane of hope grows again and one returns to the world of phenomena. (UoR MS 5003, 17r-18r; translated by Mark Nixon, original emphasis)[60]

After the war, Beckett used the image of the veil notably in the short text on the painters Bram and Geer van Velde, 'Peintres de l'Empêchement', where he speaks of:

> Un dévoilement sans fin, voile derrière voile, plan sur plan de transparences imparfaites, un dévoilement vers l'indévoilable, le rien, la chose à nouveau. Et l'ensevelissement dans l'unique, dans un lieu d'impénétrables proximités, cellule peinte sur la pierre de la cellule, art d'incarcération (*Dis* 136-7)

> An endless unveiling, veil behind veil, plane after plane of imperfect transparencies, light and space themselves veils, an unveiling towards the unveilable, the nothing, the thing again. And burial in the unique, in a place of impenetrable nearness, cell painted on the stone of cell, art of confinement. (Beckett 2011b, 880)[61]

Under the provisional title 'Le nouvel objet' Beckett wrote 'Peintres de l'empêchement' in March 1947 (Pilling 2006, 100), only a month or two before he started writing *Molloy* (see Bolin 2012, 122).

The writing in the manuscript follows Molloy's process of thinking out loud, by making frequent use of epanorthosis. Molloy says he got down on his

---

60 See Nixon 2011 (170) for a full transcription and translation.
61 This is a passage from a partial English translation of 'Peintres de l'empêchement' (without the long opening paragraph) that appeared in the catalogue of the Samuel M. Kootz Gallery in New York (1948) under the title 'The New Object', edited with an introduction by Peter Fifield in *Modernism/ modernity* 18.4 (November 2011), 878-80.

knees but immediately corrects himself to say he was standing upright: 'Je me mis à genoux, non, ça ne va pas, je me ~~mis~~ mis debout' (FN2, 02r).

On the verso (FN2, 01v), Beckett jotted down the paralipomenon 'quel pays rural, mon Dieu' ['what a land of breeders' (1955, 38; *Mo* 27)], which is not used in the body of the text until page 03r.

The manuscript is straightforward with regard to the temporal setting and announces the second day: 'Et voilà comment débuta **pour moi** cette seconde journée' (FN2, 03r). The published version leaves out 'pour moi' ['for me'] and adds instead that it might also have been the third or the fourth: '**à moins que ce ne fût la troisième ou la quatrième**' (1951, 42). Molloy regards it as a bad start because it leaves him with 'persisting doubts' (1955, 38; *Mo* 27) – 'une perplexité de longue **durée**' (FN2, 03r), later changed to 'longue **haleine**' (1951, 42) – as to the destination of the sheep. Beckett emphasizes the contrast between the white sheep and the black sheep, Molloy, by adding the adjective 'white' to the gruesome description of their thin legs crumpling under the pole-axe: 'dans un froissement ~~de leurs~~ des ^blanches^ pattes ~~absurdement~~ maigres [...] sous **l'assommoir**' (FN2, 03r). The adjective 'blanches' was left out in the published version and the possible reference to Zola's *L'Assommoir* was replaced by 'sous **le merlin**' (1951, 42) – probably not meant as an allusion to the journal *Merlin*, which showed its interest in publishing a work by Beckett only in August 1952, after the publication of the novel by Minuit on 12 March 1951. The afterthought that there is much to be said too for these little doubts was added after the manuscript version: 'Mais elles ont du bon aussi, les petites perplexités' (1951, 42). Here, Beckett introduced the sentence prepared on page 01v: 'Quel pays rural, mon Dieu' (FN2, 03r).

Paragraph 18 (FN2, 03r-04r)

'**23.[7.47]**'
(FN2, 02v)

But all the quadrupeds in the county cannot prevent Molloy from getting to his mother as quickly as possible. This 'But' marks the beginning of a new paragraph and a new writing session, dated '23.[7.47]' (FN2, 02v). Molloy's aim ('le but') is to reach his mother as quickly as possible ('~~joindre~~ ^aller vers^ ma mère le plus rapidement possible', FN1, 03r). After 'possible', Beckett has

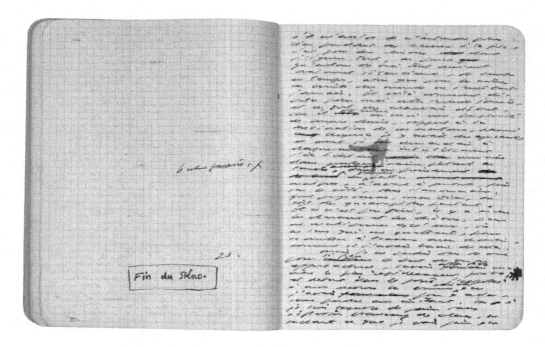

Fig. 11: The note 'Fin du Sténo', possibly indicating that Beckett had been copying separate text from an unpreserved steno pad into his notebook (FN2, 02v-03r).

written an asterisk in blue ink, which corresponds with a boxed text on the facing verso, reading 'Fin du Sténo.' (FN2, 02v; see Fig. 11) ['End of steno.'], which may refer to an unpreserved notepad (see chapter 1.1.1).

All of a sudden Molloy mentions that he is no longer lying but standing in the ditch and summoning the good reasons he had for going to his mother. But he does not mention them.

Paragraph 19 (FN2, 04r-05r)

Instead, he starts talking about the glorious weather. Molloy cannot enjoy it, though. He has killed '**Le méditerranéen**' in himself (FN2, 04r) – '**L'Egéen**' in the published version (1951, 43), 'The Aegean' in English (1955, 39; *Mo* 27). The revision may be another case of Beckett removing biographical circumstance from the text later on in the writing process. In a few days he would leave for Menton (see paragraph 20 below), which is located on the Mediterranean Sea at the border between France and Italy. While the Aegean Sea forms a part of the Mediterranean Sea, it is situated between Greece and Turkey, unrelated topograghically to the genesis of the novel, the bulk of which was written in Menton. Molloy's dissatisfaction with the weather finds its analogy in his dissatisfaction with his powers of expression in the next sentence. The gloom of rainy days, he suggests, was better fitted to his taste, but then he corrects himself twice, saying he expressed himself badly. The first writing layer reads: 'Les pâles ombres des jours de pluie répondent davantage à mon goût, **non,** je m'exprime mal.' (FN3, 04r) The epanorthosis subsequently became more elaborate, by means of an addition on the left-hand side: 'à mon humeur non plus' (FN2, 03v). When he mentions spring and the month of April, the manuscript adds that this is the month of his birth – the same as Beckett's: 'en avril, **mois de ma naissance, soit dit en ricanant**' (FN2, 04), a reference omitted from the published version (1951, 43). This act of creative undoing turns the autobiographical element into an autographic gesture, a 'mode of action taken in the moment of writing' (Abbott 1996, x).

In winter, when Molloy wraps himself in newspapers, he has a preference for the *Times Literary Supplement*. To mock the 'loutishness of learning' (*CP* 55), Beckett did not choose a French newspaper, as one might expect in a French manuscript. From the very first draft, it was the anglophone *TLS* ('Le supplément littéraire du Times', FN2, 04r) that was being derided as unmatched in terms of impermeability. In the manuscript, Molloy even says he only uses the *TLS*: '**je n'utilise que lui**' (FN2, 04r), for 'Even farts made no impression on it' (1955, 39; *Mo* 27).

When Molloy starts talking about his farting, the manuscript indicates his reticence in rather straightforward terms: 'malgré la **peine** que cela **me fait**' (FN2, 05r). The pattern in the variants indicates a tendency toward stylistic balance. There is no clear tendency from a lower to a higher register, or vice versa between the manuscript and the published version. But style does function as a means to find a certain equilibrium. Given the unsavoury subject, the style seems to be employed here to create a compensatory contrast between content and form. So, in the published version, Molloy feels obliged to mention his farts and at the same time to apologetically evoke his repugnance in a slightly higher register than in the manuscript: 'malgré la **répugnance** que cela **m'inspire**' (1951, 43). He mentions that he counted them one day, when he did not have anything special to do: 'Un jour **que je n'avais rien de spécial à faire** je les comptai' (FN2, 05r). Beckett again blurs the division between the material world – in this case the physical environment of the copybook – and Molloy's fictional world. He started calculating on the left-hand side (FN2, 04v; see Fig. 12).

After having calculated that 315 farts in 19 hours – more than 16 per hour (16.58 to be precise) – comes down to only 4 every 15 minutes, not even one every 5 minutes in the manuscript (FN2, 5r), which is changed into one every 4 minutes in the published version (1951, 44), he concludes that he hardly farts at all, that he is only a 'tout petit péteur' after all and should never have mentioned it. To Molloy's astonishment as to 'how mathematics[62] help you to know yourself' (1955, 39; *Mo* 28), the manuscript adds a comparison with psychology, which is deemed to offer less insight: 'à l'**encontre** ~~de la psychole~~ **de la psychologie**' (FN2, 05r). The auto(bio)graphical link with Beckett's own recorded interest in psychology (see Feldman 2006) is both evident and ironic.

Molloy's use of the 'mythological present' when he speaks of the past is more consistent in the manuscript than in the published text, where it is sometimes changed into a past tense, for instance when he discusses the climate of his country (his 'region' in the published version): 'il **fait** souvent du soleil le matin, dans ce x **pays**, [...] le ciel se **couvre**, la pluie **tombe**' (FN2, 05r) / 'il **faisait** souvent du soleil le matin, dans cette **région**, [...] le ciel se **couvrait**, la pluie **tombait**' (1951, 44). The rain keeps falling till the evening. Then the sun comes out, just in time for sunset. Again, the end of the writing session corresponds with the evocation of nightfall in the narrative.

---

62   The manuscript reads '**l'arithmétique**', which is changed into '**les mathématiques**' in the Minuit edition (1951, 44).

Paragraph 20 (FN2, 05r-29r)

'MENTON 27.7.47'

(FN2, 04v)

At the end of July 1947, Beckett left for Menton with his wife Suzanne (Pilling 2006, 101-2). There, on 27 July, he started a new paragraph, with Molloy back in the saddle: 'Nous voilà donc encore une fois en selle' (FN2, 05r). But the enthusiasm of a new beginning is immediately dampened by the notion of ignorance, for Molloy does not know if it was the right road. Until he sees the ramparts ahead of him. Again, the original manuscript version uses the metrical system ('100 metres'), shifting to 'paces' later on: 'à cent **mètres** devant moi' (FN2, 06r) became 'à cent **pas** devant moi' in the Minuit edition (1951, 44) – simply 'ahead of me' (1955, 40; *Mo* 28) in English. And when Molloy explains that the town where he was born had such a grasp on him that he had never succeeded in 'putting between it and me more than **ten or fifteen miles**' (1955, 40; *Mo* 28), the distance was again expressed in metrical terms in the manuscript: 'plus de **10 ou 15 kilomètres**' (FN2, 06r). The distance is the longest in the French edition, which switches to fifteen or twenty miles: 'plus de **quinze ou vingt milles**' (1951, 44). The name of the town was not yet 'X', but a sort of hiatus or placeholder: 'Pardon, monsieur, c'est bien **(ici le nom de la ville)** ici?' (FN2, 07r) ['I beg your pardon, Sir, this *is* X, is it not?' (1955, 40; *Mo* 29)]. In the manuscript, Molloy thinks it starts with '**un D**' as in Dublin (FN2, 07r), but the other letters escape him in spite of this clue, or perhaps because it is false. In the published version this suggestion that it is false is taken one step further, and the letter 'D' is replaced by the hesitation between '**un B**' or '**un P**' (1951, 45).

This moment of linguistic uncertainty is followed by a passage that was difficult to write, in which Molloy explains he was so far from words that they had lost their associations for him: ('~~Je suis si loin des mots [...] qu'ils ont perdu leurs associations~~', FN2, 07r). The situation is comparable to Watt's trouble naming one of Mr Knott's pots, or at least his impression that 'it was not a pot of which one could say, Pot, pot, and be comforted' (*W* 67). Similarly, in *Molloy* 'la condition de l'objet était d'être sans nom et celle des noms d'être sans objet' (FN2, 07r) ['there could be no things but nameless things, no names but thingless names', 1955, 41; *Mo* 67]. The theme of the Unnamable already appears: the world is lost as soon as he names it ('~~le monde aussi~~

| 186 |

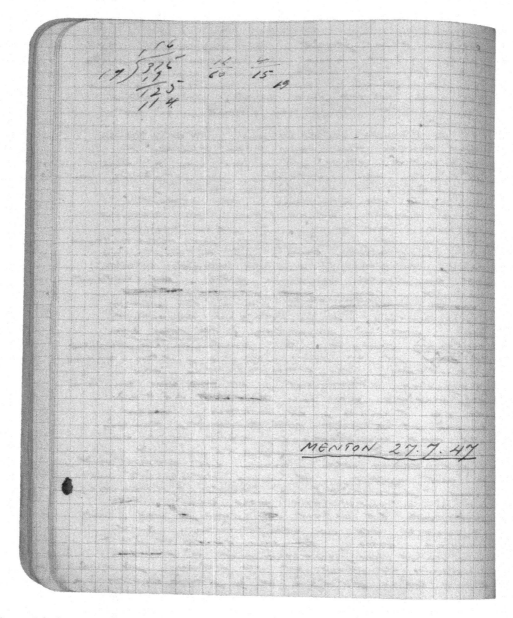

Fig. 12: Calculations with regard to the number of Molloy's farts, made just before Beckett continued the writing of *Molloy* in 'MENTON' on '27.7.47' (27 July 1947) (FN2, 04v).

m'est perdu dans l'instant où je le nomme', FN2, 07r). The passage was
so difficult to put to paper that Beckett deleted it and rewrote it on the
facing verso (FN2, 06v). This difficulty of expression is thematized in the
subsequent versions: 'I had been living so far from words so long, you
understand, that it was enough for me to see my town, since we're talking of
my town, to be unable, you understand. It's too difficult to say, for me.' (1955,
41; *Mo* 67) In the manuscript, however, it was also difficult to say, but at least
the attempt was not interrupted in mid-sentence, as Molloy explains that the
sight of his town did not enable him to utter precisely but instead barred him
from naming the slightest object: 'Il y avait si longtemps que je vivais loin des
mots, vous comprenez, que la vue de ma ville, par exemple, puisqu'il s'agit
de cela en ce moment, **loin de s'accompagner pour moi d'une précision
verbale** dénomination générique **quelconque me mettait dans l'impossibilité de
nommer avec certitude quoi que ce fût le moindre objet**.' (FN2, 06v) The
notion that he had been living so far from words for such a long time, is
reminiscent of an *Ur*-scene that frequently recurs as an allusion in Beckett's
work: Virgil's first appearance in the first Canto of Dante's *Divina Commedia*
as a figure 'who seemed faint/hoarse from long silence', 'chi per lungo
silenzio parea fioco' (Dante, *Inferno*, Canto I, l. 63). The 'long sonata of the
dead' (1955, 41; *Mo* 29) was originally a sonata of decomposition (**'la sonate
de la décomposition'**, FN2, 07r) and the 'life without tears, as it is wept'
(1955, 41; *Mo* 29) was a **'leçon'** before it became a **'pensum'** – with all its
Schopenhauerian overtones.[63]

'**28.7[.47]'**
(FN2, 07v)

The only thing one can hope, according to Molloy, is 'to be a little less, in
the end, the creature you were in the beginning, and the middle' (1955,
42; *Mo* 30). In the manuscript, the only hope is to be 'moins, à la fin, ce
qu'on était au commencement' (FN2, 09r); the middle was added in the
subsequent versions to reflect the structure of the 'sonata of decomposition':

63   Beckett first referred to Schopenhauer's *Parerga und Paralipomena* ('Das
      Leben ist ein Pensum zum Abarbeiten: in diesem Sinne ist *defunctus* ein
      schöner Ausdruck' ['Life is a *pensum* to be finished: in that sense *defunctus*
      is a nice expression']) in the closing lines of his essay *Proust* (*PTD* 93; see
      quotation above, paragraph 15).

'avec un commencement, un milieu et une fin' (FN2, 07r). Unlike this neat structure, however, the day-to-day reality of Molloy's situation is more chaotic: 'to tell the truth (to tell the truth!) I have never been particularly resolute, I mean given to resolutions, but rather inclined to plunge headlong into the shit' (1955, 42; *Mo* 30). Applied to the writing process, Molloy's is indeed an 'écriture à processus' (as opposed to 'à programme'), and even the paragraph structure starts decomposing: the paragraph that opened on page 05r continues to grow and becomes an amorphous mass of text that is not interrupted by any paragraph break until page 29r.

After his existential reflection ('Et puis merde', FN2, 08r; ['To hell with it anyway', 1955, 41; *Mo* 29]), Molloy tries to return to the matter at hand: the name of the town ('Where was I', 1955, 41; *Mo* 29). He has a plan in mind ('mon plan, dans ma tête', FN2, 09r): he will wait for a passer-by to tell him the name. But his plan is thwarted when his bicycle runs over a dog. Instead of separating these different themes, Molloy just continues without a single paragraph break.

The owner of the dog is called Sophie, '**Luce** [...] ou Lousse' in the manuscript (FN2, 11r), not yet 'Loy [...] ou Lousse' as in the first edition (1951, 49). When, after having slung the dead dog across the saddle of Molloy's bicycle, they arrive at the woman's house, he claims he cannot call her Sophie anymore and will try to call her Lousse, employing another epanorthosis: 'La maison de Sophie — non, je ne peux pas l'appeler ainsi, je vais essayer de l'appeler Lousse' (FN2, 14r).

'30.[7.47]'
(FN2, 13v)

Instead of describing Lousse and her house, Molloy decides to describe the burial of the dog first. Explaining his inability to dig the hole because he has only one leg to work with, being 'moralement unijambiste' (FN2, 15r) ['virtually onelegged' (1955, 47; *Mo* 33)], he enters into another Shandyan digression, noting that he would have been happier if he were amputated at the groin and 'if they had removed a few testicles into the bargain' (1955, 47; *Mo* 33).

In the manuscript, these testicles are called witnesses of a sperm, assassinated without joy ('~~ces témoins d'un sperme [...] assassiné sans joie~~', FN2, 15r). Beckett deleted this and replaced it by the pun '**témoins à charge [...] à décharge du procès de ma vie**' (FN2, 15r). This life then became '**ma longue mise en accusation**' (1951, 52), which in English puns on 'discharge': 'they bore false witness, for and against, in the lifelong charge against me' (1955, 47; *Mo* 33) – prefiguring Text 4 of the *Textes pour rien / Texts for Nothing*, where the 'mise en accusation' is linked to the accusative in the tension between 'I' and 'me', the narrator narrated: 'who says this, saying it's me? Answer simply, someone answer simply. It's the same old stranger as ever, for whom alone accusative I exist, in the pit of my inexistence, of his, of ours, there's a simple answer' (*TFN* 17). The lack of desire to wrest anything from them – '**plus le moindre ~~désir~~ ~~d'en tirer quelque chose~~**' – was changed to '**plus envie**' (FN2, 15r) in the manuscript and 'translated' into a reference to Giacomo Leopardi in the English version: 'non che la speme il desiderio' (1955, 47; *Mo* 33), from the poem 'A se stesso', 'To himself': 'non che la speme, il desiderio è spento' ['not only the hope, but even the desire is extinguished'] (Leopardi 2011, 234-5).[64] The accusation is turned into an accusation by the testicles for having made a balls of it ('ils m'accusaient de les avoir ~~xxx~~ couillonnés', FN2, 16r).

In the meantime, Lousse is digging the hole; 'On the whole', Molloy is just watching (1955, 48; *Mo* 34). When he starts describing her, he finds no indications that she lives 'in embarrassed circumstances', no signs that – as the manuscript specifies – her only source of income was the 'pension de guerre' ['war pension'] of her deceased husband (FN2, 18r). When she starts talking, Molloy first does not understand half ('~~la moitié~~') of what she is

---

64   Leopardi occurs frequently in Beckett's work. His name is mentioned in *Dream of Fair to Middling Women* (*D* 61) and the poem 'A se stesso' is quoted in letters (*LSB II* 509, 537) and the essay *Proust* (*PTD* 18, 63). Two books by Leopardi are still present in Beckett's personal library, *Prose, Con uno studio di Pietro Giordano* (n.d.) and *I Canti* (1936), but the poem is not marked (*BDL*, http://www.beckettarchive.org/library/LEO-PRO.html and http://www.beckettarchive.org/library/LEO-CAN.html). See Van Hulle and Nixon 2013 (116).

saying; Beckett then changed that into a quarter ('**le quart**', FN2, 19r) and by the first edition it was only a hundredth part ('**le centième**', 1951, 55). Molloy understands her parrot better than he understands her. In the manuscript, the bird only speaks French ('Putain de conasse de merde de chiaison', FN2, 19r); in the first edition, he also speaks English ('Fuck!', 1951, 55). In the English translation, the pattern is turned around: the parrot first only seems to speak English ('Fuck the son of a bitch') and then also turns out to speak French ('Putain de merde', 1955, 49; *Mo* 35).[65] The animals and the human animal Molloy are all treated in the same way: like the dog, the parrot would be buried by Lousse one day, and so would Molloy – if he had stayed.

'**1er août [1947]**'

(FN2, 18v)

In the manuscript, Molloy makes his situation more explicit than in the subsequent versions, calling it an imprisonment: '**J'étais prisonnier**' (FN2, 20r). Molloy looks for his clothes, gropingly ('en tâtonnant', FN2, 20r). In the manuscript, he does not wonder how it is possible that he was able to ferret around in the room without his crutches. This remark was added later in a tone that suggests the voice of a later self, as if Molloy were rereading what he had written, and noted a moment of his own precarious suspension of disbelief: '**Je trouve cela étrange.**' (1951, 56) ['I find it strange.' (1955, 50; *Mo* 36)]

The room is lit by the moon, framed in the window and divided in three segments by the vertical bars, of which Beckett made a drawing on the verso (FN2, 21v; see Fig. 2 in chapter 1.1.1). His description resembles the

---

65   In his notes on the translation of *Molloy*, Bowles explains how this reversal came about: 'We spent most of a morning in the Café Select swearing experimentally at each other. However, at the end of it, I was sorry to see Beckett's original searing French expletives go, so after we had worked our way round to the fairly mild American version I suggested there was no reason why the parrot should not have three masters in the English version. This was agreed and part of the original French was retained in the English, enabling the parrot to serve two masters as well as a mistress, while at the same time revealing a hitherto unsuspected talent for bilingual expression. Fortunately, there were only a few customers taking morning coffee that day in the Select, and only an occasional turning shoulder and a grin from a neighbouring table greeted our excursions below deck.' (Bowles 1994, 33)

exhaustion of possibilities in the tradition of *Watt*: the moon was moving from left to right, or the room was moving from right to left, or both together.

'2.8.47'
(FN2, 21v)

On 2 August 1947, he continued the description by adding a few other possibilities to the list: or both the moon and the room are moving 'from left to right, but the room not so fast as the moon, or from right to left, but the moon not so fast as the room' (1955, 51; *Mo* 37). When Molloy finds it hard to talk about the moon without excitement, he explains this lack of reticence by suggesting that the moon – 'si con' (FN2, 23r) – must be turning her 'arse' to the earth all the time (1955, 51; *Mo* 37). As if this were proof of his knowledgeability of the stars, Molloy subsequently admits that he took an interest in astronomy at some point, 'à un moment donné' (FN2, 23r), followed by geology.[66]

These two disciplines happen to be well represented in Beckett's 'Whoroscope' Notebook, which contains a 'Table of Geological Eras' (UoR MS 3000, 62v; see Fig. 13), preceded and followed by notes on astronomy, taken from an article called 'Is There Life in Other Worlds?' by Dr H. Spencer Jones, 'Astronomer Royal' (published in *Discovery*, New Series, Vol. II, No. 10, January 1939).[67]

Evidently, these notes were of no use for the writing of *Molloy*, but Beckett did jot them down 'à un moment donné' (probably early 1939) and he seems to be playing an autographical game with the reader when – at a later stage in the writing process – he added: **'Je ne veux pas le nier'** (1951, 58) ['I don't deny it' (1955, 52; *Mo* 37)].

Molloy's even greater interest in anthropology and its relentless definition of man in terms of what he is not, echoes the passage on 'our anthropologists' in *Watt*:

---

66   Astrology and geology are followed by anthropology and psychiatry, but in the end it is 'magic' that has 'the honour of my ruins' (1955, 52; *Mo* 38). Rubin Rabinovitz links this scene to Goethe's *Faust* (I.354ff.), where the protagonist is presented as a scholar who renounces traditional learning in favour of magic (Rabinovitz 1979).

67   See also Van Hulle 2011.

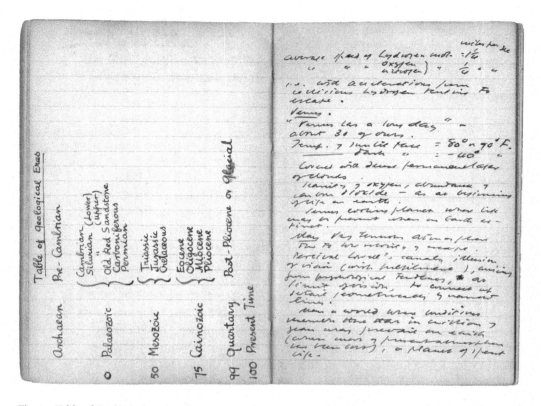

Fig. 13: Table of Geological Eras in Beckett's 'Whoroscope' Notebook (UoR MS 3000, 62v-63r).

For the only way one can speak of nothing is to speak of it as though it were something, just as the only way one can speak of God is to speak of him as though he were a man, which to be sure he was, in a sense, for a time, and as the only way one can speak of man, even our anthropologists have realized that, is to speak of him as though he were a termite. (*W* 64)

Molloy's digression on the voice he hears ('I listen and the voice is of a world collapsing endlessly', 1955, 53; *Mo* 38) was difficult to write. This passage is not just about worldmaking, but it also illustrates Nelson Goodman's suggestion in *Ways of Worldmaking* that this creative process consists of a

| 193 |

dialectic of composition and decomposition (Goodman 1978, 7): in order to write it, Beckett crossed out the first attempt on page 23v-24r and rewrote the passage on page 25r. In the French versions, the voice is clearly Molloy's, as he hears himself dictate: '~~J'écoute et m'entends dicter un monde figé en perte d'équilibre~~' (FN2, 24r).

'7.8.47'

(FN2, 24v)

The act of cancellation (or 'decomposition') coincides with the end of a writing session or the beginning of a new one. Beckett started rewriting the passage on a new page (FN2, 25r), marking the date '7.8.47' on the verso (FN2, 24v). Molloy calls it a world at an end ('un monde fini', FN2, 25r) – presaging Clov's '*Finished, it's finished, nearly finished*, it must be nearly *finished*' at the beginning of *Endgame* (*E* 6; emphasis added).

The voice becomes a whisper, and here the manuscript gives a rare hint as to the origin of this allusion: 'Et j'écouterais encore ~~cette chère voix~~ ce cher souffle **lointaine**, depuis longtemps **tue (on dirait du Verlaine)** et que j'entends enfin' (FN2, 24v-25r). The reference is to the last lines of Paul Verlaine's sonnet 'Mon rêve familier', from the first section ('Melancholia') of his *Poèmes saturniens*. This was one of the five poems whose first lines are written on a piece of paper inserted in Beckett's unmarked copy of Verlaine's *Œuvres poétiques complètes* in the Pléiade edition (Paris: Gallimard, 1968):[68]

> Je fais souvent ce rêve étrange et pénétrant
> D'une femme inconnue, et que j'aime, et qui m'aime
> Et qui n'est, chaque fois, ni tout à fait la même
> Ni tout à fait une autre, et m'aime et me comprend.
>
> Car elle me comprend, et mon cœur, transparent
> Pour elle seule, hélas ! cesse d'être un problème
> Pour elle seule, et les moiteurs de mon front blême,
> Elle seule les sait rafraîchir, en pleurant.

68   See Van Hulle and Nixon 2013 (61) and the *BDL*, http://www.beckettarchive. org/library/VER-OEU.html.

Est-elle brune, blonde ou rousse? Je l'ignore.
Son nom? je me souviens qu'il est doux et sonore,
Comme ceux des aimés que la Vie exila.

Son regard est pareil au regard des statues,
Et, pour sa **voix, lointaine**, et calme, et grave, elle a
L'inflexion des **voix chères** qui se sont **tues**. (Verlaine 1968,
63-4)

In the translation by Martin Sorrell, the last two verses read: 'And in her calm and grave and distant voice / Are modulations of loved voices gone to earth.' (Sorrell 2000, 86) The manuscript is the only version in which Beckett adds the parenthesis with the explicit reference to Verlaine; in the subsequent versions, he erases the exogenetic trace.[69] The silent voice ('qui se met à vous bruisser dans la tête', FN2, 26r ['which begins to rustle in your head', 1955 53; *Mo* 39]) prefigures the dead voices in *En attendant Godot*, which rustle like leaves, just like the voices which the shell-shocked Septimus Smith hears in *Mrs Dalloway*, 'the voices which rustled above his head' (Woolf 2000, 74). The voice also recalls 'La petite voix implorante' in *Mercier et Camier* 'qui nous parle parfois de vies antérieures' (Beckett 1995, 94) ['the faint imploring voice [...] that drivels to us on and off of former lives' (*M&C* 47)], and the verb used to describe the way the voice 'rustles' in Molloy's head ('bruisser') is the same as the one employed to describe the way Dante's words 'Lo bello stilo che m'ha fatto onore' (*Inferno*, Canto 1, l. 87; ['the fair style that has done me honour']) are said to rustle in Mercier's head: 'Ce sont des mots qui me bruissent dans la tête' (Beckett 1995, 100; untranslated in the English version). Molloy says he fears the far whisper, specifying in the manuscript: **'à l'égal des abscès [sic] et des anglo-saxons'** (FN2, 25r). By omitting this fear of abscesses and Anglo-Saxons, Beckett

---

69   'Exogenetic designates any writing process devoted to research, selection and
      incorporation, focused on information stemming from a source exterior to the
      writing. Handwritten or not, any documentary notes or copies, any quoted or
      intertextual matter, any results or inquiries or observations, any evidence of
      iconographic matter (that gives rise to a written transposition), and generally
      any written or text-image documentation, belongs by nature to the exogenetic
      category' (de Biasi 1996, 43-4). See also the *Lexicon of Scholarly Editing*
      (http://uahost.uantwerpen.be/lse/).

again removes autobiographical elements related to his physical discomforts and his unpleasant stay in London (Knowlson 1997, 186), focusing on the autography of the text instead.

The manuscript is more explicit about Molloy's writing: whereas in the published versions Molloy claims that nothing compels him 'to speak of it' (1955, 54; *Mo* 39; **'à en parler'**, 1951, 60) when it does not suit him, the manuscript mentions **'dans mes écrits'** (FN2, 26r).

When Molloy tries to finish his story about the moon, he starts talking about Diana, **'chasseresse chaste et belle'** (FN2, 26r). But this reference to Diana as a chaste and beautiful huntress was omitted in the published version. He realizes that the moon was new when he decided to go and see his mother, which makes him wonder if it is possible that fourteen days have elapsed since then (1955, 55; *Mo* 40). When his realization leads him to confess that he sometimes forgets who he is, he notes that it is at those moments that he sees the sky different from what it is – 'C'est à ces moments-là que je ~~sais~~ vois le ciel ~~autre que~~ ^{différent de} ce qu'il est' (FN2, 29r) – prefiguring the memorable moment of the mother rebuffing her son's suggestion that the sky is 'further away than you think' in *Malone Dies* (*MD* 98), or 'more distant than it appears' in *Company* (*CIWS* 5) – the moment to which the mother figure in 'The End' reacts with a violent 'Fuck off' (*ECEF* 39).

Paragraph 21 (FN2 29r-125r)

After two dozen pages, Beckett starts another, unusually long paragraph (which will turn out to be the last paragraph of Part I) by means of a rare moment of decisiveness on Molloy's part, when he demands his clothes the next day: 'Le lendemain j'exigeai mes vêtements' (FN2, 29r). While describing the valet's outfit, Molloy almost forgets to mention the valet's sandals and makes this act of almost forgetting explicit: **'Ah et puis des sandales, j'allais oubliais** [sic]' (FN2, 31r). This fine example of 'écriture à processus' is omitted in the published version (1951, 64). What is not omitted, however, is Molloy's way of addressing an audience, when he notes that it does not happen very often that he takes cognizance – 'avec une telle netteté' ['so clearly' (1955, 58; *Mo* 42)] – of the clothes that people wear and that he is happy to give 'you' the benefit of it: 'et je m'empresse de vous en faire profiter, avant d'oublier' (FN2, 32r).

When the valet brings Molloy's clothes, his hat is missing. In the manuscript, Molloy therefore asks: '**Et mon chapeau?**' (FN2, 33r) If this is barely a question, it is even less so in the published version, where he simply utters two words, '**Mon chapeau**', without the question mark (1951, 66). Nonetheless, the valet understands and brings him his hat. Molloy does not make a fuss about the sucking stone that is missing, but he does declare loudly that a knife is missing, to such effect that he receives a vegetable knife with a 'handle of so-called genuine Irish horn' (1955, 60; *Mo* 44). This (so-called) Irish element is already present in the first manuscript version: 'le manche en vraie corne d'Irlande (soi-disant)' (FN2, 35r). Molloy suggests that the moment will come when he has to draw up the list of his possessions – 'le moment viendra, s'il vient jamais, de faire l'inventaire de mes possessions' (FN2, 35r) – prefiguring the narrative situation of the next novel, *Malone meurt*.

Molloy claims it is natural that he should dilate at lesser length on what he lost than on what he could not lose, and if he does not always appear to observe this principle 'it is because it escapes me, from time to time, and vanishes, as utterly as if I had never educed it' (1955, 60; *Mo* 44). This sentence was already part of the manuscript, but not the subsequent meta-fictional comment: '**Phrase démente, peu importe.**' (1951, 68) ['Mad words, no matter.' (1955, 60; *Mo* 44)] – which is added at a later stage and therefore reads like an autographic comment, indicating a moment when the border between the narrator and the writer becomes permeable.

The linguistic scepticism is not only added, though; to some extent it is already present in the manuscript, for instance when Molloy says that 'doing' fills him with 'such a, I don't know, impossible to express' (1955 61; *Mo* 44): 'Et puis faire me remplit d'un tel, je ne sais pas, impossible à exprimer, pour moi, en ce moment, après un si long temps' (FN2, 36r). The phrase 'après un si long temps' is again reminiscent of Virgil's condition 'per lungo silenzio' in Dante's *Inferno* (see chapter 2.1, paragraph 20).

The business with the clothes had taken an entire day, until dusk, without Lousse's intervention. After this temporary absence, the next writing session opens with Lousse, sowing grass on her dog's grave. When Molloy finds his bicycle and discovers that its wheels do not turn any longer, he lies down on the grass and listens to Lousse's 'propositions' (1955, 62; *Mo* 46), convinced that she has poisoned his beer with something intended to 'mollify' him (1955, 62; *Mo* 46) – 'destiné à m'amollir' (FN2, 38r). In both the French and the English versions, the reference to Odysseus and Circe's 'moly' is incorporated in the verb.[70] In the published version, however, the phonetic correspondence with Molloy's name gets extra emphasis: 'destiné à m'amollir, **à amollir Molloy**' (1951, 70). The extra reference to Odysseus ('I was nothing more than a lump of melting wax, so to speak', 1955 62; *Mo* 46) was already part of the manuscript: 'je n'étais pour ainsi dire plus **qu'un morceau de cire, en état de fusion**' (FN2, 38r). Molloy interprets Lousse's propositions in the sense that he would, as it were, take the place of the dog he had killed. During Lousse's soliloquy, Molloy interrupts her now and then to ask what town he was in, but he does not receive any answer.

'16.8[.47]'
(FN2, 39v)

Without any obvious interruption, the writing continues on 16 August 1947. The only suggestion of a break (and of an autographic connection between the real and the fictional world) is the consciousness of time: on the verso side, Beckett writes the date of the new writing session; on the recto, Molloy mentions the chiming of the clock and starts talking about the amount of time Lousse took to cozen him: 'De temps en temps j'entendais sonner l'heure [...] c'est vous dire le temps qu'elle mit à m'avoir' (FN2, 40r). When Lousse finally gets up and walks away, Molloy stays where he is, lying on the ground, 'with regret, mild regret' (1955, 64; *Mo* 47), alluding to Goethe's

70 See Beckett's notes on Victor Bérard's French translation of the *Odyssey* in his 'Dream' Notebook, especially the entry 'molu – antidote to Circe (moly)' (*DN* 102 [entry number 712]), and the *BDL*, http://www.beckett archive.org/library/HOM-ODY.html.

Faust ('Zwei Seelen wohnen, ach! in meiner Brust', I.1112)[71]: 'Car **en moi il y a toujours eu 2 hommes**, entre autres, celui qui ne demande qu'à rester là où il se trouve, et celui qui ˢⁱᵐᵃᵍⁱⁿᵉ qu'il serait moins mal plus loin' (FN2, 41r) ['For in me there have always been two fools, among others, one asking nothing better than to stay where he is and the other imagining that life might be slightly less horrible a little further on' (1955, 64; *Mo* 47)].

On page 43r, the manuscript contains a rather long passage that is omitted in the published version and that deals with the ineluctable modality of the audible, notably the difference between listening and hearing/understanding, the latter diminishing as the former endures: '**c'est lorsqu'on a la faiblesse de ne plus écouter,** ᵖᵉᵘᵗ⁻ᵉ̂ᵗʳᵉ **parce qu'on a trop écouté (comme moi j'avais trop écouté Lousse) qu'on risque d'entendre, et alors ça devient grave**' (FN2, 43r). The words he himself utters sound to him like 'the buzzing of an insect' (1955, 66; *Mo* 49). Whereas this 'bourdonnement d'insecte' (1951, 75) in the published version announces 'the buzzing' in *Not I* / *Pas moi* (*KLT* 86-93), the manuscript compares the sound of his words with 'le pépiement d'un oiseau' ['chirping of birds'], which hits his tympanum – 'ils viennent frapper à mon tympan' (FN2, 45r), prefiguring the Unnamable's hypothesis that he is the tympanum, neither inside nor outside but between (*Un* 100).

'**16.8.47**'
(FN2, 44v)

As for his eyesight, having only one eye that functions more or less satisfactorily, Molloy can barely assess the distance separating him from 'the other world' (1955, 67; *Mo* 49). In the manuscript this other world was called the 'outside': '**monde extérieur**' (FN2, 46r). His taste and smell are equally poor – or in the slightly more elevated style of the manuscript: 'mes expériences

---

71 Beckett made copious excerpts from Goethe's *Faust*, shortly before his trip to Germany. Many of these excerpts were never used in his works, which makes it all the more striking that Beckett did *not* excerpt the passage on the 'Zwei Seelen' (Van Hulle 2006, 289). As in the case of 'non-marginalia' (Gellhaus 2004, 218-9), some of Beckett's readings seem to have made such an impact on him that he did not need to note them down and still employed them in his own works.

~~olfactives~~ olfacto-gustatives ~~avaient~~ accusaient la même pauvreté' (FN2, 46r).

Molloy claims he cannot explain why he stayed 'a good while' with Lousse (1955, 67; *Mo* 49), unless he took the trouble. In terms of ratiocination, there is an interesting sentence in the manuscript that was omitted in subsequent versions, when Molloy explains that his reasoning would often be pushed to form causes: '**il en va toujours ainsi de mes raisons, on les pousse, les pousse, jusqu'à en faire des causes**' (FN2, 46r). This is immediately followed by the reference to Arnold Geulincx, who was not named explicitly in the manuscript, where he is simply called 'the occasionalist': '**l'occasionaliste**' (FN2, 46r). According to occasionalism, matter and mind do not act on each other directly; instead it is God who intervenes on occasion of a change in one of them to bring about a corresponding change in the other. Consequently, free will is an ironic concept in Geulincx' theory: 'Just as a ship carrying a passenger with all speed towards the west in no way prevents the passenger from walking towards the east, so the will of God, carrying all things [...], in no way prevents us from resisting His will [...] with complete freedom.'[72] In Molloy's narrative, the ship becomes the black boat of Ulysses, and the allusion – not only to Homer[73] and Dante,[74] but also to Joyce – is reinforced in the English translation, which speaks of 'a sadly re*joic*ing slave' following with his eyes 'the proud and futile *wake*' (1955, 68; *Mo* 50; emphasis added). Thus, apart from the philosophical, occasionalist dimension, the futility of this minimalist sense (or illusion) of freedom also has a literary-historical dimension, possibly suggesting an indebtedness to a literary tradition that is greater than any individual writer may wish to acknowledge: if the literary tradition irresistibly moves westward, an

72   Arnold Geulincx, *Ethica* (Treatise I, Chapter 1, §2. Reason, n° 9; p. 182; see Beckett's notes in Geulincx 2006 (317). For a discussion of Beckett and Geulincx, see Tucker 2012.

73   See Beckett's notes on Victor Bérard's translation of the *Odyssey*, 'black cruiser of Ulysses' (*DN* 103 [entry number 714]), and *BDL*, http://www.beckettarchive.org/library/HOM-ODY.html.

74   On 17 February 1954, Beckett explained to the German translator Erich Franzen: 'This passage is suggested (a) by a passage in the Ethics of Geulincx where he compares human freedom to that of a man, on board a boat carrying him irresistibly westward, free to move eastward within the limits of the boat itself, as far as the stern; and (b) by Ulysses' relation in Dante (Inf. 26) of his second voyage (a mediaeval tradition) to and beyond the Pillars of Hercules, his shipwreck and death.' (*LSB II* 458)

individual writer's freedom may be limited to moving eastward only 'within the limits of the boat itself', to use Beckett's words (*LSB II* 458). Against this background, it is interesting that Beckett chose not to refer to Joyce when he explained the allusion to the German translator Erich Franzen. The *Ulysses* passage in *Molloy* can be read as a philosophical comment, but also as a tribute to Joyce, by means of which Beckett acknowledged that his hard-fought freedom from Joyce was only relative, comparable to the passenger walking towards the east on board the ship sailing westward.

In Molloy's part of the world ('dans ma région', FN2, 47r), the weather seems to be warm or cold or merely mild at any moment of the year ('chaud, ou froid, ou simplement doux, à n'importe quel moment de l'année') – to which Beckett added at a later stage: 'Ça a peut-être changé depuis.' (1951, 76) ['Perhaps things have changed since.' (1955, 68; *Mo* 50)][75] Molloy has the impression that Lousse spies on him, possibly through the hole in the lock or a little aperture among the leaves, for to get a good view you need something that 'prevents you from being seen and from seeing more than a little at a time' (1955, 71; *Mo* 52). In the manuscript, this sentence is followed by the comment that Descartes never said otherwise, 'Descartes n'a jamais dit autre chose' (FN2, 51r), which is possibly a reference to his theory of vision as developed, for example, in *La Dioptrique*.[76]

After having dwelt quite a while on this period of his life, Molloy decides that it is useless. What is not in the manuscript yet is his comment that if he goes on calling this his life he'll end up believing it (1955, 71; *Mo* 52), which is the principle of advertising: '**A force d'appeler ça ma vie je vais finir par y croire. C'est le principe de la publicité**' (1951, 80). Even though Molloy decides that it is useless, he keeps dwelling on this period. On the verso,

---

75   This added comment in the published text may have been prompted by Beckett's trip to Ireland (his 'part of the world') in June 1950 to visit his ailing mother. While the French *Molloy* had not yet been published at this time, he was already translating a passage into English for Georges Duthuit and *Transition* (see chapter 3.1).

76   In addition to Decartes, Beckett may also be alluding to Sartre's *L'Être et le néant*, which uses the keyhole or 'trou de serrure' to explain the principle of voyeurism in the chapter on 'Le regard'. Beckett also uses the concepts 'être' and 'néant' later in the manuscript of *Molloy* (FN2, 103r; see the writing session dated '30.8[.47]'). With thanks to our colleague Olga Beloborodova for drawing our attention to this source.

Beckett even makes a list of the things Molloy still needs to tell, starting with two more things about Lousse (see Fig. 14):

Encore 2 choses sur Lousse [2 more things about Lousse]
1) ~~Empoisonnement~~ [Poisoning]
2) Homme [Man]
~~Mais nourriture~~
Toujours attirance pr. les vieilles femmes. [Always attraction to old women]
Histoire d'amour [Story of love]
~~pendaison~~ [hanging]
~~Pierres à sucer~~ [Sucking stones] (FN2, 50v)

Molloy is still convinced that Lousse is poisoning him, but he does not mind. Again the system of poisoning is described according to the Wattian principle of exhausting possibilities: by slipping poison into the drink she gave him, or into the food, or both, or one day one, the next the other; in the manuscript the latter possibility was originally: '**ou un jour l'autre et l'autre l'autre**' (FN2, 52r). In spite of the list on page 50v, Molloy then starts digressing about his appetite – 'Parlons-en un peu' (FN2, 52r) ['What a subject. For conversation' (1955, 72; *Mo* 53)]. The effect of Lousse's 'miserable molys' ('les misérables molys de la Lousse', FN2, 53r) seems to be minimal, for 'coenaesthetically speaking'[77] (1955, 72; *Mo* 53) he feels more or less the same. Molloy is not sure whether these 'molys' are stimulants or depressants, for sometimes he makes a little leap in the air, and sometimes he suddenly collapses, 'à la manière d'un **mannequin** dont on lâche les ficelles' (FN2, 53r), later changed to '**pantin**' (1951, 81) ['like a puppet when its strings are dropped' (1955, 72; *Mo* 53)].

---

77 Beckett noted down the word 'coenaesthesis' (denoting the general experience arising from the sum of bodily feelings rather than the particular sensations of specific senses) from Max Nordau's *Degeneration* in his 'Dream' Notebook (*DN* 96). In the surviving drafts of the English translation the term was originally spelled '**kinaesthetically**' (ET1, 63r) before it was changed to '**coenaesthetically**' (ET2, 63r).

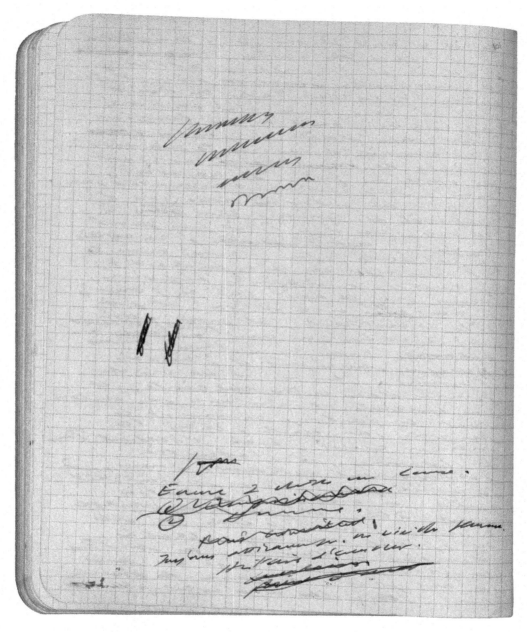

Fig. 14: A crossed-out list of the things that Molloy still needs to tell (FN2, 50v).

Nor does he know when the seeds of his future disorders were sown, such as
the loss of his toes on one of his feet. The uncertainty about which of his two
feet is expressed, again, by means of an epanorthosis: 'la chute des orteils
du pied gauche, **non, je me trompe**, du pied droit' (FN2, 55r). When Molloy,
again, concludes that it is useless 'to drag out this chapter of my... existence'
(ET1, 65r; 'my, **how shall I say**, my existence', 1955, 75; *Mo* 54), the ellipsis
suggests a moment of hesitation, corresponding with a moment of hesitation
between the gender of the possessive pronoun in the French manuscript:
'cette tranche de **ma, mon**, de mon existence' (FN2, 56r). This hesitation is
not the result of a mistake in the first version; it was deliberately written into
the body of the text from the beginning.

   After the digression on the poisoning, the text continues with the
second item in the list: '2) Homme' (FN2, 50v). Lousse is said to be 'une
femme extraordinairement plate' (FN2, 56r) ['a woman of extraordinary
flatness' (1955, 75; *Mo* 55)] to the extent that Molloy wonders whether
she is not actually a man or at least androgynous. He also claims she had a
somewhat hairy face ('légèrement poilu', FN2, 56r), but he is unsure if he is
imagining this in the interests of the narrative, thus drawing attention again
to the metafictional and the autographic dimension of the writing (in the
manuscript this passage on his imagination is written so swiftly that Beckett
forgot the personal pronoun: '**ou ne fais[-je] que l'imaginer**', FN2, 57r).
Lousse's sex does not matter much to Molloy, though. But he admits that the
person who acquainted him with love was a woman called Ruth or Edith
who was twice his age and so could have been his grandmother ('Car dans
la différence entre nos deux âges, le sien et ^{le} mien, j'aurais eu juste le temps
d'atteindre par deux fois ma majorité', FN2, 57r). The manuscript is just as
explicit about genitals, both his and hers, as the published version, but the
vocabulary took some revision: what she has between her legs turns out not
to be '**le trou** ~~béant~~ ^{rond} que je m'étais toujours imaginé' (FN2, 57r) – later '**la
bonde**' (1951, 85) ['the bunghole I had always imagined' (1955, 76; *Mo* 56)] –
and what he calls his '**verge vierge**' (FN2, 57r) became his '**membre
soi-disant viril**' (1951, 85) ['my so-called virile member' (1955, 76; *Mo* 56)].

The description of Ruth/Edith's 'dainty flat' (1955, 77; *Mo* 57) is marked by yet another epanorthosis: 'Elle avait un appartement coquet, **non, pas coquet**' (FN2, 59r).

'20.8[.47]'
(FN2, 59v)

Before she receives him, she takes a bath. The manuscript does not mention that it 'limbered her up' (1955, 78; *Mo* 57), which was added later, possibly to make another reference to the 'molys' of Lousse – '**Cela la ramollissait**' (1951, 88). In one single sentence, without hesitation, Molloy relates the story of Ruth/Edith's death when the tub overturned, the water spilt[78] all over the floor, down to the lodger below, who gave the alarm. The fluency is so remarkable that Molloy is surprised to know the story so well: 'Tiens, je ne croyais pas si bien connaître **cette histoire!**' (FN2, 60r) – thus making another autographic connection between the narrator and the writer. Molloy notes that people in his part of the world ('dans ma région', FN2, 60r) were very reserved about matters relating to sexuality ('pour tout ce qui touche aux questions de sexe', FN2, 60r). Again, it is only in later versions that this reference to Molloy's region is followed by a note to the effect that he does not know whether things have changed in the meantime, suggesting that he does not live there any longer: 'Je ne sais pas comment ça se passe aujourd'hui' (1951, 88). The fact that he never sought to repeat the experience with Ruth/Edith reassures him in the manuscript ('**me rassure**', FN2, 61r), whereas it keeps tormenting him ('**me tracasse**', 1951, 88) in the published version, because it does not solve the question whether he really experienced love or whether all his life has been devoid of it. The manuscript does not mention the chambermaid, who was added later: 'Ne me parlez pas de **la boniche**, j'ai eu tort d'en parler, c'était bien avant, j'étais malade, peut-être qu'il n'y eut jamais de boniche, dans ma vie. Molloy, ou la vie sans boniche.' (1951, 89) ['Don't talk to me about the chambermaid, I should never have mentioned her, she was long before, I was sick, perhaps there was no chambermaid, ever, in my life. Molloy, or life without a chambermaid.' (1955, 79; *Mo* 58)] After which, Molloy again makes a metafictional comment to indicate that the entire digression about Ruth/Edith only goes

---

78   The 2009 Faber edition mistakenly reads 'split all over the floor' (*Mo* 58).

to demonstrate that having 'frequented' Lousse does not prove anything as to her sex (1955, 79; *Mo* 58).

When Molloy starts talking about how he sometimes confuses Lousse and Ruth, and even his mother, thinking of them as one and the same 'vioque, aplatie et enragée par la vie' (FN2, 62r) ['old hag, flattened and crazed by life' (1955, 79; *Mo* 58)], he decides to finish his story about his stay at Lousse's house, describing how he left her on his crutches (1955, 79; *Mo* 59). In the manuscript, Beckett originally wanted to be more precise, but did not find the word, leaving open a blank space with a question mark: 'me ~~xxx~~ lançant à travers les airs, sur **le   ?   de mes béquilles**' (FN2, 62r). He did not really find 'le mot juste' in subsequent versions, circumscribing it as follows in the published version: 'me lançant à travers les airs, sur **leur point d'appui**' (1951, 89) ['springing on them through the air' (1955, 79; *Mo* 59)]. It is the small voice ('la petite voix', FN2, 63r) that tells him to go: 'Pars, Molloy, prends tes béquilles et pars' (FN2, 63r) ['Get out of here, Molloy, take your crutches and get out of here' (1955, 80; *Mo* 59)].

Without any paragraph break, the story moves from Molloy's stay at Lousse's place to the continuation of his journeys. He finds shelter, is immediately chased away by '~~un~~ une sorte de gardien de nuit' (FN2, 64r) ['a kind of nightwatchman' (1955, 80; *Mo* 60)] and wanders about the town in search of a familiar monument that would confirm that it is *his* town.

'21.8[.47]'
(FN2, 63v)

The next writing session starts with a morning scene of the town waking up: 'La ville se réveillait' (FN2, 64r). Instead of finding a familiar monument, Molloy soon slips into a narrow alley, with only a little window overlooking it on either side, face to face. Molloy not only *supposes* they are lavatory windows; for once he is *certain* about it: '**sans aucun doute**' (FN2, 64r). The exceptionality of this moment without doubt is marked by means of an extra sentence: 'Il y a quand même de temps en temps ~~une~~ des choses qui s'imposent à l'esprit, avec la force d'un axiome, sans qu'on sache pourquoi.' (FN2, 65r) ['There are things from time to time, in spite of everything, that impose themselves on the understanding with the force of axioms, for unknown reasons.' (1955, 81; *Mo* 60)] The alley turns out to be blind, '**une impasse**' (FN2, 65r). Molloy anticipates *L'Innommable*, whose narrator wonders how to proceed – 'By aporia pure and simple? Or by affirmations and negations invalidated as uttered, or sooner or later?': 'I seem to speak, it is not I, about me, it is not about me' (*Un* 1). As David Lodge notes in a chapter on 'Aporia', this sentence

> attacks the foundations of the long humanist tradition of auto-biographical fiction and fictional autobiography, from *Robinson Crusoe* through *Great Expectations* to *À la Recherche du temps perdu*, with its consoling promise of achieving self-knowledge. Beckett anticipated Derrida's notion of the inevitable 'différance' [sic] of verbal discourse: the 'I' that speaks always being different from the 'I' that is spoken of, the precise fitting of language to reality always being deferred. (Lodge 1992, 221-2).

In classical rhetoric, this 'a-poros' or 'pathless path' as David Lodge translates it, denotes doubt as to how to proceed in a discourse. In *Molloy*, Beckett puts his protagonist literally in an alley that turns out not to be an alley but a cul-de-sac. At the end there are two hidden recesses, 'deux renfonce-ments, **en replis**' (FN2, 65r). In the published version, this becomes an epanorthosis: 'deux renfoncements, **non, ce n'est pas le mot**' (1951, 92). The recesses are littered with rubbish and excrements of dogs and humans, later changed to 'masters' (1955, 81; *Mo* 60): 'de chien et **d'être humain**' (FN2, 65r; 'de chien et **de maître**', 1951, 92). As if this was not revolting enough, Beckett specifies on the verso that the ones were dry and odourless, the others still moist: '**les uns secs et sans odeur, les autres encore humides**' (FN2, 64v). After a brief exploration of the first recess he moves to the other, calling it a 'chapelle' in the published version, and adding 'voilà' (1951, 92) ['chapel, that's the word' (1955, 82; *Mo* 60)]. When it starts raining and Molloy takes off his hat to give his skull the benefit of the raindrops, he says his skull is all cracked and furrowed, to which Beckett later added '**et brûlant, brûlant**' (1951, 92) ['**and burning, burning**' (ET1, 71r)]. The English version eventually became '**on fire, on fire**' (1955, 82; *Mo* 61), possibly an intertextual reference to Petrarch's line 'chi può dir com'egli arde, è 'n picciol foco' (Petrarca 1824, 221; literally: 'who can say how he burns is in little fire'). According to Anne Atik, Beckett translated this line as 'He who knows he is burning is burning in a small fire' (Atik 2001, 80). Although Beckett had read *Le Rime di Messer Francesco Petrarca* (1824) in the original, he probably knew this line through his reading of Montaigne's essay 'De la tristesse', in which it is quoted in the context of ardent lovers' unbearable passion (Montaigne 1965, 60). He also excerpted the line in his 'Sam Francis' notebook (UoR MS 2926, 19v), and – in a similar way as the addition 'brûlant, brûlant' or 'burning, burning' in the first English typescript of *Molloy* – Beckett added the word 'burning' to the fourth typescript of *Krapp's Last Tape*, in order to emphasize the ambiguity of the 'fire' at the end of the play (*BDMP3*, ET4, 6r).[79] In a letter to Con Leventhal, Beckett explained that he interpreted 'arde' in a general sense, related to the linguistic scepticism of Gorgias: '1 Nothing is / 2 If anything is, it cannot be known. / 3 If anything is, and can be known, it cannot be expressed in speech.' (*LSB III* 136)

The suggestion, then, is that Molloy, who can still say that his skull is burning, is burning in a small fire. Nonetheless, Molloy does consider suicide. The list of things to tell on page 50v of the manuscript mentioned hanging ('~~pendaison~~'); eventually, Molloy chooses another method: 'Je pris dans ma poche le couteau à légumes, l'ouvrit et m'appliquai à m'en ouvrir le poignet' ['I took the vegetable knife from my pocket and set about opening my wrist' (1955, 82; *Mo* 61)], but in the same sentence he already mentions that pain soon got the better of him (FN2, 66r). So much for his suicide attempt – 'Voilà' (FN2, 66r) ['So much for that' (1955, 82; *Mo* 61)]. But even that does not constitute enough of an ending to justify a paragraph break. The text simply goes on. Molloy notes that 'récidiver' ['backsliding'] depresses him, although life seems made up of backsliding and death must be a sort of backsliding as well. In the French manuscript, this notion of 'récidiver' is further developed. Not even love is exempt from it, as Molloy keeps thinking about Ruth when he masturbates, which leads him to wonder if he has been cornered in that area as well: '**Récidiver récidiver. ~~Non seulement~~ J'excepte** l'amour, **mais ai-je le droit de l'excepter? Car en me masturbant je pensais à Ruth, forcément, n'ayant pas d'autre point d'appui. Alors là aussi je me serais laissé** coincer?' (FN2, 67r). Also in terms of the narrative Molloy has let himself be cornered. Stuck in this narrative cul-de-sac, he quickly changes the subject: 'Ai-je dit que le vent était tombé? Une pluie fine qui tombe, cela écarte en quelque sorte toute idée

---

79 For a more detailed discussion of Beckett's reading of Petrarch and Montaigne, especially with relation to the drafts of *Krapp's Last Tape*, see Van Hulle 2015 (176-80).

de vent, ~~n'est-ce pas?~~' J'ai des genoux énormes.' (FN2, 67r) ['Did I say the wind had fallen? A fine rain falling, somehow that seems to exclude all idea of wind. My knees are enormous.' (1955, 82; *Mo* 61)]

'**22.8.47**'
(FN2, 66v)

The next day, Beckett changes from black to blue ink and the first thing he does is cross out the '**n'est-ce pas?**' in the penultimate sentence of the previous writing session. Molloy now has two stiff legs. Before he mentions that he left the impasse, he imagines his readers saying 'Se peut-il vraiment que ça vive encore?' (FN2, 67r) ['Is it possible that thing is still alive' (1955, 83; *Mo* 61)], or: 'c'est un journal intime, ça va bientôt **s'interrompre**' (FN2, 67r), later revised as '**s'arrêter**' (1951, 93) ['Oh it's only a diary, it'll soon be over' (1955, 83; *Mo* 61)]. Thus, Molloy makes his imaginary audience determine to which genre his writing belongs.

He leaves his impasse and walks – in the rain – in the direction of the sun, out into the Leibnizian 'pre-established harmony' (1955, 83; *Mo* 62).[80] If Molloy's 'journal intime' is to be regarded as a diary, it is remarkable how often he addresses an audience. For instance, he apologizes for dwelling upon so many details, promising he will soon speed things up: 'Je m'excuse de ces détails, mais tout à l'heure nous irons plus vite, beaucoup plus vite' (FN2, 69r), without excluding the possibility of a relapse into 'a wealth of filthy circumstance' (1955, 84; *Mo* 62-3). For 'staffage' is necessary (1955, 84; *Mo* 63), 'il faut du staffage, à l'homo mensura' (FN2, 69r). In his philosophy notes, this reference to Protagoras of Abdera (480-410) is added in the margin: 'HOMO MENSURA', next to Protagoras's (underlined) dictum '<u>Man is the measure of all things, of things that are that they are, & of things that are not that they are not.</u>' (TCD MS 10967, 45r), excerpted in black ink from Wilhelm Windelband's *A History of Philosophy*. In Beckett's slightly earlier, typed notes, based on Archibald Alexander's *A Short History of Philosophy*, Protagoras is called 'The first great individualist, relativist & agnostic' (TCD MS 10967, 44r). As David Addyman and Matthew Feldman note, 'staffage

---

80   The negative theodicy is also present in Beckett's other works. For instance, Chris Ackerley calls Beckett's novel *Watt* a 'sustained critique of Leibniz's central philosophical doctrine' (Ackerley 2015, 187).

is used in sixteenth- and seventeenth-century landscape painting to denote the human (and sometimes animal) figures which are depicted in the scene, but which are not the main subject matter of the painting; they are included merely to balance the composition or in the interests of decoration' (Addyman and Feldman 2011, 768). Hence the 'wealth of filthy circumstance', as Molloy calls it.

One of the details he describes circumstantially is the knife-rest he stole from Lousse. The X-shaped legs are drawn several times on page 69v, before the object in its entirety is drawn on page 70v (see Fig. 3 in chapter 1.1.1). The object inspires Molloy with a sort of veneration as he sees it as more than merely 'un objet de vertu' (FN2, 71v),[81] whose function would always stay hidden from him. So he can puzzle over it 'sans ~~risque~~ sans fin, et sans risque' (FN2, 71r) ['endlessly without the least risk' (1955, 86; *Mo* 64)].

'**23.8[.47]**'
(FN2, 70v)

The next writing session immediately opens with a philosophical statement, building on the last sentence of the previous writing session: '**Car ne rien savoir, ~~cela ne suffit pas~~ ce n'est rien, ne rien vouloir savoir ~~non plus xxx~~ xxx non plus, non, mais ne rien pouvoir savoir, savoir ne rien pouvoir savoir, voilà par où ~~entre~~ passe la paix, dans l'âme du chercheur incurieux**' (FN2, 71r) ['For to know nothing is nothing, not to want to know anything likewise, but to be beyond knowing anything, to know you are beyond knowing anything, that is when peace enters in, to the soul of the incurious seeker' (1955, 86; *Mo* 64)]. Molloy claims there is rapture ('quelque chose d'exaltant') in the motion crutches give – or at least there should be ('~~Ou cela devrait avoir quelque chose d'exaltant~~', FN2, 72r): 'On décolle, on atterrit, parmi la foule des ~~promeneurs~~ ingambes, qui **ne ~~soulèvent jamais~~ n'osent soulever** un pied de terre ~~sans s'y être agrippés de l'autre y avoir cloué l'autre~~ avant d'y avoir cloué l'autre' (FN2, 72r) ['You take off, you land, through the thronging sound in wind and limb, who have to fasten one foot to the ground before they dare lift up the other' (1955, 86; *Mo* 64)]. Whereas he describes the

---

81   In the English translation, Beckett considered adopting the French term '**objet de vertu**' (ET1, 74r) before replacing it with '**object of virtu**' (ET2, 74r; 1955, 85; *Mo* 63).

rapture of the aerial hobble, the stylistic finetuning of this passage did take a pedestrian patience, with three cancellations to get it right.[82] Molloy ends this musing with a 'But': '**Mais** ~~c'est~~ ᶜᵉ ˢᵒⁿᵗ ˡᵃ ~~ce c'est~~ des raisonnements, fondés sur l'analyse' (FN2, 72r) ['But these are reasonings, based on analysis' (1955, 86; *Mo* 64)], as if he anticipates a Bergsonian reproach that he should be using his intuition rather than analysing and reasoning.[83]

Molloy's mind is gradually less taken up with his desire to know if he is near his mother. He is even anxious to leave the town, even if it were his mother's. He describes the night falling and the special effects of sunset, suggesting the phenomenon is characteristic of his region. The manuscript shows how Beckett complicated this statement by deleting '~~est caractéristique de ma région,~~' and introducing an element of doubt regarding the reliability of his senses: 'Ce phénomène, **est caractéristique de ma région, si je peux me fier à** ~~mes~~ **mon observation, est caractéristique de ma région.**' (FN2, 74r) Again, it is only in later versions (the pre-book publication in *Transition* and the first French edition) that Beckett adds the comment: '**Cela se passe autrement aujourd'hui peut-être** (1951, 99) ['Things are perhaps different now' (TRA, 104)].[84]

'**24.8.47**'
(FN2, 74v)

The first sentence of the next writing session (bottom of page 75r) required several attempts, with more deleted words than uncancelled ones. On the whole, the writing during this session proceeded slightly less swiftly than usual. Several passages are rewritten, such as the sentence '**~~Je ne regrettais pas du tout ma bicyclette, il me semblait~~**' (FN2, 77r), which was rewritten on the facing verso: 'Je n'avais pas du tout le sentiment de regretter ma

---

82   The expression 'sound in wind and limb' in the translation of 'la foule des ingambes' recurs in the first typescript of *Krapp's Last Tape* (HRC MS SB 4-2-1; *BDMP3*, ET1, 01r).

83   On page 72v, Beckett notes the number of pages he has already written: 'p. 53 / 72' (see chapter 1.1.1).

84   Beckett was in Ireland, during the summer of 1950, when translating the fragment from Molloy for *Transition* (see chapter 3.1). Since Minuit's first edition (March 1951) was not yet published at this time, it is possible that Beckett's stay in Ireland prompted him to change the passage about Molloy's 'région', in English and in French.

bicyclette' (FN2, 76v) ['I didn't feel I missed my bicycle, no, not really' (1955, 89; *Mo* 66)]. Molloy concludes that it is in the morning that one must hide because that is when people wake up, 'frais et dispos, assoiffés d'ordre, et ^de ^beauté et de justice, exigeants exigeant la contre-partie' (FN2, 77r), ['hale and hearty, their tongues hanging out for order, beauty and justice, baying for their due' (1955, 90; *Mo* 67)].

'**25.8[.47]**'
(FN2, 76v)

The next day started with a confirmation of the previous statement: 'Oui, de xxx huit ou neuf jusqu'à midi, c'est le passage **dangereux, car vers midi cela se tasse**' (FN2, 77r) ['Yes, from eight or nine till midday is the dangerous time' (1955, 90; *Mo* 67)]. In general, the manuscript consists of longer sentences than the published version, which often cuts sentences in two. In this case, for instance, the published version shows a full stop after 'dangereux', after which the text goes on with: '**Mais vers midi cela se tasse**' (1951, 101) ['But towards noon things quiet down' (1955, 90; *Mo* 67)].

As to the notion of death, Molloy does not exclude the possibility that it is even worse than life as a condition, 'en tant que condition' (FN2, 79v), which is why he does not rush into it. In the published version, he adds: '**C'est ma seule excuse**' (1951, 103) ['It's my only excuse' (1955, 91; *Mo* 68)]. He has no intention to say what became of him and where he went in the month or perhaps years that followed.

In order to 'blacken a few more pages' (1955, 92; *Mo* 68) ['noircir encore quelques pages' (FN2, 81r)], he does say that he spent some time at the seaside, seizing the opportunity to lay in a store of sucking stones. In the published version Molloy specifies that they are called pebbles ('cailloux') but that he calls them stones ('pierres', 1951, 105). On the verso, Beckett made several calculations and schemes to prepare the famous passage on the distribution of the sucking stones among his four pockets, notably the problem of how to suck sixteen stones one after the other and avoid sucking any stone twice (and without leaving any stone unsucked). Instead of 16 stones Beckett first considered another number, but he deleted this original number so thoroughly that it is illegible (FN2, 82r, bottom of the page). After the calculations on page 81v (see chapter 1.1.1 and cover) and after the meticulous description of the transfers of stones (FN2, 82r-85r), Beckett also jotted down the following programme:

1 Proportionner pierres aux poches. [Proportion out stones to pockets]
2 Lumière: abandonner principe de l'égale distribution. [Dawning: abandon principle of equal distribution]
3 Description de la solution [Description of the solution]
4 Il ne tenait pas tant que ça à les sucer à tour de rôle. [All the same whether the stones are sucked in turn]
5 Il les remet 4 dans chaque poche. [He puts 4 in each pocket] (FN2, 85v)

This programme is for the most part followed in the description on the next few pages (FN2, 85v-93r). The first point is integrated immediately on the facing page 86r. The revelation of a solution (point no. 2) appears on page 87r and the description of that solution (point no. 3) occupies the next several pages. Point number 4 is incorporated on page 93r as the passage on the sucking stones comes to a close. The last point is modified so that ultimately Molloy keeps only one stone. His 'calculs' (FN2, 87r) are changed into 'martingales' (1951, 108) in the first edition ['martingales' (1955, 95; *Mo* 71)]. And the 'principe de la ~~distribution~~ répartition' (FN2, 87r) becomes 'l'arrimage' (1951, 108) ['trim' (1955, 95; *Mo* 71; see chapter 3.2)]. When a solution for the problem presents itself, it sings to Molloy 'comme **un verset de l'Ecriture sainte**' (FN2, 87r). Beckett jotted down the alternative '**Kabbala**' (FN2, 86v) on the facing page, perhaps to give Molloy an esoteric leaning, but he eventually opted for '**un verset d'Esaïe ou de Jérémie**' (1951, 108) in the published text ['a verse of Isaiah, or of Jeremiah' (1955, 96; *Mo* 71)]. Molloy finds the solution inelegant, 'but sound, sound' (1955, 96; *Mo* 72). The repetition of this word was a relatively late stylistic revision. The manuscript simply reads: 'mais **solide**' (FN2, 87r); the first edition: 'mais **solide, solide**' (1951, 109). The same stylistic device is applied a few sentences further, where the manuscript reads: 'Mais j'étais **fatigué**' (FN2, 88r), and the first edition: 'Mais j'étais **fatigué, fatigué**' (1951, 109) ['But I was tired, but I was tired' (1955, 96; *Mo* 72)].[85] When he explains his solution of leaving his left coat pocket empty ('la poche gauche de mon manteau', FN2, 88r), he complicates the calculations by mentioning that 'empty' only means 'empty of stones', for this pocket contains several other objects, such as his vegetable knife and the silver. The rhetorical question 'Car où croyez-vous que je cachais mon ~~canif,~~ ^{couteau à légumes,} ~~mon argenterie~~ **mon argenterie** et le reste, que je n'ai pas encore ~~nom~~ nommé' ['For where do you think I hid my vegetable knife, my silver, my horn and the other things that I have not yet named' (1955, 97; *Mo* 72)] is followed by two vulgar options ('in the arsehole' and 'under the clitoris'), which were subsequently omitted: 'Dans le trou du cul peut-être? ~~Dans le con~~ Sous la [sic] clitoris, si je suis une femme après tout?' (FN2, 87v-88r). Instead, the published version stresses the notion of naming the objects: '... que je n'ai pas encore nommé, **que je ne nommerai peut-être jamais**' (1951, 109) ['... that I have not yet named and, perhaps shall never name' (1955, 97; *Mo* 72)]. This way of sucking the stones one after the other, 'sucer les pierres [...] **l'une après l'autre**' (FN2, 92r), is called 'sucer les pierres [...] **avec méthode**' in the published version (1951, 113) ['with method' (1955, 99; *Mo* 74)], as if it were a Cartesian discourse. Whereas, 'au fond' (FN2, 93r) ['deep down' (1955, 100; *Mo* 74-5)] it is all the same to Molloy in which way he sucks his stones. But it is not all the same to Beckett how Molloy *says* that it is all the same to him, hesitating between two verbs: 'je m'en ~~fout~~ **contre-balançais**' (FN2, 93r) eventually did become 'je m'en **foutais**' (1951, 113) ['I didn't give a fiddler's curse' (1955, 100; *Mo* 75)]. As for the stones, in the end he throws them all away, all but one.

A woman approaches Molloy one day and offers him something to eat – at least, that is what Molloy seems to remember. The uncertainty ('Je crois que ...'; 'il me semble', FN2, 94r ['I think ...'; 'it seems to me', 1955, 100-1; *Mo* 75]) was already in place in the very first version. The uncertainty also applies to his vocabulary. He claims that his stay at the seaside has a positive effect on his eyesight and on his ability to name things ['saddling with a name the rare things I saw', (1955, 101; *Mo* 76)]. But when he says that there are other needs than that of rotting in peace ('pourrir en paix', FN2, 95r),

---

85 On the second typescript of the English translation, Beckett revised the phrase to '**But I was tired, ~~but I was~~ tired**' (ET2, 84r), possibly after having corrected proofs for the *Paris Review* extract ('**But I was tired, tired**', PR, 127), but the change was reverted for the 1955 first edition by Olympia and Grove.

he adds in the published version that that is not the word ('**ce n'est pas le mot**', 1951, 115).

'**29.8[.47]**'
(FN2, 96v)

Besides rotting in peace (the earlier mentioned 'tranquility of decomposition') one of the other needs is the need to go to his mother, which is why Molloy goes back inland. But his legs are worsening, and what is more, one of them is shortening, while the other is not yet shortening, or shortening at a much slower rate so that it seemed as if it was not shortening: 'tandis que l'autre, tout en se raidissant, ne se raccourcissait pas encore, ou ~~se raccourcissait~~ avec un tel retard ^sur l'autre^ **que c'était comme si elle ne se raccourcissait pas du tout**' (FN2, 99r). Whereas this sentence makes perfect sense in the manuscript, it 'decomposes' in the subsequent versions. In the published version, Molloy does not reach the end of the sentence: '... **que c'était tout comme, tout comme, je suis perdu, ça ne fait rien**' (1951, 118) ['I'm lost, no matter' (1955, 104; *Mo* 78).[86] It takes several attempts and cancellations to write the simple question whether or not it makes any difference, as far as the pain is concerned, if he rests his leg or if he works it (FN2, 100r), and the passage caused trouble again when it had to be translated into English (see chapter 3.3).

Molloy compares his progress to a calvary, with no limit to its stations and no hope of crucifixion. But whereas he claims he has to stop more and more frequently, the writing sometimes went so fluently that some words are skipped, for instance: 'mon progrès m'obligeait à m'arrêter **de plus en * souvent**' (FN2, 101r; * indicates the skipped word 'plus'). While the writing goes on at a steady pace, the only way for Molloy to progress, is to stop (1955, 105; *Mo* 79). He wonders whether it would not be better to hang himself from a bough, but the thought of suicide has little hold on him. In the manuscript, this is formulated as a general statement, in the present tense: 'Mais les idées de suicide **ont** peu de prise sur moi' (FN2, 101r), which changes to the past tense in the published version.

---

86 In the first typescript of the English translation and the *Paris Review* extract, Molloy still said 'I'm lost, **who cares**' (ET1, 91r; PR, 133), but Beckett revised it on the second typescript to 'I'm lost, **no matter**' (ET2, 91r).

Molloy claims he could have counted the few times he could not breathe,
but the manuscript adds it is too late now and hardly worth the trouble,
'maintenant ~~il est trop tard~~ ce n'est plus la peine' (FN2, 102r), thus obliquely alluding
to the opening line of Albert Camus' essay *Le mythe de Sisyphe* (1942): 'Il n'y
a qu'un problème philosophique vraiment sérieux: c'est le suicide. Juger que
la vie vaut ou ne vaut pas la peine d'être vécue, c'est répondre à la question
fondamentale de la philosophie' (Camus 1965, 99) – but with an ironic twist.
For while it is not worth the trouble anymore, 'plus la peine', this does *not*
lead Molloy to commit suicide. Meanwhile, not only his legs but his many
other weak points ('points faibles', FN2, 103r) become weaker and weaker,
with unforeseen rapidity. From day to day, certain body parts seem to worsen,
'le trou du cul par example' (FN2, 103r) ['my arse-hole for example' (1955,
107; *Mo* 80)]. He immediately apologizes for bringing up the subject of this
orifice so often, but he blames his 'voices' (plural): 'il revient à chaque instant
dans **mes voix**, je ne peux pas toujours m'y refuser' (FN2, 103r). In the
published version, they are replaced by 'my muse': 'c'est **ma muse** qui le veut'
(1951, 122). He suggests that 'la chose nommée' (his anus) just stands for all
the things he does not name, a copula between him and the other excrement,
which – in the first writing layer – was 'le néant': 'trait d'union entre moi
(pour ne mentionner que moi) et ~~le néant~~ l'autre merde' (FN2, 103r). The
cancelled 'néant' can be read as a reference to Sartre's *L'Être et le néant*, for
the second part of the sentence mentions 'l'être': '~~alors que c'est le vrai portail
de l'être~~' (FN2, 103r) ['is it not rather the true portal of our being' (1955, 107;
Mo 81)].[87] After the change of 'le néant' into 'l'autre merde', the word 'autre'
(in 'entre moi [...] et l'autre merde') implies that Molloy regards himself as
just as much crap as for instance Krapp in the later play *Krapp's Last Tape*.
  When Molloy situates the 'desertion' of his toes (1955, 108; *Mo* 81) in this
period, he addresses the audience directly: 'Mais savez-vous seulement de
quel pied il s'agissait?' (FN2, 105r). He does not know either which foot he
is talking about, and yet he announces that he is going to tell: 'Attendez, je
vais vous le dire' (FN2, 105r), but then he doesn't and starts digressing again,

---

87   Again, the sentence is longer in the manuscript than in the published version,
      which cuts it into two sentences (sentence numbers 1654 an 1655).

in the tradition of Sterne's *Tristram Shandy*. For he does not want to give a wrong impression of his health, which 'was at bottom of an incredible robustness' (1955, 109; *Mo* 81). He must have inherited this 'robustesse inouïe' (FN2, 105r) from his mother's chromosomes, as a paralipomenon on the verso suggests: '~~Regardez ma mère. Elle me les a passés ses   ?   chromosomes.~~' (FN2, 104v). The familiar blank space with a question mark is left open for an adjective that could not immediately be found. Above this jotting, Beckett wrote another attempt, which sounds much more derogatory, referring to Molloy's mother as 'that cow': '~~Elle me les a bien passés, la vache, ses indéfectibles putains de chromosomes~~' (FN2, 104v).

'**31.8[.47]**'
(FN2, 104v)

Eventually, Beckett incorporated the paralipomenon in the text on the recto at the beginning of a new writing session, changing '**ma mère**' into '**maman**' and thus creating greater contrast between affection ('maman') and contempt ('la vache'): '**Regardez maman. De quoi x a-t-elle crevé à la fin, je me le demande. Ça ne m'étonnerait pas qu'on l'ait enterrée vivante. Ah, elle me les a bien passés, la vache, ses indéfectibles saloperies de chromosomes**' (FN2, 105r-106r) ['Look at Mammy. What rid me of her, in the end? I sometimes wonder. Perhaps they buried her alive, it wouldn't surprise me. Ah the old bitch, a nice dose she gave me, she and her lousy unconquerable genes' (1955, 109; *Mo* 82)].[88] Whereas in the case of the feet, Molloy was going to tell which foot had lost its toes, but then didn't after all,

88 The surviving drafts of the English translation show a similar hesitation as to the right tone for the subject of Molloy's mother. '**Take the case of mother**' (EM, 83v) became '**Look at Mama**' (ET1, 95r) and then 'Look at **mammy**' (ET2, 95r). The question 'What **put a stop to her** in the end?' (EM, 83v), was revised to 'What **rid me of her** in the end?' (ET1, 95r). 'I wonder' (EM, 83v), Molloy states in the manuscript fragment, which becomes 'I **sometimes** wonder' (ET1, 95r) in the first typescript. But the passage about her chromosomes proved most difficult to translate and most prone to variation. '~~Curse the old bitch and her dose of indelible chromosomes~~' was crossed out and replaced with '**Pox on the old hag and her indefectible genes**' in the manuscript fragment (EM, 83v), but further revisions were made on the second typescript: '**Ah the old bitch, a nice dose she gave me, she and her lousy unconquerable genes**' (ET2, 95r; see also chapter 3.1).

he now says he is not going to talk about his deteriorating 'weak points', but
then he does anyway: 'Que j'aie les uretères – non, je ne le dirai pas' (FN2,
106r) ['That my ureters – no, not a word on that subject' (1955, 109; *Mo* 82)].
The manuscript enumerates even more medical conditions such as muscle
spasms ('**Et la péristale**', FN2, 106r), almost as many as Beckett's list of
Samuel Johnson's symptoms in his second 'Human Wishes' Notebook, such
as 'oedema'; 'ascites'; 'hydrothorax'; 'hydorcephalus'; 'tuberculous dermatitis'
or 'scrofula'; 'sight of left eye entirely lost'; 'depression'; 'Endocrine disorder';
'asthma'; 'bad melancholy'; 'Attack of aphasia'; 'sarcocele' (tumour of the
testis) and 'urinary crisis' (UoR MS 3461/2; see Maude 2015, 181). But
Molloy is convinced that he will not die of his ailments and that, like his
mother, he will be buried alive. This is the sentence from which the original
title for the novel may derive, suggesting that 'en désespoir de cause' ['in
desperation; for want of anything better to do'] should be read in the context
of the world not knowing what to do with Molloy, rather than Molloy being
in despair about his situation: 'Moi aussi on m'~~inhumera~~ ^inhumerait^ vivant, **en
désespoir de cause**, s'il y avait une justice' (FN2, 106r). Even though he
prefers not to draw up a list of his weak points, he does consider doing it
some day, when he will take stock of his possessions: 'je la ferai peut-être un
jour, [...] quand il s'agira ~~d'établir le bilan de~~ ^Fin d'inventorier^ **mes possessions**'
(FN2, 106r). The manuscript of *Molloy* thus again anticipates the inventory
that will be the main subject of Beckett's next novel, *Malone meurt*. For
Molloy does not believe he is near the end, and he keeps the making of his
inventory for the last sprint, when he is certain that there is nothing more he
can acquire, lose, throw away or give away (1955, 110; *Mo* 83).

The published version sometimes shows (usually very short) extra
sentences such as '**Mais je peux me tromper**' (1951, 125) ['But I may be
wrong' (1955, 110; *Mo* 83)]. Frequently, however, it also cuts loquacious bits
in Molloy's narrative. Thus, for instance, the long run-up to the sentence
'**Enfin, qui trop étreint peu embrasse, c'est bien ça je crois, et je veux
simplement faire remarquer ceci,** que si [...]' (FN2, 108r) simply becomes:
'**Mais je disais** que si [...]' (1951, 126) ['But I was saying that' (1955, 111;
Mo 83)]. Apart from these stylistic revisions, most of the changes relate to
vocabulary, tenses and number. For instance, when Molloy regrets having
laid too much stress on his legs in his narrative, '**ce récit**' (FN2, 108r)
becomes '**cette promenade**' (1951, 126) ['these wanderings' (1955, 111;
Mo 83)]. As to tenses, the manuscript employs the present tense more

frequently than the published version, for instance: 'il y **a** des jours où les jambes **sont** ce que j'**ai** de mieux, abstraction faite toujours du cerveau, capable d'arriver à une telle conclusion' (FN2, 109r), which becomes: 'il y **avait** des jours où mes jambes étaient ce que j'**avais** de mieux, abstraction faite du cerveau capable de former un tel jugement' (1951, 126) ['there were days when my legs were the best part of me, with the exception of the brain capable of forming such a judgement' (1955, 111; *Mo* 83)]. And whereas the audience that Molloy reassures in the manuscript consists of multiple persons ('soyez **tranquilles**', FN2, 109r), he seems to have only one reader in mind in the published version ('soyez **tranquille**', 1951, 127).

Molloy often employs a variant of epanorthosis, suggesting it would be too much to say X, saying it all the same, and then denying it, as in the description of the forest: 'Dire que je trébuchais parmi d'impénétrables ténèbres, non, je ne dirais pas' (FN2, 109r) ['To say I stumbled in impenetrable darkness, no, I cannot' (1955, 112; *Mo* 84)]. The reason for bringing it up anyway seems to be inspired by literary tradition, notably by Dante's 'selva oscura', at the beginning of the *Divina Commedia* (*Inferno*, Canto I, l. 2); by the 'Darkness impenetrable' from Jane Austen's *Northanger Abbey* ('Darkness imprenetrable and immovable filled the room', Austen 2014, 247); by Marlow's description of Kurtz in Conrad's *Heart of Darkness* (after Kurtz's aposiopesis 'Live rightly, die, die [...]'): 'His was an impenetrable darkness' (Conrad 1990, 114); or by Proust's description of what music means to Swann in *À la recherche du temps perdu*: 'Swann tenait les motifs musicaux pour de véritables idées, d'un autre monde, d'un autre ordre, idées voilées de ténèbres, inconnues, impénétrables à l'intelligence' (Proust 1926, 189). Instead of being impenetrable, however, the darkness in the forest is a sort of blue gloom, and from time to time he arrives at a kind of crossroads: 'Mais **de temps en temps** je tombais sur une sorte de petit carrefour' (FN2, 109r). Here, the published version briefly interrupts the narrative to ponder over the phrase 'from time to time', the simultaneous tenderness and savagery of the little words: 'Mais **de temps en temps. De temps en temps. Quelle bonté dans ces petits mots, quelle férocité**' (1951, 127).

Beckett seems to have hesitated about Molloy's age. When Molloy encounters the charcoal-burner, he says he might have loved him when he was much younger: 50 or 60 years younger in the first writing layer of the manuscript ('si j'avais eu **50** ⁶⁰ ou **60** ⁷⁰ ans en moins', FN2, 110r), 70 in the published version ('**soixante-dix** ans de moins', 1951, 128). But, of course, as with everything in Molloy's narrative, 'ce n'est pas sûr' (FN2, 110r) ['it's not certain' (1955, 112; *Mo* 84)]. And it is not even certain whether this uncertainty applies to the seventy years or to the possibility that he might have loved the charcoal-burner. This briefly reminds him of Ruth/ Edith, whose name he cannot remember and with whom he nonetheless experienced true love: 'aucun rapport avec – comment s'appelait-elle encore – ~~Edith – non?~~ Rose? non – Reine? – non plus – enfin vous voyez qui je veux dire' (FN2, 109v-110r). When Molloy asks the charcoal-burner the way to the nearest town, the published version adds a comment on his linguistic abilities: '**je trouvai les mots qu'il fallait, et les accents**' (1951, 128) ['I found the necessary words, and accents' (1955, 113; *Mo* 85)]. And when he asks him for the nearest way out of the forest, the extra comment in the published version is that he grew eloquent: '**Je devenais éloquent**' (1951, 128). The eloquence might corroborate the intertextual link with *Heart of Darkness*, given the importance of this notion and its link with self-deception in Conrad's story.

'1.9[.47]'
(FN2, 110v)

After he has hit the charcoal-burner on his head with his crutch and given him a few kicks in the ribs on either side – '**J'ai toujours eu la manie de la symétrie**' (1951, 130) ['I always had a mania for symmetry' (1955, 114; *Mo* 86)] is again an addition that was not yet in the manuscript – the narrative just jumps from a most cruel scene to the banal question whether Molloy did eat from time to time: 'Mais est-ce que je mangeai du moins, de temps en temps' (FN2, 113r). One of the words Beckett couldn't find immediately, leaving open a space with a question mark, was the word 'caroubes': '**quoi encore, des   ?**   , si chers aux chèvres' (FN2, 113r) ['What else, ah yes, carobs, so dear to goats' (1955, 115; *Mo* 86)]. Physically speaking, Molloy could stay in the forest, but he has the feeling that if he were to stay he would go against an imperative of the voices, his prompters, 'mes souffleurs' (FN2, 115r), whose imperatives nearly always bear on the question of his relations with his mother (1955, 117; *Mo* 88). Molloy claims the purpose of going to his mother is to establish their relations on a less precarious footing, 'afin de mettre nos rapports sur une base moins ambigue' (FN2, 117r).

The voice is called an intimate voice, 'une voix ^intime^' (FN2, 118r), which becomes 'une voix **interne**' in the published version (1951, 134) ['far away inside me' (1955, 118; *Mo* 89)], and Molloy also speaks of 'une sorte de conscience' (FN2, 118r) ['a kind of consciousness' (1955, 119; *Mo* 89)]. The little adjustments, 'as between Galileo's vessels' (1955, 119; *Mo* 90), were originally compared to adjustments 'entre deux **valves de pression**' (FN2, 119r), before becoming '**les vases de Galilée**' (1951, 135).[89]

While in the manuscript, Molloy thinks it was winter, he adds in the published version that perhaps it was only autumn: 'C'était peut-être seulement **l'automne**' (1951, 136). The issue of the voices becomes more complex when Molloy starts speaking about what he says to himself. For instance, the gloom turning less blue makes him explain it is because there is less green, even though it is still dense, because of the lead-sealed winter sky: 'Elle est moins bleue parce qu'il y a moins de vert, mais elle est toujours aussi épaisse, à cause du ^grâce au^ ciel plombé d'hiver. **Et des branches noires il tombe du noir. Ça c'est ajouté**' (FN2, 120r). The last few words do not appear in the other versions, where the addition is no longer rendered as direct speech: '**Puis quelque chose sur les branches noires dont il tombait du noir, quelque chose dans ce goût-là**' (1951, 136) ['Then something about the black dripping from the black boughs, something in that line' (1955, 120; *Mo* 90)]. Moreover, there are the forest murmurs, which sound like a gong (FN2, 121r). In the published version, Molloy adds the sound of the horn which he had taken off his bicycle (1951, 137).

When Molloy realises he can also crawl and starts explaining how he goes about it, he notes that he keeps losing his hat. This was a sloppy moment in the narrative, for in order not to lose his hat Molloy had attached a lace. In the published version, this small narrative anomaly is solved with the least effort, by means of the addition: '**il y avait longtemps que le lacet s'était cassé**' (1951, 138) ['the lace had broken long ago' (1955, 122; *Mo* 92)].

Falling into the ditch at the end of the forest, Molloy sees the plain as far as the eye can see, but immediately corrects himself. This epanorthosis was already in place in the manuscript: 'Je regardai la plaine déferlant devant

---

89   In English, Beckett considered the phrase '**Galileo's jars**' (ET1, 104r).

moi à perte de vue, non, pas tout à fait à perte de vue' (FN2, 123r), for he sees the towers of a town, 'faintly outlined against the horizon' (1955, 123; *Mo* 92). Worried that, even if this were his town, he would never be able to reach it, he 'heard a voice' (1955, 123; *Mo* 93) according to the English versions, whereas in the French versions it is Molloy who literally hears himself saying not to fret, that help was coming: **'je m'entendis dire** de ne pas me biler, qu'on venait à mon secours. Textuellement' (FN2, 124r). The verb 'biler' probably triggers the memory of the little boy who said thanks to Molloy when he stooped and picked up his marble ('sa bille') – and the manuscript makes this strange association explicit: **'Mais quelle extraordinaire association d'idées'** (FN2, 124r).

Finally, the closing line of the novel's first part famously shifts from the first-person narrator to the third person. This shift was not yet part of the first writing layer of the manuscript; it was added after a cancellation (and again the sentence is longer in the manuscript than in the published version, which cuts it into three short sentences): 'J'avais envie de retourner dans la forêt, ~~oh pas vraiment.~~ oh pas une vraie envie, **~~je restais là où j'étais,~~ Molloy pouvait rester, là où il était.**' (FN2, 125r) ['I longed to go back into the forest. Oh not a real longing. Molloy could stay, where he happened to be.' (1955, 124; *Mo* 93)] Underneath this last sentence, Beckett has drawn a line and the word count (boxed): '40.000 app.' (see Fig. 15)[90]

---

90 On the verso (FN2, 124v), Beckett has also written the number of pages he had written so far ('125') (see chapter 1.1.1).

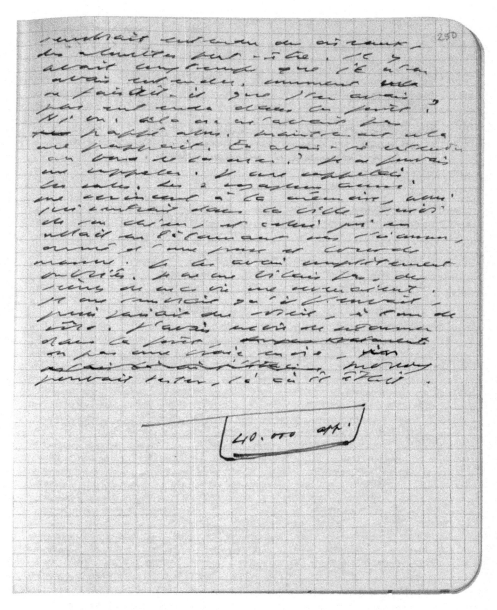

Fig. 15: Beckett finishes with a horizontal stroke to end Part I, under which he later writes a word count, '40.000 app.', underlined then framed (FN2, 124r).

| 223 |

2.2 PART II

When Molloy alludes to Wordsworth's definition of poetic composition to explain that it is 'in the tranquility of decomposition' that he remembers and judges 'the long confused emotion which was my life' (1955, 32; *Mo* 22), this 'tranquillité de la décomposition' (1951, 36) concisely summarizes not only Molloy's character but also Beckett's approach to characterization. This approach had its roots in his lectures on 'Racine and the Modern Novel' at TCD in 1931. In his lectures on Gide, Beckett advised his students to read Gide's essay *Dostoïevsky* (consisting mainly of a series of lectures presented at the Vieux-Colombier in Paris in 1922), and to 'Apply remarks to [Gide] himself' because Gide would have written this essay 'pour exprimer [s]es propres pensées' (TCD MIC 60, 19; see Le Juez 2008, 33-48). Beckett must have read several passages from this essay to his students, because Rachel Burrows's notes contain numerous quotations. Almost all of them stress the complexity and integrity of incoherence of Dostoevsky's characters,[91] usually presented against the contrastive background of Balzac's works.

Of all of Balzac's works, Gide notes, *Louis Lambert* is undoubtedly the least accomplished.[92] As opposed to Balzac, Dostoevsky allows his characters to be incoherent, which Gide compares to Rembrandt's *clair-obscur*.[93] Beckett seems to have positioned himself against Joyce the way

---

91 Also the 'tranquility' of Molloy's decomposition is presaged by what Gide calls Dostoevsky's 'quietism': 'c'est à une sorte de bouddhisme, de quiétisme du moins, que nous conduit Dostoïevsky' (Gide 1923, 226-7) – summarized as 'Dost's quietism' by Rachel Burrows in her notes on Beckett's lectures (TCD MIC 60, 24).

92 'De tous les livres de Balzac, *Louis Lambert* est sans doute le moins réussi; en tout cas, ce n'était qu'un monologue. Le prodige réalisé par Dostoïevsky, c'est que **chacun de ses personnages**, et il en a créé tout un peuple, **existe d'abord en fonction de lui-même**, et que chacun de ces êtres intimes, avec son secret particulier, se présente à nous dans toute sa **complexité problématique**' (Gide 1923, 71; TCD MIC 60, 21; bold typeface in the quotation indicates the words noted down by Burrows in her notes).

93 'Ses principaux personnages restent toujours en formation, toujours **mal dégagés de l'ombre**. Je remarque en passant combien profondément il **diffère par là de Balzac** dont le **souci principal** semble être toujours **la parfaite conséquence du personnage**. Celui-ci dessine comme David; celui-là peint comme Rembrandt' (Gide 1923, 75; TCD MIC 60, 21).

Gide positioned Dostoevsky against Balzac. As Andy Wimbush has shown,[94] Beckett presented both Balzac and Joyce as masters of their material: in *Dream*, Balzac is said to be the 'absolute master of his material' (*D* 119); after Beckett's 'revelation,' Joyce is presented as someone who went as far as one could go in the direction of 'being in control of one's material' (qtd. in Knowlson 1997, 352), 'a superb manipulator of material' – against whom Beckett positioned himself as a writer who is 'not master of [his] material' (Shenker 2005, 162).

This may create the impression that, from Beckett's point of view, Joyce was on a par with Balzac, which seems an unfair analysis, given that Beckett kept admiring Joyce until the very end of his life, even paying homage to him by adding an allusion to the end of *Finnegans Wake* – 'a way a lone a last a long the' (Joyce 1939, 628) – in 'what is the word': 'afaint afar away' (*CIWS* 134). But Gide's contrastive analysis does seem to have provided Beckett with a strategy to position himself with regard to Joyce. And the notion of being master of one's material (or not) is a crucial element in his poetics. *Molloy* can be read as a demonstration or performance, rather than an explanation, of this aesthetic vision. What is explained in *Dream of Fair to Middling Women* is enacted in *Molloy*.

In *Dream*, as John Bolin notes (2012, 151-2), the content of Beckett's lectures (especially the Gidean analysis of Dostoevsky vs. Balzac) is concentrated as a mini-lecture: 'The procédé that seems all falsity, that of Balzac, for example, and the divine Jane and many others, consists in dealing with the vicissitudes, or absence of vicissitudes, of character in this backwash, as though that were the whole story' (*D* 119). This procedure is characterized as a 'nervous recoil into composure,' 'a backwash of composure,' 'a kind of centripetal backwash that checks the rot' (*D* 119):

---

94   Andy Wimbush, '"Omnipotence and Omniscience": Beckett's Joyce vs. Beckett's Gide from *Dream of Fair to Middling Women* to *Molloy*', paper presented at the conference 'Beckett and Modernism', University of Antwerp, 27-30 April 2016.

To read Balzac is to receive the impression of a chloroformed world. [...] he can write the end of his book before he has finished the first paragraph, because he has turned all his creatures into clockwork cabbages[95] and can rely on their staying put wherever needed or staying going at whatever speed in whatever direction he chooses. (*D* 119-20)

The question, however, is what is human about his *Comédie humaine*: 'Why *human* comedy?' (*D* 120). In *Dream*, the character of Lucien is presented as 'a stew of disruption and flux,' he *is said to be* 'disintegrating' (*D* 116-7; emphasis added). The flaw of *Dream*, however, was not that it attacks Balzac's tendency towards explanation, but that it does so by using the same explanatory strategy. In his lectures, Beckett had said about the 'darkness' and 'unexplained mysticism' of Alissa in Gide's *La Porte étroite*: 'If Balzac treated this he'd establish train of motives & explain it all' (TCD MIC 60, 27). As opposed to Balzac, there are 'no explanations in Dost[oevsky]' (27). In *Molloy*, Beckett seems to have found a way to *apply* or *enact*, rather than *explain*, the Dostoevskian method. And this is also where the Balzacian and Joycean methods diverge. What Beckett admired in Joyce's work was the convergence of form and content: 'his writing is not *about* something; *it is that something itself*' (*Dis* 27; original emphasis). Later on, Beckett spoke of his poetics in terms of finding a form that 'accommodates the mess' (Driver 2005, 219). One could argue about the nuances between the form *being* the content and the form *accommodating* the content, but the result is that the character of Molloy is not *said to be* disintegrating (like Lucien in *Dream*), but that he *is* disintegrating.

Almost all the characteristics mentioned in the statements quoted from Gide's *Dostoïevsky* during the TCD lectures are applicable to Molloy: the contradictions and inconsistencies[96]; the humility and complexity[97]; the self-

---

95   As Andy Wimbush notes, the narrator's comment on Balzac's characters being 'clockwork cabbages' (*D* 119) echoes Rachel Burrows's note 'B[alzac] considers humanity as so much vegetable inertia' (TCD MIC 60, 58; Wimbush 2015, 7).

96   'Je ne connais pas d'écrivain plus **riche en contradictions et en inconséquences** que Dostoïevsky; Nietzsche dirait: "**en antagonismes**".' (Gide 1923, 83; TCD MIC 60, 23)

97   'Cette **humilité** [...] le disposait à la soumission devant ce qu'il reconnaissait supérieur. Il s'est **incliné** profondément **devant le Christ**; et la première et la

abnegation.[98] But the analogy goes even further. Gide quotes Jacques Rivière, who distinguishes two types of characterization: either the novelist can insist on a character's complexity, or he can stress its coherence; either he shows all its obscurity[99] or he can suppress it; either he preserves and respects its caverns or he exposes them.[100] In his lectures, Beckett summarized this as follows: 'You can either respect a cavern or go about it with an electric torch as Stendhal & Balzac' (TCD MIC 60, 29). Thus, whereas Molloy is stumbling in 'impenetrable darkness', Moran makes sure he does not leave on his quest without a 'Lampe!' (as indicated in a paralipomenon on FN4, 03r; see writing session dated '16.10.47' below).

In Beckett's lectures, he also referred to a passage from Rivière (as quoted by Gide) in which he discusses the unfathomable gulfs ('abîmes [...] insondables') marking Dostoevsky's characters.[101] These 'abîmes' or

plus importante conséquence de cette soumission, de ce **renoncement**, fut [...] de préserver la **complexité** de sa nature.' (Gide 1923, 116; TCD MIC 60, 23)

98 **'C'est cette abnégation**, cette résignation de soi-même, **qui permit la cohabitation en l'âme de Dostoïevsky des sentiments les plus contraires,** qui préserva, qui sauva l'extraordinaire richesse d'antagonismes qui combattaient en lui.' (Gide 1923, 117; TCD MIC 60, 23)

99 This obscurity may be alluded to in the 'darkness I have always struggled to keep under', as it is called in *Krapp's Last Tape* (*KLT* 9).

100 'L'idée d'un personage étant donnée dans son esprit, il y a, pour le romancier, deux manières bien différentes de la mettre en œuvre : ou il peut insister sur sa complexité, ou il peut souligner sa cohérence ; dans cette âme qu'il va engendrer, ou bien il peut vouloir produire toute l'obscurité, ou bien il peut vouloir la supprimer pour le lecteur en la dépeignant ; ou bien il réservera ses cavernes, ou bien il les exposera. (*Nouvelle Revue française*, 1er février 1922)' (Rivière qtd. in Gide 1923, 166-7). Gide comments on this passage as follows: 'Vous voyez quelle est l'idée de Jacques Rivière : c'est que l'école française explore les cavernes, tandis que certains romanciers étrangers, comme Dostoïevsky en particulier, respectent et protègent leurs ténèbres.' (167)

101 **'Dostoïevsky s'intéresse** avant tout **à leurs abîmes** et c'est à suggérer ceux-ci **les plus insondables** possible qu'il met tous ses soins' (Rivière qtd. in Gide 1923, 167; TCD MIC 60 29). In the rest of the quotation, Rivière develops the idea by means of contrasting it with the 'French school': 'Nous [l'école française], au contraire, placés en face de la complexité d'une âme, à mesure que nous cherchons à la représenter, d'instinct nous cherchons à l'organiser. [...] nous supprimons quelques petits traits divergents, nous interprétons quelques détails obscurs dans le sens le plus favorable à la constitution d'une unité psychologique.' (Rivière qtd. in Gide, 167-8) And again Gide applies this idea to Balzac: 'Ce qui lui importe, c'est d'obtenir des personnages conséquents avec eux-mêmes – c'est en quoi il est d'accord avec le sentiment de la race

'gulfs' characterize Molloy, who enjoys the 'spurious deeps' (1955, 27; *Mo* 18), whereas Moran presents himself as 'a sensible man, cold as crystal and free from spurious depth' (1955, 154; *Mo* 117). Andy Wimbush therefore insightfully interprets the two-part structure of *Molloy* as a demonstration of the Dostoevsky/Balzac dichotomy: 'in Balzac's novels, Beckett said, "charcters can't change their minds or artistic order crashes – must be consistent" [(TCD MIC 60, 41)]. Similarly, Moran declares: "I [...] never changed my mind before my son", implying that he sees it as shameful or weak to do so [(1955, 141; *Mo* 107)]' (Wimbush 2015, 12). In the beginning of the novel's second part, Moran indeed seems to represent the Balzacian 'nervous recoil into composure,' 'the centripetal backwash that checks the rot' (*D* 119). His task is to 'see about Molloy' (1955, 125; *Mo* 95), 'restoring the novel to order' as Andy Wimbush notes (2015, 12).

But of course, even before his TCD lectures, Beckett already warned us that 'the danger is in the neatness of identifications' (*Dis* 19). When we read the Molloy/Moran opposition in terms of the Dostoevsky/Balzac dichotomy the question is whether Beckett had this dichotomy in mind as a programme for his novel and, if so, whether he is not guilty of the same kind of programmatic writing of which he accused Balzac. According to the analysis in *Dream of Fair to Middling Women*, Balzac 'can write the end of the book before he has finished the first paragraph' (*D* 119-20), and that is indeed how Moran begins his journey: 'how can you decide on the way of setting out if you do not first know where you are going' (1955, 134; *Mo* 102). Even if conceived as a parody, the neatness of the identification would suggest a programme on Beckett's part. But that would contradict what Beckett told Charles Juliet, namely that he did not know where he was going when he wrote the first sentence of *Molloy*: 'Quand j'ai écrit la première phrase de *Molloy*, je ne savais pas où j'allais' (Juliet 1995, 19). It can never be excluded that there are notes that have not yet surfaced, but so far we have not found any evidence that contradicts Beckett's statement. The extant manuscripts suggest that the idea of introducing a second narrator in a second part developed *during* the writing process, as part of Beckett's 'écriture à processus,' rather than 'à programme' (Hay 1984).

française, car ce dont nous, Français, avons le plus besoin, c'est de logique.' (169)

At numerous instances in *Molloy* Part I the narrative 'composure' is complicated – and to a certain extent de-composed – by means of additions (very often metacomments that undermine Molloy's reliability as a narrator) between the manuscript and the first edition, which indicates that the idea of emphasizing Molloy's de-composition came at a relatively late stage in the writing process. The paragraphs in the manuscript gradually became longer and longer, until Beckett, in a subsequent version, decided to undo the paragraph breaks and turn the majority of Part I into an amorphous mass of text, unstructured by paragraphs. While the novel's first part gradually becomes less 'paragraphed' in the manuscript, the contrast with the second part's regular compartmentalization in paragraphs indicates that the idea of creating a contrastive, two-part structure suggested itself during the writing process and was then developed by emphasizing the contrast, eventually eliminating the paragraph structure in Part I and adding numerous metafictional interjections that complicate Molloy's narrative.

Moreover, as we will see, towards the end of Part II, Moran's own decomposition is staged by means of several elements that Beckett 'cogged' from an anonymously published book by Pierre Gustave Brunet, called *Curiosités théologiques*, which enumerates hundreds of the most bizarre theological theories and practices. Moran's initial, 'Balzacian' composure is questioned in the form of 16 unanswered questions, based on Brunet's *Curiosités théologiques*, until he starts reciting his 'quietist Pater' (1955, 229; *Mo* 175), also based on Brunet, which indicates that Moran eventually (and gradually) becomes less of a 'Balzacian' character, more in line with 'Dost[oevsky]'s quietism' (TCD MIC 60, 24). Moran's initial composure and self-command is based on a rigid application of religious rules. By making Moran ask questions derived from a bibliographical work that ridicules the most extravagant excesses of religion, Beckett makes effective use of exogenetic material to infiltrate Moran's composure and expedite its decomposition. So, it seems fair to read the two parts of *Molloy* as an illustration of the Balzac/Dostoevsky dichotomy (Wimbush 2015), and as a de-composition of the Balzacian composure, but the manuscripts also provide us with indications that what, with hindsight, looks like a rather schematic programme – a programme to make an aesthetic statement about being non-programmatic – was apparently not the result of programmatic writing ('écriture à programme') but of 'écriture à processus'.

Paragraph 1 (FN2, 126r)

'3.9.47'
(FN2, 125v)

In the first writing layer of the manuscript, the famous opening of the second part at midnight was limited to 'Il est minuit. **L'heure de se coucher.**' The sentence 'La pluie fouette les vitres' (FN2, 126r) ['The rain is beating on the windows' (1955, 125; *Mo* 183)] was added later, but certainly before Beckett switched to black ink for the remainder of the manuscript on '9.10. 47.' (FN3, 71v; see below) Because of this addition, 'L'heure de se coucher' ['Bedtime'] was replaced by **'Je suis calme'** (1951, 142) ['I am calm' (1955, 125; *Mo* 95)] in the published versions. The first-person narrator gets up and goes to his desk, which (instead of **'bureau'**, 1951, 142) is called **'écritoire'** in the manuscript (FN2, 126r), emphasizing the act of writing.

Paragraph 2 (FN2, 126r)

He mentions a 'report' (1955, 125; *Mo* 95) and declares that it will be long, before he mentions his name.

Paragraph 3 (FN2, 126r; paragraph 2 in 1951)

His name is 'Moran, Jacques' (1955, 125; *Mo* 95), just like his son. As opposed to Molloy's narrative (especially towards the end), Moran's report is structured by means of numerous – often very short – paragraphs (in the manuscript even more than in the published version).

Pargraph 4 (FN2, 127r; paragraph 3 in 1951)

Moran remembers the day he received the order 'de m'occuper de Molloy' (FN2, 126r) ['see about Molloy' (1955, 125; *Mo* 95)], on a Sunday.

Paragraph 5 (FN2, 127r; paragraph 4 in 1951)

While he is watching the coming and going of his bees, he hears his son's footsteps on the gravel, caught up in a fantasy of flight and pursuit, 'ravi dans je ne sais ~~quel monde~~ quelle fantaisie **de fuites et de poursuites**' (FN2, 127r). The suggestion to read this second part of the novel as a pursuit, turns the composition into a fugue – a theme that recurs much later in Beckett's oeuvre, in the abandoned sections of *Stirrings Still*, in which the protagonist is characterized as someone who had not always failed in his attempted flights and pursuits.[102]

Paragraph 6 (FN2, 127r-128r, paragraph 5 in 1951)

In an uncharacteristically idyllic paragraph, Beckett describes how Moran enjoys his Sunday, looking at his lemon-verbena.

Paragraph 7 (FN2, 128r, paragraph 6 in 1951)

But Moran reports that these were his last moments of peace and happiness. This one sentence constitutes a separate paragraph.

Paragraph 8 (FN2, 128r-130r; paragraph 7 in 1951)

And then the peace is disturbed by a man who enters the garden and comes straight to where Moran is sitting, under a tree. The tree ('~~un arbre~~') is cancelled and replaced by the more specific description '**mon pommier**' (FN2, 128r), which will become even more specific in the English translation: 'my Beauty of Bath' (1955, 127; *Mo* 96; see chapter 3.2).[103] As such, Beckett does not parody Balzac without mastering the realist techniques of novel

---

102 'Revenu à lui ou à ce qui avait jadis passé pour tel son premier mouvement fut finalement de se demander s'il l'était vraiment. [...] Etait-ce donc bien à nouveau celui qui n'avait pas toujours échoué jadis dans ses tentatives de fuite et de poursuite?' (UoR MS 2933/4; see *BDMP1*). See also Van Hulle 2011.

103 The housekeeper does not yet have a name in the manuscript; she is described as '**ma domestique**' (FN2, 128r), whereas the published version introduces her simply as '**Marthe**' (1951, 144), anglicized to '**Martha**' in the translation (1955, 127; *Mo* 96).

writing. 'Stendhal expressed particular at expense of general' he told his students during his TCD lectures (Burrows notes, TCD MIC 60, 49; see also paragraph 86).

Moran is displeased by the disturbance, but he is 'mollified' (1955, 128; *Mo* 97) by the reflection that after all the man was only acting as a go-between. Originally, Beckett wrote that Moran was relieved, '**adouci**' (FN2, 129r), which became '**amolli**' in the published version (1951, 145), thus echoing the 'molys' in Part I. Beckett even adds on the verso that suddenly Moran had pity: '**Oui, soudain j'eus pitié de lui, pitié de moi**' (FN2, 129r). The addition of pity in this context of piety on a Sunday recalls the 'great phrase' in Beckett's early story 'Dante and the Lobster', when Belacqua tries to translate the line 'Qui vive la pietà quand'è ben morta'[104] and wonders why it is not possible to show 'piety and pity both' at the same time (*MPTK* 13). Moran observes how he, in his turn, is being observed by his thirteen- or fourteen-year-old son, whose intelligence was above average in the manuscript: 'Son intelligence également **dépassait la moyenne**' (FN2, 129r); in the published version his intelligence is little short of average, which is followed by the afterthought '**Mon fils quoi**' (1951, 145) ['My son, in fact' (1955, 128; *Mo* 97)]. As in Part I, these kinds of short interjections or sentences were added here and there after the manuscript stage. The relationship between father and son is immediately made explicit in the manuscript: 'Je l'appelai **violemment**' (FN2, 129r; the adverb was dropped in the published version, 1951, 145). He orders him to bring them some refreshing drinks, '**des boissons rafraichissantes**' (FN2, 129r). Again, this rather vague description had to make room for something more specific: '**de la bière**' (1951, 145) ['some beer' (1955, 128; *Mo* 97)]. Moran sends the boy inside to get ready for mass, but he is interrupted: 'He can stay, said Gaber' (1955, 128; *Mo* 97). The rather abrupt introduction of Martha and Gaber in the published version

---

104 'Here *piety* lives when *pity* is quite dead' (Dante 2002, 362-3; *Inferno*, Canto XX, l. 28; emphasis added). In Canto IV, Virgil explains that he takes pity [*pietà*] on the unbaptised patriarchs and illustrious pagans in Limbo because they were simply born too early to be saved by Christ; but in Canto XX, it is not appropriate to feel the same pity for the soothsayers in *Inferno*. So, here 'piety' [*pietà*] lives only when 'pity' [*pietà*] is dead. Later in the story, Belacqua wonders 'Why not piety and pity both' (*MPTK* 13). With a 'superb pun' (*MPTK* 11), Dante (formally at least) accomplishes precisely what Belacqua has in mind: the word *pietà* simultaneously performs its double semantic function, 'piety and pity both'.

differs markedly from the manuscript, where Moran's wooden style of writing is (perhaps over)emphasized with repetition: 'Il vaut mieux qu'il reste, dit **le messager. Le messager** s'appelait Gaber' (FN2, 130r).[105]

Paragraph 9 (FN2, 130r-131r; paragraph 8 in 1951)

Gaber gives the instructions. The manuscript is slightly more explicit about the nature of the enquiry (**'une enquête'**, FN2, 131r) than the published version, which simply calls it a job: **'ce travail'** (1951, 146). When Gaber says he could do with another beer, Moran suddenly feels very nervous in the manuscript: **'Je me sentais très nerveux'** (FN2, 131r) – which was omitted in the Minuit edition. He sends him into the kitchen, where 'the maid' (1955, 129; *Mo* 98) would serve him (**'~~Marthe vous servira~~ la servante** vous servira', FN2, 131r). The end of the paragraph reads like the original of what is parodied in *Waiting for Godot* when Pozzo, Didi and Gogo bid farewell: '**~~Au revoir~~** Adieu, Monsieur Moran, dit-il. **~~Au revoir~~** Adieu Monsieur Gaber, répondis-je.' (FN2, 131r) ['Goodbye, Moran.' (1955, 129; *Mo* 97)][106]

Paragraph 10 (FN2, 131r-134r; paragraphs 9 and 10 in 1951)

Moran is too late for mass. The whole passage, full of exclamation marks, about his missing mass, is an addition on the verso:

> Moi qui ne ratais jamais la messe, l'avoir ratée justement ce dimanche-là! Quand j'en avais un tel besoin! Pour me mettre en train! Je pris la résolution de soliciter [sic] une communion particulière, au courant de l'après-midi. Je me passerais de déjeuner. Avec le bon père Ambroise on ~~peut~~ pouvait toujours s'arranger. (FN2, 131v)

---

105 The passage '**Nous avions essayé de nous tutoyer. En vain. Moi je ne dis, ne disais, tu qu'à deux personnes.**' (1951, 145) was not yet part of the manuscript and later dropped again in English.

106 The published version reduces this drastically to: '**Salut Moran, dit-il.**' (1951, 147)

[I who never missed mass, to have missed it on that Sunday of all Sundays! When I so needed it! To buck me up! I decided to ask for a private communion, in the course of the afternoon. I would go without lunch. Father Ambrose was always very kind and accommodating. (1955, 129-30; *Mo* 98)]

He calls his son,[107] but Jacques junior probably went to mass alone, which causes him to think about the verger's surveillance and other matters related to church.

Paragraph 11 (FN2, 134r-135r)

Moran does not yet take the matter of his mission seriously. But his report interprets Gaber's words as a foreshadowing. Gaber and Moran's 'chief' (1955, 131; *Mo* 100) is called 'le directeur' ['boss'] at this instance in the manuscript, which was written with some difficulty:

> ~~Comment~~ Même si, **en écoutant l'exposé** de Gaber, l'affaire m'avait **semblé presque** indigne de moi, l'insistance du **directeur** pour m'avoir, plutôt qu'un autre, aurait dû ~~me mettre la puce à l'oreille~~ m'avertir que je faisais erreur. Et la nouvelle que **Jacques** allait m'accompagner, **qui m'avait fait tressaillir** ~~qua~~ au moment de l'apprendre, ~~aurait était dû m'aiguillonner dans le même sens,~~ était un indice, non moins ~~significatif~~ sinistre, ~~qu'il s'agissait d'une affaire exceptionnelle~~ que l'affaire avait quelque chose d'exceptionnel. (FN2, 134r)

The passage underwent quite a few extra revisions before publication:

> Même si, à **la lecture du rapport** de Gaber, l'affaire m'avait **paru** indigne de moi, l'insistance du **patron** pour m'avoir, **moi Moran,** plutôt qu'un autre, et la nouvelle que **mon fils** allait m'accompagner, auraient dû m'avertir **qu'il s'agissait d'un travail sortant de l'ordinaire.** (1951, 49)

---

107 In the published version, this is the beginning of a new paragraph; in the manuscript (FN2, 132r) the text runs on without indentation.

[Even if, as set forth in Gaber's report, the affair had seemed unworthy of me, the chief's insistence on having me, me Moran, rather than anybody else, ought to have warned me that it was no ordinary one. (1955, 131; *Mo* 100)]

'**4.9[.47]**'
(FN2, 134v)

The next writing session opens with the afterthought that he should have started preparing his mission immediately, instead of 'dreaming of [his] breed's infirmities' (1955, 131; *Mo* 100). But, with hindsight, he recognizes that the poison was already acting on him, creating an echo with Lousse's 'molys' in Part I.

Paragraph 12 (FN2, 135r)

Again, Beckett pays special attention to the Stendhalian specificity of the particulars. The beer becomes 'lager' and when Moran wonders whether he will be granted the body of Christ after a pint, the beer even gets a brand name: 'M'accorderait-on le corps du Christ après un verre d̶'̶U̶r̶q̶u̶e̶l̶l̶?̶ de **Wallenstein?**' (FN2, 135r; see 'Whoroscope' Notebook, UoR MS 3000, 72r).

Paragraph 13 (FN2, 135r-136r)

Moran goes inside and asks if his son has returned: '**J̶a̶c̶q̶u̶e̶s̶ ̶n̶'̶e̶s̶t̶ ̶p̶a̶s̶ ̶r̶e̶n̶t̶r̶é̶?̶**' (FN2, 135r) The direct question is immediately cancelled and replaced by indirect speech: '**Je demandai si Jacques était rentré**' (FN2, 135r) ['I asked if Jack was back' (1955, 132; *Mo* 100)]. When Moran says he won't eat lunch, Marthe asks if he is unwell: '**V̶o̶u̶s̶ ̶ê̶t̶e̶s̶ ̶m̶a̶l̶a̶d̶e̶?̶**' Which is again immediately replaced by indirect speech: '**Elle répondit en me demandant si j'étais malade**' (FN2, 136r) ['She asked if I were ill' (1955, 132; *Mo* 100)]. He ruins her day off, then offers her to take off the next day. The only reason for the 'mollifaction' is the realization that she would be capable of poisoning him – another echo of the 'molys' in Part I, referring to

Circe in the *Odyssey*.[108] So, the mere realization of the possibility of being poisoned becomes a 'moly' in and of itself, mollifying Moran. He leaves her and goes out: '~~Je s~~' (FN2, 136r) – but before the verb is written, Beckett cancels it and decides to start a new paragraph.

Paragraph 14 (FN2, 136r-137r)

'Je sortis et allai sur la route' (FN2, 136r). His neighbour is surprised that he is not in church, for everyone knows Moran's Sunday habits, especially the chief – still called '**le directeur**' (FN2, 137r) rather than '**le patron**' (1951, 151) – in spite of his remoteness.

Paragraph 15 (FN2, 137r)

On Jacques junior's return, Moran looks at him: '**Je le regardai**' (FN2, 137r). To Marthe, he says that she can serve lunch, '**Jacques est rentré**' (FN2, 137r). These two superfluous sentences were cut in the published version. Instead, the manuscript lacks the sentence '**Je ne faisais qu'aller et venir**' (1951, 151) ['I did nothing but go to and fro' (1955, 133; *Mo* 101)]. What follows is a nice example of how the complex 'autographic' relationship between Beckett and Moran, writer and character, functions. After Moran's praise to Irish stew and 'the land it has brought before the world' (1955, 133; *Mo* 101), he repeats to Marthe (who has wept) that he will eat at 4 pm sharp: 'Je me mettrai à table à 4 heures **tapantes**, dis-je' (FN2, 137r). In the published version 'tapantes' has been omitted, but Moran adds an extra sentence to the effect that he did not need to add 'sharp': '**Je n'avais pas besoin d'ajouter tapant**' (1951, 151). Moran thus appears (at least at this instance in the published text) as someone who masters his language with perfect economy of words. At the same time, it reads as a reprimand by Beckett to himself because it was unnecessary to add 'tapantes' in the manuscript version. The result is that this sentence is as ambiguous as the 'great phrase' in Dante's line 'qui vive la pietà quand'è ben morta' (see paragraph 8 above), and the word 'I' (referring to both the real author and the fictional character) arguably becomes an equally 'superb pun' as Dante's 'pietà' performing its double

108   Derived from Victor Bérard's translation (*DN* [entry 712]). See also the *BDL*, http://www.beckettarchive.org/ library/HOM-ODY.html.

semantic function, 'piety and pity both'. Only when Moran goes to his room, does he make his first attempt to grasp 'l'affaire Molloy' (FN2, 137r) ['The Molloy affair' (1955, 133; *Mo* 101)].

Paragraph 16 (FN2, 137r)

Still, Moran keeps shirking the core of the affair and feels 'une grande confusion' (FN2, 137r) ['a great confusion' (1955, 134; *Mo* 101)] coming over him.

Paragraph 17 (FN2, 138r-139r)

The question with which Moran, being 'un esprit méthodique' ['a methodical mind' (1955, 134; *Mo* 101)],[109] begins in dealing with the Molloy affair is whether he should set out on his 'vélomoteur' (FN2, 138r) ['autocycle' (1955, 134; *Mo* 101)]. Moran's question is related to a more general one: 'how can you decide on the way of setting out if you do not first know where you are going, or with what purpose you are going there?' (1955, 134; *Mo* 102). Normally he would deal with these questions first, before deciding on the problem of transport, but not this time. In the context of the writing process of Beckett's novel, this becomes a matter of poetics. As indicated above, during his lectures at Trinity College Dublin, Beckett had repeatedly expressed his dislike of writers in whose work 'characters can't change their minds or artistic structure crashes' (Rachel Burrows notes, TCD MIC 60, 41). Moran's customary approach resembles the method of writers in the category of Balzac and Corneille (according to Beckett's lectures), but although he calls the Molloy case 'une affaire banale' (FN2, 137r) ['The affair is banal' (1955, 134; *Mo* 102)] it already starts undermining his preconceptions and habitual structures. As a character, Moran gradually becomes more Racinian in the sense that, not unlike Andromaque, he is 'faced with a multiplicity of conflicting demands' (UoR, Daiken notes, 8). And Moran's son will serve as a parody of a 'confidant' on his journey, whose function – as in Racine's plays – is 'to express a fragment in the mind of the protagonist' (according to Leslie Daiken's student notes, UoR, Daiken notes, 8) or the 'division in

---

109   The characterization 'un esprit méthodique' suggests a reference both to Descartes and to Balzac (as construed by Gide) in opposition to Dostoevsky.

mind' (according to Rachel Burrows's notes, TCD MIC 60, 65). Against this background, it is noteworthy that Moran and his 'confidant' have the same name.

Paragraph 18 (FN2, 139r)

Moran's favourite mode of transport is his 'vélomoteur'. That this preference is the sole basis for his decision to leave on his autocycle is linked to Freud's *Jenseits des Lustprinzips* in a remarkable meta-comment: '**Remarquez de quelle manière** s'inscrivait', au seuil de l'affaire Molloy, le funeste principe du plaisir' (FN2, 139r). In the published version ('**Ainsi** s'inscrivait [...]', 1951, 153) ['Thus was inscribed, on the threshold of the Molloy affair, the fatal pleasure principle' (1955, 135; *Mo* 102)] the reader is not addressed directly as in the manuscript. The pleasure principle is called 'fatal', thus foreshadowing the adversities to come, but the first-person narration also seems to guarantee that everything will turn out to be less 'fatal' than Moran presents it, since apparently he is still capable of writing it all down. Thus, as a narrator, Moran demonstrates Beckett's favourite lines from Shakespeare's *King Lear* (IV.1), 'The worst is not, So long as one can say, "This is the worst"' ('Sottisier' Notebook, UoR MS 2901, 14v), and from Petrarch's sonnets, 'chi può dir com'egli arde, è 'n picciol foco' ('who can say how he burns is in little fire'; see above, writing session dated '21.8[.47]').

Paragraph 19 (FN2, 139r)

The next paragraph opened with a rift in the curtains: '~~Par la fente entre les rideaux~~' (FN2, 139r). Beckett crossed it out and decided to open the sentence with the image of dust motes floating in the sunlight: 'Les rayons du soleil entraient par la fente entre les rideaux, ~~faisaien~~ rendant visible **le mouvement** de la poussière' (FN2, 139r). The movement of the dust motes became a '**sabbat**' (1951, 153). Moran keeps basing his preparation on a lack of information. Instead of looking outside to see what the weather is like, he relies on the sparse information based on what enters the room through the rift in the curtains.

Paragraph 20 (FN2, 139r-140r)

When Jacques junior asks his father if he can go out, Moran – who abhors vagueness – asks his son where exactly he wants to go.

Paragraph 21 (FN2, 140r)

This creates another interesting tension between the narrator and the writer, for Beckett does not yet know the name of the place Moran's son has in mind: '**Au ? ** répondit-il' (FN2, 140r), later replaced with '**Aux Ormeaux**' (1951, 153) ['To the Elms, he replied' (1955, 135; *Mo* 103)], the name of their 'petit jardin public' (1951, 153) ['little public park' (1955, 135; *Mo* 103)]. Moran's methodical and 'rational' approach is emphasized in the manuscript by means of a short sentence that was later omitted: '**On a des raisons, pour sortir**' (FN2, 140r). Moran does not believe his son when he says he wants to go over his botany, and would (almost) have preferred him to say he was going to look at the ducks in the park ('Regarder les **canards**', FN2, 140r) – which become girls in the Minuit edition ('Regarder les **filles**', 1951, 154) ['To look at the tarts' (1955, 135; *Mo* 103)].[110]

Paragraph 22 (FN2, 140r-142r)

When Moran starts talking about his nap, he reminds himself that he should shorten his narrative ('Raccourcissons', FN2, 140r) and move on. But then he continues babbling away, about the baroque jesuit style of the church door and about father Ambrose offering him a cigar and 'un digestif' (FN2, 141r) ['a little glass of something' (1955, 136; *Mo* 103)]. In the manuscript, the conversation with father Ambrose is much shorter than in the published version. When father Ambrose guesses Moran wants communion and Moran bows his head, Ambrose immediately goes and fetches what he calls his 'trousse' (FN2, 141r) ['kit' (1955, 137; *Mo* 104)]. In the published version, Beckett added the scene in which father Ambrose urges Moran not to tell anyone that he will give him communion, and to let it 'remain between us and –' (1955, 137; *Mo* 103), pointing upwards and noticing a '**tache**

---

110   Beckett introduced the cruder variant for 'girls' in the second typescript of the translation: 'To look at the **girls** ᵗᵃʳᵗˢ' (ET2, 10r; see chapter 3.3).

d'humidité' (1951, 155), on the ceiling. So instead of a secret between them and God, it is something that remains between them and a damp stain that was not there yet in the manuscript. While father Ambrose is fetching his kit, Moran asks the Lord ('le Seigneur') for guidance, but 'Sans résultat' (FN2, 142r) ['Without result' (1955, 137; *Mo* 104)].

Paragraph 23 (FN2, 142r – FN3, 01r)

After communion, Moran allows father Ambrose eight minutes for small talk. Again, the conversation is shorter in the manuscript: when Moran tells Ambrose about his grey hen, which neither broods nor lays, and only sits in the dust, 'dans la poussière' (FN2, 143r), Ambrose refers to Job and laughs, which leads to a short reflection on laughter being 'le propre de l'homme' (1951, 157) ['It is peculiar of man' (1955, 138; *Mo* 105)], possibly alluding to Bergson's *Le rire: Essai sur la signification du comique.*[111] This short scene was not yet part of the manuscript, which continues with Ambrose asking Moran what he feeds his hen on (FN2, 143r) and his advice to give her bicarbonate of soda.

When Beckett arrived at the design of a crossword puzzle (in another hand, possibly Suzanne's) at the back of the notebook and at the brief autobiographical note and the draft of the letter requesting an estimate for work to be done at the Villa Irlanda in Menton (see chapter 1.1.1), he simply stopped in mid-sentence and continued in the third notebook. The autobiographical note is quite interesting, as Beckett suggests in it that he is not aware of any major influences and that he has no projects:

> Né à Dublin 1906 de parents irlandais
> 1923-27 études à Trinity College l'université de Dublin en Irlande.
> 1928-30 lecteur en x d'anglais à Normale
> 1928–1938 publi publications diverses (ess Poèmes, Nouvelles, Essai sur Proust, Nouvelles, Poèmes, Roman publié à Londres en langue anglaise
> 1 essai livre sur Proust, 1 livre de Nouvelles, 1 livre de poèmes, 1 roman. Depuis 1945 écrit en français. exclusivement.

---

111   See Salisbury 2012 and Gontarski 2015.

Ne se connaît pas d'influences majeures. N'a pas de projets.
(FN2, 144v)

Beckett's deletion of **'exclusivement'** is significant, as it indicates his uncertainty about ever returning to English as a language of composition after *Molloy*.

Paragraph 24 (FN3, 01r)

> **'5.9.47' / Menton**
> (FN3, inside front cover)

Sometimes the published version undoes a revision that took place in the manuscript. The host lies heavy on Moran's stomach. The manuscript first calls it ~~'l'hostie'~~, which is replaced by **'la nourriture divine'** (FN3, 01r), but in the published version it is **'l'hostie'** again (1951, 157).

Paragraph 25 (FN3, 01r)

> **'6.9.[47]'**
> (FN3, inside front cover)

By the time he arrives home in the rain, he is in a bad mood. The stew is a great disappointment.

Paragraph 26 (FN3, 02r-03r)

Moran goes up to his room and opens the curtains on 'a calamitous sky' (1955, 139; *Mo* 106) ['un ciel de désastre' (FN3, 02r)]. He tries to pull himself together, in vain, when his son comes in. In the manuscript Beckett often uses the present tense where the published version features the past tense, for instance when Moran notes that his son has a special way of saying 'papa' when he wants to hurt his father: 'Il **a** une façon de dire papa, mon fils, quand il veut me blesser, très particulière' (FN3, 03r; 'Il **avait** une façon', 1951, 159). Moran tells his son to wear his green school suit, which turns out to be blue, as his son points out. 'Blue or green, put it on' Moran says violently, adding for good measure in the manuscript: **'Est-ce compris?'** (FN3, 03r)

['Understood?'].[112] Again, a manuscript cancellation ('tes ~~affaires~~ **choses** de toilette', FN3, 03r) is undone in the first edition: 'tes **affaires** de toilette' (1951, 159) ['your toilet things' (1955, 140; *Mo* 106)].

Paragraph 27 (FN3, 03r)

'**7.9.[47]**'
(FN3, 02v)

The next day, Beckett started a new paragraph in which Moran starts doubting his own instructions to his son, wondering whether they would stand the test of second thoughts. It took Beckett several attempts to write this question: '~~Ne serai-je pas amené, à la réflexion Ne serais[je] pas obligé, à la réflex Ne serais[je] pas amené~~ Résisteraient-elles à la réflexion? ~~Ne serais[je] pas obligé, xx~~ Ne serais-je pas amené, dans très peu de temps, à les rapporter? **A avouer que je m'étais trompé?**' (FN3, 03r). The latter question, in which he considers that he might have to admit that he had been mistaken, was omitted in the published version (1951, 159). The passage in which Moran states that he never changed his mind before his son is also interesting in the autograph because Beckett changes his mind a few times in order to get this sentence formulated: 'Moi ~~que mon fils n'avait jamais vu changer qui n'avait jamais~~ qui ne changeais jamais d'avis, devant mon fils' (FN3, 03r).

Paragraph 28 (FN3, 03r-05r)

When his son says that he has an appointment with Monsieur Py, the manuscript version explains that '**Py était le dentiste**' (FN3, 04r), which is left out in the published version, since three sentences further on this information is implicit in Moran's remark that Py is not the only dentist, 'pas **le seul** dentiste **du pays**' (FN3, 04r), 'pas **l'unique** dentiste **de l'hémisphère**

---

112 This uncertainty about the blue or green outfit finds a curious echo in Beckett's reply to Alan Schneider's question why the characters in *Endgame* have red and white faces: 'Faces red and white probably like Werther's green coat, because the author saw them that way' (*LSB III* 94) – the irony being that Goethe did not see Werther's coat that way, for Werther's coat is blue (Goethe 1999, 168-9).

septentrional' (1951, 160) ['of the northern hemisphere' (1955, 141; *Mo* 107)].

Paragraph 29 (FN3, 05r)

Here and there, the direct speech of the manuscript is replaced by indirect speech in the published version. For instance, when Moran asks his son what he is waiting for: '**Qu'est-ce qu**$^{e\,tu}$ **attends, dis-je**' (FN3, 05r) becomes '**Je lui demandai ce qu'il attendait**' (1951, 161). Sometimes, the change from direct to indirect speech already takes place in the manuscript: when Jacques junior asks if he can bring his stamps, Moran's reply is originally presented as direct speech: '~~Tu peux emporter le petit album, dis-je~~' (FN3, 05r), which is deleted and replaced by: '~~Je lui~~ **Je l'autorisai à emporter ce dernier**' (FN3, 05r) ['I authorised him to bring the latter' (1955, 142; *Mo* 108)].

Paragraph 30 (FN3, 06r-08r)

Moran needs to plan his journey, but finds himself thinking of the neighbours instead, the Elsner sisters and their dog Zulu.

Paragraph 31 (FN3, 08r)

In a rebellious moment he wonders what compelled him to accept this commission. Again, the direct question in the manuscript ('**Qu'est-ce** qui m'obligeait à accepter ce travail?', FN3, 08r) is turned into indirect speech in the published version: '**Je me demandai [...] ce** qui m'obligeait à accepter ce travail' (1951, 163).

Paragraph 32 (FN3, 08v-09r)

Moran keeps trying to defer the journey but eventually makes an irrevocable decision ('**inébranlable**' in the manuscript, FN3, 08r): they will leave just before midnight.

Paragraph 33 (FN3, 09r)

Finally, his thoughts turn to 'l'affaire Molloy' (FN3, 09r), but not before
Moran has made a last reflection on the unfathomability of the mind, 'now
beacon, now sea' (1955, 145; *Mo* 110) – which was originally likened to an
alternation of earth and light: 'tantôt ~~terre, tantôt lumière~~ mer, tantôt
phare' (FN3, 09r).

Paragraph 34 (FN3, 09r-12r)

The difference between Moran and Gaber is that the latter was 'un **simple**
messager' (FN3, 09r) ['a messenger' (1955, 145; *Mo* 110)] and was therefore
entitled to a notebook, whereas Moran as an agent never took anything
in writing. Gaber understood nothing about the messages he carried,
which is why the comments of the messengers made the agents impatient,
as an extra sentence in the manuscript specifies: '**C'est pourquoi les
commentaires des messagers impatientaient les agents. Car Gaber
croyait ~~comprendre~~ comprendre ce dont il était question, dans les
messages**' (FN3, 09r-10r). Gaber is an extreme example of what Andy Clark
and David Chalmers call the 'extended mind' (1998). Just like their fictitious
example of the Alzheimer's patient, 'Otto', whose memory is beyond the
brain, Gaber's memory is so bad that his messages only exist in his notebook,
not in his head, 'pas dans la tête, mais ~~dans le calepin~~ uniquement dans le
calepin' (FN3, 10r). In the manuscript, Gaber is also called a hierographer,
'**hiérographe**' (FN3, 11r).

His weekly wage is expressed in dollars (40 dollars, against Moran's of
only 32 dollars), whereas the currency in the published versions is pounds.
This revision of dollars to pounds resembles the previously noted shift from
kilometres to miles between the manuscript and the published text (see
chapter 2.1, paragraphs 11 and 20), emphasizing the Anglo-Irish context of
the novel. In this case, however, Beckett considered using American rather
than French currency at first, which suggests that rather than inscribing
Molloy within one cultural context in particular, he sought to destabilize
such straightforward identification. Even though the French text suggests 'an
adherence to anglophone norms of measurement' (Morin 2009, 60), other
evocations of a French setting remain in the published version. This process
of cultural destabilization or decentralization even continues in translation

(see chapter 3.2), so that 'comparing English and French versions forbids a straightforward alignment with an Irish setting and Irish origins', as Emilie Morin points out (2009, 61).

Paragraph 35 (FN3, 12r-13r)

The expression 'le partage diminue **le malheur**' in the manuscript (FN3, 12r) is changed into 'le partage diminue **l'infortune**' in the published version (1951, 166), and the translation alludes to this change: '**trouble** shared, or is it **sorrow**, is trouble something, I forget the word' (1955, 147; *Mo* 111). The 'chief' is still simply called 'le **directeur**' in the manuscript (FN3, 13r); in the published text, Beckett added his name: 'le **patron (un nommé Youdi)**' (1951, 166) ['one Youdi' (1955, 147; *Mo* 112)]. In the French manuscript of *L'Innommable*, an interesting jotting sheds some light on the way Beckett may have come up with the idea of calling this figure Youdi: 'Dieu / Ideu / Udie' (HRC-MS-SB-3-10, *BDMP2*, FN1, 67r; Van Hulle and Weller 2014, 152).

Paragraph 36 (FN3, 13r-14r)

In the kitchen, Moran finds Marthe in her '**fauteuil à bascules**' (FN3, 13r) ['rocking-chair' (1951, 167; *Mo* 112)], one of Beckett's favourite philosophical images, based on Arnold Geulincx's image of the cradle.[113]

---

113   As Anthony Uhlmann notes, Geulincx 'suggests that what we want to happen often does happen. We think we bring it about, but in fact something else brings it about. He likens this to a newborn baby (the epitome of powerlessness). The baby cries because it wants the cradle in which it lies to be rocked. And the cradle is rocked, but not by the baby; rather, it is rocked by the hand of the mother [...]. To the baby it might seem that there is a direct relation between the desire and the action, but the action is in fact brought about by another. Geulincx likens this to our situation in relation to God' (Uhlmann 2006, 80).

Paragraph 37 (FN3, 14r-16r)

Moran enters his son's room. Jacques junior is transferring a few rare and valuable stamps from the one album to the album of duplicates. 'Show me your new Timor, the five reis orange' (1955, 149; *Mo* 113), Moran says in the published version, 'ton **Timor** neuf, le cinq reis jaune' (1951, 168). Phil Baker has suggested an interesting psychological reading of this 'Timor' stamp with its moustached figure, in terms of the fear of the father in Part II, *timor patris*, which constitutes the counterpart of the *amor matris* in Part I (Baker 1997, 41). In the manuscript, Beckett did not have a name yet for the specific stamp: 'Montre-moi ton (**nom de timbre**), dis-je.' (FN3, 15r). Moran also mentions that the stamp had cost '**40 cents**' in the manuscript (FN3, 15r), which became '**un florin**' in the published version (1951, 168). Emphasizing the patriarchal model, Moran employs the same 'futur prophétique' as Youdi in his message to him: 'Tu laisseras tes deux albums à la maison' / 'Votre fi[l]s vous accompagnera' (FN3, 15r-16r). This 'prophetic future' (ET2, 22r) eventually became a 'prophetic present' (1955, 149; *Mo* 113) in the translation: 'You leave both your albums at home' / 'Your son goes with you' (1955, 149; *Mo* 113). After taking the two albums, he says he withdrew without a word. The exclamation mark in the manuscript ('sans un mot!', FN3, 16r) was omitted in the published version. And the paragraph ends with the remark that sorrow does more harm when dumb, which may be an allusion to Seneca's 'Curae leves loquuntur, ingentes stupent' ('Light sorrows speak, deeper ones are silent', from *Hyppolytus* Act 2, scene 3, line 607), which Beckett jotted down in the 'Super Conquérant' Notebook (UoR MS 2934, 1r), containing drafts of *Stirrings Still* (BDMP1).[114]

Paragraph 38 (FN3, 16r-18r)

Here and there, Beckett's mother tongue seems to influence his word choice in the manuscript, for instance when young Jacques' temptation of putting his most cherished stamps in his pocket is described with the verb 'chérir' (FN3, 17r), which is perfectly possible, but may have been judged too close

114   It is possible that Beckett's source for this quote from Seneca's *Hyppolytus* was again (see above) Michel de Montaigne's essay 'De la tristesse' (Montaigne 1965, 61). See also Van Hulle and Nixon 2013 (114).

to the English verb 'to cherish': 'les quelques timbres qu'il **chérissai[t]'**
(FN3, 17r) becomes 'qu'il **affectionnait**' in the published version, to become
'**cherished**' in the English versions (1955, 150; *Mo* 114). The lesson Moran
wants to 'impress' ('inculquer') upon his son is *'Sollst entbehren'* ['you must
abstain'] from Goethe's *Faust* (I.1548).[115]

Paragraph 39 (FN3, 18r-21r)

Whereas Goethe's Faust claims he is too young to be without wishes, this
Schopenhauerian negation of the will does seem to be the state Moran tries
to achieve momentarily when he lies down in his room (1955, 151; *Mo* 114).
In this condition he is able to pierce the 'veil of maya'[116]: 'C'est allongé, bien
au chaud, dans l'obscurité, que je pénètre le mieux la ᶠᵃᵘˢˢᵉ turbulence du
dehors' (FN3, 18r) ['It is lying down, in the warmth, in the gloom, that I best
pierce the outer turmoil's veil' (1955, 151; *Mo* 114-5)]. Moran is well aware
of the delusive nature of his sensations, 'qu'heureusesment je sais illusoires'
(FN3, 19r).

Paragraph 40 (FN3, 21r)

When Moran starts focusing on the man he is supposed to look for, he calls
him 'Molloy, or Mollose' (1955, 152; *Mo* 116). What may look like a hesitation
between two names in the published versions was less ambiguous in the
first layer of inscription of the manuscript, when Moran stated that Molloy
was simply more generally known as Mollose: 'Molloy, ~~plus généralement
connu sous le nom Mollose~~' (FN3, 21r). Beckett cancelled it and replaced
it by ᵒᵘ ᴹᵒˡˡᵒˢᵉ above the line in the same blue ink as the body of the text. This
Molloy or Mollose was no stranger to Moran.

---

115   See Kern 1959 (185). Beckett made extensive excerpts from Goethe's *Faust*
      shortly before he went to Germany in 1936 (Van Hulle 2006). The passage
      from which these words derive is the moment just before Faust makes his pact
      with Mephistopheles: 'In jedem Kleide werd ich wohl die Pein / Des engen
      Erdelebens fühlen. / Ich bin zu alt, um nur zu spielen, / Zu jung, um ohne
      Wunsch zu sein. / Was kann die Welt mir wohl gewähren? / Entbehren sollst
      du! sollst entbehren! / Das ist der ewige Gesang, / Der jedem an die Ohren
      klingt' (I.1544-51).
116   For a thorough examination of Beckett's reading of Schopenhauer, see Pothast
      2008.

Paragraph 41 (FN3, 21r-22r)

Nor was 'La mère Molloy, ^{ou Mollose}' (FN3, 21r) ['Mother Molloy, or Mollose' (1955, 153; *Mo* 117)]. At least, she was known to him in so far as such a son bears the stamp of his mother – 'dans la mesure où un tel fils en porte les traces' (FN3, 22r). The English version creates an interesting symmetry through the word 'stamp' (1955, 153; *Mo* 117), which is not that prominent in the French version: Molloy bears his mother's 'stamp' the way Jacques junior bears his father's.

Paragraph 42 (FN3, 22r-23r)

The name 'Mollose' seems more correct to Moran, but what he hears in his heart of hearts ('dans mon for intérieur') is the first syllable 'Mol', followed by a second that is smothered by the first. Beckett first wrote '~~étouf~~', interrupted the writing in the middle of the word, cancelled it and replaced it by '**cotonneuses**' (FN3, 22r) ['very thick, as though gobbled by the first' (1955, 153; *Mo* 117)]. In the manuscript, Moran gives more alternatives than in the published versions: 'oy', 'ose', 'ote', '**one**' or even 'oc' (FN3, 22r). The reading 'one' was later left out, possibly because 'Mollone' would have made the resemblance with 'Malone' too obvious. It is the insistence with which Gaber pronounces the name 'Molloy' that compels Moran to admit that 'Mollose' is wrong. In stylistic terms, the writing process shows a tendency towards a simpler vocabulary. For instance, Beckett deletes two verbs before he chooses the simple verb 'dire': 'Gaber avait **~~prononcé~~** ~~articulé dit~~ Molloy' (FN3, 22r) ['Gaber had said Molloy' (1955, 154; *Mo* 117)]. The idea that all these names might somehow relate to the same 'self', is slightly more prominent in the manuscript, where the word 'soi' is originally used in the following sentence: 'Que l'homme est peu d'accord avec **~~soi~~** ^{lui-même}, c'est fou' (FN3, 23r) ['How little one is at one with oneself, good God' (1955, 154; *Mo* 117).

Paragraph 43 (FN3, 23r)

Moran then starts enumerating what little he knows about Molloy, in a sequence of very short paragraphs that are all marked by indentations in the manuscript as in the published version. The writing is extremely smooth, without any cancellation in the first few paragraphs of the following enumeration.

Paragraph 44 (FN3, 23r)

Molloy had little room and his time was limited: 'Tantôt, prisonnier, il se précipitait vers je ne sais quelles étroites limites, tantôt, poursuivi, il se réfugiait vers le centre.' (FN3, 23r) ['Now, a prisoner, he hurled himself at I know not what narrow confines, and now, hunted, he sought refuge near the centre.' (1955, 154; *Mo* 117)]

Paragraph 45 (FN3, 23r)

Molloy panted.

Paragraph 46 (FN3, 23r)

Molloy did not so much walk as charge ('Il chargeait plus qu'il ne marchait', FN3, 23r), and yet he advanced but slowly. In addition to charging, Molloy swayed like a bear.

Paragraph 47 (FN3, 23r)

Molloy rolled his head, uttering 'des mots inintelligibles' (FN3, 23r) ['incomprehensible words' (1955, 155; *Mo* 118)].

Paragraph 48 (FN3, 24r)

Molloy was heavy, even misshapen and of a dark colour, without being black: 'difforme même'. ~~Et sombre sans être noir.~~ Et, sans être noir, de couleur sombre.' (FN3, 24r).

Paragraph 49 (FN3, 24r)

Molloy was always on the move.

Paragraph 50 (FN3, 24r)

This is how Molloy appeared to Moran: 'C'est ainsi qu'il ~~m'apparaissait~~ ^me visitait^' (FN3, 24r). The original verb 'apparaissait' recalls the Ur-scene in Dante's *Inferno* (Canto I), when Virgil appears to Dante as a faint figure, hoarse from long silence (see chapter 2.1, paragraphs 20 and 21; chapter 2.2, paragraph 106). The verb 'to appear' retains the suggestion that each Murphy, Molloy or Moran in Beckett's fictional world is narrated into existence by the next in line. The replacement of the verb by 'me visitait' still suggests that the 'visit' could also be a 'visitation' in the sense of the appearance of a fictional being. The point Moran tries to make is that Molloy was just the opposite of himself: 'Tout le contraire de moi, quoi' (FN3, 24r).

Paragraph 51 (FN3, 24r)

The autographic ambiguity between the narrative progression and the writing's progress or dysteleological 'gress' comes to the fore again in this shortest of paragraphs: 'Quant à savoir où il voulait en venir, je n'en avais pas la moindre idée' (FN3, 24r). More than the English translation ['what it was all about' (1955, 155; *Mo* 118)], the French original ['what he was getting at, what he had in mind, where he was heading'] questions the teleology of both Molloy's journey and (implicitly) of the writing process.

Paragraph 52 (FN3, 24r-25r)

Moran has no idea how old Molloy might be. It seems unlikely to him that Molloy would die a natural death, but then he wonders whether his own death would not at the same time be Molloy's: 'ne serait-elle pas ~~aussi~~ ^en même temps^ la sienne à lui?' (FN3, 25r), suggesting the identity of Molloy and Moran.

Paragraph 53 (FN3, 25r)

As to Molloy's face, Moran has no information.

Paragraph 54 (FN3, 25r-26r)

In the next paragraph, Moran admits that he is a contrivance: 'car j'étais une fabrication' (FN3, 25r). He even calls it the '**inénarrable menuiserie** qu'était mon existence' (FN3, 26r) ['the inenarrable contraption I called my life' (1955, 156; *Mo* 119)]. By translating 'inénarrable' by 'inenarrable', rather than the more regular translations 'indescribable' or 'hilarious', Beckett draws extra attention to the literal meaning of 'inénarrable', incapable of being narrated. And yet, this is exactly what this autography seems to be trying to do: narrate the inenarrable. Moran claims that he would not mention 'ces présences' (FN3, 26r) ['these apparitions' (1955, 156; *Mo* 119)] if he were to tell the story of his life, but then again that would be an auto*bio*graphy rather than an autography.

Paragraph 55 (FN3, 26r-27r)

The workings of this autography are hinted at in the deleted verb 'se recomposer': 'Et le Molloy que je ~~me recomposais~~ renflouais, ce mémorable dimanche, n'était certainement pas tout à fait celui de mes fonds' (FN3, 26r) ['And the Molloy I brought to light, that memorable August Sunday, was certainly not the true denizen of my dark places' (1955, 156; *Mo* 119)]. This reflexive 're-composition' implies more than just composition; it requires decomposition before it can be recomposed.

Paragraph 56 (FN3, 27r)

'Deux remarques' ['Two remarks' (1955, 157; *Mo* 119)], Moran writes, and he immediately starts a new paragraph. What follows, however, are not two but three remarks.

Paragraph 57 (FN3, 27r)

First: the resemblance between the 'Molloy I stalked within me' (1955, 157; *Mo* 119) and the '**réel** Molloy' (FN3, 27r) or '**vrai** Molloy' (1951, 177) ['true Molloy' (1955, 157; *Mo* 119)] cannot have been great.

Paragraph 58 (FN3, 27r)

Second: perhaps Moran is mixing elements of the Molloy described by Gaber with the 'Molloy ~~qui existait en moi~~ **récupéré** en moi' (FN3, 27r) ['my private Molloy' (1955, 157; *Mo* 119)]. Before arriving at this compact phrase in English, Beckett first tried a more literal translation: '~~the~~ ^my private^ **Molloy,** ~~thus retrieved within me~~' (ET2, 29r)

Paragraph 59 (FN3, 27r-28r)

Three: Moran concludes, with an epanorthosis, that there were three, no four Molloys at present: 'Il y avait en somme trois, non, quatre Molloy ~~au moment où nous en sommes~~' (FN3, 27r):

  1 'Celui de **mon intimité**' (cf. 'Celui de **mes entrailles**', 1951, 178);
      ['He that inhabited me' (1955, 157; *Mo* 119)]
  2 'la caricature que j'en faisais';
      ['my caricature of same' (1955, 157; *Mo* 119)]
  3 'celui de Gaber';
      ['Gaber's' (1955, 157; *Mo* 119)]
  4 'celui qui, en chair et en os, m'attendait' (FN3, 27r).
      ['The man of flesh and blood somewhere awaiting me' (1955, 157;
      Mo 119)]

To which he needs to add 'celui **du directeur**' (FN3, 28r; 'celui **de Youdi**', 1951, 178) ['Youdi's' (1955, 157; *Mo* 119)]. This multiplicity corresponds with Gide's account of the Dostoevskyan character, as opposed to Balzac's – and according to Gide the entire French school's – fixation on 'la constitution d'une unité psychologique' (Gide 1923, 167-8; see chapter 2.2, note 101). And the multiplicity was even more manifold in the manuscript, which speaks of an infinity of others, '**une infinité d'autres**' (FN3, 28r). But Moran limits himself to the 5 Molloys, which are called five versions, '~~ces 5 versions~~' (FN3, 28r), in the manuscript, thus presaging Daniel C. Dennett's 'multiple drafts model' of consciousness, which suggests that 'at any point in time there are multiple "drafts" of narrative fragments at various stages of editing in various places in the brain' (Dennett 1991, 113): 'These distributed content-discriminations yield, over the course of time, something *rather* like a narrative stream or sequence, which can be thought of as subject to continual editing by many processes distributed around in the brain, and continuing indefinitely into the future' (113). This indefinite continuation into the future accords with the 'continuing incompletion' that characterizes autography according to H. Porter Abbott (Abbott 1996, 20) and with the infinity of other versions ('une infinité d'autres', FN3, 28r), suggested by the manuscript.

Paragraph 60 (FN3, 28r)

Moran admits that he has just made three remarks, instead of the two he announced, which is also an interesting autographic moment, since – like Moran – Beckett originally announced two remarks and then wrote three remarks instead.

Paragraph 61 (FN3, 28r)

Moran feels equal to facing Gaber's report, but although he is ready to finally start the enquiry, the manuscript shows three false starts:

> ~~L'enquête~~ ~~commen~~ ~~allait commencer.~~ Il me semblait que l'enquête **allait** ~~commencer~~ **enfin commencer.** (FN3, 28r)

In its autograph version, this sentence can again serve as the counterpart to Clov's opening line in *Endgame*: 'Finished, it's finished, nearly finished, it must be nearly finished.' (*E* 6)

Paragraph 62 (FN3, 28r-30r)

At that moment, the sound of the gong fills the house. As a rule, Moran is at the table a few minutes before the appointed hour, fiddling with the cover and playing with the knife-rest. This echo of the knife-rest in Part I was not yet part of the manuscript (FN3, 29r), but added later: '**jouant avec le porte-couteau**' (1951, 179). Jacques junior does not show up for supper. In the manuscript, Marthe explains that he is not feeling well: '**Il ne se sent pas bien, dit-elle**' (FN3, 29r). But Moran is more occupied with his own joke on the French idiomatic expression for not feeling well: '**C'est donc moi qui ne**

suis pas dans mon assiette. Ce trait d'esprit me plut énormément, je j'en ris tellement que je me mis à hoqueter' (FN3, 29r). The expression (literally 'out of my plate') also occurs in Part I, when Molloy confuses east and west (see chapter 2.1, paragraph 11). There, Beckett opted for the English phrase 'out of sorts' to render more or less the same meaning, but that would have been a feeble substitute in the dinnertable context of Moran's part. Instead, Beckett left out the pun but highlighted its absence in the translation: 'I then made a joke which pleased me enormously, I laughed so much I began to hiccup' (1955, 158; *Mo* 120). Moran adds that the joke 'was lost on Martha' (1955, 158; *Mo* 120) ['fut perdu pour Marthe' (FN3, 29r)]. While she simply did not get it, the joke is completely lost on English readers because they are not even given the chance to get it – unless they consult the French version of *Molloy*, to which they are subtly directed. This is an instance where a textual scar, a remnant of something that was cut from the text, is deliberately left behind to mark the translation with the traces of a decision made during the transition from one language to another, which extends the notion of 'autography' to translation (see chapter 3.2).

Paragraph 63 (FN3, 30r-31r)

When Jacques junior finally comes down, he is scarlet in the face: 'Jacques était rouge' (FN3, 30r). The comparison to a cherry (^{'comme une cerise'}) was added, and replaced in the published version by a peony, 'comme **une pivoine**' (1951, 179). The boy still does not feel well.

Paragraph 64 (FN3, 31r-38r)

Jacques junior says he has a stomach-ache. He takes his temperature and shows his father the thermometre. In the manuscript Moran specifies that he has forgotten what it showed: '**Je n'ai pas retenu le chiffre**' (FN3, 34r). His son turns out to have a fever, but Moran says there is nothing wrong with him. He gives him an enema in the bathroom and suddenly feels an acute pain in his knee. After Jacques junior has gone to bed, Moran goes down to the kitchen and prepares a bowl of hot milk and a slice of bread and jam, after which the Minuit edition interrupts the narrative with a meta-comment, which is not in the manuscript: '**Il a voulu un rapport. Il l'aura, son rapport**' (151, 185) ['He asked for a report, he'll get his report' (1955, 164;

Mo 125)]. Moran sees Marthe sitting in her rocking-chair in the kitchen – to which the published version adds: '**On aurait dit une Parque en panne de fil**' (1951, 185) ['Like a Fate who had run out of thread' (1955, 164; *Mo* 125).

Paragraph 65 (FN3, 37v)

The longish paragraph is interrupted by an addition on the verso (FN3, 37v), which became a separate paragraph about the exceptional way in which Moran takes leave of Marthe, shaking her hand for a long time. Normally, he always left her 'off-handedly' (1955, 165; *Mo* 125). In the manuscript, Beckett did not immediately find the right word to express this manner, resorting to the usual method of leaving open a blank space with a question mark, in order not to interrupt the flow of writing: 'toujours avec   ?   ' (FN3, 37v), filling in the blank later: 'toujours avec **désinvolture**' (1951, 186).

Paragraph 66 (FN3, 38r-39r)

On the recto, the body of the text continues with the minutest details of how Moran dissolves a sleeping powder in the milk. Again, the Minuit edition adds a meta-comment that is not in the manuscript: '**Je ne lui ferai grâce de rien**' (1951, 187) ['He asked for a report, he'll get his report' (1955, 165; *Mo* 126)]. When Moran enters his room, he notices the two albums with stamps on his desk and looks for a few stamps at random. Again, in the manuscript Beckett does not waste any time searching for the right names and leaves open two blank ellipses: '**le .. mettons, le ...**, et quelques autres' (FN3, 39r). The blanks were filled in later: '**le Togo un mark carmin avec le beau bateau, le Nyassa dix reis de 1901**, et quelques autres. **J'aimais beaucoup le Nyassa. Il était vert et représentait une girafe en train de brouter la cime d'un palmier**' (1951, 187) ['the Togo one mark carmine with the pretty boat, the Nyassa 1901 ten reis, and several others. I was very fond of the Nyassa. It was green and showed a giraffe grazing off the top of a palm-tree' (1955, 165-6; *Mo* 126)].[117] Moran's son is already asleep and yet he wakes him up to make him drink the milk with the sleeping powder. A rare, tender moment ensues, which was prepared by the paralipomenon

---

117   In the second typescript of the translation, Beckett tried out the variant 'a giraffe ~~nibbling~~ grazing off the top of a palm-tree' (ET2, 36ar).

'~~Nous n'avions plus besoin de mots, pour l'instant~~' on page 38v. Beckett developed this scene on the verso pages 38v-39v, starting with the line: 'Nous n'avions plus besoin de mots, pour l'instant. ~~Nous~~ Il était d'ailleurs rare que mon fils me parlât le premier' (FN3, 38v) ['We had no further need of words, for the time being. Besides my son rarely spoke to me unless I spoke to him' (1955, 166; *Mo* 126)].

Paragraph 67 (FN3, 39r-40r)

Moran's nightly thoughts shirk the Molloy affair, and so does his pen: 'Et ~~de même~~ ^{ainsi} qu'alors ma pensée se refusait à Molloy, de même cette nuit ma plume' (FN3, 39r-40r).

Paragraph 68 (FN3, 40r)

With bitter satisfaction, Moran reflects that if his son would die during their journey, it would be none of his doing ('ce n'était pas moi qui l'aurais voulu', FN3, 40r).

Paragraph 69 (FN3, 40r-41r)

Moran goes down to the garden. In the manuscript, he refers to the place where he lives as '**mon village**' (FN3, 40r), which became '**Shit**' in the published French version (1951, 189) and '**Turdy**' in the English (1955, 167; *Mo* 127). He wonders what he would have done that day without his son, his job probably: 'Mon devoir peut-être' (FN3, 41r).

Paragraph 70 (FN3, 41r)

Moran is thoroughly disoriented by what he calls 'anéantissement' (FN3, 41r) ['nothingness' (1955, 168; *Mo* 128)].

Paragraph 71 (FN3, 41r-43r)

When he looks into the kitchen, Marthe appears to have gone to bed (FN3, 43r).

Paragraph 72 (FN3, 43r)

He goes upstairs again, stops at his son's door and hears nothing. The first layer of inscription is more explicit, stating that Moran has never heard anyone sleep so silently and still: '~~Je n'ai jamais vu personne dormir aussi silencieusement, q aussi immobile, que mon fils à cette époque~~' (FN3, 43r). Finally, he enters his own room.

Paragraph 73 (FN3, 43r-45r)

The first sentence of the new paragraph shows several cancellations and substitutions in the manuscript. Moran describes his exceptional situation: ready to go but without knowing where he is going, '**n'ayant** ~~rien arrêté à l'itinéraire au chemin à suivre et aux étapes expédients~~ [...] ~~insouciant des perspectives météorologiques~~' (FN3, 43r) ['having consulted neither map nor time-table, considered neither itinerary nor halts, heedless of the weather outlook' (1955, 169; *Mo* 129)]. Again, the text seems to be thematizing its own unplanned development – an 'écriture à processus' rather than 'à programme' (Hay 1986-7). He stuffs a minimum of clothes into his haversack.

Paragraph 74 (FN3, 45r)

Moran notes that conspicuousness is the ABC of his profession.

Paragraph 75 (FN3, 45r-46r)

Seen with his son, he would be taken for a widower and his antics would be viewed as 'un effet de la ~~douleur~~ ^viduité^' (FN3, 46r). The word 'viduité' emphasizes the text's autographic nature, given that – more than ten years after the writing of *Molloy* – Beckett wrote the scene in *Krapp's Last Tape* in which Krapp no longer remembers the meaning of the word 'viduity' (*KLT* 7).

Paragraph 76 (FN3, 46r-47r)

'**19.9[.47]**'
(FN3, 45v)

Beckett marked the date of this paragraph, in which Moran claims he is actually happy to leave his house, his garden and his village.

Paragraph 77 (FN3, 47r)

But instead of leaving, Moran keeps digressing, this time by going into detail about his enormous bunch of keys.

Paragraph 78 (FN3, 47r-51r)

Finally, the moment of leaving arrives. Moran takes action and wakes his son, who – according to the manuscript – is only 14 years old, '**n'a que 14 ans**' (FN3, 48). All of a sudden, he changes the subject and starts talking about his boater ('mon canotier', FN3, 48r) and the elastic he attached to it – another echo of Part I. It is almost midnight. They enter the little wood in the dark, not unlike the 'selva oscura' at the beginning of Dante's *Divina Commedia* (*Inferno*, Canto I, l. 2; see chapter 2.1, writing session dated '31.8.[.47]'). When Moran unlocks the wicket-gate, he turns back to have one last look at his house.

Paragraph 79 (FN3, 51r-53r)

Moran notes that his son always loses his way so easily whenever they walk together, yet when alone he seems to know all the shortcuts. When he sends him for instance 'on the road to V' (1955, 175; *Mo* 133) for grain, he is back in half the time Moran would have taken for the journey himself. In the manuscript the road to '**V**' (1951, 198) is 'la route de **B.**' (FN3, 52r).

Paragraph 80 (FN3, 53r-55r)

While Moran tells his son to walk behind him, he starts wondering whether Jacques is actually capable of keeping behind him. He imagines himself turning around one day 'pour constater sa disparition' (FN3, 53r) ['find him gone' (1955, 176; *Mo* 134)]. Facing the word 'disparition', Beckett marked the date on the verso.[118]

'22.9.[47]'
(FN3, 52v)

The text continues with Moran's observation that, a few minutes later, his son is no longer behind but in front of him.

Paragraph 81 (FN3, 55r-58r)

Moran explains that it is the summer holidays. Shortly after midnight strikes, he asks his son if he has brought his scout-knife. Just like in the case of the Timor stamp, Moran notes that he had given it to his son himself (1955, 178; *Mo* 136): 'C'est moi qui le lui avais donné' (FN3, 55v). This is the opening line of a sizeable addition on the verso about Jacques junior's extraordinary ability to remember the dates of battles and other exploits of the human race. In the first layer of inscription, their futility was emphasized more explicitly by speaking of unimportant dates and altitudes of mountains: 'les dates ~~sans importance et l'altitude des montagnes~~' (FN3, 55v). Again, the currency ('chaque **cent** qu'il recevait', FN3, 57r) is changed according to the pattern noted above: 'chaque **penny** qu'il recevait' (1951, 202) ['every penny he received' (1955, 179; *Mo* 136)]. When Moran orders his son to give him his pocket-knife, he has no doubt that young Jacques would at that moment have cut his throat with pleasure: 'Il m'aurait à ce moment-là sans doute volontiers égorgé, avec ce même couteau' (FN3, 57r).

---

118   As this example indicates, the dates in Beckett's manuscript do not always coincide with a paragraph break.

Paragraph 82 (FN3, 58r-61r)

After having dwelt upon the nonevents on the day of his departure, Moran now states that he has no intention of telling everything that happened to them during their journey to the Molloy country, 'le pays de Molloy' (FN3, 58r). Beckett needed a few attempts to write the ironic comment that this would be tedious: '~~Non pas que ce~~ ~~Ce serait même peut-être fastidieux~~ **Ce serait fastidieux**' (FN3, 58r). Moran calls his scrivening 'ce triste travail de clerc' (FN3, 58r) and, like Molloy, he speaks of a 'voice' in slightly more elaborate terms in the manuscript than in the published version:

> Et la voix à laquelle je me soumets ~~est d'abord une voix intérieure, qui m'ordonne~~ je n'ai pas eu besoin de Gaber pour me la transmettre, car elle est en dedans de moi, et elle m'exhorte d'être jusqu'au bout ~~un fidèle~~ ce ~~et serviteur, même~~ fidèle serviteur que ~~j'ai toujours été~~ je fus toujours, d'une cause qui n'est pas la ~~mienne.~~ **Si elle me dit** ~~cette même voix me dit~~ et de remplir patiemment mon rôle jusque dans ses dernières ~~ame~~ amertumes et extrémités, ~~non pas ce~~ comme je ~~voudrais que les autres remplissent~~ voulais, du temps de mon vouloir, que les autres remplissent les leurs (FN3, 59r)

> ['And the voice I listen to needs no Gaber to make it heard. For it is within me and exhorts me to continue to the end the faithful servant I have always been, of a cause that is not mine, and patiently fulfil in all its bitterness my calamitous part, as it was my will, when I had a will, that others should. (1955, 180; *Mo* 137)']

It is a voice that is 'not always easy to follow' (1955, 180; *Mo* 137), for which Beckett uses a key word in his aesthetics: 'c'est une voix assez ambiguë' (FN3, 59r; 1951, 180). The description turns into a meta-comment that also applies to Beckett's autography when Moran has the impression he will follow this ambiguous voice from now on, 'no matter what it commands' (1955, 181; *Mo* 137).

Paragraph 83 (FN3, 61r-62r)

Moran starts telling what little he knows about Molloy's country, 'si différent du mien' (FN3, 61r) ['so different from my own' (1955, 182; *Mo* 138)], as he considers this part of his 'pensum' (FN3, 61r) ['penance' (1955, 182; *Mo* 138)]. He would not be surprised if he deviated (or digressed in Shandyan fashion) from 'la marche ˢᵗʳⁱᶜᵗᵉ ᵉᵗ réelle des évènements' (FN3, 62r) ['the true and exact succession of events' (1955, 182; *Mo* 139)], and he refers to Camus' essay on the absurd, *Le Mythe de Sisyphe*, noting that not even Sisyphus is required to scratch himself always at the same appointed places, 'suivant ˢⁱ ˡ'ᵒⁿ ᵉⁿ ᶜʳᵒⁱᵗ **une doctrine en vogue**' (FN3, 62r) ['as the fashion is now' (1955, 182; *Mo* 139)]. Moran uses the verb **'récidiver'** for the Sisyphean labour, which recalls Molloy's 'Récidiver récidiver' on page 66r of FN2 (see chapter 2.1): for Moran, hope is 'hellish' (1955, 182; *Mo* 139), 'la disposition infernale par excellence' (FN3, 62r), whereas 'récidiver' or 'doing the same thing endlessly over and over' (1955, 182; *Mo* 139) fills him with satisfaction.

Paragraph 84 (FN3, 62r-64r)

Molloy's country is situated in the north, in relation to Moran's village, and is called Bally. The facing verso (FN3, 62v) shows a drawing of a square within a square (see Fig. 16). Moran expresses the size of the country's surface area in square miles ('5 ou 6 milles carrés') rather than kilometres (FN3, 63r). In the manuscript, he also explicitly addresses a French audience: 'C'était ce qu'on appelle en Fra ce que les Français appellent une commune on appelle en une com **En France** on appelle ça une commune' (FN3, 63r). In the partial typescript and the published version 'En France' becomes '**Dans les pays évolués**' (FT, 212r; 1951, 207) ['In modern countries this is what I think is called a commune' (1955, 183; *Mo* 139)], which at the same time obscures the cultural context and emphasizes the backward nature of the Molloy country. Bally is the hub of Ballyba, just like Moran's village 'Shit' is 'la perle ᶜʰᵉᶠ⁻ˡⁱᵉᵘ de Shitbaba' (FN3, 64r) ['hub of Turdyba' (1955, 183; *Mo* 139)]. The manuscript adds a passage about the inventor of this nomenclature – a huguenot priest – its falling into disrepute and subsequent revival, which was removed in the typescript (see chapter 1.2.1):

C'est ~~C'est~~ ^{Ce fut} un prêtre qui ~~a invint~~ inventé ^{inventa} cette ~~nomenclature~~
~~terminologie~~ nomenclature, au 16ème siècle, en pleine persécution
huguenote, et elle fut reprise, ~~au siècle suivante~~ [sic] abandonnée,
reprise et abandonnée, selon les fortunes des idéologies en
présence, jusqu'au triomphe définitif de la vraie croyance. (FN3,
63r-64r)

Paragraph 85 (FN3, 64r-65r)

Ballyba can boast a certain diversity: pastures, bogland, copses and towards
its confines some undulating aspects, '~~quasiment~~ ^{presque} rieurs, comme si
Ballybaba était content de ne pas aller plus loin' (FN3, 64r) ['almost smiling
aspects, as if Ballyba was glad to go nu further' (1955, 183; *Mo* 140)]. But
the major attraction of the region was a strangled creek. On the facing
verso, Beckett has drawn a few images that show a bean-like shape, which
may depict the strangled creek or the comma-shaped bacterium ('bacille-
virgule') mentioned a few pages later (paragraph 88 below). All inhabitants
agreed that their town was on the sea, like the inhabitants of Blackpool (in
the English versions, 1955, 184; *Mo* 140) and like the inhabitants of Isigny-
sur-Mer (in the French versions), 'à l'instar des Isignais' (FN3, 65r), they had
'Bally-sur-mer' (FN3, 65r) printed on their notepaper.[119]

Paragraph 86 (FN3, 65r-66r)

Moran notes that the population of Ballyba was small. The pastures are
meagre and strewn with boulders. So, this raises the major question about
the source of Ballyba's prosperity (1955, 184; *Mo* 140): 'D'où tirait donc
Ballyba ses richesses?' (FN3, 66r; see Fig. 17). As a good confidence-inspiring
narrator, Moran says: 'Je vais vous le dire.' But in the published versions this
confidence is immediately shattered when he adds: '**Non, je ne dirai rien.
Rien.**' (1951, 208) ['I'll tell you. No, I'll tell you nothing. Nothing.' (1955, 184;
Mo 140). This sentence was introduced as an addition in pencil to the partial
typescript (FT, 214r). The hand is somewhat atypical. Emilie Morin suggests

119   On the facing verso (64v), Beckett writes '(II) 83', which is probably a page
       count that includes the pages of Part II (18 pages in FN2 plus 65 pages in
       FN3; see chapter 1.1.1).

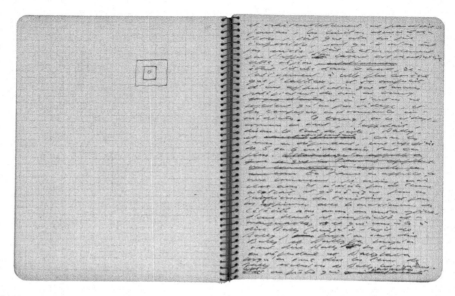

Fig. 16: The beginning of Moran's description of Bally, with a drawing of a square within a square on the facing verso (FN3, 62v-63r).

that the addition is Maya 'Mania' Péron's (2009, 89), but as indicated in chapter 1.2.1 we think it is possible that it is Beckett's and that the idea to cut the passage on Ballyba's economy was his.[120] In the manuscript and the typed layer of the typescript Moran does start explaining the economy of Ballyba, which is based on the excrements of its inhabitants: 'Je vais vous le dire. ^{Non, je ne dirai rien.} Des selles de ses habitants. Et cela depuis ~~les~~ ^{des} temps immémoriaux. Quelques mots à ce sujet' (FT, 214r).[121] And before Moran starts elaborating on the topic, he notes that this might be the last time he will have the opportunity to surrender himself to his passion for local particulars – echoing the 'demented particulars' in *Murphy* (*Mu* 11) and Beckett's own lectures, based on Gide's *Les Faux-monnayeurs*: 'En localisant et en spécifiant, l'on restreint. Il n'y a de vérité psychologique que particulière, il est vrai; mais il n'y a d'art que général. Tout le problème est

120 A translation of this excised passage is included in the Appendix.
121 For an early discussion of this thirteen-page omitted passage, focussing on the topic of faeces in relation to Buddhist thought and Schopenhauer, see O'Reilly 2006.

là précisément: exprimer le général par le particulier; faire exprimer par le particulier le général' (Gide qtd. in Rachel Burrows's notes, TCD MIC 60, 49). According to Burrows's notes, Beckett summarized this rule by referring to Stendhal and contrasting him with Balzac: 'Novel is a method of expressing general by means of particular. Stendhal expressed particular at expense of general, stated the type of the period. Balzac never stated a "cas particulier": expressed general at expense of particular' (TCD MIC 60, 49).

Paragraph 87 (FN3, 66r-71r; FT, 214r-218r)

The passion for local particulars also applies to the stylistic precision with which Beckett – following Flaubert's example – kept looking for the right word. Right from the start, in the first sentence about Bally's outstretched agricultural zone – 'Bally était entouré de toutes parts d'une zone maraîchère' – Beckett already used his fuchsia pen to change 'entouré de toutes parts' into 'ceinturé' in the typescript (FT, 214r). Every year thousands of tons of superb vegetables of all kinds were carted off from Ballyba to national and foreign markets. All of this was made possible thanks to the citizens' excrements. Moran realizes this may sound strange and immediately adds: 'Je m'explique' (FN3, 66r) ['Let me explain'], which brings him closer to Balzac's tendency to 'explain it all' than to Dostoevsky, who offers 'no explanations', according to Beckett's TCD lectures (Burrows, TCD MIC 60, 27). Starting from the age of two, every person who was a resident of Ballyba owed the agricultural organisation 'O.M.B' (Organisation Maraîchère de Ballyba) a certain amount of fecal matter every year, to be delivered on a monthly basis (which was changed to 'bi-mensuellement' in the typescript, FT, 214r). Beckett also changed 'Chaque personne' into 'every soul': 'Chaque <u>personne</u> âme' (FT, 214r; fuchsia ballpen). The expression 'ayant domicile' is changed into 'ayant un domicile' with a blue pencil in the left margin, where an alternative ('étant domicilié') is also suggested in the same blue pencil, possibly in Mania Péron's hand.

The required quantities of fecal matter to be delivered differed according to, for instance, the age or the temperament of the contributor, and special circumstances were taken into account, for example in case of sickness; 'en cas de maladie' was made more specific by means of an addition (fuchsia ballpoint) to the typescript: 'certaines maladies, telle par exemple une obstruction intestinale' (FT, 215r). Travellers had to compensate in cash what

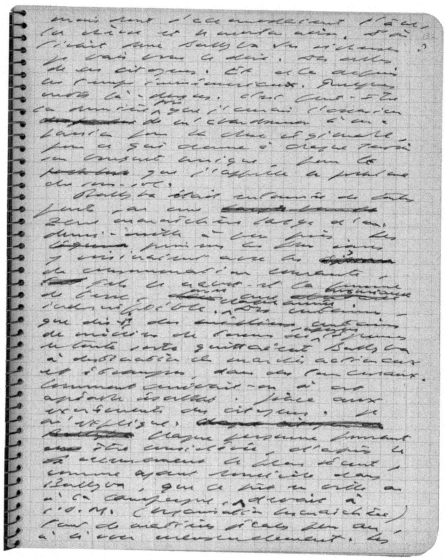

Fig. 17: After the question 'D'où tirait donc Ballyba ses richesses?' (l. 2-3), Moran starts explaining the economy of Ballyba, based on the excrements of its citizens (FN3, 66r).

they owed to the 'O.M.B.' in kind, up to 12 or 15 cents per kilo (FN3, 67r-68r). With the same fuchsia ballpoint pen, Beckett changed 'douze à quinze cents' into '~~onze~~ cinq à sept pence' in the typescript (FT, 215r), following the previously noted tendency. He also inserted an extra paragraph break at this point. The price was enough to dissuade most of the inhabitants of Ballyba from travel; most of the residents stayed home. In the manuscript, this was the end of a writing session.

'**25.[9.47]'**
(FN3, 67v)

The next writing session continues to expand on this topic with the introduction of a new character: the Obidil. The typescript adds an extra sentence, 'On l'appelait l'Obidil' (FT, 216r), emphasizing the act of naming. Certain officials could be absent without recompense for a period never exceeding 8 days, on the condition that they could justify their absence with a travel order. The Obidil was the person who delivered these travel orders, which were very difficult to obtain. He did not belong to any party or sect, according to the manuscript; in the typescript, '**secte**' has been replaced with '**confession**' (FT, 216r) ['denomination']. In the manuscript, the character's name was initially a different anagram of libido, **Odibil** (FN3, 68r), not yet its mirror image Obidil, as in the published text; in the partial typescript, the Odibil is already changed into **Obidil** (FT, 216r).[122] The Obidil was the only person who could decide whether a departure from Ballyba was indispensable or whether it could be avoided: for the word 'évité' the alternative 'écarté?' ['dismissed'] was cautiously suggested with a question mark in the left margin. With similar caution (a question mark) and with the same writing tool (grey pencil), the expression 'entrer en fonctions [sic]' (FT, 216r) was marked in the left margin to indicate that it should be written without an –s ('sans s?'). Before taking up office, the Obidil had to swear an oath, which obliged him to live virtuously, to wear only clothes of an immaculate whiteness, and never to leave his house: 'sortir ~~du bourg~~ de sa maison' (FN3, 69r) was changed with fuchsia ballpoint into 'sortir ~~de sa~~

---

122   This section is an expanded and revised version of the section '*Molloy* and the Obidil: Ballyba's Disnarrated Economy' in 'The Obidil and the Man of Glass: Denarration, Genesis and Cognition in Beckett's *Molloy, Malone meurt / Malone Dies* and *L'Innommable / The Unnamable*' (Van Hulle 2014, 27-31).

~~maison~~ ^{chez lui'} (FT, 216r). It was believed that only death could relieve the Obidil of his obligation to perform his duties (FN3, 69r). Even in his death throes, people consulted him when required with the same confidence and the same submissive air as when he had been in perfect health (FN3, 69r).

Having given this brief description of the Odibil, Moran in his capacity as narrator decides not to add anything because he says he will have the chance to behold the Odibil of Ballyba from closeby (FN3, 69r): 'Mais j'aurais l'occasion de voir de plus près cet étrange fonctionnaire et je n'ajouterai sur lui à cet endroit que les quelques remarques suivantes' (FT, 217r). The only extra information he gives in this connection is that the old Odibil has deceased. There are no applicants for the post (and here, the manuscript switches from Odibil to Obidil), but the entire population gathers on the large square in front of his house, where it designates its preferred successor. Again, a few changes are suggested in grey pencil:

> Il n'y avait pas ⟨**de candidats**⟩^{candidature} à l'office d'Obidil. Mais la population toute entière se réunissait, sur la **~~grande place~~** ~~grand'place~~ devant la maison de celui que la mort venait enfin de délivrer, et là, dans un délire de douleur d'abord, ensuite de joie, et au moyen de je ne sais quel instinct collectif, sans urne ni bulletins, ^{~~la populace~~} désignait en hurlant son successeur. (FT, 217r)

Whoever is empowered with the position of the Obidil does not have the right to reject it, but has to go and live in his new, splendid abode without delay, putting on the obligatory white clothes, white gloves and white hat, in order to appear on the balcony and present himself to the crowd: '**se montrer** à la foule' (FN3, 70r) became '**répondre aux ovations** de la foule' in the typescript (FT, 217r). In the typescript, Beckett hesitates between tenses when the Obidil is said to raise his head and let his gaze dwell upon the village and the vegetable fields: 'il lev<u>ait</u> ^{levât? oui} la tête et parcour<u>ait</u> ^{parcourût?} du regard la ville, les vastes champs de légumes et, plus loin, la maigre campagne' (FT, 217r). The additions in fuchsia ballpoint, followed by question marks, seem to be answered by the comment in pencil ('oui'), suggesting that the third-person singular imperfect (*imparfait*) is the correct tense. This would also determine the chronology of the fuchsia and grey pencil corrections. The description concludes with a simple statement that this should suffice: 'Et **cela suffira sur l'~~Obid~~**^{dib}**il**, pour le moment'

(FN3, 71r). The typescript shows a form of inertia in that the description cannot stop, as it were, and runs on until it is stopped definitively with a second reminder that this is enough ('cela suffit'): 'Et **cela suffit, sur l'Obidil**, pour le moment. Et quand je dis qu'il n'avait ni parti ni confession, je veux dire qu'à partir de son élection il n'en avait plus, comme il n'avait plus de famille. Et **cela suffit, sur l'Obidil**' (FT, 218r). When, later in the manuscript, Moran refers back to this description, he simply mentions it as the moment when he stopped talking about the Obidil, saying that he was going to see him from closeby (FN4, 47r; see paragraph 113 below).

Paragraph 88 (FN3, 71r-72r; FT, 218r)

After the paragraph closing with 'cela suffit', Beckett made a small 'to do' list for the narrator, indicating the order of things to tell:

> ~~Retour au sujet des voyageurs.~~ [Return to the subject of the travellers]
> ~~Le clergé.~~ [The clergy]
> ~~Les visiteurs.~~ [The visitors]
> ~~Retour à la merde.~~ [Return to the shit]
> ~~Le mode de collecte.~~ [The method of collection]
> Pas payée. [Not paid]
> Les W.C. de Ballyba [The toilets of Ballyba]
> question de maladie (choléra). [question of disease (cholera)]
> bacille-virgule. [comma-shaped bacterium] (FN3, 70v)

Beckett immediately started with the first two items in the list, returning to the subject of travel and the travel orders, which were not limited to public officials, military staff, and civic notables. Members of the clergy, numerous in Ballyba, were entitled to them as well, in principle. But in practice they never obtained any. One of the other measures undertaken to discourage them from leaving Ballyba was the residence bonus, 'la prime de séjour' (FN3, 71r). Studies on the influence of profession on the stools of the people had shown that the average clergyman did not defecate in quite the same manner as the layman, and that the fecal matter in particular contained substances of incomparable fertility, above all with regard to lettuce – 'surtout pour les **salades**' (FN3, 71r), changed to '**romaines**' (fuchsia ballpoint) in the typescript (FT, 218r) – which some people did not hesitate to attribute to the presence, in the bowl, of seminal elements going wherever they could. On the opposite verso in the manuscript, the word 'semen' (FN3, 70v) is written in blue ink and encircled; in the typescript, the annotator with the grey pencil has marked this sentence with an x and two vertical lines in the left margin (FT, 218r). The first line on the next page in the manuscript admits that this was a rather unscientific theory, no doubt (FN3, 72r).

'PARIS 9.10.47'
(FN3, 71v)

Here, the manuscript changes from blue ink to black ink. The date and place name on the verso are written in the same black ink. The text continues in mid-sentence, noting that the other theory regarded the phenomenon merely as an effect of the sacrament, extending its habitual grace to the digestive tract.

Paragraph 89 (FN3, 72r-73r; FT 219r)

Beckett started a new paragraph for the next item in the list: visitors and tourists were granted a three-day delay, after which they became tributary to the O.M.B. in the same way as the residents, obliging them to show compliance, in the form of a deposit slip, before leaving the territory. This was to answer to the case of those staying with private individuals, who did not make use of the public toilets that were directly linked up with the agricultural periphery through a radial system of cesspits, 'un système **de cloaques** rayonnants' (FN3, 72r) – changed into a sewage system, 'un système **d'égouts** rayonnants' in the typescript (FT, 219r). Moran promises he will come back to this topic: 'Nous y reviendrons d'ailleurs' (FN3, 72r) – to which Beckett adds in fuchsia ballpoint in the typescript: 'Je l'espère sincèrement' (FT, 219r). Because of the shortness of this three-day delay, the expression 'Ballyba weekend' had come to be used to refer to brief suspensions of pain spoiled by the certainty that it would soon come back: 'gâtée par la certitude que celle-ci ~~reviendra~~ doit bientôt revenir' (FN3, 72r). In the typescript, 'doit bientôt revenir' is underlined in pencil and the alternative '**Ne tardera pas à**' is added above the line (FT, 219r). Moran gives two examples, the first being people saying about a convalescent whose relapse seemed imminent: 'Le pauvre, ce n'est qu'un week-end de Ballyba' (FN3, 72r) – in the typescript: 'Pah, ce n'est que le week-end de Ballyba' (the alternative 'qu'un weekend de Ballyba' is suggested in pencil in the left margin; FT, 219r). The second example is possibly a comment on the Irish poet Austin Clarke, whom Beckett had ridiculed before in *Murphy* as Austin Ticklepenny: according to Moran, the metaphysical poet 'Clark' (FN3, 72r) – changed to 'Clarke' in the typescript (FT, 219r) – had gone as far as to compare the Ballyba weekend to the period of love that ranges from dating to mating: 'qui va depuis la rencontre jusqu'à l'accouplement' (FN3, 72r) – changed in fuchsia ballpoint in the typescript to: 'qui s'écoule entre les premiers baisers et le coït proprement dit' (FT, 219r). People cited other verses by him, composed at the age of '75' (FN3, 73r; changed to 85, 'quatre-vingt-cinq ans', in the typescript, FT, 219r), where, in a surge of irresistible optimism, Clark(e) applied the same comparison not only to human life, but to eternity itself: 'non seulement la vie elle-même ^{de l'homme}, mais l'éternité toute entière. elle-même' (FN3, 73r). The typescript reads: 'non seulement la vie de l'indiv[id]u, mais celle du genre humain' (FT, 219r). The word 'vers' is underlined (fuchsia ballpoint) in the typescript and linked to a note in the bottom margin suggesting that these 'verses' should be made more specific: 'spécifier' (FT, 219r) – according to Gide's principle 'exprimer le général par le particulier; faire exprimer par le particulier le général' (Rachel Burrows's notes, TCD MIC 60, 49; see paragraph 86 above) – but the entire passage was omitted from the published version instead.

Paragraph 90 (FN3, 73r-74r; FT, 219r-220r)

Beckett starts a new paragraph to elaborate the next two items on his list: 'Retour à la merde. / Le mode de collecte.' The collection of excrements took place on the first and fifteenth of each month. In the typescript, the word 'au' is underlined at two instances in blue pencil, 'au premier et au quinze', with an alternative suggestion in the left margin: 'le premier ou le quinze' (FT, 219r). The manuscript further explains that half the population started counting on the first, the other half on the fifteenth, but this sentence was omitted in the typescript. The word '**collecte**' is underlined in grey pencil in the typescript, and with the same characteristic caution the alternative '**ramassage?**' is added in pencil with a question mark in the left margin

(FT, 219r). The collection was done by means of enormous carts, pulled by grey asses, which halted at every house in front of which the dustbins were aligned, shining like silver, 'brillant comme de l'argent' (underlined in blue pencil in the typescript, FT, 220r). The bins were marked with a name, 'chacune **avec son nom**' (FN3, 73r) – changed in the typed layer of FT to 'chacune **avec s̶o̶n̶ ̶n̶ le nom de son propriétaire**', and subsequently in fuchsia ballpoint to '**portant** chacune **le nom de son propriétaire**' (FT, 220r). They had stood there[123] since the previous evening and people competed zealously to scrub and polish them for there was a fine on lack-lustre bins. The manuscript specifies that the fine was more or less high depending on whether the bins were very lack-lustre, moderately lack-lustre or a bit lack-lustre: '**plus ou moins élevées suivant qu'elles étaient très ternes, modérément ternes ou peu ternes**' (FN3, 73r); this was omitted in the typescript. The disposal team carried out a preliminary verification, paid out money, loaded the dustbins onto the carts, and replaced them with empty ones. A more scrupulous checkup took place at the warehouse. If everything was finished before noon, the afternoon could be spent at will. In the evening, a ball would be held in the main square (again the annotator with the blue pencil suggested '**grande place**' should be changed to '**grand'place**', FT, 220r). Sometimes it would fall on a Sunday, which in that case was deferred to the next day; this latter detail was typed out, but then deleted with fuchsia ballpoint.

Paragraph 91 (FN3, 74r; FT, 220r)

Still following the list on page 70v, the next paragraph deals with financial matters. At the end of the year the accounts were closed and whoever was in deficit had to compensate for it in cash, at the average rate of the previous year, '**au cours moyen** de l'année écoulée' (FN, 74r), which became three times as expensive in the typescript: '**au triple du cours moyen** de l'année écoulée' (FT, 220r). People who had exceeded their required contribution received certificates, which were very much sought after. They were of different colours, depending on the extent of merit. The yellow diploma from the O.M.B. was highly desirable as it facilitated access to certain high offices.

---

123 In the sentence 'Elles y̲ attendaient' the word 'y' is underlind in blue pencil with the corresponding note 'attend. là' in the left margin (FT, 220r).

Paragraph 92 (FN3, 74r-76r; FT, 220r-222r)

According to Moran's account, some odd characters managed to keep a small portion of excrements, even beyond their personal needs, and sold them to the deficient, doing good business: 'même au delà de leurs besoins personnels, ~~de sorte qu'ils le revendaient~~ et pouvaient en revendre [...] **aux déficitaires**' (FN3, 75r); in the typescript: 'même au-delà de leurs besoins ᵖᵉʳˢᵒⁿⁿᵉˡˢ, **au point de pouvo'r en faire un ~~petit~~** ᵛᵉʳⁱᵗᵃᵇˡᵉ [ˢⁱᶜ] **commerce**' (FT, 221r). In particular, Moran mentions a certain Colbert, famous throughout the entire country, who amassed a considerable fortune simply by eating and defecating. The 'fortune **considérable**' (FN3, 75r) was changed to 'fortune **coquette**' in the typescript and subsequently changed to 'fortune ~~coquette~~ ʳᵒⁿᵈᵉˡᵉᵗᵗᵉ' (FT, 221r) in black ink. The choice of the name 'Colbert' is remarkable and could be a reference to Jean-Baptiste Colbert, the famous Minister of Finances under Louis XIV, who reformed the domestic economy, introduced a fairer tax system and improved the mode of collection in France.[124] He also suffered from stomach aches, reducing his meals to bread soaked in broth. Whereas the reference to the poet 'Clarke' suggests a satire that is unequivocally linked to the local setting of Dublin and environs along the lines of Adam Winstanley's reading of the passage as a comment on '[Éamon] de Valera's vision of a self-sufficient Ireland' (Winstanley 2014, 97), the reference to Colbert delocalizes and widens out the complex satire, in line with other decentralizing strategies that Beckett employs in the two language versions of *Molloy*. Colbert is described as a skin-and-bones little old man, extremely haggard – to which the typescript adds that he was thought to defecate up to six or seven times a day: '**On lui attribuait jusqu'à six et sept selles**

---

124   Beckett may have known Alexandre Dumas the Elder's novel *Le Vicomte de Bragelonne ou Dix ans plus tard*, the third book of the *Three Musketeers* series, in which Colbert is a major character. Although there is no direct evidence that Beckett read *Le Vicomte de Bragelonne*, *Le Comte de Monte-Cristo* is referred to by Moran in *Molloy*: 'Oui, il devait se croire une âme de petit Dantès, dont les singeries lui étaient d'ailleurs familières, telles que les éditions Hatchet se permettent de les rapporter.' (1951, 203) ['Yes, he must have felt his soul the soul of a pocket Monte Cristo, with whose antics as adumbrated in the Schoolboys's classics he was needless to say familiar.' (1955, 179; *Mo* 137)] A general familiarity with Alexandre Dumas the Elder is also suggested in *Mercier and Camier*, when the two protagonists meet Watt: 'A pity Dumas the Elder cannot see us, said Watt' (*M&C* 92).

par jour' (FT, 221r). Colbert's cellars were full of fecal matter: **'matières fécales'** (FN3, 75r) became **'ses évacuations'** in the typescript, which was changed in fuchsia ballpoint to: **'ses ~~évacuations~~ ^{déjections'}** (FT, 221r). People suspected him of adulterating it with bird shit, as the manuscript specifies: **'On le soupçonnait de** les adultérer avec de la fiente' (FN3, 75r); in the typescript, this is changed to: **'Les méchantes langues disaient qu'il** les adultérait avec de la fiente ^{d'âne'} (FT3, 221r), with the addition of the marginal ass ('d'âne') in fuchsia ballpoint. Colbert sold his fecal matter at the official price as he obviously did not care about the yellow diploma. Every year larger quantities were demanded from him, but he always retained a surplus. He could have been charged with monopolization, restrictive actions could have been undertaken against him, but civil upheavals were feared: the rough version of the manuscript ('On **aurait pu** invoquer le ^{principe du} monopole, prendre contre lui des mesures de contrainte ^{on craignait les réactions populaires'}; FN3, 74v-75r) was rephrased in the typescript: 'On **n'osait** invoquer le principe du monopole **ni** prendre contre lui des mesures de contrainte, **de peur** ^{crainte} **des** réactions **populaires'** (FT, 221r; the underlining and the alternative 'crainte' are in blue pencil). At some point, the O.M.B. offered to buy all of Colbert's surplus. He refused. He was outraged, and made no secret of it that the annual deficits were paid for at a rate that was three times higher than the official one: 'il était outré, et ne s'en cachait pas, que le^s déficits annuels se **soldent** ^{? dassent} à un cours trois fois supérieur à l'officiel' (FT, 221r). With his fuchsia ballpoint pen, Beckett underlined '-dent' in 'sol<u>dent</u>' and indicated his uncertainty about the tense with a question mark in the left margin, to which the annotator with the grey pencil (most probably Mania Péron) added the correct ending ('[sol]dassent'). Moran then inserts a direct quotation: 'Je ne vends qu'aux déficitaires ~~pauvres~~ ^{indigents}, **proclamait-il'** (FN3, 76r). The typescript follows a pattern that emerges throughout the genesis of *Molloy*: the overly pompous tags ('proclamait-il') are usually changed to a more neutral register, as in this case in the typescript: 'Je ne vends qu'aux indigents, **disait**-il' (FT, 221r). Beckett thus took to heart the lesson of the 'Eumaeus' episode in *Ulysses* where Joyce hilariously ridicules the 'Bloomian' style of writing and its misguided efforts to never use the same tag.[125]

---

125 For instance: 'Mr Bloom unaffectedly concurred' (Joyce 1986, 509.365),
'Stephen rejoined' (509.384), 'Mr Bloom pursued' (510.409), 'Mr Bloom

Moran concludes that Colbert was loved by all the poor and explicitly repeats that the name of this extraordinary being was Colbert, adding that one day they would make a statue of him, hopefully seated: '**Assis j'espère**' (FT, 222r). Some people already talked about him as if he were a saint, praying: '**Saint-Colbert, chiez pour nous**' (FT, 222r). Again, this may be a reference to Jean-Baptiste Colbert, whose statue in front of the Assemblée nationale depicts him seated with the left hand raised.

Paragraph 93 (FN3, 76r; FT, 222r)

In accordance with the list on page 70v, Moran mentions he would like to devote a paragraph to the curious and ingenious toilet facilities of Ballyba – the typescript adds: 'avant de **quitter** ce sujet', which Beckett changed to 'avant de ~~**quitter**~~ ᵐ'ᵃʳʳᵃᶜʰᵉʳ ᵃ ce sujet' (FT, 222r; fuchsia ballpoint). But then Moran adds that the desire seems to have left him, adding (and hoping) that perhaps it would come back: 'Il reviendra peut-être. Je l'espère' (FT, 222r).

Paragraph 94 (FN3, 76r-78r; FT, 222r-224r)

Still following the list on page 70v, the text continues with the question of illness (the penultimate item on the list). Moran has to admit he does not know whether public health, exposed continuously to this accumulation of organic matter, was worse or better than elsewhere. Probably a few cases of typhoid or cholera morbus from time to time (corresponding to the 'choléra' and the 'bacille-virgule' mentioned in the list on page 70v). He presumes that, when you are born in excrement and when you live your entire life in

confided' (510.414), 'he inquired generally' (512.484), 'Mr B interrogated' (515.618), 'Stephen expostulated' (518.772), 'he ventured to say' (519.807), 'his good genius urged' (519.811), 'Stephen interposed with' (521.882), 'Mr Bloom dittoed' (521.884), 'Mr Bloom acceded' (521.889), 'Mr B. proceeded to stipulate' (525.1092), 'Stephen assented' (525.1104-5), 'remarked he audibly' (526.1116), 'Stephen retorted' (527.1160), 'Mr Bloom insinuated' (527.1163), 'Stephen interrupted' (527.1164), 'queried Mr Bloom' (527.1166), 'Bloom ejaculated' (532.1418), 'our hero eventually suggested' (537.1643). For a stylistic analysis of this chapter, see O'Neill 1996; see also Onno Kosters, 'From "Little Pills Like Putty" to "Three Smoking Globes of Turd": 'Eumaeus' as a Writers' Lab', paper presented at the James Joyce Symposium ('Anniversary Joyce'), London, June 2016.

its proximity, you can adapt to it quite easily (FN3, 77r). In the typescript, the adverb was omitted in the typed layer and added in the margin in blue pencil: 'on peut très ^bien^ s'en accom^m^oder' (FT, 222r).

Moran brings up the issue of visitors, which were few in number since people did not go to Ballyba for pleasure, fearing the robust reception of the excremental man, 'cette **robuste** acceptation de l'homme excrémentiel' (FN3, 77r; '**rude** acceptation' in the typescript, FT, 222r). Even Moran, in all his lucidity – '**tout lucide que j'étais**' (FN3, 77r) – approaches it with anxiety: '**je m'en approchais avec inquiétude**' (FN3, 77r). The affirmative sentence becomes a negative construction in the typescript ('**je ne m'approchais pas de Ballyba sans inquiétude**', FT, 222r) and the remark about his lucidity was cut in fuchsia ballpoint. Apart from the fuchsia revisions and the blue and grey pencil annotations, there are also a few annotations in black ink, usually corrections of basic grammatical mistakes, such as '~~de la~~ ^du^ cloaque' (FT, 222r).

The typescript introduces more paragraph breaks than the manuscript. Fond of catechistic reasoning, Moran asks himself questions and tries to answer them, for instance: he wonders what he knew about Ballyba's odour and can only reply that he does not know anything about that aspect of Molloy's country. As for testimonials about Ballyba by foreigners, he is only aware of one book in German, called *Letters from a Shithole* ('Briefe aus einem Scheissdorf'), by the balneotherapist Kottmann, inventor of the fecal bath as a treatment for mental illness: '~~Il préconisait l'emploi de bains d'excrément pour les maladies nerveuses~~ ^Il était l'inventeur du bain fécal pour ~~les~~ le traitement des maladies ~~nerveuses~~ mentales^' (FN3, 77v-78r). In the typescript, mental illness is replaced (with fuchsia ballpoint) by anguish (and the change from 'pour' to 'dans' is suggested in blue pencil): 'Il était l'inventeur du bain fécal **pour** ^dans^ le traitement **~~des maladies mentales~~** ^de l'angoisse^' (FT, 223r). Kottmann proposed to the O.M.B. to build reservoirs where the excrement could be stored for this kind of balneotherapy, before being spread out. Nothing would be lost for the crops. The O.M.B. objected that the bodies of the bathers constituted a source of pollution. But it had seemed to Kottmann that this was just a pretext and that the real motivations behind the refusal were entirely different. Moran does not expand on those real motivations. Instead, he just gives a very brief review of Kottmann's book, a scientific work that did not lack considerations of a more general nature, on the charm (*Reiz*) of Ballyba and the merits of its inhabitants. And as for impartial witnesses in the flesh, neither Moran himself nor anyone else that he knew of had ever encountered one.

In the typescript, Beckett added a one-sentence paragraph that clearly indicates the end of the set piece: '**Ici se termine ce ~~passage~~** ^{morceau} **d'anthologie.**' (FT, 224r)

Paragraph 95 (FN3, 78r-79r; paragraph 87 in 1951)

'**11.10.47**'
(FN3, 77v)

In the manuscript, Moran provides closure to his description of Ballyba's economy with a concluding '**Voilà**' (FN3, 78r): that then was a part of what he thought he knew about Ballyba when he left home (1955, 184; *Mo* 140). In the published versions, this is followed by only one sentence, stressing the unreliability of Moran as a narrator: 'Je me demande si je ne confondais pas avec un autre endroit' (1951, 208; FT, 224r) ['I wonder if I was not confusing it with some other place' (1955, 184; *Mo* 140)]. In the manuscript and the typescript,[126] however, Moran continues and mentions that this was only the first part of what he knew, the other part was about the bad condition of the means of communication, about the rustic customs, about the precautions foreigners were advised to take, '**etc.**' (FN3, 79r). But he decides not to dwell upon these aspects.

Paragraph 96 (FN3, 79r-80r)

Talking about Ballyba is almost impossible, Moran explains. About Shit he would be able to talk without passion and with precision, but not about Ballyba.[127]

126 'L'autre partie mériterait qu'on s'y arrête. Elle avait trait à la mauvaise condition des voies de communication, aux moeurs campagnardes, aux précautions à prendre par les étrangers, **etc.**' (FT, 224r)

127 On ne s'y arrêtera pourtant pas. Ces notions étaient certainement fausses pour la plupart. Il est des sujets qu'il est difficile de traiter. Ballyba en était un. Des auteurs dont _{je viens de} ^{j'ai failli} parler n'étaient pas forcément de mauvaise foi. On pouvait s'étendre froidement sur Shit, sans passion et avec précision. Pas sur Ballyba. Y être viciait le jugement, ne plus y ~~ren~~ être ne rendait pas le calme. N'y avoir jamais été semblait sa meilleure chance, à condition de ne

Paragraph 97 (FN3, 80r; paragraph 88 in 1951)

After this digression, Moran concentrates on the situation at hand: his son and he are leaving his village. The lane skirts the wall of the graveyard where Moran has a 'plot in perpetuity' (1955 184; *Mo* 141). The manuscript specifies that it had not been easy to get the authorization to erect a cross on it before his death: **'J'avais dû me batailler pour avoir l'autorisation de planter la croix'** (FN3, 80r).

Paragraph 98 (FN3, 80r-82r; paragraphs 89-96 in 1951)

Moran and his son walk for several days by sequestered ways, 'des chemins obscurs' (FN3, 80r). On the first day, Moran finds the butt of Father Ambrose's cigar in his pocket. This passage (paragraph 90 in 1951) is not part of the manuscript and was added later on. On the third day, Jacques junior gets his knife back. They make all kinds of detours at a snail's pace, and Moran openly admits that he was clearly not in a hurry to arrive (FN3, 82).

Paragraph 99 (FN3, 82r-84r; paragraph 97-98 in 1951)

Meanwhile, Moran gives thought to Gaber's instructions, preferably in foetal position, with his back against a tree (FN3, 82r). What is unclear to Moran is what he is supposed to do with Molloy once he is found, which is normally part of the instructions for a mission, as in other cases such as 'l'affaire Yerk'[128] (FN3, 83r) ['The Yerk affair' (1955, 187; *Mo* 142)]. The remark that he never had to deal with a woman was added in the published version (1951, 212). To the exclamation 'Oh je pourrais vous raconter des histoires' (FN3, 84r) the published version adds **'si j'étais tranquille. Quelle tourbe dans ma tête, quelle galerie de crevés. Murphy, Watt, Yerk, Mercier et tant d'autres'** (1951, 212) ['Oh the stories I could tell you, if I were easy. What

---

pas faire attention aux racontars. C'est là une chose que je ne savais pas en partant de chez moi. Je croyais que j'allais tout voir de mes propres yeux, me faire une opinion ne devant rien ~~pâ~~ personne, ajouter Ballyba aux endroits où j'étais passé. Serait-ce à qui ne l'a jamais ~~connu~~ subi que l'amour livre le mieux ses <u>secrets</u>?' (FT, 224r)

128   The first time 'Yerk' is mentioned, the name seems to be spelled 'York' (FN3, 83r).

a rabble in my head. What a gallery of moribunds. Murphy, Watt, Yerk, Mercier and all the others' (1955, 188; *Mo* 143)]. These names were not yet part of the manuscript. The subsequent, enigmatic epanorthosis is also a late addition that was not yet in the manuscript: **'Je n'aurais pas cru que – si, je le crois volontiers. Des histoires, des histoires. Je n'ai pas su les raconter'** (1951, 213) ['I would never have believed that – yes, I believe it willingly' (1955, 188; *Mo* 143)].

Paragraph 100 (FN3, 84r; paragraph 99 in 1951)

Moran is convinced that he has forgotten Gaber's instructions as to what needed to be done with Molloy once he was found.

Paragraph 101 (FN3, 84r-85r; paragraph 100 in 1951)

'**12.10.47**'
(FN3, 84v)

He considers sending Gaber a telegram from Ballyba, adding between brackets in the manuscript that he did not know there was no telegraph in Ballyba: '**(j'ignorais qu'il n'y eût pas de télégraphe dans Ballyba)**' (FN3, 85r). But he also tells himself that the longer it took him to find Molloy the greater his chances were of remembering what to do with him (1955, 189; *Mo* 144).

Paragraph 102 (FN3, 85r-89r; paragraph 101-102 in 1951)

One night, he feels a terrible pain in his knee: 'une douleur fulgurante ~~me s'empara~~ traversa mon genou' (FN3, 85r). He wonders whether it is the same knee as the one that hurt him in the bathroom just before he left, when he rubbed it 'avec ~~du Baume Bengué~~ ᵈᵉ ˡ'ⁱᵒᵈᵉˣ' (FN3, 86r; see Fig. 18). This brand name originally created a parallel with Molloy's story, who also rubs 'du baume Bengué' (1951, 87) on Ruth/Edith's rump – 'winter cream' in English (1955, 77; *Mo* 57) – but the change to 'iodex' undoes the symmetry between the two parts (see chapter 3.2).

Moran explains the pain away by telling himself that it is just a touch of neuralgia. The subsequent meta-comment was not yet in the manuscript:

Fig. 18: 'du Baume Bengué', deleted on page FN3, 86r.

'**Telle est la rapidité de la pensée. Mais ce n'était pas fini**' (1951, 215) ['Such is the rapidity of thought. But there was more to come' (1955, 190; *Mo* 145)]. The next day, however, he is unable to get up when he wakes with a mild erection. The erection is a supralinear addition in the manuscript: 'et la verge en légère érection' (FN3, 87r). Again, the published version adds an extra meta-comment to the effect that this detail is simply added to make things more lifelike: '**pour plus de vraisemblance**' (1951, 215), emphasizing the sustained engagement with the techniques of realist fiction.

Paragraph 103 (FN3, 89r)

Moran considers what he should do if his leg gets worse.

Paragraph 104 (FN3, 89r)

'**14.10.47**'
(FN3, 88v)

He writes a transitional paragraph in which he notes that he will not expound his reasoning, but that its conclusion enabled the composition of the following passage (1955, 192; *Mo* 147).

Paragraph 105 (FN3, 90r – FN4, 04r)

Moran sends his son to the nearest village – which is not called '**Hole**' (1951, 218; 1955, 193; *Mo* 147) but '**Carrick**' (FN3, 90r)[129] in the manuscript – to buy a bicycle for up to an amount that is expressed in dollars, before it is

129 Further on, 'Carrick' is spelled '**Carrig**' (FN3, 94r). There are several places called Carrick in Ireland and Beckett himself used to play golf at

converted to pounds ('**40 dollars**', FN3, 90r; '**cinq livres**', 1951, 218) ['five pounds' (1955, 193; *Mo* 147)]. Moran asks Jacques if he is content: '**Es-tu content?**' (FN3, 90r), which – according to the pattern noted above – is turned into indirect speech in the published version: '**Je lui demandai s'il était** content' (1951, 218). According to the manuscript, Carrick is 'à 15 **kilomètres** d'ici' (FN3, 91r), whereas Hole (in the published version) is 'quinze **milles** d'ici' (1951, 218) ['fifteen miles away' (1955, 193; *Mo* 147)]. Moran frequently interrupts his narrative – not unlike Hamm and his chronicle in *Fin de partie / Endgame* – to make meta-comments such as: 'Que c'est soulageant, un peu de dialogue de temps en temps' (FN3, 91r) ['What a boon it is from time to time, a little real conversation' (1955, 193; *Mo* 147)]. Moran asks his son to listen carefully for he will not say it twice: '**car je ne le dirai pas deux fois**' (1951, 221). This was not yet in the manuscript, in which Moran says and writes that he will repeat himself: 'Je répète. Je répétais' (FN3, 94r). After which the published version adds again: '**Moi qui avais dit que je ne répéterais pas**' (1951, 221) ['I who said I would not repeat' (1955, 196; *Mo* 149)]. And then he asks his son to repeat what he has just said, adding that he has to keep a distance for his breath stinks. Here, the manuscript shows a short aposiopesis: '**Tu ne . .**' (FN3, 94r). These first two words of another reprimand are left out in the published version, which only says what Moran refrains from saying, namely that his son does not brush his teeth and complains of abscesses: 'J'allais dire, Tu ne te laves pas les dents et tu te plains d'avoir des abcès, mais je me retins à temps' (1951, 221). He lets his son repeat the assignment, to go to Carrick/Hole, and continues interrogating him: 'Pour quoi faire.' '~~Pour acheter une bicyclette~~', his son replies. But then Beckett cancels this sentence and makes Moran say that he cannot go on: 'Non, je ne peux pas **continuer**' (FN3, 94r), which is even shorter in the published version: '**Non, je ne peux pas**' (1951, 221). This moment prefigures the famous last line of *The Unnamable* ('you must go on, I can't go on, I'll go on', *Un* 134) and the subsequent, late insertion of 'je ne peux pas continuer' in the closing line of the 1971 Minuit edition of *L'Innommable*: 'il faut continuer, *je ne peux pas continuer*, je vais continuer' (Beckett 1971b, 212; emphasis added; Van Hulle and Weller 2014, 45). In the manuscript of *Molloy* this 'I can't go on' is striking because Beckett actually

Carrickmines Golf Club; Carrig is more directly derived from the Irish word 'caraig', 'rock'.

crosses out the continuation of the conversation: 'Pour quoi faire. ~~Pour acheter une bicyclette~~ Non je ne peux pas continuer' (FN3, 94r). But then both he and Moran go on nonetheless.

'16.10.47'
(FN4, front flyleaf)

The text continues on the front flyleaf of the fourth notebook, mentioning that in the end Moran almost chases away his son, who takes to his heels.

'17.10.47'
(FN4, front flyleaf)

On the inside of the front flyleaf, next to the date, Beckett has written **'Lampe !'** On the corresponding recto, Moran mentions the 'lanterne' ['lamp' (1955, 198; *Mo* 149)] of the bicycle, but immediately adds that he would only need it later, 'pour les courses nocturnes **et d'hiver**' (FN4, 03r). This reference to winter was left out in the published version: 'to light his way in the night' (1955, 198; *Mo* 151).

Paragraph 106 (FN4, 04r-18r)

The day seems very long to Moran. This sentence echoes the odd sentence 'Venus has a long day', which Beckett excerpted from the article 'Is There Life in Other Worlds?' by Dr H. Spencer Jones in the 'Whoroscope' Notebook (UoR MS 3000, 63r; see chapter 2.1, paragraph 20).[130] Moran misses his son. After a while, a man appears, wearing a heavy coat and leaning on a massive stick, who asks Moran to give him a piece of bread. His accent is that of a foreigner, according to the manuscript. Later, Beckett added **'ou d'un homme qui a perdu l'habitude de la parole'** (1951, 226) ['or of one who had lost the habit of speech' (1955, 200; *Mo* 153)], alluding again to the moment Virgil appears to Dante, 'per lungo silenzio [...] fioco' (see chapter 2.1, paragraph 20). And when Moran says to himself, 'C'est un étranger', he adds

---

130 'Venus has a long day; its length is not known exactly but it is somewhere about thirty of our days. This explains the great difference between the midday and midnight temperatures on Venus' (Spencer Jones 1939, 44).

(only in the manuscript), that it is not necessarily a question of nationality: **'Je ne pensais pas seulement à la question de nationalité'** (FN4, 09r). Moran gives him some bread, takes a look at his stick, and the man leaves. Before he concludes his report on the second day, he needs to note one incident – for which he starts a new paragraph.

Paragraph 107 (FN4, 18r-30r)

Moran has just lit his fire when he is hailed by a man, whose face resembles Moran's (FN4, 21r) and who asks him if he has seen an old man with a stick pass by. In the manuscript, the man adds that it is a satyr and that he violates girls: **'C'est un satyre, dit-il, il viole les fillettes'** (FN4, 23r). Moran says he has not seen the old man, whereupon the man orders him to show his papers (only in the manuscript): **'Montrez-moi vos papiers'** (FN4, 23r). A little later, the man is stretched on the ground, 'la tête en bouillie' (FN4, 23r) ['his head in a pulp' (1955, 207; *Mo* 158)]. The inexplicable act of violence recalls Beckett's lectures at Trinity College, Dublin, when – according to Rachel Burrows's notes – he referred to two concepts introduced by Gide to discuss the role of irrationality in literature: the 'geste gratuit' (TCD MIC 60, 39) and the 'crime immotivé' (14). Beckett valued acts that 'cannot be reduced to motive', as Burrows noted (TCD MIC 60, 14). With regard to the excessive explanations à la Balzac, Beckett criticizes the 'Snowball act' (see chapter 2.1, paragraph 7), which releases purely mechanical setting of circumstance: 'enchaînement mécanique fatale [sic] de circonstances', with its 'arbitrary direction' and 'constant acceleration to crisis' (TCD MIC 60, 40; see above, chapter 2.2, paragraph 7). The notions of the inexplicable 'geste gratuit' and the 'crime immotivé' seem to inform Moran's gratuitous act of violence. He cannot explain what happened. It would have been a nice piece of reading, he says, but at this stage of his report he does not intend to '~~commencer à inventer~~ me lancer dans **la littérature**' (FN4, 24r) ['give way to literature' (1955, 207; *Mo* 158)].

Moran himself only has a few scratches. His leg is bending normally again. By the time he has dragged the man into the shelter, Moran's leg is stiffening again. At dawn, he drags him into the copse, dismantles the shelter and throws the branches over the body. He strikes camp and makes himself comfortable a little further, on the crest of a rise ('au sommet d'un monticule', FN4, 27r). On the verso, Beckett adds a remark that recalls his observations on visual art in his German diaries, namely that the land and the clouds gently led the eyes to the camp, 'as in a painting by an old master' (1955, 210; *Mo* 160): 'Et je fis cette remarque curieuse, que la ~~campagne~~ terre ici, ~~était ainsi disposée~~ et même les nuages du ciel, de quelque côté qu'on regardât, étaient disposés de façon à amener doucement les regards vers le camp, à la manière **d'un tableau de maître**' (FN4, 27v). To kill time, he asks himself a number of questions, such as: What had happened to the blue felt hat? Whereas the published version notes that this is followed by a '*Réponse*' (1951, 238), the answer in the manuscript is: '**Néant**' (FN4, 29r). To the question whether his son would denounce him, Moran's answer (only in the manuscript) is that you never know with Jacques: '~~Avec mon fils on ne pouvait être sûr de rien.~~ **Impossible de savoir**' (FN4, 29r). To the last question how it was to be explained that after the incident he felt much as usual, the answer (only in the manuscript) is again: '**Néant**' (FN4, 30r).

Paragraph 108 (FN4, 30r)

It took Beckett several attempts (ten lines of deleted text) to write the first sentence of the next paragraph, that is, to let Moran explain that these questions were separated by more or less prolonged intervals of time.

Paragraph 109 (FN4, 30r-31r)

Moran tries to imagine himself at the moment he wrote 'tout ce passage' (FN3, 30r) and claims that it was written with a firm hand ('d'une main ferme'). If this passage refers to the passage of the questions, it is indeed remarkable how smoothly it was written in Beckett's manuscript, with very few deletions. This autographic moment is even extended in the epigenesis, when Moran's words 'Me **rapportant** maintenant en imagination à l'instant présent' are translated as '**Translating** myself now in imagination to the present moment' (1955, 212; *Mo* 161; see chapter 3.1 and 3.2).

Paragraph 110 (FN4, 31r-36r)

Thus the third day wears away and around 7 p.m. his son arrives with a bicycle, about which Moran says he could easily write 4000 words. Jacques junior asks his father what happened to his leg. Moran says he had a fall ('je suis tombé'), which is followed by Moran's claims that he would have experienced it as a relief to be arrested and collared, even in front of his son: **Au fond, je m'en foutais qu'on m'arrête. Je sais que que**[131] **cela m'aurait été d'un grand soulagement, qu'on vienne me mettre la main au collet, oui, devant mon fils, à l'instant même.** (FN4, 32r-33r) This passage was omitted and instead, the published version reads: '**Je cherchai le nom de la plante née des éjaculations des pendus et qui crie quand on la cueille**' (1951, 241) ['I tried to remember the name of the plant that springs from the ejaculations of the hanged and shrieks when plucked' (1955, 213; *Mo* 162)]. The name he is looking for is mandragore/mandrake. The association between the fall and this plant becomes clear in Beckett's play *En attendant Godot*, written in the period between the writing of *Molloy* in 1947 and its publication in 1951. In the play, Gogo suggests to Didi they could hang themselves, to which Didi replies that it would give them an erection ('Ce serait un moyen de bander'), with all that follows: 'Là où ça tombe il pousse des mandragores' (Beckett 1999b, 21) ['Where it falls mandrakes grow' (*WFG* 13)]. The French version contains a nice pun ('ça tombe'/'sa tombe'), suggesting the 'wombtomb' theme of life and death, and explaining Moran's association between the fall ('je suis tombé') and the mandrakes.

Jacques junior tells his father that the bicycle cost 30 dollars and that he has spent the other 5 on food, after which Moran starts ranting again: '**tu as dépensé 5 dollars? dis-je. Oui, dit-il. C'était inoui [sic]. A quoi? dis-je. A manger, dit-il. Tu t'es empiffré pour 5 dollars, dis-je, ~~et moi qui ai failli mourir de faim~~** ~~penda~~ **pendant que moi je mourais de faim en t'attendant**' (FN4, 33r). This passage is omitted in the published version, which replaces it with the comment '**Assez, assez**' (1951, 241) ['Enough, enough' (1955, 213; *Mo* 163)].

---

131   The word 'que' is inadvertently written twice in the manuscript.

Again, in comparison with the autograph manuscript, the replacement reads like a meta-comment that characterizes the autographic nature of this text. In the end, they manage to get to Ballyba on the bicycle.

Paragraph 111 (FN4, 37r-42r)

Moran admits that he would not have got there without his son. He repeatedly notes that he thinks a lot about himself ('Je pensais beaucoup à moi', FN4, 38r), and that they arrived in Ballyba without knowing it. One day, Moran sees a shepherd – which is where the writing session ends.

'24.10.47'
(FN4, 37v)

The new writing session of 24 October starts with the description of the black sheep. Moran writes a long pastoral description to simply say that the shepherd indicates the direction to Bally, to the north.

Paragraph 112 (FN4, 42r)

That night, Moran has a violent scene with his son. He insists that this may be important.

Paragraph 113 (FN4, 42r-53r; paragraphs 113-120 in 1951)

But in the next paragraph he denies it, saying they have had many scenes like that before: 'Non, je ne sais pas, j'ai eu tant de scènes avec mon fils' (FN4, 42r-43r). At the time, it must have seemed a scene like any other, but the next morning Moran realizes his mistake. His son has left him, with a considerable amount of money. He has only left his father a little sum (**'cinq dollars'**, FN4, 45r; **'quinze shillings'**, 1951, 250; ['fifteen shillings' (1955, 221; *Mo* 169)]), just enough to keep him going until help arrives. For several days, he remains where he is, in Ballyba but still far from Bally, which he can see in the distance. At that moment Moran suddenly brings up the subject of the Obidil (see paragraph 87 above). After Beckett removed the passage about Ballyba's economy (see FN3 66r-80r; FT 214r-224r) he did not cut this reference to the Obidil, thus creating a disruption in the narrative. The Obidil's story, which remains 'unactualized' in the text, is a special case of disnarration, for it *was* actualized in the manuscript.[132] Here, on page 47r of the fourth notebook, Moran refers back to this description and simply mentions it as the moment when he stopped talking about the Obidil, recalling that he was going to see him from closeby. Now he can only say that eventually he never saw him. In the published versions of the text, this simple *announcement* that he was going to see him was changed into a *longing*:

> Et cet Obidil, dont **je me suis arrêté** de parler **en disant** que **j'allais le** voir de plus près, **et** bien je ne le vis jamais, ni de près ni de loin, et il n'existerait pas que je n'en serais que modérément **surpris**. (FN4, 47r).

> Et cet Obidil, dont **j'ai failli** parler, que **j'aurais tellement voulu** voir de près, **eh** bien je ne le vis jamais, ni de près ni de loin, et il n'existerait pas que je n'en serais que modérément **saisi**. (1951, 251)

> [And with regard to the Obidil, of whom I have **refrained from** speaking, until now, and whom I so **longed to** see face to face, all I can say with regard to him is this, that I never saw him, either face to face or darkly, perhaps there is no such person, that would not greatly surprise me. (1955, 222; *Mo* 170)]

132 For a more elaborate discussion of de- and disnarration in Beckett's 'trilogy' of novels, see Van Hulle 2014a. In 'Denarration in Fiction: Erasing the Story in Beckett and Others' (2001) Brian Richardson defines denarration as 'a kind of narrative negation in which a narrator denies significant aspects of her narrative that had earlier been presented as given' (168). He contrasts this working definition with Gerald Prince's concept of the 'disnarrated', denoting 'possible events that, though referred to, remain unactualized in a text' (169). Richardson subsequently identifies a series of instances of denarration and presents them as a continuum of narrative negation. This continuum ranges from denarration 'light' to substantial narrative negations as forms of 'extreme narration' (Richardson 2006). The 'unactualized' story of the Obidil could be regarded as an example of what Gerald Prince, by way of Elyane Dezon-Jones, refers to as 'predisnarration', i.e. 'sequences of events, story-like passages that the teller of a narrative chooses to eliminate from a public, official "final" version of that narrative' (Prince 1988, 8).

In the manuscript, Moran says he has stopped (rather than refrained from) speaking of him, announcing that he was going to (rather than longing to) see him from close by (FN4, 47r). The difference between the variant readings 'stopped' and 'refrained from' may seem small, but from a narratological point of view it is as big as the difference between narration and disnarration.

In the published version, Moran introduces a character and no sooner has he uttered his name than he doubts this person's existence within the storyworld. Instead of an Obidil whom he confidently expected to be seeing soon, the character becomes the object of yearning or even desire. The obvious link with libido suggests a parody of Freud's theories (see for instance O'Hara 1992) and other works on psychology which Beckett read in the 1930s (see Feldman 2006). Possibly, even the very act of cutting the passage on Ballyba's economy – thirteen pages in FN3, eleven pages in FT – can be read as a parody of forms of repression, but what is being disnarrated here is more than a reference to Freud.

With regard to the excremental aspect of Ballyba's economy, Irish literature has a long tradition of scatological satire, Jonathan Swift's poems such as *The Lady's Dressing Room* and *Cassinus and Peter* being among the most famous examples. The tension between the immaculate appearance of the Obidil as the mirror image of libido versus the shit that keeps the economy going is just as strong as the tension in Swift's poems between the idealized Celia and the realization that she is also merely a human animal – 'Oh! Celia, Celia, Celia shits!' (Gilmore 1976, 38).

Apart from his capacity as a satirist, Swift was the Dean of Saint Patrick's Cathedral in Dublin, the city after which Bally is probably modelled (Morin 2009, 62). There are instances in the manuscripts of the three novels that corroborate this hypothesis. In the earliest French manuscript of *L'Innommable*, Beckett originally wrote 'Baile atha Cliath'[133] (followed by the narrator's disclaimer that he cannot guarantee that it is spelled correctly). The Irish name for Dublin ('town of the hurdled ford') was later replaced by 'Bally'. It is not surprising that Bally is modelled after Dublin, but this direct connection does strengthen the hypothesis that what is being disnarrated in *Molloy* is related to a historical economic context (see Winstanley 2014). Following Adam Winstanley's suggestion to read the satire alongside Joseph

133   MS-HRC-SB-3-10, *BDMP2*, FN1, 5v.

Hone and Mario M. Rossi's biography *Swift: or, The Egotist* (1934), to which Beckett assisted (Pilling 2011, 238), it may be useful to zoom in on Hone and Rossi's suggestion that 'not only does he [Swift] urge upon his countrymen the duty of cultivating their own garden, but he proposes to nullify English law within the Constitution' (260). To a student and ex-lecturer of French literature at TCD, the cultivation of one's own garden would most probably have sounded like a direct quotation from Voltaire's *Candide*. This Voltairian element adds an extra intertextual dimension to the complex parody. Beckett was familiar with Voltaire's satirical sneers, as indicated by the references to the *Lettres d'Amabed* in his Italian Bible, marking scatological passages to which Voltaire draws attention, for instance Ezekiel 4:15: 'Then he said unto me, Lo, I have given thee cow's dung for man's dung, and thou shalt prepare thy bread therewith' (Van Hulle and Nixon 2013, 181-3).[134]

The Voltairian twist to the Swiftian satire also complicates the religious dimension to Beckett's omitted passage, which seems to include a critique of the presence of Catholicism in Irish politics and economics of the 1930s. For in addition to the many ways in which the figure of the Obidil may be interpreted, several aspects of his description (the obligation to live virtuously, the whiteness of his clothes, the crowd gathering on the large square, his appearances on the balcony, the fact that he is usually only replaced when he dies) suggest a reference to the pope. From such a papal figure, one might expect that his function would be the prerogative to decide, for instance, who can 'travel' to heaven and who cannot; and against such a celestial background, the excrement-based economy of Ballyba by extension might even stand for earth as a whole, 'die Erde' in German, which Beckett turned into 'merde' when he quoted Goethe's *Faust* with a twist in the addenda to *Watt*: 'Die Merde hat mich wieder' (*W* 219).

But as in Swift's line 'Oh! Celia, Celia, Celia shits' the revered Obidil's function, within the satirical context of the omitted passage, seems to be related to much more mundane or down-to-earth business. The link between religion (the pope-like figure of the Obidil) and economic policy (the excrement-based economy of Ballyba) is perhaps not self-evident at first sight, but as Geert Lernout notes, the Catholic hierarchy and the Irish movement for home rule were inextricably intertwined (2010, 42). This close relationship, which began in 1878 with the death of the conservative cardinal Cullen (42),

134 See the *BDL*, http://www.beckettarchive.org/library/SAC-BIB.html.

was 'instrumental in establishing the equation of Irishness and Catholicism [...] that would have a crucial influence on the formation of the new Irish state in 1922' (48). This interconnection was still in place when, in the 1930s, Ireland chose to pursue a policy of economic protectionism and to build an 'indigenous' industry, 'producing primarily for the home market' (Neary and Ó Gráda, 250).

The focus on indigenous production, sprung from the land, was a theme Beckett had already tried to satirize before. In 1934, he had been toying with the idea of a satire, modeled after Daniel Defoe's *The True-Born Englishman* – 'A true-born Englishman's a contradiction, / In speech an irony, in fact a fiction' (Defoe 1889, 195). With 'a strong weakness for oxymoron' (*MPTK* 32), Beckett's 'Trueborn Jackeen' notes not only focus on the ethnic mixture that constitutes the contradiction of a 'trueborn' Dubliner; they also contain details about the effects of insularity, notably the retarded development of Irish flora and fauna after the ice age (TCD MS 10971/2/8).

To the extent that these are all elements of narratives connected to a homeland or hometown (Bally – Baile Átha Cliath – Dublin), they partially define Molloy's identity. And their omission may consequently be relevant in connection with what Eric P. Levy has termed the 'repudiation of selfhood' (2007, 101). Evidently, there are many possible answers to the question what is being satirized or parodied in the omitted passage, and why it was eventually omitted. But from a narratological perspective, the most pressing question is why it was *not entirely* omitted. For Beckett deliberately left a few traces. While the omitted passage with its prospective encounter with the Obidil was 'disnarrated' (a possible event that remains unactualized in the text), Beckett gave the act of *dis*narration a *de*narrative twist. As a result, the omitted passage is part of what Daniel Ferrer calls 'mémoire du contexte' (2011, 120). Beckett could easily have refrained from including the question 'What then was the source of Ballyba's prosperity?' but he chose to mark the long omitted answer by leaving a textual scar. What remains of the whole episode is the mere promise of its telling ('I'll tell you'), and the epanorthosis 'No, I'll tell you nothing' (1955, 184; *Mo* 140). And the same goes for the sudden mention of the Obidil in notebook 4 (FN4, 47r), which is another textual scar.[135]

135   Instead of reopening the wound, the aim of genetic criticism is to reconstitute the contextual memory, as Daniel Ferrer notes: 'La démarche du généticien

Moran has not eaten for several days and grows gradually weaker, aware that he is going to lose consciousness very soon. Until suddenly Gaber arrives: 'Mais l'arrivée de Gaber mit fin à ces ébats' (FN4, 48r). In a similar way as the end of Part I, the end of Moran's story (in the manuscript) is also characterized by a lack of paragraphs (or at least fewer than in the published version). Whereas in the published version, Gaber's arrival is marked by a new paragraph (1951, 252; paragraph number 120), the manuscript simply continues (FN4, 48r). Gaber reads from his notebook: 'Moran, Jacques, rentrera chez lui toutes affaires cessantes' (FN4, 49r) ['Moran, Jacques, home, instanter' (1955, 224; *Mo* 171)]. Gaber does not seem to notice any change in Moran, in spite of his terrible outward appearance and his 'grandes métamorphoses intérieures' (FN4, 50r) ['great inward metamorphoses' (1955, 224; *Mo* 171)]. Indeed, in the Gidean dichotomy between Dostoevsky and Balzac, Moran has changed from a Balzacian to a Dostoevskyan character. Moran wants to know if Youdi is angry. Gaber assures him he is not. The only thing Youdi has told him is: 'la vie est une bien belle chose, Gaber, une chose extraordinaire' (FN4, 52r) ['life is a thing of beauty, Gaber, and a joy for ever' (1955, 226; *Mo* 172)], invoking the first line of John Keats's poem 'Endymion': 'A thing of beauty is a joy forever' (Keats 2001, 61). If the allusion is already implied in the French text – which calls life a beautiful and extraordinary thing but not a 'joy forever' – it is more explicit in the English version, marking self-translation as an opportunity for Beckett to emphasize or insert new intertextual references. When Moran opens his eyes, Gaber is gone.

vise moins à réparer la blessure de l'arrachement du contexte, à suturer, à compléter, qu'à réactiver les contextes fossiles, à réveiller la mémoire qui y est inscrite, à en faire une véritable mémoire vive' (Ferrer 2011, 121). See also Van Hulle 2014c.

Paragraph 114 (FN4, 53r-56r; paragraphs 121-124 in 1951)

That night he sets out for home, where he arrives in spring, from which he deduces that he must have been on the way all winter. Anyone else ('Un autre que moi') would have lain down in the snow, resolved never to rise again, but not Moran: 'Pas moi' (FN4, 54r) ['Not I' (1955, 227; *Mo* 173). This phrase recurs several times throughout the narrative, prefiguring the title of the later play *Not I* / *Pas moi*.

Paragraph 115 (FN4, 56r-57r; paragraphs 125-126 in 1951)

Moran starts listing a series of questions 'd'ordre théologique' (FN4, 56r) ['of a theological nature' (1955, 228; *Mo* 174)]. In Beckett's personal library there is a book called *Curiosités théologiques par un bibliophile* by Pierre Gustave Brunet (Paris: Garnier Frères, nouvelle edition, [1884]; see Van Hulle and Nixon 2013), which he had already used during the composition of *Watt*, and many of the passages cited in *Molloy* are marked with grey pencil in his copy of the book.[136] In the manuscript, the order of the questions is slightly different (questions 9 and 10 are swapped) and there are only 15 questions (the manuscript lacks question 14 of the published version – 'Might not the beatific vision become a source of boredom, in the long run?', 1955, 229; *Mo* 175). The following list of passages from which the questions are derived follows the text and the order of the 16 questions as they appear in the published version of *Molloy* (1951, 258-9; 1955, 228-9; *Mo* 174-5):

> Certaines questions d'ordre théologique me préoccupaient bizarrement. En voici quelques unes.
> [Certain questions of a theological nature preoccupied me strangely. As for example.]
> 1° Que vaut la théorie qui veut qu'Ève soit sortie, non pas de la côte d'Adam, mais d'une tumeur au gras de la jambe (cul ?) ?
> [1. What value is to be attached to the theory that Eve sprang, not from Adam's rib, but from a tumour in the fat of his leg (arse?)?]

---

136 See the *BDL*, http://www.beckettarchive.org/library/CUR-THE.html.

Brunet p. 3: (*Curiosités théologiques* : Première partie[137] : Judaïsme et Christianisme : Idées singulières relatives à l'histoire de l'ancien et du nouveau testament): 'D'après divers Orientaux, ce ne fut pas de la côte d'Adam que sortit Ève, mais d'une tumeur qui lui vint au gras de la jambe et qui, s'ouvrant au bout de six mois, laissa sortir la première femme.'

> 2° Le serpent rampait-il ou, comme l'affirme Comestor, marchait-il debout ?
> [2. Did the serpent crawl or, as Comestor affirms, walk upright?]

Brunet p. 5: 'Les Orientaux et les rabbins ont avancé bien des contes au sujet du serpent ; on a prétendu qu'avant son crime il avait quatre pieds, qu'il était ailé et d'une beauté admirable. [...] Pierre Comestor affirme qu'il marchait debout comme l'homme ; Bède dit qu'il avait le visage d'une jeune fille (*virgineum habens vultum*).'

> 3° Marie conçut-elle par l'oreille, comme le veulent Saint-Augustin et Adobard ?[138]
> [3. Did Mary conceive through the ear, as Augustine and Adobard assert?]

Brunet p. 11: 'Des idées singulières ont été mises en avant au sujet de la Vierge ; on a pensé que Marie avait conçu par l'oreille : c'est ce qu'ont dit saint Augustin, saint Éphrem, Agobard, le Bréviaire des Maronites. Les artistes se sont parfois inspirés de cette tradition ; dans une ancienne image conservé à Sainte-Marie-Majeure, à Rome, Jésus entre sous la forme d'une colombe dans l'oreille de Marie.'

---

137 *Curiosités théologiques* consists of three parts. Most of Moran's theological questions derive from the first part. The title of the second part is: DEUXIÈME PARTIE : Opinions religieuses étrangères au christianisme (197ff.); the TROISIÈME PARTIE (297ff.) is an annotated bibliography of 'certains ouvrages qui se rattachent à des questions religieuses, ou que les bibliographes rangent du moins dans la classe de la théologie' (297).

138 Beckett used the name '**Agobard**' in the French manuscript (FN4, 56r) but switched to '**Adobard**' thereafter.

4° L'antéchrist combien de temps va-t-il nous faire poireauter encore ?
[4. How much longer are we to hang about waiting for the antechrist?] [139]

Brunet p. 13: (*Curiosités théologiques* : Première partie : Judaïsme et Christianisme : 'L'Antéchrist'): 'Un savant Hollandais, C. Wytachius, a composé une dissertation publiée à Amsterdam, en 1666, afin de prouver que Mahomet est l'Antéchrist. [...] D'autres savants modernes ont supposé qu'il n'avait point paru encore.'

5° Cela a-t-il vraiment de l'importance de quelle main on s'absterge le podex ?
[5. Does it really matter which hand is employed to absterge the podex?]

Brunet p. 19: (*Curiosités théologiques* : Première partie : 'Judaïsme et Christianisme : 'Idées singulières des Rabbins'): 'Plusieurs docteurs juifs n'ont pas hésité à faire une description détaillée du cérémonial qu'il faut observer lorsqu'on obéit aux plus tristes besoins de la nature humaine. Ils recommandent d'examiner d'abord les quatre points cardinaux et l'horizon afin de se tourner vers le nord ou le midi, jamais du côté de l'orient ou du couchant. Il faut attendre pour abaisser ou élever son vêtement qu'on soit accroupi ; enfin il n'est permis que de se server de la main gauche (*Podex non dextrâ sed senestrâ manu abstergenda sit... legis hœc arcana sunt*).' [140]

6° Que penser du serment des Irlandais proféré la main droite sur les reliques des saints et la gauche sur le membre viril ?

---

139 Although the spelling of '**antechrist**' was changed to '**ante^jchrist**' on ET2 (90r), the original spelling was retained for the Grove and Olympia first editions of *Molloy* (1955, 229). It was later corrected to '**antichrist**' for the 1965 Grove Press Black Cat edition (166) and to '**Antichrist**' for the 1966 Calder and Boyars Jupiter Books edition (179), the latter based on Beckett's corrected galleys (see 1.4.3 and 1.4.4). The 2009 Faber edition of *Molloy* follows the 1966 Calder edition: '**Antichrist**' (*Mo* 175).

140 Beckett clearly tried to retain as much of the Latin vocabulary as possible in Moran's fifth question.

[6. What is one to think of the Irish oath sworn by the natives with the right hand on the relics of the saints and the left on the virile member?]

Brunet p. 20: (*Curiosités théologiques* : Première partie : Judaïsme et Christianisme : 'Idées singulières des Rabbins'): 'Qu'on parcoure les lois souvent étranges qu'Howel, le bon roi du pays de Galles,[141] donna à ses sujets au dixième siècle ; on y verra que, lorsqu'une femme violée veut poursuivre en justice celui qui l'a outragée, elle doit, en proférant le serment qui dénonce le crime et le criminel, poser la main droite sur les reliques des saints et la gauche sur le membre viril de l'accusé.'

> 7° La nature observe-t-elle le sabbat ?
> [7. Does nature observe the sabbath?]

Brunet pp. 20-1: (*Curiosités théologiques* : Première partie : Judaïsme et Christianisme : 'Idées singulières des Rabbins'): 'L'observation du sabbat chez les Juifs a été l'objet de trente-neuf règles diverses […] On prétendait que l'observation du sabbat était respectée même par la nature, et on citait, comme preuve de cette assertion, le fleuve sabbatique en Syrie : selon Josèphe, après avoir coulé six jours avec abondance, il sèche tout à coup le jour du sabbat ; suivant quelques rabbins, il ne coule au contraire que le jour du sabbat, et il est à sec le reste de la semaine. Les voyageurs modernes n'ont pu retrouver cette rivière miraculeuse.'

> 8° Serait-il exact que les diables ne souffrent point des tourments infernaux ?
> [8. Is it true that the devils do not feel the pains of hell?]

Brunet p. 25: (*Curiosités théologiques* : Première partie : Judaïsme et Christianisme : 'Le diable, ses œuvres, ses suppots et son domaine'): 'Du reste, des savants démonologues affirment que les diables ne souffrent point des tourments infernaux, ce qui les découragerait et les empêcherait de chercher à tromper les hommes.'

---

141   Beckett replaced Wales in Brunet's text by Ireland in Moran's sixth question.

9° Théologie algébrique de Craig. Qu'en penser ?
[9. The algebraic theology of Craig? What is one to think
of this?]

Brunet p. 142: (*Curiosités théologiques* : Première partie : Judaïsme et
Christianisme : 'Quelques idées bizarres avancées par des théologiens'): 'le
mathématicien écossais John Craig, mort en 1709, conçut l'idée d'appliquer
les calculs de l'algèbre à la théologie, il rechercha quelle devait être
l'affaiblissement des preuves historiques suivant l'intervalle des temps et la
distance des lieux, et il trouva que la force des témoignages sur lesquels est
appuyée la vérité de la religion chrétienne ne pouvait subsister que quatorze
cent cinquante-quatre ans, à partir de 1699, année où il mit au jour ses
Theologiæ christianæ principia mathematica. Il en conclut qu'il y aurait un
second avènement de Jésus-Christ, une seconde révélation pour rétablir la
foi chrétienne dans toute sa force.'

10° Serait-il exact que Saint-Roch enfant ne voulait téter ni les
mercredis ni les vendredis ?
[10. Is it true that the infant Saint-Roch refused suck on
Wednesdays and Fridays?]

Brunet p. 33: (*Curiosités théologiques* : Première partie : Judaïsme et
Christianisme : 'Singularités des légendes de quelques saints. – Miracles'):
'Saint Roch est un des saints sur lesquels les légendaires s'exercèrent le plus ;
on dit qu'il vint au monde avec une croix rouge sur la poitrine ; dévot dès le
maillot, il ne voulait téter ni les mercredis ni les vendredis.'

11° Que penser de l'excommunication de la vermine au seizième
siècle ?
[11. What is one to think of the excommunication of vermin in
the sixteenth century?]

Brunet p. 91: (the opening words of the paragraph are underlined in
Beckett's copy of the *Curiosités théologiques*: 'L'excommunication des
animaux durant le moyen âge est un fait étrange, mais il est attesté de la
façon la plus irrécusable dans le recueil des consultations de Barthélémy
de Chassanée, jurisconsulte célèbre dans la première moitié du seizième

siècle ; cette collection, imprimée à Lyon en 1531, in-folio, a obtenu plusieurs éditions. La première de ces consultations est intitulée : De excommunicatione animalium insectorum.' (see Van Hulle and Nixon 2013, 185-91, 255)[142]

12° Faut-il approuver le cordonnier italien Lovat qui, s'étant châtré, se crucifia ?
[12. Is one to approve of the Italian cobbler Lovat who, having cut off his testicles, crucified himself?]

Brunet p. 121: (*Curiosités théologiques* : Première partie : Judaïsme et Christianisme : 'Eunuques volontaires. – Flagellants'): 'En 1808, un cordonnier italien, nommé Lovat, établi à Venise, se crucifia lui-même après avoir opéré sur sa personne l'opération de la castration ; il fut soigné à temps, et il échappa à ses terribles blessures.'

13° Que foutait Dieu avant la création ?
[13. What was God doing with himself before the creation?]

Brunet p. 341: (*Curiosités théologiques* : Troisième partie – 'certains ouvrages qui se rattachent à des questions religieuses'): '*Le Lucidaire en français*, Paris 1506. On trouve sous ce titre une série de questions et de réponses dans lesquelles sont abordées avec naïveté "diverses matières subtiles et merveilleuses en matière d'interrogatoire." La plupart de ces questions se rapportent à la religion. Le disciple demande à son maître : "Quelle chose est Dieu ? Où il estoit devant qu'il fist le monde ?"'

14° La vision béatifique ne serait-elle pas une source d'ennui, à la longue ?
[14. Might not the beatific vision become a source of boredom, in the long run?]

---

142   See the *BDL*, http://www.beckettarchive.org/library/CUR-THE.html.

It is possible that this question was added without direct recourse to Brunet's *Curiosités théologiques*. The question was not yet part of the manuscript and was added later on, between the stages of the manuscript and the first publication. The following passages in Brunet deal with beatitude, but do not explicitly thematize tedium (*ennui*).

Brunet pp. 333-4: (*Curiosités théologiques* : Troisième partie – 'certains ouvrages qui se rattachent à des questions religieuses'): 'Geoffroy Vallée [...] consigna ses folles imaginations dans un opuscule intitulé : *la Béatitude des Chrétiens, ou le Fleo de la Foy*, 1572. Ce livret, de 8 feuillets, est extrêmement rare. Dès le frontispice de son écrit, l'auteur donne à connaître le dérangement de son cerveau.' Brunet describes the book as a 'tissu de sottises, où se montre aussi un mécontentement prononcé contre les puissants du jour qui "au lieu de contempler et méditer nuit et jour ce que c'est de l'Éternel et de l'homme, n'ont le mot de justice, charité, religion, qu'en leur bouche et en leur bourse."'

Brunet p. 237: (*Curiosités théologiques* : Deuxième partie : Opinions religieuses étrangères au Christianisme : 'Les Japonais'): 'Divers voyageurs racontent qu'au Japon les adorateurs du dieu Amida s'imaginent qu'en se suicidant en l'honneur de cette divinité, ils sont certains d'obtenir une béatitude immense dans l'autre monde. Il n'est donc pas rare qu'un dévot se noie pour donner un témoignage éclatant de sa piété.'

Brunet p. 285: (*Curiosités théologiques* : Deuxième partie : Opinions religieuses étrangères au Christianisme : 'Croyances en vigueur aux îles Marquises et chez d'autres insulaires océaniques'): 'A Tikopia (autre île de la Polynésie), les insulaires croient à une vie future, et ils sont persuadés que toutes les âmes jouissent de la béatitude céleste. Un de ces sauvages, auquel on demanda s'il n'y avait pas de récompense pour les bons et de châtiment pour les méchants, répondit fièrement : "Il n'existe aucun méchant parmi nous."'

> 15° Serait-il exact que le supplice de Judas est suspendu le samedi ?
> [15. Is it true that Judas' torments are suspended on Saturdays?]

Brunet p. 270: (*Curiosités théologiques* : Deuxième partie : Opinions religieuses étrangères au christianisme : 'Judas Iscariote'): 'D'après quelques vieilles traditions relatées dans des écrits du moyen âge, Judas est, jusqu'au jugement dernier, ballotté par les flots toujours agités d'une mer furieuse. Quelques trouvères ajoutent que, chaque samedi, son supplice est suspendu, par un effet spécial de la miséricorde divine.'

16° Si l'on disait la messe des morts pour les vivants ?
[16. What if the mass for the dead were read over the living?]

Brunet pp. 71-2: (*Curiosités théologiques* : Première partie : Judaïsme et Christianisme : 'Singularités relatives aux sacrements'): 'Peut-on dire des messes de morts pour les vivants ? Quelques anciens auteurs ont répondu par l'affirmative et ont cité un exemple tiré de la vie de saint Théodose, abbé au sixième siècle, lequel fit célébrer l'office des trépassés pour un religieux nommé Basile, qui était plein de vie et qui expira lorsque les prières furent terminées ; mais ce trait est tiré de la *Vie des Saints* écrite en grec par Siméon Métaphraste, et l'on sait combien ce recueil abonde en récits apocryphes.'

Et je récitais le joli Pater quiétiste, **Dieu qui n'êtes plus au ciel que sur la terre et dans les enfers, je ne veux ni ne désire que votre nom soit sanctifié, vous savez ce qui vous convient.** Etc.

[And I recited the pretty quietist Pater, Our Father who art no more in heaven than on earth or in hell, I neither want nor desire that thy name be hallowed, thou knowest best what suits thee. Etc.]

Brunet pp. 170-1: (*Curiosités théologiques* : Première partie : 'Judaïsme et Christianisme' : 'Quiétisme'): 'On sait que vers la fin du dix-septième siècle quelque dévôts, à force de vouloir s'élever aux plus sublimes hauteurs de la contemplation, s'imaginèrent que leur âme pouvait se réunir à l'essence divin, et qu'alors ce que faisait le corps était chose très indifférente.' Brunet refers to Jean de la Bruyère's work *Dialogues posthumes sur le quiétisme* (1699) and quotes the quietist version of the Lord's Prayer: 'Nous citerons l'Oraison dominicale réformée, à l'usage des quiétistes : "**Dieu qui n'êtes** pas plus au ciel que sur la terre et dans les enfers, je ne veux ni ne désire que votre nom soit sanctifié ; vous savez ce qui vous convient ; si vous voulez qu'il soit, il le sera sans que je le veuille et le désire ; que votre royaume arrive ou n'arrive pas, cela m'est indifférent. Je ne vous demande pas que votre volonté soit faite en la terre comme au ciel ; elle le sera malgré que j'en aie. C'est à moi à m'y résigner. Donnez-nous à tous notre pain de tous les jours qui est votre grâce, ou ne nous la donnez pas ; je ne souhaite ni de l'avoir, ni d'en être privé ; de même, si vous me pardonnez mes crimes comme je pardonne à ceux qui m'ont offensé, tant mieux. Si vous m'en punissez, au contraire, par la damnation éternelle, tant mieux encore, puisque c'est votre bon plaisir. Enfin, mon Dieu, je suis trop abandonné à votre volonté pour vous prier de me délivrer des tentations du péché.'"[143]

Paragraph 116 (FN4, 57r; paragraph 127 in 1951)

Moran describes his theological questions as a way of taking refuge in a frivolous and charming world (1955, 230; *Mo* 175).

Paragraph 117 (FN4, 57r-58r; paragraph 128 in 1951)

Then he makes a list of other questions he asked himself. In question 10, whether we all meet again in heaven, he only enumerates himself, his mother, his son, his son's mother, Youdi, Gaber, Molloy and Molloy's mother. To this list the published version adds Yerk, Murphy, Watt, Camier **'et les autres'** (1951, 260) ['and the rest' (1955, 230; *Mo* 176)].

---

143 Andy Wimbush's translation is based on la Bruyère; minor differences with Brunet's citation of the passage are indicated in bold: 'Our Father, who art no more in heaven than on earth or in hell, **who art everywhere,** I neither want nor desire that thy name be hallowed, thou knowest best what suits **us**; if thou wilt, it shall be, unless I want or desire it. That thy kingdom come or not come, it is all the same to me. I do not ask thee that thy will be done on the earth as it is heaven: it will be so no matter what I do, I can only resign myself to it. Give us this day our daily bread, which is thy grace, or give it not to us: I neither wish to have it nor to be without it. Likewise, if thou forgivest my trespasses as I forgive those who trespass against me, that is all well and good. But if thou wouldst rather punish me by **damnation**, then so much the better, since it is thy pleasure. Finally, Father, I am too abandoned to thy will to ask thee to deliver me from temptation and from evil.' (Wimbush 2015, 3-4)

Paragraph 118 (FN4, 59r)

In the manuscript, the list is followed by a very short one-sentence paragraph that is omitted from the published version, in which Moran states that these are the things keeping him busy in his rare spare time: '**Voilà quelques-unes des considérations dont je meublais mes maigres loisirs**' (FN5, 59r).

Paragraph 119 (FN4, 59r-62r; paragraph 129 in 1951)

Moran wishes to say that he often thought of his bees, especially of their dance. One of the few extra sentences that are not in the manuscript is again a meta-comment about writing for the public: '**On dirait quelquefois que j'écris pour le public**' (1951, 262). Against the background of Beckett's lectures at TCD in the early 1930s (especially his emphasis on the integrity of incoherence and complexity) it is interesting that it is the complexity of the bees' dance that stupefies Moran. He concludes with rapture: 'Voilà une chose que je pourrai étudier toute ma vie, sans jamais la comprendre' (FN4, 61r) ['Here is something I can study all my life, and never understand' (1955, 232; *Mo* 177)].

'**30.10.[47]**'
(FN4, 60v)

After some concluding remarks about the dance of his bees, Moran suddenly starts talking about something completely different: the voice.

Paragraph 120 (FN4, 61v; paragraph 130 in 1951)

This paragraph about the voice is an addition on the verso. Moran explains that it was on the way home that he heard it for the first time, without paying attention to it.

Paragraph 121 (FN4, 62r-63r; paragraph 131 in 1951)

He notes that, physically speaking he was becoming rapidly unrecognizable.

Paragraph 122 (FN4, 63r-64r; paragraph 132 in 1951)

He discards many of his clothes, but keeps his tie, knotted round his bare neck. The published version adds the detail that it was a spotted tie, but Moran forgot what colour: **'C'était une cravate à pois, mais j'oublie de quelle couleur'** (1951, 265).

Paragraph 123 (FN4, 65r-67r; paragraph 133 in 1951)

On the verso (64v), Beckett writes a paralipomenon ('**manne**', foreshadowing the manna mentioned on page 66r), and he notes a voice beginning to speak: '**voix qui commence**' (FN4, 64v). Moran explains what he did when it rained, preferring the shelter of his umbrella even though it was reduced to a few flitters of silk fluttering from the stays (1955, 236; *Mo* 179).

Paragraph 124 (FN4, 67r; paragraph 134 in 1951)

A few very short paragraphs follow in quick succession. The thought of taking to the road, to get a lift, never crossed Moran's mind.

Paragraph 125 (FN4, 67r; paragraph 135 in 1951)

Actually, the thought of turning for help would have displeased him if it had occurred to him.

Paragraph 126 (FN4, 67r; paragraph 136 in 1951)

Moran notes that he reached home with his '**cinq dollars**' (FN4, 67r), later changed to '**quinze shillings**' (1951, 266) ['fifteen shillings' (1955, 236; *Mo* 180)], but then he corrects himself: 'Non. J'en dépensai **un**' (FN4, 67r) – in the published text: 'Non, j'en dépensai **deux**' (1951, 267) ['No, I spent two' (1955, 236; *Mo* 180)] – after which Moran starts explaining how.

Paragraph 127 (FN4, 67r)

In the manuscript he immediately starts telling about that day he was waiting under his umbrella, '~~Un jour que j'attendais, sous mon parapluie,~~' (FN4, 67r), but then the narrative is interrupted.

Paragraph 128 (FN4, 67r; paragraph 137 in 1951)

Moran mentions other molestations, but decides not to record them.

Paragraph 129 (FN4, 68r-71r; paragraph 138 in 1951)

He resumes: one night he was accosted by a big ruddy farmer who asked him what he was doing on his land. Moran replied he was on a pilgrimage to 'la madone de Shit' (FN4, 69r) ['the Turdy Madonna' (1955, 237; *Mo* 181)]. When the farmer asks 'The black one?', Moran again uses the same 'Not I' construction: 'Un autre se serait démonté. Pas moi' (FN4, 69r) ['Another would have lost countenance. Not I' (1955, 237; *Mo* 181)]. Moran asks a little hot tea, takes '**un dollar**' (FN4, 70r; '**un florin**', 1951, 269) from his pocket and gives it to the farmer. Beckett adds a sentence on the verso in which Moran talks about himself in the third person: 'Ah ce vieux Moran, rusé comme un serpent' (FN4, 69v) ['Ah Moran, wily as a serpent' (1955, 238; *Mo* 182)]. That was how he spent his dollar/florin.

Paragraph 130 (FN4, 71r; paragraph 139 in 1951)

In a very short, one-sentence paragraph Moran suddenly states: 'Maintenant je vais pouvoir conclure' (FN4, 71r) ['Now I may make an end' (1955, 239; *Mo* 182)].

Paragraph 131 (FN4, 71r-74r; paragraph 140 in 1951)

And what follows is the closing paragraph. It is night and Moran skirts the graveyard, along his plot in perpetuity. He bursts open the locked wicket. All his bees have died during winter. At that moment, Moran is sure that he can make an end: 'Oui, maintenant je peux conclure' (FN4, 72r). He finds a letter from Youdi, asking for a report. In the meantime it is summer again. His son has returned. He has crutches now. And all of a sudden Moran brings up the topic of the voice again, who tells him this and that: 'J'ai parlé d'une voix qui me disait ceci et cela' (FN4, 74r) The narrative briefly shifts to the third person (by means of a cancellation of the first person): 'Elle ne se servait pas des mots qu'on m'avait appris au petit Moran.' (FN4, 74r) ['It did not use the words that Moran had been taught when he was little' (1955, 241; *Mo* 184)]. The voice tells him to write the report. He goes back into the house and writes: 'Il est minuit. La pluie fouette les vitres.' Which is followed without any hesitation by: 'Il n'était pas minuit. Il ne pleuvait pas' (FN4, 74r) ['It is midnight. The rain is beating on the windows. It was not midnight. It was not raining' (1955, 241; *Mo* 184)].[144]

Underneath these closing lines, Beckett wrote 'FIN 1/11/47' (see Fig. 19). This is one of the most famous 'explicits' of twentieth-century fiction, but these closing lines were not the end of the writing process. The end was in the beginning.

Paragraph 1: The Incipit

In addition to Louis Hay's categories of 'écriture à programme' and 'écriture à processus', Bernhild Boie and Daniel Ferrer regard the incipit as 'a third variant', *hors-catégorie* so to speak (Boie and Ferrer 1993, 17). The space opened up by the tension between the beginning of the writing process and the beginning of the novel is particularly interesting in the case of the opening paragraph of *Molloy*. The last date written in black ink in the manuscript is 30 October 1947 (FN4, 60v); the last words ('Il ne pleuvait pas.') are followed by 'FIN 1/11/47' (FN4, 74r), but this date is written in blue pencil, so it is possible that it was added later on, after Beckett had finished the incipit, also dated '1.11.47', on the first verso pages of the first notebook (FN1, 01v–02v; see Figs. 20 and 21): 'Je suis dans la chambre de ma mère' (FN1, 01v) ['I am in my mother's room' (1955, 7; *Mo* 3)]. By this time the first-person narrator is slightly different from the 'je' of the rest of the first notebook: the first-person narrator has replaced his mother. 'Il ne

144   Brian Richardson refers to these closing sentences as an illustration of extreme denarration, in which 'very little (if anything) is left over after the assaults of textual negation the narrative performs upon itself' (Richardson 2001, 171).

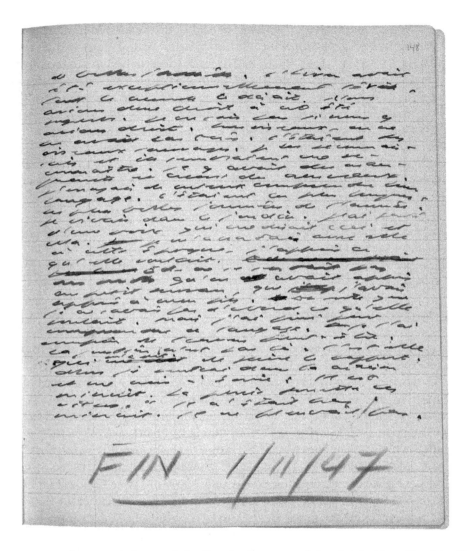

Fig. 19: After Moran's famous closing line that it was not raining, despite his earlier claim, Beckett wrote the date 'FIN 1/11/47' (1 November 1947) in large thiumphant capitals, using blue pencil (FN4, 74r).

manque plus qu'un fils' (FN1, 02v) ['All I need now is a son' (1955, 8; *Mo* 3)], and indeed it seems to him that he even knew his son. The paragraph is written in one smooth movement, almost without cancellations, and it differs hardly from the published version.[145] But after the introduction of the man who comes every week to fetch the new pages the 'I' has written, the published version shows three sentences that are not in the manuscript: **'Quand il vient chercher les nouvelles feuilles il rapporte celles de la semaine précédente. Elles sont marquées de signes que je ne comprends pas. D'ailleurs je ne les relis pas'** (1951, 7) ['When he comes for the fresh pages he brings back the previous week's. They are marked with signs I don't understand. Anyway I don't read them' (1955, 7; *Mo* 3)]. Again, Beckett added a meta-comment that thematizes the process of revision, adding an extra layer to the autography, which culminates in the passage that ends the opening paragraph: 'C'est lui qui m'a dit que j'avais mal commencé et qu'il fallait commencer autrement' (FN1, 02r) ['It was he told me I'd begun all wrong, that I should have begun differently' (1955, 8; *Mo* 4)]. At the end of notebook 4, Beckett also decided that he had begun 'all wrong', that he should have begun differently. So he added the incipit. The following comment by the 'I' therefore applies to Beckett as well: 'J'avais commencé au commencement, figurez-vous, comme un vieux con' (FN1, 02r) ['I began at the beginning, like an old ballocks, can you imagine that?' (1955, 8; *Mo* 4)].[146] As a result, the genesis of *Molloy* ends with the beginning, like a snake biting its own tail: 'Voici mon commencement à moi [...] Le voici' (FN1, 02r) ['Here's my beginning [...] Here it is' (1955, 8; *Mo* 4)].

145 One of the few variants is: 'Le vrai amour était **avec** une autre' (FN1, 02v), which became 'Le vrai amour était **dans** une autre' in the Minuit edition (1951, 8) ['The real love was in another' (1955, 8; *Mo* 3)]. Between the manuscript and the Minuit edition, Beckett also added a few details to suggest that this man who fetches and brings the papers is the same as Gaber, who visits Moran on a Sunday: 'C'est un drôle de type, celui qui vient me voir. **C'est tous les dimanches qu'il vient, paraît-il. Il n'est pas libre les autres jours.** Il a toujours soif.' (1951, 8) ['He's a queer the one who comes to see me. He comes every Sunday apparently. The other days he isn't free' (1955, 8; *Mo* 3)] As if to emphasize the queerness of this character even more, Beckett called him **'a queer card'** in the earlier drafts of the translation (Sp1-3, 02r; ET1, 02r; MER, 89; NWWT2, 02r; NWWG, 01r; NWW, 317), predating ET2.
146 Earlier versions of the translation, before ET2, were milder on the narrator: 'like an old **fool**' (Sp1-3, 02r; ET1, 02r; MER, 89; NWWT2, 02r; NWWG, 01r; NWW, 317; see chapter 3.2)

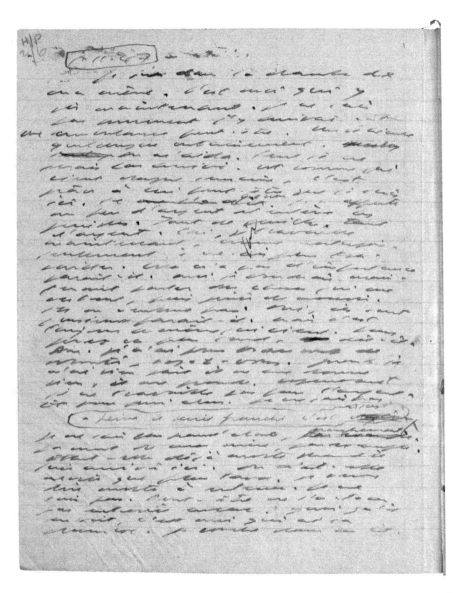

Fig. 20: Beckett added the first paragraph of *Molloy* last, on '1.11.47' (1 November 1947), facing the paragraph he had written first in the chronology of the novel, six months earlier (FN1, 01v).

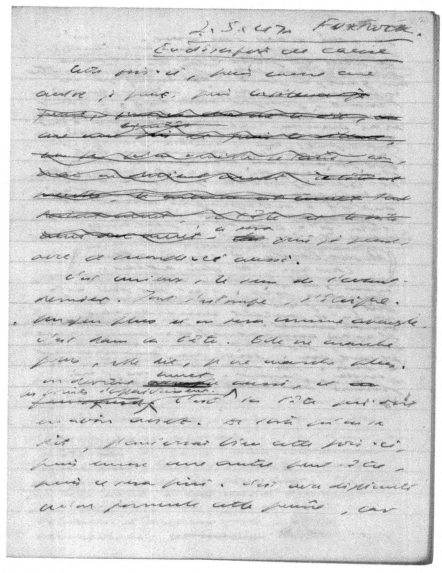

Fig. 21: The original opening paragraph in the first notebook of *Molloy*, begun on '2.5.47' (2 May 1947) in 'Foxrock' under the heading 'En désespoir de cause' (FN1, 02r).

3 Genesis of *Molloy* (English)

3.1 Translating *Molloy*

When the French *Molloy* was first published by Les Éditions de Minuit in 1951, Beckett's experience with self-translation was still rather limited. In the previous two decades, he had taken on quite a lot of 'bread and butter work' translating others (Knowlson 1997, 168) but, except for a handful of poems, Beckett's only sustained efforts at rendering writing of his own into a different language were the story 'Love and Lethe' from *More Pricks Than Kicks* – as 'Mort plus précieuse', now lost (*LSB I* 212) – and the novel *Murphy*. Both translations were made from English to French with the help of native speaker Alfred Péron (see chapter 1.2.1, note 19). Translating himself from his newly adopted language into his mother tongue was a relatively new and strange experience for Beckett. Still, in early 1953, he did embark – unassisted – on an English version of the stage play *En attendant Godot*, but for the first part of the 'trilogy' he again acquired assistance. On their title pages, the first English editions of *Molloy* published by Grove Press and Olympia Press, introduce the text as 'translated from the French by Patrick Bowles, in collaboration with the author'. But the actual genesis of the translation was more complicated and when Beckett finally set to work with Patrick Bowles, they did not always proceed in the strict sense of a 'collaboration'.

The first tentative plans for an English version of *Molloy* date back to July 1948, a mere eight months after Beckett had finished the original French. George Reavey informed him that Cyril Connolly was looking for an English text to include in his London magazine. 'I fear there is little chance of my having 30.000 words for Horizon by the date you mention', Beckett answered on 8 July 1948: 'If French was not a bar I could let them have the first half of *Molloy*, about that length' (*LSB II* 80). Beckett would know, as he kept word counts in his French notebooks (see chapters 1.1.1 and 2). While the actual timeframe is not mentioned in the letter, according to Deirdre Bair, Beckett 'thought it unlikely that he could get the piece translated by the deadline' and the plans did not materialize (Bair 1978, 402). Instead of losing time on self-translation which, Beckett would later complain, interfered with his writing, he typed up *Malone meurt* and started working on the holograph of *En attendant Godot*. The 'frenzy of writing', also known as the 'siege in the room', proceeded apace, yielding a first draft of *L'Innommable* – the final part of the 'trilogy' – by January 1950.

In mid-June of that year, Beckett was called back to Ireland by his brother, Frank. Their mother had been diagnosed with Parkinson's disease a few years before, but now her condition was rapidly worsening and Beckett arranged for May to be taken into a nursing home. 'When not at her bedside', Ruby Cohn writes, 'he typed up *L'Innommable* and translated into English passages of *Molloy* and *Malone meurt*' (Cohn 2005, 193), which appeared in the October 1950 issue of *Transition Fifty* no. 6. These 'Two Fragments', as Beckett called them, were only distinguished by the Roman numerals 'I' (*Molloy*) and 'II' (*Malone Dies*), without reference to the novels from which they had been lifted. This isolated appearance allowed him to use the *Molloy* extract as a homage to his late mother, as Molloy talks about 'settling this matter between my mother and me' and the fragment closes on the words 'without mother' (TRA, 103, 105). The reason for these extracts remains unclear. It is possible that Beckett turned to translating his new French writings back into English as a last resort, because so many publishers in Paris had rejected them. Even Jérôme Lindon of Les Éditions de Minuit was yet to accept *Molloy* and *Malone meurt* when Beckett worked on the English samples in Dublin. His wife, Suzanne Déchevaux-Dumesnil, had brought them to the attention of Minuit by the time *Transition* came out, but no decision had been made and no contract signed (Weller 2011, 113). And so *Molloy*, originally written in French, made its public *entrée* in English. Lindon eventually published the novel in March 1951, and it was soon followed by *Malone meurt* in November of that year.

A few months later, Richard Seaver noticed the 'blue titles' staring out at him as he passed the shop window of Minuit in the rue Bernard-Palissy (Seaver 1991, x). An American student at the Sorbonne, writing a thesis on Joyce, Seaver vaguely recalled Beckett's essay in *Our Exagmination Round His Factification for Incamination of Work in Progress* from 1929. In the following weeks, he started collecting as much of Beckett's work as he could find in Paris, and brought it to the attention of Alexander Trocchi, who had founded a new English literary magazine called *Merlin*.[147] 'Stop talking,

147   The story of *Merlin* and its most loyal members (Alexander Trocchi, Jane Lougee, Austryn Wainhouse, Patrick Bowles and Christopher Logue) is well-documented. The most important sources are Seaver 1991, Girodias 1990, de St Jorre 2009, Campbell 2013, Logue 1999, Seaver 2012, Murray Scott 2012 and Calder 2014, all of which are loosely drawn upon for the factual details concerning *Merlin*, unless a specific source is cited.

Mon, and put it on paper', Trocchi advised Seaver in his Scottish brogue: 'There's a deadline next Thursday!' (Seaver 1991, xiv). 'Samuel Beckett: An Introduction' was printed in the second issue of the magazine (vol. 1, no. 2, Autumn 1952), and Seaver – now an editor of *Merlin* himself – offered Beckett and his publisher a copy.[148] From Lindon he learned that the author was sitting on an unpublished novel in English entitled *Watt*. Because Beckett sympathized with the 'Merlin juveniles', as he dubbed them in a letter to George Reavey (12 May 1953, *LSB II* 376), he allowed them to include an 'Extract from Watt' in the third issue of *Merlin* (vol. 1, no. 3, Winter 1952-53), and even to publish the complete novel in their Collection Merlin, a book series operating under the aegis of Maurice Girodias and his recently set up Olympia Press. While this publishing house was mostly popular for its 'dirty books' or 'DBs' – especially with tourists – John de St Jorre notes that 'Olympia was in fact capitalising on erotic fantasy to earn the money needed to publish otherwise unpublishable authors such as Beckett' (2009, 96).

With the extract from *Watt* that he forwarded to Trocchi on 27 September 1952, Beckett added a cover letter in which he stated: 'No objection, as far as I am concerned, to your eventually publishing a passage from the texts which have appeared in French. I thought you wanted an inédit. But you would have to get the consent of the Editions de Minuit' (SU, Austryn Wainhouse Papers, box 3). As soon as he returned from Spain on 19 October 1952, to look for a cheaper printer, Trocchi acknowledged his receipt of the *Watt* extract and told Beckett: 'I am still very interested in publishing a translation from "Molloy" or "Malone meurt" and I intend if you have no objection to speak again to the Editions de Minuit about the possibility of that for Number Four (February 15, 1953)' (SU, Austryn Wainhouse Papers, box 3). Permission would not be a problem, but Beckett wanted to settle more important matters first. 'May I count on you to send me proofs of the Extract from Watt?', he asked Trocchi on 21 October 1953 (SU, Austryn Wainhouse Papers, box 3). Beckett returned them corrected on 4 December 1952, requesting

148   On 12 August 1952, Lindon told Beckett that he had received a visit from the 'director' of a new English-language review entitled *Merlin*, who asked for permission to include a fragment from *L'Innommable* in the next issue. Lindon felt that 'une nouvelle' would perhaps be better still, but it is not clear whether he is alluding to one of the 'nouvelles' ('La Fin', 'L'Expulsé', 'Premier amour' and 'Le Calmant') or a 'new' and unpublished work (IMEC, Fonds Samuel Beckett, Boîte 1, Correspondance 1946–1953).

a 'Rendez-vous day after to-morrow. Saturday at 2 o'clock at the Brasserie Lipp, Bd. St. Germain (terrasse)' to discuss translations from his French novels (SU, Austryn Wainhouse Papers, box 3). The plan that emerged from this encounter was to have *Molloy* follow *Watt* as soon as possible, first in the magazine, then in the Collection Merlin. In order to have a fragment ready for next issue, *Merlin* began to work on an English version straight away. Trocchi submitted a preliminary draft of a section from the novel around late 1952 or early 1953, which Beckett started revising at the back of the so-called 'Tara MacGowran Notebook' (EM).[149] The fragment takes up folios 77v to 85v and terminates abruptly with the draft of a letter to an unspecified addressee (Figs. 22 and 23):

> You may put[150] your translation of the <u>Molloy</u>
> extract. I can make nothing of it.
> The passage I suppose ~~is begins~~ is from the
> top of p. 117 "Et maintenant ma progression..."
> to the end of Part I.
> Yours sincerely (EM, 86r)

The passage in the notebook does start on p. 117 of Minuit's first *Molloy* edition, but it ends sooner, at the top of p. 126, i.e. fifteen pages before the end of Part I (p. 141). Beckett seems to have anticipated the space needed in the notebook to revise the translation – as folios 87 to 96 are left blank – but he gave up before reaching the halfway point. The short note that follows the interrupted draft is probably connected to a longer letter to Alexander Trocchi, in which Beckett tried to express his difficulties with the revision. The actual letter has not been found, but a heavily revised draft survives in the 'Sam Francis Notebook' (UoR MS 2926):

---

149 According to Ackerley and Gontarski, the draft in the Tara MacGowran Notebook is related to the October 1950 prepublication of *Molloy* in *Transition* (Ackerley and Gontarski 2006, 556). This is impossible, as the fragment in the magazine is not the same selection of text. The other material in the notebook also suggests that Beckett did not start using it until early 1952, after he translated the *Molloy* fragment while staying in Ireland with his mother during the Summer of 1950.

150 Though difficult to decipher, it is also possible that Beckett wrote 'pub' (short for 'publish') instead of 'put'.

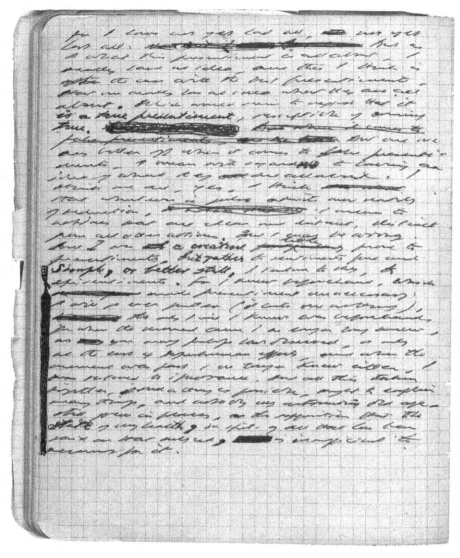

Fig. 22: Last page of the English holograph fragment in the 'Tara MacGowran' notebook, with several revisions and marginal doodles (EM, 85v).

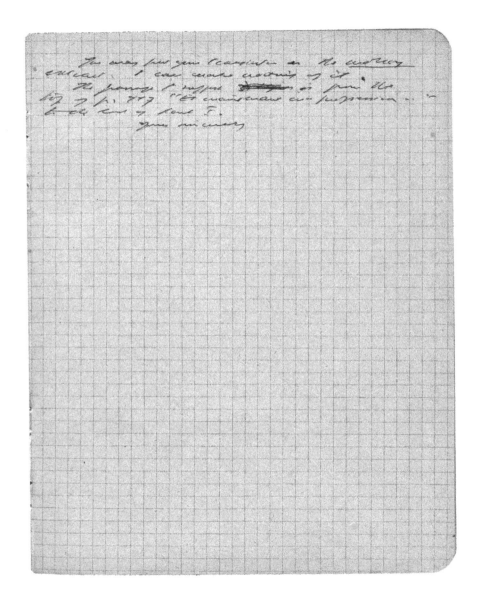

Fig. 23: Draft of a letter concerning the *Molloy* fragment in the 'Tara MacGowran' notebook to an unspecified addressee, probably Alexander Trocchi (EM, 86r).

I have been ~~thinking~~ ~~over~~ ~~trying to reflect on~~ ~~the possibility of Molloy in~~
~~English~~ ~~trying to imagine~~ ~~Watt~~ ~~in~~ ~~Molloy in English~~ I have been
thinking over the possibility of Molloy in English and ~~came to~~
~~the conclusion~~ feel that we had far better drop this project for the
moment at least. ~~It won't~~ ~~It does~~ It won't go into English, I don't
know why. It would have to be entirely rethought and rewritten,
which ~~is~~ is ~~not~~ ~~only a job I can only do myself~~ I fear ~~is~~ a job only
myself can ~~do and on~~ undertake and ~~and~~ which I simply can't face ~~it~~
at present. ~~You~~ You may of course publish ~~the~~ ~~tr~~ ~~translation of~~
the extract in Merlin, if you still wish to. ~~In spite of its merits~~
~~I think it has great~~ ~~The translation has great possibilities~~ I am
revising the translation, which ~~has~~ has great qualities. ~~I am~~ I'm
~~I think over-correcting it~~ ~~am~~ afraid ~~am making~~ am making a lot
of changes, probably too many. My English is queer. I can't do
much at a time and progress very slowly and don't know when
it will be ready. Hardly before the end of this month. (UoR MS
2926, 6v, 7v)

The editors of Beckett's correspondence date the draft 'on or before
5 February 1953' (*LSB II* 356), because on that day he also contacted Jérôme
Lindon about the extract, mentioning a letter to Trocchi. While the reasons
he gives for dropping the translation are similar, Beckett is much more
honest and straightforward about the merits of the attempt when writing to
his French publisher:

> La traduction en anglais de l'extrait de Molloy n'est pas bonne.
> Je suis en train de la réviser et elle pourra quand même passer
> dans Merlin. Mais j'ai écrit à Trocchi qu'il vaut mieux laisser
> tomber pour le moment son projet de traduction intégrale. Il
> faudrait que je le fasse moi-même, très librement, et je n'en ai
> pas le courage en ce moment. D'une façon générale je sais que je
> ne supporterai pas mon travail traduit en anglais par un autre.
> Et réviser, comme j'essaie de le faire en ce moment, me donne
> encore beaucoup plus mal que de traduire moi-même, et pour un
> résultat déplorable. (*LSB II* 357)

[The English translation of the passage from *Molloy* is not good. I am busy revising it, and, even as it stands, it will do for *Merlin*. But I have written to Trocchi that it would be better if he dropped for now the project of a complete translation. It would have to be myself that did it, very freely, but I haven't the heart for that at the moment. Broadly speaking, I know that I shall not be able to bear my work being translated into English by someone else. And revising, as I'm trying to do right now, is even more trouble than doing my own translating, and for a dire outcome. (*LSB II* 358)]

Three weeks later, on 25 February 1953, he was still complaining to the Irish writer Aidan Higgins that *Molloy* 'proves untranslatable. Too awful in English' (qtd. in Beplate 2011, 100).

Beckett's frankness in correspondence with Lindon and Higgins contrasts sharply with the care he took in the Trocchi letter to couch his opinion of the draft in kindness, eventually putting the blame on himself and his 'queer' English. At first sight, Beckett's gentle tone, and the fact that he was writing to Trocchi directly, suggests that the editor of *Merlin* himself was responsible for the *Molloy* fragment. However, Trocchi's answer of 26 February 1953, sent upon his return from London to promote the literary magazine abroad, proves that he was merely the spokesperson for someone else's work:

I was sorry to hear you felt you couldn't allow us to go ahead with 'Molloy' – I found it exasperating having to explain in England who you were and what you had written. Of course you can probably do something better with 'Molloy' if you don't merely translate. Nevertheless, I would like to have your corrected version of the Seaver translation of the part for publication in 'MERLIN'...we can if you like call it a tentative something or other, even putting a note that you intend yourself at a future date to rewrite in English. [...] I'd be grateful to have the piece from 'Molloy' just as soon as you can let me have it. (SU, Austryn Wainhouse Papers, box 3)[151]

151   In his introduction to *I can't go on, I'll go on*, Seaver obliquely refers to the fragment that Beckett was revising in the Tara MacGowran Notebook: 'I

Trocchi's belligerent tone annoyed Beckett to such an extent that, in his answer of 28 March 1953, he started coming back on his earlier decision to let *Merlin* have Richard Seaver's translation – revised or not – as a gesture for their efforts and their interest in his work:

> Re[garding] Molloy extract I can only repeat what I have already told you. It seems quite impossible to me in English and my corrections of Seaver's translation don't make it any more readable. I can't see how the publication of such a text in Merlin could help with the sales of Watt. I am very sorry to disappoint you in this. (SU, Austryn Wainhouse Papers, box 3)[152]

With Beckett's rejection of the specimen, and his refusal to further revise it, all plans to publish *Molloy* in English, either partly or in full, were temporarily put on hold. Trocchi's brazen insistence, in his letter to Beckett of 13 April 1953, that *Merlin* should also have the first option on subsequent works in English, and that 'although this perhaps rests with Les Editions de Minuit rather than with you, we still feel that should you succeed in your translation of "Molloy" and the other French works we are entitled to the same consideration' did little to sway the author (SU, Austryn Wainhouse

began work on a draft but had not progressed far when the financial pressures on *Merlin* became such that I landed a job that paid me enough not only to live on but to finance a couple of issues of the magazine. The hitch was that it took me out of Paris for six months' (Seaver 1991, xxiii). In his later memoirs, Seaver explains that he moved to Chaumont, a small town in the Haute-Marne region, to work there as the 'official translator-interpreter for an American construction company under contract with the U.S. Air Force to build a base in eastern France' (Seaver 2012, 166). He recalls that he 'boarded the train one Sunday morning in early February' of 1953 (168), which indeed situates his leaving Paris at the time of Beckett's exchange with Trocchi about the early draft. Seaver was a logical choice because he had already translated a few snippets from *Molloy* for his article on Beckett in *Merlin*.

152 Beckett also drafted this letter in a notebook (TCD MS 4662) first but, unlike the earlier mentioned draft letter to Trocchi in the 'Sam Francis' notebook, this one is only slightly revised. The relevant passage reads: 'Re[garding] Molloy extract, I can only repeat what I have already told you, i.e. that I can't succeed in making anything of it seems to me quite impossible in English. My corrections of th of Seaver's translation don't make it any more readable and I don't think cannot see how the publication of such a text in Merlin would could help with the sales of Watt. I am very sorry to disappoint you in this' (TCD MS 4662, 30v).

Papers, box 3). The project lay dormant until Barney Rosset of Grove Press, New York wanted to publish *Molloy* together with *Waiting for Godot*. Through Lindon, Rosset made an agreement with *Merlin* to release a joint edition in Europe and America. Trocchi, warning Rosset from his recent experience, set out the terms as follows in his letter of 15 June 1953:

> Your main difficulty will be to translate in a way which satisfies Beckett, and without omissions. [...] If you produce a satisfactory translation, then, to produce our edition for the continent of Europe we shall require not only o[u]r present option from Les Editions de Minuit but also an option on your translation. I'm sure, if you can, you will make this easy for us. If on the other hand you cannot produce what is according to Beckett a satisfactory translation – and you shouldn't be over-confident, I know Beckett very well – and we are able to do so, we shall only be too pleased to make it accessible to you. (MU, Collection Merlin Files, box 3, folder 18)

Rosset did not let his confidence be swayed, answering Trocchi on 18 June 1953:

> I am not too worried about the translation because I will be very amenable to anything Beckett has to say, and of course I also will have to be satisfied with the translation, so if Beckett is hard to please I am too, and therefore we should get along perfectly. Naturally my preference for a translator is Beckett himself. (MS, Collection Merlin Files, box 3, folder 18)

However, knowing how difficult it was to translate *En attendant Godot*, and wanting Beckett to focus on new work as much as possible, Rosset contacted him the same day about '[a] young man, Belgian by birth, who moved to this country some seven years ago'. At first he was writing in French, but now he had turned to English, which he mastered as a native language (*LSB II* 386n5). The anonymous Belgian had also started translating *Godot* – unnecessary now that Beckett was doing his own version – but perhaps 'he could be capable of doing the novels', Rosset suggested (*LSB II* 387n5).

On 25 June 1953, Beckett clarified his terms, informing Rosset that *Merlin* was already on the lookout for their own translator:

> With regard to the novels my position is that I should greatly prefer not to undertake the job myself, while having the right to revise whatever translation is made. But I know from experience how much more difficult it is to revise a bad translation than to do the thing oneself. That is why I should like to see a few brief specimens of translation before coming to a decision. Trocchi has kindly undertaken to produce three specimens of the first 10 pages of <u>Molloy</u> and <u>Malone</u>. If your Belgian (whose beginning of Godot it would interest me to see) could do a few pages of Molloy I should be very glad too. My idea was that it would be easier to collaborate with a translator living here. In any case it is a job for a professional writer and one prepared to write in his own way within the limits of mine, if that makes any sense, and beyond them too, when necessary. (*LSB II* 385)

Three weeks later, on 18 July 1953, Beckett told Rosset he had made his choice: 'I think I have found a suitable translator here for the no[vel] if I can judge from the specimen he showed me. Unless I prefer [the] translation of your acquaintance, which I have not yet receive[d, I] shall submit to you the specimen in question' (*LSB II* 387-8). The man he had selected was Patrick Bowles, a young South-African writer, translator and editor of *Merlin*, who not only matched Beckett's profile but also lived close by.[153] Trocchi had promised Beckett there would be three specimens of the novel's opening ten pages to choose from, but a letter from Austryn Wainhouse to Trocchi of 22 July 1953 suggests there were no other samples, or that Beckett made up his mind after seeing only one:

---

153   The most complete biograpical information on Patrick Bowles can be found in James Campbell's obituary for *The Guardian* entitled 'Waiting for Beckett' (18 January 1996, p. 13) and Christopher Logue's memoir *Prince Charming* (1999).

Beckett appears to have fixed, stubbornly, firmly, irreducibly, upon Pat as translator, although Grove Press, sweating in its drawers, has cried from the other shore that it too has a first-class man, and would Beckett look at a sample translation that is being sent. Beckett's chosen Pat; but for the sake of form he must wait for the Grove Press' contribution. (WU, Alexander Trocchi Papers, box 37, folder 11)

The editors of Beckett's correspondence note that Rosset did send him a sample from the young Belgian's translation of *Godot* on 31 July 1953, but there is no evidence of a *Molloy* specimen (*LSB II* 398n1). Richard Seaver – who had left Paris for Chaumont by this time – was not part of the selection either, as he explained to Trocchi in his letter of 3 August 1953: 'Lack of time prevented me from ever resubmitting a section of <u>Molloy</u> to Beckett. I'm not really hot about doing it. More power to Pat if he wants & can do it' (WU, Alexander Trocchi Papers, box 37, folder 6).[154] It was too late in any case. As Beckett urged Rosset on 1 September 1953, thanking him for the *Godot* sample: 'It has as you say great merits, but I think all things considered it is better for Bowles to go on with the job he has so well begun' (*LSB II* 397).

In the notes that Bowles later published about his collaboration with Beckett, 25 July 1953 is given as the starting date of their collaboration: 'Samuel Beckett has chosen my translation for *Molloy*', he records, 'for the reason that I wasn't a translator, rather than that I was: he wanted a writer rather than a translator' (Bowles 1994, 24). Bowles now 'began meeting with Beckett on a regular basis to revise the draft translation':

---

154 The fact that he speaks of 'resubmitting' a sample again confirms that he made the earlier fragment, revised in the 'Tara MacGowran' notebook, not Trocchi. There is a problem, however, with Seaver's reconstruction of events in his memoir. He claims that Beckett first asked him to translate *Molloy* during their work on the English version of 'La fin', which appeared in the sixth issue of *Merlin* (vol. 2, no. 3, Summer – Autumn 1954). After having 'actually translated half a dozen pages', he declined and suggested that Patrick Bowles should do it instead (Seaver 2012, 211-2). Although Seaver was involved with *Molloy*, Beckett's letter to Pamela Mitchell of 25 November 1953 (Pilling 2006, 121) situates the translation of 'La fin' much later – i.e. six months after Beckett and Bowles started collaborating.

It was slow, painstaking work, a quarter of a century before the era of word processors. It was wrung and thrashed and hammered out. Every day we revised a few pages, pen in hand, but debating virtually every word. Occcasionally Beckett would throw the cat among the chickens by saying, 'Give it a bit of rhythm'. That could mean re-casting an entire paragraph. One could not just inject a drumbeat into one phrase alone. It had to play its part in the paragraph. Every night, not much sleep, re-typing the day's work. Then the draft for the next day. (Bowles 1994, 24-5)

They were noticed by George Plimpton, editor of the *Paris Review*, who describes how '[t]he two sat at a café table and argued about the correctness of a word as if they were scholars working on a medieval manuscript by a Flemish monk' (Plimpton 1981, 372). However, the most important source to track the progress of the translation is Beckett's letters. On 27 July 1953, he reported to his friend Mania Péron: 'Je commence à traduire Molloy en anglais avec un jeune Sud-Africain. <u>Je fais dans son vase</u> devient <u>I piss and shit in her pot</u>, j'espère que ce n'est pas trop tirer sur la portée de faire' (*LSB II* 393) ['I am beginning to translate *Molloy* into English with a young South African. "Je fais dans son vase" becomes "I piss and shit in her pot." I hope that is not pushing the scope of "faire" too far' (*LSB II* 394)].

Although they had been at it for just a few days, the translation Beckett gives for the passage – thirty-six sentences into the novel, on p. 8 of the first Minuit edition – is exactly how it appeared in the published text. Also the fact that it is not a literal transposition reveals how intensely they had been labouring on the first few pages from the start. As Bowles told Alexander Trocchi on 27 July 1953: 'What is worth saying is that those first 9 pages over which Beckett and I have now gone twice-meticulously twice(!) are now truly Joyceanly polished' (WU, Alexander Trocchi Papers, box 36, folder 12). On the next day, Beckett showed the draft to Barney Rosset:

Herewith the specimen translation I told you about, as revised by me. I find it satisfactory. If you do too, will you get in touch with the translator, Patrick Bowles, 5 Cité Vaneau, Paris 7me. It is going to be a slow job and we are both anxious to get on with it. All that is required now is your approbation and that the question of the translator's fee should be settled to the satisfaction of Bowles and yourself. (SU, Grove Press Records, box 84)

Barney Rosset was sceptical at first, having written to Beckett on 18 June 1953: 'I really do not see how anybody else can get the sound quality, to name one thing, but I am willing to be convinced' (Rosset 2016, 71). After reading the first specimen of the English *Molloy*, Rosset was 'most favourably impressed with it' and he officially approved Bowles on 4 August 1953: 'Short of doing the work yourself the best would be to be able to really guide someone else along – and that situation you seem to have found', he told Beckett (Rosset 2016, 72). The same day Rosset contacted Trocchi: 'We have the first part of MOLLOY on hand, translated by Bowles, and I consider it to be fine – so perhaps there will not be too much difficulty in that direction' (MU, Collection Merlin Files, box 3, folder 18). Difficulties arose in another area, when Rosset offered Bowles his contract on 10 August 1953 (*LSB II* 398n2). Two weeks later, on 25 August 1953, Bowles asked Rosset to 'modify what appear at first sight to be very sympathetic terms' because what he and Beckett were actually doing was rewriting *Molloy*, not just translating it (see chapter 3.2):

You see, for a conventional translation of a straightforward novel I could work in the conventional straightforward manner producing a first draft, a typed and revised one and perhaps a third finally revised manuscript. However it may astonish you to learn that the draft of ten pages Mr. Beckett sent you, after his co-operation with me, was, when it came to your hands, the eighth draft. Now this is exceptional yet, for the book has many of the time-honoured infuriating obstacles one is more accustomed to expect in verse-translation, I expect it to be the rule with this translation. The fact that it is a lengthy job does make your apparently generous terms not so adequate as

I am sure they appeared to you when you drew them up. This translation will take six months. At the end of this period I think I can promise you will be able to take it to press. I shall, when the contract is finally signed by both of us, give you a deadline and make every effort to keep to it. (MU, Collection Merlin Files, box 3, folder 18)[155]

Bowles's estimate of 'six months' for the completion of the translation would turn out to be grossly optimistic, but the collaboration seemed to have gotten off to a good start.

Meetings continued in between rehearsals for the late September reprise of *En attendant Godot* (Knowlson 1997, 398), for example on 15 September 1953 at the Café François Coppée. Beckett had witnessed the opening night of *Warten auf Godot* in Berlin a week earlier, which he complained to Bowles was 'very unsatisfactory', the producer having fallen off stage and the actors changing lines (Bowles 1994, 26). He also talked about Joyce and his own work on the French 'Anna Livia Plurabelle'. Joyce's poem 'Ecce Homo', written on the death of his father, triggered a whole series of associations when Beckett and Bowles next convened on 30 September 1953: Pound, Eliot, Balzac, Hugo, Samuel Johnson, but also W. B. Yeats, who came up in the context of *Molloy*, as Bowles recalls:

---

155   Rosset's proposed rate in the original contract for the *Molloy* translation was $6.00 per 1,000 words, $150 paid in advance, the rest upon completion of the manuscript. Bowles accepted the advance terms but countered Rosset's offer with a lump sum of 260,000 francs or $740, which he felt was 'hardly excessive', and Rosset agreed. Bowles also said he could only offer Grove the American rights of the translation, but Rosset cabled Beckett on 15 September 1953: 'we must own translation outright'. The Grove Press Records also contain an unsigned note reading: 'It is cust[omary] to receive a small fee for use of trans!' Since Bowles thanked Rosset on 28 October 1953 for sending him an additional cheque for $30 up, this is probably how they agreed to settle the matter when they met in Paris in late October to sign the contract. At roughly 79.630 words, the total due for the translation was $278,71. With $180 already paid, this left a balance of $98,71 upon completion (SU, Grove Press Records, box 98). On top of the translator's fee, Bowles received a 2.5% commission for every copy sold over 3.000. This was to be a small though regular source of income for Bowles in the following decades.

We were trying to find the proper word to express the sense that in this toppling, crumbling, collapsing world of Molloy nothing remained vertical. The word 'upstanding' came up and one of us, I forget which, myself I think, recalled Yeats' poem with – 'and young upstanding men' – objecting to its moral connotations – then Beckett, looking up, 'Dirty old man he was'. (Bowles 1994, 26)

It may have been Beckett who thought of Yeats's poem 'The Tower', as in 1934 he had cited the phrase in 'Recent Irish Poetry' to exemplify 'the virtues of a verse that shall be nudist' (*Dis* 72). More importantly, the discussion of Yeats offers an indication of their progress with the translation. On p. 46 of the first typescript (corresponding to 1951, 59), *Molloy* mentions the voice in his mind, which is 'of a world collapsing endlessly', of 'wastes where true light never was, nor any upright thing, nor any true foundation, but only these leaning things, forever lapsing and crumbling away' (1955, 53; *Mo* 38). The English translation was anything but crumbling, with talks between Beckett and Bowles becoming more personal and open. Everything seemed to be going perfectly. The first 'Extract from *Molloy*' appeared on 15 September in the fourth issue of *Merlin* (vol. 2, no. 2, Autumn 1953) and two weeks later – on 28 September 1953 –Lindon even officially certified Bowles as his approved translator for the next two years, implying they would take on the entire Trilogy together (Pilling 2006, 120).[156]

In mid-October Barney Rosset and his wife Loly visited Paris. They met Patrick Bowles, who gave them a second, more substantial as well as more polished sample of the translation in progress. Beckett had approved the specimen, writing to Rosset on 14 October 1953: 'I am quite pleased with the result and hope you are too' (SU, Grove Press Records, box 84). On 19 October 1953, the Rossets conveyed their delight to Beckett in writing from New York: 'We like the <u>Molloy</u> translation very much, and we are looking forward very keenly to seeing more. My congratulations to you and Patrick for the good work' (Rosset 2016, 75). This second specimen consisted of the first thirty-seven typescript pages from Part I, up to the point when Molloy, whose bicycle accidentally ran over Lousse's dog, Teddy, is stopped

---

156 The Minuit files in the Fonds Samuel Beckett at IMEC contain a copy of this 'Attestation' (Boîte 1, Correspondance 1946–1953).

from running away by a police constable (1951, 48; see chapter 1.2.2). The translation had already advanced far beyond this point, as Beckett's next letter to Rosset of 27 October 1953 shows: 'Work with Bowles proceeds apace, i.e. about a page an hour. Yesterday we did the unpleasant Ruth or Edith idyll which I fear may shake you in English' (*LSB II* 412). Having reached p. 85 in the French text, there were fifty pages left to go before the end of Part I. A week later, on 4 November 1953, Beckett reported: 'We are getting on slowly but well with translation and hope to have first part finished in about ten days' (SU, Grove Press Records, box 84). His timing was spot on. Bowles's note of 14 November 1953 reads: 'I met Beckett in the Select at 10.30 a.m. [...] It should have been ten but I was late. I had stayed up till 8 a.m. this morning typing up the first half of *Molloy*, which we finished a day or two ago' (Bowles 1994, 26).

It seems likely that they used the next few days to go over the entire Part I again and make minor adjustments, as Bowles waited till 18 November 1953 to send Rosset the typescript:

> Here also of course, minus the 30 odd pages you already have, is the complete M.S. of the first half of MOLLOY, there may be a few corrections to follow but it is very nearly the final version: one or two errors in punctuation, and a word here and there perhaps, may have to be changed, but it is accurate enough to be sent round to magazines etc. (SU, Grove Press Records, box 98)

In fact, Beckett would make a few hundred additional changes to the second typescript of Part I later on – nearly all very minor (see chapters 3.2 and 3.3). As his letter of 20 November 1953 to the Rossets indicates, he needed some distance from the text first to be able to assess it properly: 'I leave it to you to judge the result, I am beyond doing so. I don't think it stinks too much of a translation, but it certainly doesn't take kindly to English' (*LSB II* 419). Rosset liked it, writing to Bowles on 30 November 1953: 'It reads extremely well and I think that it is a fine job' (SU, Grove Press Records, box 98). That Beckett was still on very good terms with his translator is not only suggested by the fact that he borrowed and read his copy of *The Catcher in the Rye*. It is also confirmed by his letter of 25 November 1953 to Pamela Mitchell. 'Bowles is very pleasant to work with', he wrote, but their task was clearly beginning to take its toll: 'I was kilt entirely co-translating in Paris, and the result not very satisfactory. Wish I could discover why my cursed prose won't go into English' (*LSB II* 420).[157]

Molloy was not the only translation on his mind at this time, and English not the only language he struggled with. He was also assisting Erich Franzen with a German translation of the novel, revising Daniel Mauroc's (abandoned) French *Watt*, vetting the Spanish version of *Godot*, correcting proofs for its American publication, and working on *Malone stirbt* with Elmar Tophoven. Consequently, '*Molloy* hasn't advanced much further', Beckett confided to Barney Rosset on 12 December 1953, 'I am tired and most of the time in the country. But part 2 will go faster' (*LSB II* 432). Bowles too had taken a break, in London. When Beckett saw him on 15 January 1953, he wrote to Rosset: 'He is getting going on second part of <u>Molloy</u>' (SU, Grove Press Records, box 84). Yet Bowles's notes reveal that he was slow to start again: 'Suddenly realize that I began translating *Molloy* in July '53 and now it is January 26 1954, and the damned thing is only half-finished' (Bowles 1994, 27).

While Part I of the book had been wrapped up in four months, Part II would take nearly a year. The cause of this delay is revealed by Richard Seaver in his memoirs:

> Patrick turned his back on the project and reimmersed himself in his own work, the long-planned novel he had, two years before, sketched out in his mind from start to finish, three volumes that, he announced, he would submit only to Jonathan Cape in London, whose list he found compatible with his taste. (Seaver 2012, 213)

Christopher Logue, too, remembers him talking about his novel: '"I want my reader hardly to know my book has started," Bowles used to say. "To slide into it by accident, as it were. But to emerge changed"' (Logue 1990, 124). One fine day he would 'walk into Jonathan Cape and place it on the table, beautifully typed, in green binders', but Logue comments dryly: 'He never wrote it' (123). Like many aspiring authors, Bowles had difficulties

---

157   In the draft of his letter to Mitchell, preserved in notebook TCD MS 4662, Beckett referred to the translation more negatively as 'pretty poor' instead of 'not very satisfactory' (29v), which shows that his opinion of the text was subject to change, depending on the moment.

carving out time to write from his busy schedule. In order to earn a living, he was teaching in Le Havre, some 200 km outside of Paris, making the long journey on his bicycle because he did not like the train. Luckily, the school had agreed to clear his schedule on Monday mornings and Friday afternoons, leaving him free to spend long weekends in the city. What little free time remained was taken up entirely by the *Molloy* translation, which left Bowles hardly any room to pursue interests of his own. The original note for 26 January 1954 – which he edited before publication in the *P.N. Review* – illustrates his mounting frustrations. Looking back on his collaboration with Beckett (begun in July 1953) Bowles laments:

> Admittedly I have done other things since then as well. But not enough to fill 6 long months. Besides which I want to read several thousand books! Here I am half-way through the [Farraday Slaughter][158] piece, page 15 – I ought to be a hermit, fossilizing in a cave: and making journeys in three directions only per day: from the bed to the table, the table to the pantry, the pantry to the shithouse: and of course variations on these.[159]

158 Lois More Overbeck transcribes this as 'Rockenhalter' (e-mail to Pim Verhulst, 8 January 2013), but it is probably 'Faraday Slaughter'. The sixth issue of *Merlin* (vol. 2, no. 3, Summer-Autumn 1954), contains a prose contribution by Bowles entitled 'from *Faraday Slaughter*' (201-5). Given the dense and highly poetic nature of the piece, as well as its heavy reliance on Joycean wordplay, it is more likely to be an extract from a short prose experiment than a full-length novel, hence Bowles's reference to p. 15 as 'half-way through'. Understandably, he would not have wanted to draw attention to this never republished or even unfinished piece forty years later, as it only confirms what Campbell notes in his obituary for *The Guardian*: 'while the other juveniles achieved success in seniority in their respective fields, Bowles's own literary work never broke free of his term of hard labour with Beckett' (Campbell 1996, 13).

159 Bowles's 'Notes on Talks with Samuel Beckett' are preceded by an introduction in which he explains their origin: 'The following notes are attempts to reproduce without embellishment what was said by Samuel Beckett or myself in the course of our meetings for work on the translation of his novel, *Molloy* [...]. Except for passages described as a folly, they are not inventions and nothing is fictitious. Most of these notes were written about forty years ago. I have carried them around the world since then in their original form, namely a scrawl on odd bits of paper, mercifully in ink. They even spent about fifteen years with me in Equatorial Africa. [...] Had I tinkered with them, I would probably have tarnished what appeal they may have. What Mr. Beckett had said was what he had said. Why change it?' (Bowles 1994, 24). Despite this

Any aspiring writer too deeply immersed in the work of a still living penman is bound to emulate his style, something Beckett himself knew all too well. The passage that Bowles excised from his notes does indeed emit a whiff of Beckett, much like Beckett's own earlier writing 'stinks of Joyce' (SB to Charles Prentice, 15 August 1931, *LSB I* 81). 'I'm not really indifferent to this kind of thing', Bowles admitted to Alexander Trocchi in the summer of 1953, 'particularly when my admiration for Beckett increases the more I do on Molloy and see him, himself' (WU, Alexander Trocchi Papers, box 36, folder 12).[160] For Beckett, it was necessary to have a writer as his co-translator, but he may have underestimated the adverse effect it could have on that individual's own artistic development – even though in 1930 he had experienced a similar anxiety of influence when translating the 'Anna Livia Plurabelle' episode from Joyce's 'Work in Progress'. To put some distance between himself and Beckett, Bowles started 'avoiding him', as Richard Seaver recounts in his memoir:

> Now, with Pat gone silent, Beckett found himself obliged to reverse their roles: while it had been agreed that whenever Patrick had a dozen or so pages translated, he would contact Beckett either directly or via Lindon, now, when two or three of his *pneumatiques* had gone unanswered, Beckett became the stalker. (Seaver 2012, 213)

From this point on, the English translation of *Molloy* would no longer develop as a true 'collaboration'. Instead of going over the text together, Bowles would occasionally mail chunks of typescript to Beckett for revision. Richard Seaver also claims he had another 'peripheral involvement' in the project at this point:

elaborate disclaimer, Bowles did edit the notes slightly, mostly those parts about himself, as the example above shows. We are grateful to Lois More Overbeck for comparing the *P.N. Review* transcript to Bowles's original holograph and for giving us permission to quote from it (e-mail to Pim Verhulst, 8 January 2013). For a more detailed analysis of the notes in their historical context see Verhulst and Dillen 2014.

160   The letter itself is not dated, but reference to the impending publication of *Watt* in the Collection Merlin situates it between late July – when Beckett and Bowles started working on *Molloy* – and late August 1953 – when *Watt* was published.

I suggested again, having the experience of 'La fin,' that Pat force himself on a schedule of twelve to fifteen pages a week and show me them before they were sent to Beckett. For the next three weeks he did, and I found them strong and faithful, returning them with a few emendations and suggestions, which he said helped greatly. (Seaver 2012, 213)

While there is no material evidence to support Seaver's claim, it would be another plausible explanation for the many delays that set back the Moran section.

Because of the growing interest in Beckett's work from England and the snail's pace at which *Molloy* was progressing, he started rethinking the partnership with Bowles and his colleagues for the Trilogy. 'My convention with Merlin concerns Molloy only and I do not intend to extend it to the other works for the moment', he assured Rosset on 22 January 1954, adding: 'Sick of all this old vomit and despair more and more of ever being able to puke again' (*LSB II* 448). Aside from the troublesome collaboration with Bowles, Beckett needed a break from translation in general because it exhausted him too much to write anything new. He only felt 'compelled to do it by a foolish feeling of protectiveness towards the work', as he explained to his American publisher on 11 February 1954 (*LSB II* 456). After a good two months of silence, Rosset asked Beckett for an update on 14 April 1954, something he would do incessantly for the next six months: 'It has been long since we have heard from you. What has been happening with the translation... I'm almost afraid to ask, but we would like to know' (Rosset 2016, 82). Beckett answered with an exasperated letter – his first in a series of many – on 21 April 1954:

> With regard to translation I fear I have been very remiss. The revision of the German *Molloy* finished me. I have not seen or heard from Bowles for a long time. I revised the first few pages of Part II of *Molloy* and that was our last contact. With the delayed appearance of *Godot* I suppose there is no great hurry about *Molloy*. Sometimes I feel the only alternative is to wash my hands of it entirely or to do it entirely myself. (*LSB II* 480)

Grove Press would not publish *Waiting for Godot* until 8 September 1954 (Federman and Fletcher 1970, 76), buying them some extra time for the English markets. Two more extracts from the first part of *Molloy* had also appeared, in the *Paris Review* 5 (March 1954) and *New World Writing* 5 (April 1954). But the German *Molloy* – out since 24 May 1954 – strangely preceded the English translation by almost a year (*LSB II* 498n3).

Because the situation with Bowles became increasingly untenable from a business point of view as well, Rosset made Beckett a proposition on 5 May 1954:

> We have a contract with Bowles whereby he was to translate Molloy for us and be paid at the rate of $3.50 per 1000 words of translation plus a royalty of 2.5% per copy for each copy sold over 3000 copies. We paid him $180.00 thus far and I would be very happy to switch the same terms over to you. I do not know whether the sections translated cover the advance paid or not. We have the first 108 pages here and you mention having done the first few pages of part two with Bowles. That should come fairly close to the mark. Let me know what you plan to do – we of course will hope that you either renew contact with Bowles or plough on by yourself. [...] We put off the publication date as you know, but if we want to do Molloy in the foreseeable future you must get on with the translation. Hope you see your way clear to getting it done, with or without Bowles. (Rosset 2016, 83)

Beckett's initial response is unknown as Rosset mislaid a briefcase that contained his last two letters, but he had 'offered to take on the translation of Malone Meurt and L'Innommable' in correspondence with Bowles, who relayed the news to America on 17 May 1954:

> Since I have not merely one, but two books of my own I am attempting to finish, one in the early stages, another farther on, and shall be grateful of the time it will leave me to work of my own, I have accepted, pending your approval, which I am sure you will be glad to give. (SU, Grove Press Records, box 98)

The problem was that Beckett not only wanted a fee higher than that of Bowles, but also than what was agreed on with Grove for his own translation of *Godot*, as his next letter of 8 June 1954 makes clear. Rosset carefully explained that his financial situation did not allow this and that he could only offer the same terms: 'As for your being a better translator than Bowles – no argument, and I am very pleased to know that you want to do the job yourself, but it is not exactly a situation where better gets paid better' (Rosset 2016, 85). Negotiations were temporarily suspended because, at the end of May 1954, Beckett received a telephone call from his sister in law Jean, informing him that his brother Frank had been diagnosed with terminal lung cancer. So he rushed to Dublin and stayed at the Shottery in Killiney for three and a half months (Knowlson 1997, 400).

In addition to keeping Frank company as much as he could, helping Jean around the house and entertaining their children, Beckett was also trying to 'get on anew with revision of Bowles's <u>Molloy</u>', which he found 'a loathsome task', as he wrote to Pamela Mitchell on 10 June 1954 (UoR MIT 027). 'I thought I might get to Paris for 48 hours or so, but I fear that is out of the question', he mused on 15 June 1954. Instead, he would 'vaguely try and correct the incorrigible Bowles' (UoR MIT 028). Working in these conditions was a grim repeat of 1950, when Beckett made his first translation from *Molloy* – and *Malone meurt* – for *Transition*. Preoccupied with his mother then, his personal situation resembled that of Molloy. Now, it was closer to that of Malone, who also tries to come to terms with death.[161] Beckett's letter of 30 June 1954 to Mitchell, in which he complains there is '[n]o getting on with that cursed revision of Bowles at all', contains a description of himself which could easily have come straight out of *Malone Dies*: 'The least difficulty stops me, I start looking out of the window, at the old wordless world. Then can't turn back to <u>Molloy</u>' (UoR MIT 031). As if to complete the striking parallels with the events of 1950, Beckett also turned to translating *Malone meurt* on his own, commenting in his letter to Jérome Lindon of 12 July 1954:

---

161 In his letter to Henri Hayden of 28 August 1954, sent from Dublin, Beckett would also compare his brother's condition to that of Moran: 'Ici, pas grand'chose à raconter. Sa pente est bien longue. L'y suivre jusqu'au bout, souvent ça semble impossible. Ça me fait un peu l'effet du retour de Moran.' (*LSB IV* 742) ['Here nothing much to report. The slope he's on is very long. To follow him on it right to the very end often seems impossible. To me it feels a bit like Moran's return journey.' (*LSB IV* 743)]

'Ça me donne beaucoup moins de mal que la révision Bowles' (*LSB II* 488)
['It is giving me far less trouble than revising Bowles' (*LSB II* 489)].[162]

The ease at which *Malone Dies* progressed, did not move Beckett to discharge Bowles from his duties. When Rosset urged him, 'Do tell us what you think about the translating job, etc., and the status of Molloy' on 7 July 1954 (Rosset 2016, 87), Beckett replied five days later: 'It is better that Bowles shd. finish *Molloy*. I am waiting for him to send me more pages to revise', adding for Rosset's reassurance: 'I have begun to translate Malone' (*LSB II* 487). With Beckett still in Dublin and Bowles dividing his summer between Barcelona, Tossa and Lloret de Mar, communications between the two were very patchy. A letter from Bowles to Trocchi, undated but clearly written from Spain over the summer, gives a good impression of the situation: 'Have you heard from Beckett: I sent him a thick wad of Molloy MS' (WU, Alexander Trocchi Papers, box 36, folder 12).[163] The package had reached its destination by 21 August 1954, when Beckett updated Rosset, who kept asking about the translation:

> I am slowly and with great difficulty continuing the revision of Bowles's text. The last pages he sent me bring us up to p. 208 of the book. I expect the next 100 will be to the end. When he last wrote he was in Spain. He seems to be having bad health. I am sorry for all this delay, it has really been from every point of view an unsatisfactory job. When the revision is finished and clean copy made by Bowles we shall have to go through it rapidly again. I really do not think you can count on having our final version much before November. I have so much to do here that an hour's continuous work is exceptional. (*LSB II* 496-7)

162 For a more detailed study of this novel's genesis, see Dirk Van Hulle and Pim Verhulst, *The Making of Samuel Beckett's Malone meurt / Malone Dies*, Brussels and London: University Press Antwerp and Bloomsbury (forthcoming).

163 The letter is undated but the return address line states: 'c/o [care of] Amer. Express / Barcelona.' The archivist responsible for cataloguing the material guesses '[1952?]' but, given the reference to *Molloy* and the context of the translation in general, this should rather be 1954.

Beckett's letter to Henri Hayden of 24 August 1954 gives an impression of the mistakes that Bowles made in his translation: 'J'essaie d'avancer la révision du <u>Molloy</u> anglais. Un mal fou. Le traducteur se fait de + en + sublime. "Un parapluie à manche massif" [(1951, 192)] devient en anglais "Un trench-coat à manches massives."' (*LSB IV* 742) ['I'm trying to push ahead with the revision of the English *Molloy*. Terrible trouble. The translator gets more and more sublime. "Un parapluie à manche massif" becomes in English "Un trench-coat à manches massives."' (*LSB IV* 743)] Beckett alludes to Moran's decision to leave home his 'black cloak' in favour of a 'massive-handled winter umbrella' (1955, 170; *Mo* 129), which Bowles had apparently misunderstood to mean a 'trench-coat with massive sleeves' instead of an 'umbrella with a solid wooden shaft' (*LSB IV* 743n3). Incidents such as these gave Beckett the feeling he was 'rewriting' rather than 'revising' the translation, as he complained to Jérôme Lindon on 2 September 1954: 'J'essaie toujours de réviser, plûtot de récrire, le texte de Bowles.' (IMEC, Fonds Samuel Beckett, Boîte 1, Divers Correspondance 1950–1956).[164]

Two weeks later, on 7 September 1954, he told Pamela Mitchell: 'finished at last Bowles revision, at least the pages I had', adding ominously: 'there are more to come' (UoR MIT 038). Having reached the point in the novel when Moran refuses to answer the question 'D'où Ballyba tirait-il donc son opulence?' (1951, 208) – sixty-six pages into the second part – there were still sixty-four pages to go in the French edition before a final overhaul could even start. Beckett's November estimate would turn out to be rather accurate, but working conditions did not improve. When Beckett prepared to go back to Paris on 17 September 1954, he had little news to offer Barney Rosset, who was eager to start preparing for the novel's publication together with *Merlin* (see chapters 1.4.2 and 1.4.3):

---

164 This suggests that Beckett's following comment to Lindon, made in his letter of 18 October 1955, is to be read with scepticism: 'Comme je n'ai fait que "réviser" la traduction de Molloy faite par Bowles, je n'ai reçu aucune rémuneration de Merlin.' (*LSB II* 557) ['As I did no more than "revise" the translation of *Molloy* done by Bowles, I have received no remuneration from Merlin.' (*LSB II* 557)]

I have finished revision of *Molloy* up to p. 209 and am waiting for Bowles to send me from there to end. Si ça ne dépendait que de moi you'd have the finished article next month. I'll chivvy Patrick when I get back to civilization. Make yr. mind easy the authorised version will go to you and them simul et semel whatever that means. I used to know. (*LSB II* 502)

Although Rosset had written to Bowles on 28 September 1954, hoping that 'nothing happens to prevent an uninterrupted run to the finish' (SU, Grove Press Records, box 98), it was not so easy to 'chivvy Patrick' as Beckett had expected, judging from his letter to the publisher of 18 October 1954, three weeks later: 'Bowles too is hopeless. No acknowledgement of my last corrections and no sign of the concluding pages. I do not even know where he is. I wish as heartily as you that it was finished and out of the way' (*LSB II* 507) – even more so now that Beckett was fiddling with a new play, *Fin de partie*. Bowles was certainly back in Paris, as *Merlin*'s meeting agenda of 6 October 1954 lists him as present and records his promise that 'the MS would be ready in a month at the outside' (MU, Collection Merlin Files, box 3, folder 4). This time he was true to his word, and on 25 October 1954 Beckett informed Lindon that he had received the last part of the translation, asking for a copy of the French *Molloy* to check his revisions of the English version against the original (Pilling 2006, 125). Because it was ten days since Beckett's last letter, and Christopher Logue told Rosset that Bowles had sent his final corrections, anxious letters started arriving from New York.

On 27 November, Rosset wanted to know: 'How goes it with MOLLOY? Not a word for so long' (SU, Grove Press Records, box 84). The question had crossed Beckett's letter of 25 November 1954, in which he set his publisher's mind at ease: 'I thought that you would like to know that I have finished revising Bowles's text and have sent it to him to type out clean. Then I go through it rapidly once again and then off it goes to you' (*LSB II* 512). Two weeks later, Beckett had 'seen Bowles', telling Rosset on 7 December 1954: 'He has finished typing out clean the revised text of *Molloy* and I am at present giving it a final go-through. It will certainly go off to you next week. I am not satisfied with it but have reached the stage when I simply do not see it anymore' (*LSB II* 512). In fact, Beckett took three weeks to finetune the translation, explaining the delay to Rosset on 18 December 1954:

I was on the point of writing to tell you that final text of Molloy is alas again held up because of ill health of your humble and obedient. I can't get on with it at the moment. I have written to Bowles telling him he may count on it for second week of January. I hope to get to the country next week and to finish it there. Any way I suppose you couldn't do much about it at this season. (SU, Grove Press Records, box 84).

On 27 December 1954, he wrote to Pamela Mitchell: 'Putting the finishing daubs at last to Bowles's *Molloy*, that makes about the 10th re-reading and it has my soul drowned in vomit' (*LSB II* 514n2). After a terrible Christmas and New Year, he declared Molloy *bon à tirer* on 7 January 1955, writing to Mitchell: 'Can't do any more with <u>Molloy</u> and am leaving it at that' (UoR MIT 048).[165]

Beckett submitted his corrected typescript for final approval to Patrick Bowles on 12 January 1955, writing to Rosset the next day:

I handed over to Bowles yesterday the final text of <u>Molloy</u> and you should receive it in the course of next week. I am far from being satisfied with the translation but really can do nothing more with it for the moment. Perhaps I shall see it more clearly in proof and be able to improve it a little more. But I think you may take it that the text as it now stands is about the best we can do. Shall welcome any suggestions you may have to make. (SU, Grove Press Records, box 84)

Bowles needed about ten days to process Beckett's annotations, dispatching copies of the final typescript on 20 January 1955 simultaneously to Maurice Girodias and Barney Rosset (*LSB II* 520n2), who acknowledged receipt on 7 February 1955 (SU, Grove Press Records, box 84). Because Grove arranged with *Merlin* and Girodias to photographically reproduce the Olympia edition, Beckett had to read just one set of proofs. Rosset's only wish was for him to be 'reasonably dilligent in getting them corrected' (24 February 1955;

165   The letter was postmarked in January but only mentions 'Friday' as the date of composition. Since Beckett suggests he and Mitchell should meet again some day, and he proposes Wednesday 12 January in his letter of Monday the 10th, 'Friday' must refer to the first Friday of 1955, i.e. the 7th of that month.

SU, Grove Press Records, box 84). The next day, Bowles delivered the Olympia proofs to Minuit, with the message that the line spacing would be increased by one point. Because Girodias needed the proofs back quickly, they were forwarded to Ussy, where Beckett set about correcting them (letter from Les Éditions de Minuit to SB, 25 February 1955, IMEC, Fonds Samuel Beckett, Boîte 1, Divers Correspondance 1950–1956). Three weeks later, on 13 March 1955, he was relieved to tell Pamela Mitchell: '*Molloy* at last finished and done with, i.e. page proofs corrected, you'll get a copy in due course' (*LSB II* 531). The Olympia Press text appeared at the end of March, with the Grove Press edition trailing in August 1955 (Pilling 2006, 127). Despite Beckett's fierce judgment of the English version during the translation process – the combination of 'affreuse' ('frightful') and 'cauchemar' ('nightmare') in his letter to Jacoba van Velde of 20 August 1954 (*LSB II* 496) being one of the more annihilating epithets – he grew more positive as the memory of the experience itself faded and he was more capable of assessing the result fairly. According to Bowles, 'Beckett did in fact later say that he thought it was better in English' (Bowles 1994, 33).

While at times he became frustrated with Bowles, he never held a grudge against the young man. They remained on friendly terms for many years to come, meeting in Paris and corresponding occasionally.[166] Beckett knew first-hand how (self-)translation got in the way of his own writing, and he always expressed a genuine concern for Bowles, as his fellow Merlinite, Christopher Logue, recalls:

---

166 While the letters that Beckett and Bowles exchanged during the translation process of *Molloy* have not been located, some later correspondence survives, transcripts of which are available in the James and Elizabeth Knowlson collection at the University of Reading (folder entitled 'Bowles, Patrick', JEK/A/2/37). The letters, extending into the early 1980s, mostly concern attempts to meet and Beckett helping Bowles to further his career, for example by commenting on his poetry and encouraging him to do more translation work. The folder also contains a few letters between Knowlson and Bowles from the 1990s. They occasionally deal with *Molloy* but disclose no new information about the translation process. With thanks to David Tucker for drawing our attention to this material.

He was friendly, generous, always asking after others, particularly Patrick: 'How is he? Is he working at his own work? I don't want to take him away from his own work. We worked at writing my book again. This time in English. I could not have done it alone. I needed someone who knew English as I once did.' (Logue 1999, 173)

This is also the answer Bowles received from Beckett when he asked him why he did not translate *Molloy* on his own: 'he replied that not having spoken or worked in English for seventeen years he felt out of touch with the language and wanted to work with an English writer for a while so as to feel his way back into the language' (Bowles 1994, 27). While it is surely an exaggeration to say that Beckett had not used English for seventeen years, the uncertainty he felt at writing in his mother tongue was genuine, having lived in France since the late 1930s, and French having become his primary means of expression. Yet it seems that working on the second part of *Molloy*, isolated from Bowles, was actually more decisive for Beckett to overcome his reserve than the months he spent truly collaborating on the novel. It was this experience – and the subsequent decision to translate *Malone* alone – that led to the crucial insight recorded in his letter of 4 January 1956 to Cyril Lucas, who asked permission to do *Malone meurt* and *L'Innommable*: 'I am by no means a good translator, and my English is rusty', Beckett told him, 'but I simply happen to be able still to write the queer kind of English that my queer French deserves' (*LSB II* 591-2).

Perhaps no variant between the twin texts of *Molloy* captures this insight better than Moran's reflection on his own story towards the end of Part II, when a movement of the mind in the French text becomes a self-reflexive comment on the act of self-translation in English: '*Me rapportant maintenant en imagination à l'instant présent, j'affirme avoir écrit tout ce passage d'une main ferme et même satisfait, et l'esprit plus tranquille que depuis longtemps.*' (1951, 239; emphasis added) ['*Translating myself now in imagination to the present moment, I declare the foregoing to have been written with a firm hand and a mind calmer than it has been for a long time.*' (1955, 212; emphasis added)]. As this variant illustrates, the notion of autography can also be extended to the English self-translation of *Molloy*, which continues the genesis of the French text as a form of 're-writing'.

3.2 Translation as Re-Writing

During their work on the English *Molloy*, Beckett would frequently say to Bowles that what they were trying to do was to 'write the book *again* in another language – that is to say, write a *new* book' (Bowles 1994, 27; emphasis added). This combination of the words 'again' and 'new' leads to a definition of translation as *re-writing*, a double entendre that encompasses the notions of fidelity (writing *again*) and change (writing *anew*), between which there is a constant tension. As Bowles explains in the 'Translator's Preface' to his English version of Friedrich Dürrenmatt's tragicomedy *Der Besuch der alten Dame – The Visit* – referring to his experience with Beckett: 'One translates within the dilemma of literalness and readability, the one tending to rise as the other falls' (Bowles 1962, n.p.). This rising and falling movement between 'literalness' on the one hand, and 'readability' on the other, can be traced in the drafts of the English *Molloy* as well, which offer insight into the 'dilemma' its translation posed. Because the author himself partook in the English version of *Molloy*, it more accurately becomes an act of self-translation, which perhaps allows for more leeway from 'literalness' in the direction of 'readability' than a standard translation by a third party would. However, as the drafts of the novel illustrate, it was still a difficult balancing act in which alternatives were frequently weighed against each other.

Sadly, we can now only partially reconstruct this process. As explained in chapter 1 (see 1.2.2), Bowles lost most versions that document his collaboration with Beckett on *Molloy*, which imposes considerable limitations on a genetic analysis of the translation process. The two most substantial surviving documents on which this chapter is based are relatively late typescripts – one partial (ET1, Part I), the other complete (ET2, Parts I & II) – and the late changes they record are few and mostly local, generally leaving the sentence structure intact. All that remains of the earlier, undoubtedly more dynamic stages is a very short extract in *Transition* – not very different from the published text – a longer but still brief holograph fragment in the 'Tara MacGowran' Notebook (EM) – Beckett's revision of Richard Seaver's sample – and a short typescript specimen (Sp1-3) – already the eighth draft of the novel's opening pages (see chapter 1.2.2). Unlike *Malone Dies* or *The Unnamable*, the other two novels in the translated 'trilogy', *Molloy* is a patchwork of different influences and creative energies. 'Whether teamwork of that sort should also be considered self-translation, is a worthwhile but complex question', as Rainier Grutman observes (2013, 203n2).[167] But, unfortunately, the Seaver-Beckett-Bowles collaboration on the English *Molloy* will not provide an answer, as it is near impossible to clearly disentangle and study the role or share of each party in the constitution of the text, because of gaps in the genetic record. All surviving documents are palimpsests of at least two translators, and the versions compiled independently by Seaver or Bowles have not been preserved, some of which – in the case of Bowles – were collaborative from the start, when he and Beckett met in cafés to translate the text on the spot. At best, we can generally reconstruct Beckett's final tweakings of the text, with cursory digressions into the earlier surviving fragments.[168]

In order to do so, this chapter makes a subdivision between revisions that mark the English *Molloy* as a self-translation, and thus as a continuation of the writing process (3.2), and changes that are more characteristic of translation in general (3.3). The former category offers illustrations of how Beckett 're-wrote' or 'wrote the book again' in another language, sometimes drawing attention to the result as a translation rather than 'original', which makes the English *Molloy* an integral part of the autographic project that Beckett had started in French in 1947. As mentioned in 3.1, when Moran reflects on his act of writing, he uses the words '*Translating myself* now in imagination to the present moment' (1955, 212; *Mo* 161-2; emphasis added) instead of '*Me rapportant* maintenant en imagination à l'instant présent' (1951, 239; emphasis added). This transition from writing to translation is also reflected in the altered references to *Molloy* as part of a 'trilogy' in the first part of the novel.

As explained in the introduction to this volume, when Beckett embarked on *Molloy*, he had possibly already conceived of a follow-up novel, *Malone meurt*, which leads Molloy to the following autographic comment at the

167   In addition to Rainier Grutman's article cited above, see also his entry on 'Self-Translation' in the *Routledge Encyclopedia of Translation Studies* (2nd edition, 2009) and Cordingley 2013 for a broader perspective on the practice of self-translation beyond the familiar case of Samuel Beckett.

168   The goal of this chapter is therefore to highlight significant changes in the extant drafts of the translation (genetic variants), not to launch a full-scale, bilingual comparison of the French and English versions. For more in-depth studies of the differences between the 'original' and the translation of *Molloy*, see Hill 1990, Morin 2005, 2009 and Mooney 2012.

start of his narrative: 'Cette fois-ci, puis encore une je pense, puis c'en sera fini je pense, de ce monde-là aussi' (1951, 8). This flash-forward to a second instalment is twice repeated in the preamble – 'C'est le sens de l'avant-dernier' (1951, 9) and 'De sorte qu'on se dit, J'arriverai bien cette fois-ci, puis encore une autre peut-être, puis ce sera tout' (1951, 9) – but also a fourth time when Molloy reaches the seashore: 'Mais je confonds peut-être avec un autre séjour, antérieur, car ce sera celui-ci mon dernier, mon avant-dernier, il n'y a jamais de dernier, au bord de la mer' (1951, 114). These meta-fictional comments reflected Beckett's situation when he was writing the French version of *Molloy*, but by the time he was translating it into English, he had also completed a third novel, turning *Molloy*, *Malone meurt* and *L'Innommable* into a 'trilogy' – although he did not like the term, possibly because the third novel was an afterthought and he did not conceive of them as such (see chapters 1.4.2, 1.4.3 and 1.4.4). The references are updated in the English version of *Molloy* to reflect this altered situation, but not until the first and the second typescripts. The three passages that featured in the early specimens (Sp1-3) still followed the French original, and Beckett did not adjust the fourth reference to the 'trilogy' until the second typescript, which explains why the *Paris Review* extract was not yet up to date, as opposed to the *Merlin* and *New World Writing* fragments:

> This time, then once more I think, then I think it'll be over, with that world too. (Sp1-3, 02r)
> This time, then once more I think, **then perhaps a last time,** then I think it'll be over, with that world too. (ET1, 02r)
> This time, then once more I think, **then perhaps a last time,** then I think it'll be over, with that world too. (MER, 89)
> This time, then once more I think, **then perhaps a last time,** then I think it'll be over, with that world too. (NWW, 317)
>
> Premonition of the last but one. (Sp1-3, 03r)
> Premonition of the last but one **but one**. (ET1, 02r)
> Premonition of the last but one **but one**. (MER, 89)
> Premonition of the last but one **but one**. (NWW, 317)
>
> So that you say, I'll manage this time, then perhaps once more, then nothing more. (Sp1-3, 03r)

So that you say, I'll manage this time, then perhaps once more,
then perhaps a last time, then nothing more. (ET1, 03r).
So that you say, I'll manage this time, then perhaps once more,
then perhaps a last time, then nothing more. (MER, 89).
So that you say, I'll manage this time, then perhaps once more,
then perhaps a last time, then nothing more. (NWW, 317).

But perhaps I am thinking of another stay, at an earlier time, for
this will be my last, my last but oj^{n}e, there is never a last, by the
sea. (ET1, 88r)
But perhaps I am thinking of another stay, at an earlier time, for
this will be my last, my last but one, there is never a last, by the
sea. (PR, 131)
But perhaps I am thinking of another stay, at an earlier time, for
this will be my last, my last but oj^{n}e, ~~or but two~~ or two there is never a
last, by the sea. (ET2, 88r)

Instead of making the English text a more up-to-date or more 'complete'
version of *Molloy* than its French counterpart, the passages may be
understood to reflect different autographic moments in both languages, the
one connected to the act of writing, the other to the act of (self-)translation
or 're-writing'. In this respect, it is telling that Beckett chose not to alter the
French passages when he had a chance to do so for the reset 1971 hardback
edition of *Molloy* by Minuit – as he did for the ending of *L'Innommable* (see
Van Hulle and Weller 2014, 45-6).

Since *Molloy, Malone meurt* and *L'Innommable* were never collected as
a 'trilogy' in French, unlike their English counterparts (see chapter 1.4.1), the
mention of only one follow-up narrative instead of two need not raise the
reader's suspicion, as it may well refer to the story of Moran, which comes
after that of Molloy. In English, however, it is a more direct foreshadowing
of *Malone Dies* and *The Unnamable*, so that here, too, nothing seems out of
place at first sight. It is not until we compare the two versions of the novel
that we start noticing the numerous, though mostly small contradictions
between the two accounts. Perhaps the most innovative aspect of *Molloy* as a
bilingual novel is that it uses (self-) translation as a means to further subvert
the reliability of its narrators, which seem to claim one thing in French and
another in English, as the examples below illustrate.

Narrative unreliability

A dissimilarity between the French and English *Molloy* that is comparable to the 'trilogy' references discussed above has to do with the names of the two men about whom Molloy tells a story at the beginning of the novel. In French, they are consistently called A and B, but the English translation uses A and C. This transition is recorded piecemeal in the drafts. The early specimen translation that Beckett sent to Barney Rosset still follows the French. The first typescript, however, changes B to C, but only on three occasions (ET1, 07r, 12r, 13r), retaining B in four other places. In the second of these instances, Molloy seems confused about which letter to use: 'Not that I was so conclusively, I mean confirmed, in my first impressions with regard to – wait – ~~B.~~ C.' (ET1, 12r) Beckett may have deliberately used this hesitation as an opportunity to cast doubt on Molloy's ability as a narrator, by having him jumble together the letters A, B and C. Assuming this was not merely an oversight, it was only a brief consideration because in the second typescript all B's were changed to C's.[169] Ruby Cohn connects the letters to Abel and Cain, the biblical allusion fitting the violent context of the *Molloy* preamble (Cohn 2005, 399). Considering Beckett's fondness for the letter M – the thirteenth letter of the alphabet – it is also possible that the combination of A and C – the first and third letters of the alphabet – was intended to create yet another M-avatar in the novel, in addition to Molloy and Moran, following the logic: 1 (A) & 3 (C) = 13 (M).

There are other passages in the English translation where Molloy seems less certain as a narrator than in French, for example when he talks about his stiffening legs. In the early holograph fragment, he still appears to be confident about his story: 'But now ~~this~~ ^this^ ~~other~~ ^latter^, as a result ^no doubt^ of its stiffening, and ~~the~~ the commotion thus set up among its nerves and tendons, began to be even more tender than the other' (EM, 77v), which follows the French version: 'du fait de son radissement sans doute' (1951, 117). But Beckett turned it into a supposition in the first typescript: 'as a result of its stiffening **I suppose**' (ET1, 90r).

---

169   Though both were based on ET1, the extracts in *Merlin* and *New World Writing* differ in their use of A and C. MER adopts C consistently, whereas NWW always follows ET1, thus confusing A, B and C. This is due to the fact that Beckett corrected proofs for MER but not for NWW (see chapter 1.3.1).

Together with Molloy's diminishing confidence, his tendency to lose track of his sentences or to be at a loss for words also became more prominent in the later stages of the translation's genesis, as the following example illustrates. '**What I may venture to assert, without fear of covering myself with ridicule**', Molloy states in the early *Transition* pre-publication, 'is that I gradually lost interest in knowing among other things what town I was in and if I should soon find my mother and settle the matter between us' (TRA, 103). But in the first typescript, the possible consequence of his assertion is left out, causing Molloy's sentence to derail: 'What I can assert, **without fear of --- without fear**, is that I gradually lost interest in knowing' (ET1, 75r). In this sense, the genesis of the English translation reflects that of the French version, where 'Ce que je peux assévérer sans crainte de tomber dans le ridicule' (FN2, 72r) was also changed to 'Ce que je peux affirmer, sans crainte de – sans crainte' (1951, 97).[170]

Molloy even draws attention to the untrustworthiness of his account when he talks about his encounter with the sheep. He wonders 'if they had safely reached some commonage or fallen, their skulls shattered, their thin legs crumpling, first to their knees, then over on their fleecy sides, under the pole-axe' ('le merlin', 1951, 42), immediately adding '**though that is not the way they slaughter sheep**' (ET1, 32r). This metacomment, which is not part of the French version, at the same time confirms and undermines Molloy's reliability as a narrator, as he appears to be both knowledgeable and ignorant about the way sheep are usually slaughtered. Beckett exaggerated the effect even more in the second typescript of the English translation by adding the correct method: '**but with a knife, so that they may bleed to death**' (ET2, 55r). Instead of correcting the phrase, Beckett makes the change of mind an integral part of the text, thereby complicating Molloy's narrative voice even further in translation.

Such remarks are accompanied by additions that emphasize the fabricated nature of Molloy's story. When he states that he will some day return to the town and meet again the 'sergeant and his merry men', it is because 'to ~~define~~ ^{conjure up} a being, a place, I nearly said an hour, but I ~~don't~~

---

170 This similarity between the French and English geneses is due to the fact that the early *Transition* fragment, published in October 1950, was based on a version of *Molloy* predating the 1951 first edition of Minuit, probably the typescript of which only a small fragment survived as FT (see chapters 1.2.1 and 1.3.1).

~~want to hurt anybody's~~ ^{would not hurt anyone's} feelings, and then to use them no more, that would be, how shall I say, I don't know' (ET1, 30r). The sentence was already inconclusive in French, but the phrase 'camper un être' (1951, 40) – to 'sketch' or 'depict' something – is revised to draw attention to Molloy's narrative as a fictional account, which becomes even more explicit in the second typescript: 'to ~~define~~ ~~conjure up~~ ^{contrive} a being' (ET2, 30r). The same tendency to fabulate can be noted in Moran's part, for example when he lends his son a helping hand on their journey: 'I put my hand behind me and my son grasped it, gratefully I ~~felt~~ ^{fancied'} (ET2, 43r). The original choice of words is more affirmative than the original French – 'il me sembla' (1951, 197) – but in Beckett's revision it becomes more uncertain, based on self-deceit rather than genuine feeling or impression.

Molloy's method of ratiocination is stranger in English as well, evinced by his trying to remember the colour of the dog that accompanied B: 'Oui c'était un poméranien orangé, plus j'y songe plus j'en ai la conviction' (1951, 15). This conventional phrase is turned upside down quite early on in the translation process: 'Yes, it was an orange pomeranian, the ~~more~~ ^{less} I think of it the more certain I am' (Sp1-3, 08r). A similar revision occurs when Molloy explains his difficulty to hear words properly as a 'defect of the under-standing perhaps, which only began to vibrate on repeated solicitations, or which did vibrate, if you like, but at a ~~lesser~~ ^{lower} frequency, ^{or a higher,} than that of ratiocination' (ET2, 58r), which expands on the original French: 'un niveau inférieur à celui de la ratiocination' (1951, 74). Molloy is clearly not a conventional character, and certainly not a traditional narrator who inspires confidence and functions according to our reader expectations, even more so perhaps in English than in French.

Even Molloy's state of mind can be questioned, for example when he mentions saying his goodbyes at the start of Part I, adding it would be 'foolish' not to do so ('bête', 1951, 9) – a metacomment not yet present in the French manuscript. Apparently, the word 'foolish' was not strong enough to express the sentiment that Molloy wanted to convey, as Beckett tried out several alternatives in the subsequent versions of the translation, ranging from '**stupid**' (Sp1, 03r) in the early specimens, to '**folly**' (ET1, 03r) in the first typescript, and eventually '**madness**' in the second typescript and the published versions (ET2, 03r; 1955, 9; *Mo* 4), making Molloy more prone to exaggerate. The English drafts show him gradually sliding on that scale.

Although less draft material survived for Moran's part, some of the revisions that Beckett made to it can also be read as autographic reflections casting doubt on his reliability as a narrator. In French, Moran explains that on Sunday evening they usually have 'les restes de la volaille, poulet, caneton, oie, dinde, que sais-je' (1951, 180). The list is the same in English, but it is followed by a significantly different comment: 'the remains of a fowl, chicken, duck, goose, turkey, ~~and suchlike~~ I can think of no other fowl' (ET2, 31r). Apart from stressing Moran's ignorance, this change also creates an autographic effect. It must have been easier for Beckett to think of other types of fowl in his mother tongue than in his adopted language, but instead of expanding the list in translation, his more limited knowledge of French is projected onto Moran in the English version. In the case of young Jacques' pocket knife, however, Beckett did expand the list of features. As Moran explains: 'Ce couteau comportait, outre les cinq ou six lames de première nécessité, un tire-bouchon, un ouvre-boîte, un poinçon, un tournevis, un pied-de-biche et je ne sais quelles autres futilités encore' (1951, 201). In the translation he can think of one additional futility – 'a corkscrew, a tin-opener, a punch, a screw-driver, a claw a gauge for removing stones from hooves' (ET2, 46r) – which is yet another reflection of Beckett's greater vocabulary range in English than in French. The effect is that when we read the French and English *Molloy* in conjunction, the unre-aliability of the narrators is increased because of these slight shifts.

As with Molloy, Moran's linguistic failures are sometimes more emphasized in translation. Having asked his son if he knows what to do with the thermometer – 'You know which mouth to put it in?' – Moran admits: 'I had turned my phrase badly, ~~I should rather have said, Don't go to the wrong door.~~ mouth was not the word I should have used.' (ET2, 32r). In French he also says 'Ne te trompe pas d'entrée' (1951, 182), but Beckett decided to stress Moran's failure without providing the correct alternative, increasing the negativism of the text – a tendency already to be observed in some of the revisions to the French drafts (see chapter 2).

Metacomments on language

In the French version of the text, Beckett – by way of the narrator Molloy – makes what can be read as a comment on the intricacies of the language and its various tenses, for example after the sentence: 'Alors voilà, je suis fixé sur certaines choses, je sais certaines choses sur lui, des choses que j'ignorais, qui me tracassaient, des choses même dont je n'avais pas souffert' (1951, 16). Having used a passé composé, an indicatif présent, two times the passé simple and finally a plus-que-parfait, Molloy concludes: 'Quelle langue' (1951, 16). Since he does not say 'langage' but 'langue', the observation refers to the French language rather than his personal use of the idiom – calling to mind Ferdinand de Saussure's famous distinction between 'langue' and 'parole' from his *Cours de linguistique générale*. Molloy's remark was first rendered as '**What language**' (ET1, 09r) before being revised as '**What rigmarole**' (ET2, 09r), no longer pertaining to the English language but the nonsense Molloy chooses to express with it.

Other comments about to the French language could not be simply transferred into English and therefore had to be adjusted slightly in translation. When Molloy comes up with a principle to avoid sucking the same stones without increasing the number of his pockets, he refers to it with 'le terme arrimage, que je ne connaissais pas' (1951, 108). In French, it is a very specific word that can mean little else. In English, Beckett uses 'the word trim', which has a variety of other meanings, so that Molloy adds it is a word he 'had never met with ^{in this sense}' (ET2, 83r). So, unlike 'arrimage' in French, Molloy is familiar with 'trim', just not in this particular meaning. Each version of the text therefore reflects a different linguistic reality and Molloy's explanation of the term slightly differs in each language. In French, he states that 'le terme arrimage ne pouvait signifier rien d'autre', whereas in English he adds a word to highlight the multiple meanings of the term: 'this word trim could not ^{here} mean anything else, anything better, than the distribution of the sixteen stones in four groups of four, one group, in each pocket' (ET2, 83r-84r)

Sometimes Beckett also generalizes specific comments about the French tongue to language in general, heightening the linguistic scepticism of the text, as when Molloy stops talking about his time at Lousse's house, because it has no significance: 'ce n'est pas la peine que je prolonge le récit de cette tranche de ma, mon, de mon existence, car elle n'a pas de signification, à mon sens' (1951, 84). Molloy's uncertainty about the correct gender of the word 'existence', and his consequent hesitation between the female ('ma') and male ('mon') inflexions of the personal pronoun, betrays a sense of unfamiliarity or uneasiness with the French language and its grammatical rules. Whether this slip is an autographic reflection of Beckett's proficiency is hard to verify, but he chose to highlight the moment in the original version of *Molloy* instead of correcting it (see chapter 2.1, writing session dated '19.8[.47]'). Because English is not an inflected language, Beckett turned it into a search for 'le mot juste' in translation, stressing the general inadequacy of language as a means of expression: 'But it is useless to drag out this chapter of ~~my....~~ ^{my, how shall I say, my} existence, for it has no sense, to my mind' (ET2, 65r).

Molloy ascribes his incompetence with language to the fact that he had 'been living so far from words so long', and when he tries to explain why he could not remember the name of his town, he concludes: 'It's too difficult to say, for me' (1955, 41; *Mo* 29). Even his 'sense of identity was ~~veiled~~ ^{wrapped} in a nameles⁵ness often hard to penetrate' he adds, in a reference to Schopenhauer's 'veil of Maya', which has to be penetrated for true knowledge to emerge (see chapter 2.1, paragraph 17 and chapter 2.2, paragraph 39). The translation of 'anonymat' (1951, 45) as 'namelessness' especially invokes Mauthner and the language veil that Beckett mentioned in the famous Kaun letter (*LSB* 512-21), but he 'vaguened' the link by rendering 's'enveloppait' (1951, 45) more literally as 'wrapped'.

Dehumanization and decay

Some of Molloy's comments about language are connected to the concept of 'humanity', for example when he explains what he meant by saying that he had his bellyful of walking to Lousse's house, carrying the dead dog: 'That is to say I didn't have it really. You think you have your bellyful but you seldom have it really. It was because I knew I was there that I had my bellyful, a mile more to go and I would only have had my bellyful an hour later' (1955, 46; *Mo* 33). In French, Molloy concludes this exposé with the comment 'Voilà comme on est' (1951, 51), which is at first translated as a remark pertaining to him alone but is then expanded into a general human trait: 'That's the way with you. ^{Human nature. Marvellous thing.}' (ET2, 40r)

Running counter to Molloy's description of himself as a human being, his worsening physical condition gradually reduces him to roaming the earth like an animal. As he puts it, 'leaves or no leaves I would have abandoned ~~walking upright, the way men do~~ ^{erect motion, that of man'} (ET2, 105r). The adjective 'erect' more readily invokes *Homo sapiens*'s ancestor *Homo erectus*, thus contrasting Molloy's development with the evolutionary history of mankind and marking the regressive process that he goes through as one of devolution. By the end of Part I, when Molloy has completed his dehumanizing process, his downfall was first described fittingly with the motion of a snake: 'I **slithered** ^{lapsed} down to the bottom of the ditch' (ET2, 107r). But then it was revised to reflect the sense of the French version more accurately: 'Je me laissai dégringoler jusqu'au fond du fossé' (1951, 140).[171]

Moran's animality, too, is increased in the drafts. Unable to walk, just like Molloy, he has to sit on the carrier of their bicycle, relying on his son for motion. When the bulges of the carrier start digging into his buttocks, he explains that the more things resist him, the more 'rabid' he gets and the passage that follows is revised in subsequent drafts to emphasize this animal behaviour: 'With time, and nothing but my teeth and nails, I would **toil up** from the bowels of the earth to its crust, knowing full well I had nothing to gain' (ET2, 77r), which was changed to '**rage up** from the bowels of the earth' for the published text (1955, 214), a notably more violent reaction than the French 'je remontais' (1951, 242). His decay, too, is further emphasized in the drafts when he rubs and slaps every part of his body with his free hand, only to 'keep the blood ~~running~~ ^{trickling} freely' (ET2, 96r), which still flowed profusely in the French: 'afin d'y entretenir une circulation abondante' (1951, 266).

171 Additionally, 'Tous ceux qui dégringolent' ('crash down'/'collapse') is an alternative title for the French version of his radio play *All That Fall* (*Tous ceux qui tombent*) – translated together with Robert Pinget – that Beckett used in correspondence, for example in his letter to Barbara Bray of 17 November 1958 (TCD 10948-1-012). One reason why Beckett liked the title in particular was because he considered the French translation a failure, even more so its television/cinema adaptation by the (O)RTF. For a detailed study of the genesis of *All That Fall* / *Tous ceux qui tombent*, see Pim Verhulst, *The Making of Samuel Beckett's Radio Plays*, Brussels and London: University Press Antwerp and Bloomsbury (forthcoming).

Parallels between Molloy and Moran

Molloy and Moran share many other traits apart from their dehumanized or decayed states, and several revisions to the English translation of the novel may be read as attempts to create more parallels between the two characters. With regard to the general rule that all cyclists must step down upon entering the town, Molloy remarks: 'It is a good rule and I observe it **meticulously**, in spite of the difficulty I have in advancing on my crutches pushing my bicycle at the same time' (ET1, 19r). His observance of the rule is already a little more meticulous in English than in French ('avec soin', 1951, 27), but it becomes almost zealous in the second typescript, resembling Moran's obsession over rules and codes of conduct, especially with regard to faith: 'I observe it **religiously**' (ET2, 19r). Like Moran, Molloy also develops a more personal relationship with God in the English translation, when he states that he will judge his life 'as it is said that **God will judge us**, and with no less impertine͏ᵉnce' (ET1, 27r) – in French, 'Dieu nous jugera' (1951, 36) – which is later revised to 'God will judge **me**' (ET2, 27r), echoing Moran's visit to Father Ambrose to take the communion.

The parallels also extend to food consumption. In the Ruth/Edith episode, Molloy uses a term to describe his meals with her that establish a link with the Irish stew Martha cooks for Moran: 'Whereas I flung myself at the ~~Eintopf~~ ᵐᵉˢˢ, ~~swallowed~~ ᵍᵘˡᵖᵉᵈ ᵈᵒʷⁿ the half or the quarter of it in two mouthfuls ~~worthy of a fish of prey, I mean~~ without chewing (with what would I have chewed?)ᐟ then pushed it from me with loathing.' (ET2, 63r) 'Eintopf', the initial translation of 'plat unique' (single-course meal, 1951, 81), refers to a German stew typically consisting of broth, vegetables, potatoes and meat, though it comes in a number varieties and the term signifies a way of cooking the ingredients in one pot rather than a specific recipe. The Kassel area, for example, where Beckett frequently visited the Sinclair family between 1928 and 1932 (Knowlson 1997, 109), has a dish called 'Lumpen und Fleeh' ('rags and fleas'), which is quite similar to Irish stew.[172] While Beckett severs the

---

172   Beckett uses the word several times in the diaries he kept during his trip through Germany from 1936 to 1937 (UoR MS 5006). He often complains of uneatable Eintopf and mocks it as 'arish stew = neues nationalgericht der deutschen [new German national dish]' in the German vocabulary notebook that he carried with him (qtd. in Nixon 2011, 206n6). Also mentioned in Beckett's diary are the so-called 'Eintopf-Sonntage', a propagandist initiative by

connection with Moran's part by preferring the more general 'mess' over 'Eintopf', it does create another kind of resonance, namely with his comment that the task of the artist now is 'to find a form that accommodates the mess' in an interview with Tom Driver (2005, 219). Consequently, the passage could be read as an aesthetic statement about the form of *Molloy*, especially in relation to Gide and Balzac (see chapter 2).

Beckettian vocabulary

Other revisions to the drafts of *Molloy* connect with specific Beckett texts, especially those written after the French original, creating a kind of intratextual core vocabulary on which each subsequent work builds, even in (self-)translation.

A good example occurs when Molloy briefly interrupts his story of A and B (C in English) at the beginning of the novel to reflect on the reliability of his narrative: 'I can't believe it. No, I will not lie, I can easily conceive it. No matter, no matter, let us go on, xx as if all arose from one and the same weariness, ~~accumulate, and cumulate,~~ on and on hoarding, until there is no room, no light, for any more' (ET1, 12r). The expression that Molloy used in French was 'meublons, meublons' (1951, 19), but Beckett revised his translation for the retyped section of the second typescript: 'on and on, **heaping up and up**' (ET2, 12r), creating a link with the opening lines of Clov in *Endgame*: 'Finished, it's finished, nearly finished, it must be nearly finished. [*Pause.*] Grain upon grain, one by one, and one day, suddenly, there's a heap, a little heap, the impossible heap' (*E* 6), an image that is reinvoked later in the play: 'Moment upon moment, pattering down, like the millet grains of... [*he hesitates*] ... that old Greek' (*E* 42). Matthew Feldman, who has studied Beckett's notes on the Pre-Socratics from Wilhelm Windelband's *A History of Philosophy*, points out that the reference is not to one person in particular but to 'an entire philosophical movement, built on extreme scepticism and the primacy [of] individual perception' (2006, 34). Concerning the 'art

the Nazi government ordering the people and restaurants to eat or serve only cheap stew dishes on every first Sunday of the month from October to March (see 'Becketts Blick auf Berlin' in *Der Spiegel* 51, 2005, p. 152).

of logomachy or eristic' – which values winning a discussion by means of rhetoric over expressing the truth – Beckett noted that:

> Euclid's adherents Eubulides and Alexinus were famous for a series of such catches, among which the Heap (which kernel of grain by being added makes the heap?) and the Baldhead (which hair falling out makes the head bald?), were fundamental thought [sic] far back to Zeno, who used it to ^argue that the composition of magnitudes out of small parts is impossible. (TCD MS 10967/42, qtd. in Feldman 2006, 34)

This impossibility of composing magnitudes out of small parts may also be read as a critique on the traditional novel form, in particular as practised by Balzac, which Beckett seems to take issue with in *Molloy*. All attempts at creating such a magnitude, be it the preamble about A and B or the narratives of Molloy and Moran, deliberately break down into smaller parts. While this idea was already part of the French version as a structuring principle, the link with Zeno and the Pre-Socratics was not made explicit until Beckett applied the final revisions to the English *Molloy*, possibly under the influence of *Fin de partie*, which he was working on around that time.[173]

Another revision to the drafts of *Molloy*, this time to the part narrated by Moran, can also be placed in the context of *Fin de partie*. The play has often been connected to the death of Beckett's brother Frank in 1954, with whom he spent his final months (Knowlson 1997, 400-2). The experience further shook Beckett's belief in the existence of a merciful God, prompting Hamm's famous line about the Almighty: 'Le salaud ! Il n'existe pas !' (Beckett 2010a, 74) ['The bastard! He doesn't exist!' (*E* 34)] The French version of *Molloy*, written seven years before Frank's death, was already sceptical about God, but the terms in which this scepticism is expressed became more aggressive in the English version. Moran's bold statement that 'there are men and there are things, ~~let me have no talk of~~ ^to hell ^with animals' (ET2, 89r) is extended to the creator in the next line: '~~Nor of~~ ^And ~~with~~ ^with God' (ET2, 89r). The French version is milder on this account: 'ne me parlez pas des animaux. Ni de Dieu'

---

173 For a more detailed study of the play's genesis see Dirk Van Hulle and Shane Weller, *The Making of Fin de partie / Endgame*, Brussels and London: University Press Antwerp and Bloomsbury (forthcoming).

(1951, 256). While it brings to mind the anarchist slogan 'ni Dieu ni maître' – also featured in Friedrich Nietzsche's *Jenseits von Gut und Böse* – the English version is more combative and blasphemous. These two examples illustrate how the genesis of one text can affect the (self-) translation process of another and vice versa, even across language barriers, which is an important though seldom studied dynamic in the bilingual writing of Samuel Beckett.

Other revisions have less far-reaching consequences apart from adding to a sense of Beckettian vocabulary, for example '~~bursting~~ ᵒᵒᶻⁱⁿᵍ with obsequiousness' (ET2, 78r) – 'prêt à l'obséquiosité' (1951, 101) – which is so frequently used in *Worstward Ho*: 'In it ooze again. Ooze alone for seen as seen with ooze. Dimmed. No ooze for seen undimmed. For when nohow on. No ooze for when ooze gone.' (*CIWS* 100) Similarly, the revision of '~~brooding on endless~~ ʳᵉᵛᵒˡᵛⁱⁿᵍ ⁱⁿᵗᵉʳᵐⁱⁿᵃᵇˡᵉ martingales' (ET2, 83r) evokes V's recurrent phrase 'Will you never have done ... revolving it all' in the play *Footfalls* (*KLT* 110, 114). In the story of A and B/C, the 'manteau' (1951, 10) they are wearing was also first translated as '**overcoats**' (ET1, 04r), before it was replaced with the archetypal Beckettian attire: '**greatcoats**' (ET2, 04r).

Intertextuality

Apart from these intra-textual resonances, Beckett introduces an intertextual reference on two occasions, only to delete it again later on. The first occurs in Molloy's part, when he admits: 'j'aurais fait l'amour avec une chèvre, pour connaître l'amour' (1951, 86). Beckett first translated this confession with a reference to Virgil, which he then revised in the second typescript: 'I would have made love with a goat, to know ~~quid sit Amor~~ ʷʰᵃᵗ ˡᵒᵛᵉ ʷᵃˢ' (ET2, 67r; see Fig. 24). In *Eclogues*, VIII, the shepherd Damon relates how he, as a twelve-year-old boy, first saw his love Nysa guided by her mother in an apple orchard, only to see her snatched away by his rival Mopsus. Damon ascribes the cruelty of the God of Love to his birth in a bare, remote region and his inhuman ancestry: 'Nunc scio, quid sit Amor: duris in cotibus illum / aut Tmaros, aut Rhodope, aut extremi Garamantes / nec generis nostri puerum nec sanguinis edunt' (Virgil 1999, 76, l. 43-5). Of course, Beckett's appropriation of the verse is not as lofty, referring to carnal rather than emotional 'love' – aimed at animals. The revised expression is still a paraphrase of Virgil's line

– more literal than the French 'pour connaître l'amour' (1951, 86) – but the link has been 'vaguened' (Pountney 1998, 149).

The second example occurs in Moran's part. Having discovered that his son has been letting air escape from the tire to prevent them from carrying on, he exclaims: 'Tu es un misérable, dis-je' (1951, 242). In the English translation, Moran does not speak directly to Jacques and first uses a term that invokes the Bible – not coincidentally, perhaps, the Old Testament: '**My son is vile, I said**' (ET2, 77r). This could be a reference to *Samuel* 3:13, in which the Lord tells Samuel that he will judge the house of Eli 'for ever for the iniquity which he knoweth; because his sons made themselves vile, and he restrained them not'. Moran will not make that mistake, as he constantly rebukes Jacques for his misconduct. His choice of words is fitting, not only because of his severe and authoritative parenting, but also because he is a regular churchgoer familiar with Scripture. Yet Beckett eventually replaced the Biblical phrase with God's general punishment of the vile: '**I cursed him.**' (ET2, 77r)

Although Beckett undid this biblical reference, he left another one standing, which already featured in the typed text of ET2, the earliest surviving draft for Part II of the novel. Moran complains that the seat of his breeches sawed his crack '**from Dan to Bersheeba**' (1955, 234) – 'depuis le coccyx jusqu'à l'amorce du scrotum' (1951, 264) – a common Biblical measurement of distance between two cities. Moran's profane use of the expression proves how far the Molloy case has removed him from Father Ambrose, God and religion.

Cultural specificity

Biblical phrases must have come easier to Beckett in English than in French because he was so familiar with the language of the *King James Bible*, due to his religious upbringing in the Protestant circles of Dublin. As the genetic analysis of the French *Molloy* has shown, Beckett removed some of the more explicit references to Ireland in the original manuscript, such as the place name starting with a 'D' or the two canals that evoke Dublin (see chapter 2.1, paragraphs 15 and 20). To a certain extent, Beckett thus universalized the setting of the novel, suggesting rather than stating an Irish context. At the same time, he grounded the narrative more locally in the French

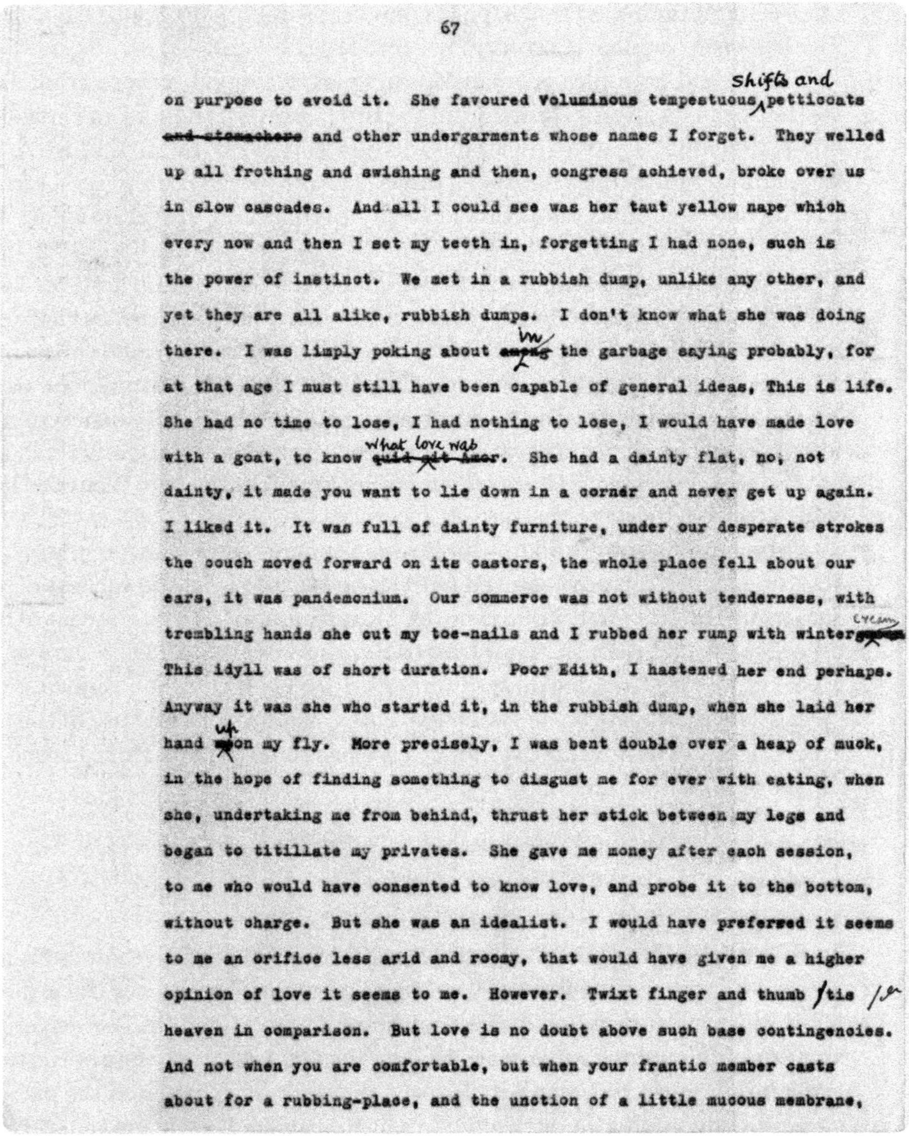

on purpose to avoid it. She favoured **voluminous** tempestuous ^shifts and^ petticoats
~~and stomachers~~ and other undergarments whose names I forget. They welled
up all frothing and swishing and then, congress achieved, broke over us
in slow cascades. And all I could see was her taut yellow nape which
every now and then I set my teeth in, forgetting I had none, such is
the power of instinct. We met in a rubbish dump, unlike any other, and
yet they are all alike, rubbish dumps. I don't know what she was doing
there. I was limply poking about ^in^ ~~among~~ the garbage saying probably, for
at that age I must still have been capable of general ideas, This is life.
She had no time to lose, I had nothing to lose, I would have made love
with a goat, to know ^what love was^ ~~quid sit Amor~~. She had a dainty flat, no, not
dainty, it made you want to lie down in a corner and never get up again.
I liked it. It was full of dainty furniture, under our desperate strokes
the couch moved forward on its castors, the whole place fell about our
ears, it was pandemonium. Our commerce was not without tenderness, with
trembling hands she cut my toe-nails and I rubbed her rump with winter ^cream^ ~~greens~~.
This idyll was of short duration. Poor Edith, I hastened her end perhaps.
Anyway it was she who started it, in the rubbish dump, when she laid her
hand ^up^ ~~up~~on my fly. More precisely, I was bent double over a heap of muck,
in the hope of finding something to disgust me for ever with eating, when
she, undertaking me from behind, thrust her stick between my legs and
began to titillate my privates. She gave me money after each session,
to me who would have consented to know love, and probe it to the bottom,
without charge. But she was an idealist. I would have preferred it seems
to me an orifice less arid and roomy, that would have given me a higher
opinion of love it seems to me. However. Twixt finger and thumb ^'tis^ /ˢ
heaven in comparison. But love is no doubt above such base contingencies.
And not when you are comfortable, but when your frantic member casts
about for a rubbing-place, and the unction of a little mucous membrane,

Fig. 24: Beckett replaces the quotation from Virgil's *Eclogues* ('quid sit Amor') with a literal translation of the phrase, 'what love was' (ET2, 67r, l. 11).

manuscripts by exchanging the globalized American currency of dollars and cents for pounds, shillings and florins, or by replacing the European-French usage of metres and kilometres with the Anglo-Saxon system of miles (see chapter 2.1, paragraphs 11 and 20; and chapter 2.2, paragraphs 34, 84, 105, 110, 113 and 126). The latter trend continued in the English drafts, but not without hesitation.

For example, Molloy's 'six pots de bière' – after which he would 'drink nothing for a week' – first became '**six Imperial pints of porter**' (ET1, 63r), a measurement equal to 1/8th of an Imperial gallon that is only used in the UK and Ireland. Beckett downplayed the Anglo-Irish reference again to '**mugs of beer**' (ET2, 63r) on the second typescript, but in other cases he replaced neutral French terms with English equivalents that emphasize the Anglo-Saxon context of the novel. Moran's 'pommier', for example, becomes 'my ~~apple tree~~ ^Beauty of Bath^' (ET2, 02r), a popular kind of dessert apple no longer grown commercially because the fruit bruises easily, but which is still a common garden variety. Another instance occurs in Part II, when Moran refers to his 'carpette' (FN3, 15v), later his 'moquette' (1951, 168) in the Minuit first edition, possibly playing on the phrase 'fumer la moquette' (talk nonsense). The English version hesitates between two brand names '~~Axminster~~ ^Wilton^' (ET2, 22r), types of carpet manufactured in Devon and Wiltshire, eventually settling on the latter.

The reverse also occurs, when a specific brand name in the French version is replaced with a more general term in the translation. An interesting example is 'baume Bengué' (1951, 87; see chapter 2.2, paragraph 102), an ointment to soothe muscle pain that Molloy puts on the rump of Edith/ Ruth. In English, Beckett doubted between '~~wintergreen~~^cream^' (ET2, 67r), the first being a blanket term for oil extracted from the Gaultheria plant, which is used as a folk remedy for arthritis, poor blood circulation, rheumatism, inflammation or tendinitis, and the latter a general term for ointments with a similar function. The term 'baume Bengué' stands out in the original *Molloy* because the story is vaguely set in an Anglo-Irish context, in which a French brand name seems exotic. Beckett also used the term in Part II, when Moran feels a sharp pain in his knee and asks his son Jacques to bring him '~~du Baume Bengué~~ ^de l'iodex^' (FN3, 86r), an English brand which is unknown to French readers. So, what originally created symmetry between the novel's two parts was subsequently used to disrupt the cultural unity of *Molloy* as a novel, one character using a French brand, the other an English one to remedy ailments in the original. By opting for 'wintercream' and 'iodex' in the English version, Beckett smoothes over the dissimilarity, but he destabilizes the cultural context elsewhere in the translation.

When Moran's sore knee plays up again later in the story, he claims it is only a touch of neuralgia and promises himself to procure 'une boîte de thermogène, avec le joli démon dessus' (1951, 215). The reference is to a brand of thermogenic cotton, produced in France, which became very popular after 1909 thanks to a successful marketing campaign using the artwork of French-Italian designer Leonetto Cappiello. As William H. Helfand explains, the image of a 'fire-eating circus performer holding the product close to his chest [...] has become an icon of creative advertising imagery' (Helfand 1991, 34). Though common in Europe, the product was little used in the UK and the USA, so Moran's reference to '**a packet of thermogenie**ᵉ **wool, with the pretty demon on the outside**' (ET2, 57r) must have been foreign to English and American readers alike. It not only disrupts the Anglo-Saxon context of the story – strengthened by some of the brand names mentioned above – but it also harks back to the novel's French origin, which is further emphasized by Beckett's preference for the unusual Gallic spelling of 'thermogene' over 'thermogenic' in the typescript.

Fig. 25: Cappiello's design for the packaging of 'le thermogène' with the demon, as mentioned by Moran.

Use of Irishisness

In connection to cultural specificity, particular mention should be made of Beckett's revisions with regard to his use of Irish in the drafts of *Molloy*. Quite early in the translation process, on 4 August 1953, having read the first specimen by Beckett and Bowles, Barney Rosset made a critical comment which he referred to as 'a mention of words':

> Those such as skivvy and cutty are unknown here, and when used they give the writing a most definite British stamp. That is perfectly all right if it is the effect you desire. If you are desirous for a little more vagueness as to where the scene is set it would be better to use substitutes which are of common usage both here and in Britain. (Rosset 2016, 72)

Though Beckett understood Rosset's point, and was amenable to suggestions, he also pointed out that it was a 'far-reaching' problem in his reply of 1 September 1953:

> I understand your point about the Anglicisms and shall be glad to consider whatever suggestions you have to make in this connexion. But the problem involved here is a far-reaching one. Bowles's text as revised by me is bound to be quite unamerican in rhythm and atmosphere and the mere substitution here and there of the American for the English term is hardly likely to improve matters, on the contrary. We can of course avoid those words which are incomprehensible to the American reader, such as skivvy and cutty, and it will be a help to have them pointed out to us. (*LSB II* 397-8)

Beckett replaced the word **'skivvy'** on Sp1-3 (02r) – 'boniche' in French (1951, 8) – with the more neutral term **'chambermaid'** on ET1 (02r), but **'cutty'** (1955, 14; *Mo* 8) – a short tobacco pipe – was retained, and many other decidedly un-American words were added to the English text of *Molloy* during the translation process, even to the passage covered by this early specimen. In Sp1-3, for example, Molloy explains that he 'began at the beginning, like an old **fool**, can you imagine that' (Sp1-3, 02r), which Beckett replaced with the more Irish-British term **'ballocks'** in the retyped pages of ET2 (02r; see chapter 2.2, Paragraph 1: The Incipit).

Other late revisions of the novel's opening sequence give the text a more distinctive Anglo-Irish tone. Beckett altered the sentence 'It was **he who told me** I'd begun all wrong, that I should have begun differently' (Sp1-3, 02r) – referring to the man who comes to collect his pages every Sunday – to 'It was **he told me** I'd begun all wrong, that I should have begun differently' on ET1 (02r). This same type of revision also occurs further on in the text, when Molloy speaks of Lousse's dead dog, 'her Teddy ~~whom~~ she had loved like ~~her own~~ ^{an} only child' (ET2, 42r). In both cases the pronoun is deleted, which is a typical characteristic of Hiberno-English.

Beckett's emphasis on the 'text as revised by me' in his letter to Rosset is therefore important, as it suggests that he deliberately enhanced its un-American character. At the same time, he destandardized the text by making it less 'English' or, perhaps more correctly, less 'British'. This notion of substandard English relates to the comment Beckett made in his earlier cited letter to Cyril Lucas of 4 January 1956, about his 'queer kind of English' and 'queer French' (*LSB II* 591-2; see chapter 3.1). As several critics have noted (Fletcher 1967; Morin 2009; Mooney 2011), Beckett's use of French in *Molloy* often deviates from the norm, infusing it with Irish inflexions. Hiberno-English traits appear to fulfil a similar destabilizing function in the English version of the text, but this is not to say that Beckett 'naturalized' *Molloy* as an Irish novel. While he did introduce several explicit and outspokenly Hiberno-English elements in the early stages of the translation process, he removed them again later on. As a result, the 'queer' Anglo-Irish flavour of the novel remains as subtle as the 'queer' nature of his French, which is just slightly off-standard and evokes a sense of Irishness while keeping a distance from it.

The most interesting example in this respect is the word **'puckaun'**, which Beckett used in ET1 (31r) as a translation for 'le bouc' (1951, 41), but later replaced with the more neutral term **'buck-goat'** on ET2 (31r). Beckett had also used the word in *Watt*, just before the Addenda, when 'a goat emerged, dragging its pale and chain' and Mr Nolan complains: 'Riley's puckaun again [...] I can smell him from here' (*W* 213). 'Puckaun' is a markedly Hiberno-English word, derived from the Irish *pocán*, diminutive of the male goat *poc*. This status may explain why the term was problematic in a deliberately bi-cultural, Anglo-French text like *Molloy*, but not in a more openly

Hiberno-English novel such as *Watt*. According to the *OED*, the earliest use of 'puckaun' is found in the writings of Jonathan Swift, more particularly his 'Dialogue in Hibernian Style between A and B'. In vol. VII of *The Works of Jonathan Swift*, edited by Sir Walter Scott, this burlesque is presented as a 'specimen of Irishisms, or what Swift condemned as such [...] taken from an unfinished copy in the Dean's handwriting, found among Mr Lyon's papers' – a clergyman attending to him during his last years (Swift 1824, 156). Swift packs many examples of Irish words, phrases and syntax into a twenty-four line conversation between two characters called A and B, ending with the question:

a Do you make good cheese and butter?
b Yes, when we can get milk; but our cows will never keep a drop of milk without a Puckaun. (Swift 1824, 157)

As Swift uses the word differently, meaning a bull instead of a male goat, it may not be the actual source of Beckett's 'puckaun', but the fact that it functions there as a specimen of Hiberno-English is relevant for *Molloy* and may explain why it was eventually replaced – evoking an Irish context all too strongly.

As Molloy himself points out, he is not an expert on the Irish language, claiming as much ignorance about this subject as about the meaning of tears and laughter: 'they are so much **Gaelic** to me' (1955, 49; *Mo* 35).[174] This was a very late addition, probably on the proofs, as both typscripts still have **'Hebrew'** (ET1; ET2, 42r) for the French 'je m'y connais guère' (1951, 54). Some of the strongest Irishisms having been removed from the text at this stage, Molloy's comment does not seem out of place.

174 Molloy's remark echoes a comment about bilingualism that Beckett had made in his letter of 17 February 1954 to Hans Naumann: 'Je ne considère pas l'anglais comme une langue étrangère, c'est bien ma langue. S'il en est une qui m'est parfaitement étrangère, c'est la gaélique.' (*LSB II* 461) ['I do not consider English a foreign language, it is my language. If there is one that is really foreign to me, it is Gaelic.' (*LSB II* 464)]

Minor improvements

Finally, Beckett used his translation of *Molloy* to make minor changes or even improvements to the text which, as Marilyn Gaddis Rose observes in her entry on Beckett for *The Oxford Guide to Literature in English Translation*, 'truly make the translating seem like an excuse for bilingual copy editing' (2000, 295). While these are mostly isolated instances with local impact rather than examples of a pattern, they do alter the text slightly.

In the following example, Beckett clarifies Molloy's statement that he watched B 'recede, **overtaken** by his anxiety' (ET1, 06r) – 's'éloigner, gagné par son inquiétude' (1951, 12) – by pointing out the subject in the second typescript: '**overtaken (myself)** by his anxiety' (ET2, 06r).

In addition to clarifying, Beckett also corrects the original. In French, Moran felt the Molloy affair was beneath him as he read Gaber's report ('à la lecture du rapport de Gaber', 1951, 149), but since no such physical document is mentioned in the text, Beckett revises the translation to leave it open as to how the message was conveyed: 'Even if, ~~on hearing~~ as set forth in Gaber's report, the affair had seemed unworthy of me, the chief's insist~~ing~~ence on having me, me Moran, rather than anybody else, ought to have warned me that ~~the commission~~ it was no ordinary one' (ET2, 06r).

Sometimes Beckett also changed the sense of the text slightly to better fit the context, without any broader ramifications, for example when he translates the 'jumelles' with which Ruth spies on Molloy ('m'épiait', 1951, 79) first literally as '**a pair of field glasses**' (ET1, 62r) but then as '**a spy-glass**' (ET2, 62r). The same occurs when Molloy talks about '**the noise** that old pump makes' (ET1, 105r) – 'le bruit' (1951, 137) – when speaking of his heart, which is changed to a '**squelch**' (ET2, 105) in the second typescript because it better fits the reference to hydraulics.

Other examples of this category merely add detail, for example the 'femme' (1951, 114) that approaches Molloy on the beach, spurred on by her companions, who is specified as '**a** young **woman**' (ET2, 88r). Similarly, at the beginning of Part II, Moran claims that Gaber had 'journeyed from afar, on purpose to disturb me' (ET2, 02r), which makes him look even more unsympathetic than in French, which simply states: 'il était venu de loin, me déranger' (1951, 144).

3.3 Other Patterns of Revision

While 3.2 discussed some of the revisions in the drafts of the English *Molloy* that mark it as a self-translation, this section discusses a selection of traits that are more common to the act of translation in general. Leaving aside matters of punctuation, such as the removal or addition of question marks, exclamation marks and commas, the lengthening of contractions, as well as the merging and splitting up of sentences, 3.3 focusses on style and word order, repetition, literalness, idiomatic use of language, register, expressions, puns and minor corrections.

Style and word order

Beckett's revision of Richard Seaver's fragment in the Tara MacGowran Notebook offers rare insight into his frequent complaint that the novel 'won't go into English' (see chapter 3.1), as well as his struggle with the syntax and the rhythm of the text.

Judging from this early draft, it seems that Beckett's remark mainly pertains to the peculiar style of the original and his difficulties to render especially the longer and more complex constructions of the French text into English. Whoever was responsible for choosing the passage translated in EM, it was a very difficult one to begin with. Unlike the easygoing preamble of the novel about the characters A and B (C in English), it begins with a series of meandering and syntactically convoluted sentences, in which Molloy tries to explain how his 'progress' on crutches was always 'slow and painful' because his short, stiff leg continued to worsen, while at the same time his good leg grew stiffer every day. As he struggles to get his story straight, Beckett struggles to capture the rambling style of the French in English. As a starting point, few other passages in *Molloy* could have been more cumbersome as well as discouraging:

Et maintenant ma progression, toujours lente et pénible, l'était
plus que jamais, à cause de ma jambe courte et raide, celle
qui depuis longtemps me faisait l'impression d'avoir atteint
les limites de la rigidité, mais allez vous faire foutre, car
elle se faisait plus raide que jamais, chose que j'aurais crue
impossible, et en même temps se raccourcissait chaque jour
davantage, mais surtout à cause de l'autre jambe, qui elle aussi
devenait rapidement raide, de souple qu'elle avait été, mais ne se
raccourcissait pas encore, malheureusement. (1951, 117)

And now my progress, **at all times slow and painful**, was **so
more** than ever, because of my short stiff leg, the same ~~which
I had so long regarded~~ which had so **long seemed to me** as
stiff as a leg could be, **to my** ~~xxx~~ ˢⁱⁿᵉˣᵖᵉʳⁱᵉⁿᶜᵉ inexperience, for it **now grew** stiffer
than ever, ∗ a thing **which I should** not have thought possible,
and at the same ~~time shortene~~ **grew daily shorter**, but above
all because of the other leg, **which now also rapidly stiffened,
it supple so long,** but **did** not yet **shorten, unfortunately.**
(EM, 77v)

And now my progress, **slow and painful at all times**, was **more
so** than ever, because of my short stiff leg, the same **which I
thought had long been** as stiff as a leg could be, **but ~~nothing
doing~~** ~~not on your life~~ damn the bit of it, for it **was growing** stiffer than ever,
a thing **I would** not have thought possible, and at the same time
shorter every day, but above all because of the other leg, **supple
hitherto and now growing rapidly stiff in its turn** but not yet
shortening, unhappily. (ET2, 90r)

EM offers many more examples of this kind. Deviations from the original are
few and mostly limited to word order, as Beckett seems above all concerned
with approximating the style and transferring the sense of the French text.
While at times the later typescripts still show minor stylistic changes to word
order, they are always local, rarely affecting an entire sentence, as in the
example above.

Repetition

Beckett often revised the translation to avoid repetitions of words or phrases in the original French. One of the most basic examples is the reoccurrence of a noun in the same sentence, which is then deleted in English: 'Dear **bicycle**, I shall not call you bike, you were green, like so many ~~bicycles~~ of your generation' (ET1, 14r). Repetitions do not have to occur in the same sentence to be removed, and they can also be replaced with a pronoun. 'But would **this gentleman** come from afar' (Sp1-3, 08r) was changed to 'But would **he** come from afar' (ET1, 08r) between the early specimen and first typescript of Part I, because 'gentleman' had already been mentioned in the previous sentence. If the original text already has a pronoun and it is repeated, the English translation sometimes leaves it out, which is not so easy to do in French because of grammatical restrictions. Such pronouns are usually copied in the earlier stages of the translation but discarded later on, for example when Moran explains how he managed to catch runners faster than himself: 'They stop and ~~they~~ wait for me, rather than prolong such a horrible ourburst at their heels' (ET2, 63r) ['On s'arrête et on m'attend' (1951, 224)].[175] To avoid repeated verbs, also difficult to leave out in French, Beckett often uses a synonym: 'Don't **talk** to me about the chambermaid, I should never have ~~talked about~~ ᵐᵉⁿᵗⁱᵒⁿᵉᵈ her' (ET2, 68r).

Occasionally, repetitions are inserted where the original French has none, usually removed again later, for example when Molloy explains why the police compel cyclists to dismount and cars or carriages to slow down upon entering the town: 'The reason of this regulation is I think this, that **the ways into** and of course **the ways out of** town are narrow and darkened by enormous vaults' (ET1, 19r). On the second typescript, Beckett revised the repetition of 'ways' to accord with the French: '**the ways into** and of course **out of** this town' (ET2, 19r). The same happens when Molloy expresses his dislike of the police station: 'I am weary of **this place**, I want to **leave this place**' (ET1, 25r), later revised as 'I am weary of **this place**, I want to **go**' (ET2, 25r), to mirror the original: 'je suis las de cet endroit et je veux aller ailleurs' (1951, 34), which does not repeat 'endroit' either. These are clearly sites of hesitation and sometimes they go back to the French manuscript,

---

175   In addition to deleting '~~they~~', Beckett also boxed the pronoun.

like the passage where Molloy receives a mug of greyish concoction from the social worker:

> Le liquide débordait, ~~le~~ le bol vacillait avec un bruit **de dents** qui claquent (où [sic] ~~éta~~ étaient-ce effectivement **mes dents** que j'entendais ? Non, car **je n'avais déjà plus de dents**, à ce moment-là) et le pain ruisselant se penchait de plus en plus. (FN1, 59r)

> Le liquide débordait, le bol vacillait avec un bruit **de dents** qui claquent, ce n'était pas **les miennes, je n'en avais pas**, et le pain ruisselant se penchait de plus en plus. (1951, 34)

> The liquid overflowed, the mug rocked with a noise of chattering **teeth**, not **my teeth**, I had **no teeth**, and the sodden bread ~~drooped~~ ˢᵃᵍᵍᵉᵈ more and more. (ET1, 25r)

> The liquid overflowed, the mug rocked with a noise of chattering **teeth**, not **mine**, I had **none**, and the sodden bread sagged more and more. (ET2, 25r)

In the first draft, 'dents' was repeated three times in the same sentence, cut back to just one in the published text. On ET1, however, the word 'teeth' again occurs three times, as in the French manuscript, but was finally reduced to one, in line with the French edition on which it was based.

Such repetitions imbue the narrative with a sense of monotony, but apart from that – or rhythmic concerns – they have no clear function. The following examples are different. In the first, Beckett repeats words in the translation for emphasis. Speaking about the women on the beach, who look like black specks in the far distance, Molloy adds that he 'could follow ~~all~~ their ~~anties~~ ᵐᵃⁿᵒᵉᵘᵛʳᵉˢ, saying, It's getting **smaller ~~and smaller~~**, or, It's getting bigger ~~and bigger~~' (ET2, 88r).

Another case is the passage where Moran claims he can think of no worse situation than the one he is in at present: 'C'est-à-dire que pour m'en faire une idée il me faudrait plus d'imagination que je n'en ai' (1951, 203). In English, Moran's lack of creative imagination is put into practice by his repetition of the word, first as a noun then as a verb, for want of a better alternative: 'That is to say, I have not enough **imagination** to ~~conceive~~ ^{imagine} it' (ET2, 48r). At first, 'conceive' was meant to avoid repetition, but then this device was used to make the form of the sentence enact its content.

Literal translation

A revision pattern of which many examples are to be found in the surviving drafts of *Molloy* concerns literal translation. The English version generally follows the French text in the earlier drafts, shifting to a freer translation in later versions, but as the following examples show, it was also a gradual process and revisions of this kind are to be found at all recorded stages of the translation process. One of the earliest instances occurs in the A and B (C) preamble, when B (C) picks up his dog and '**plunged** his face in the orange fleece' (Sp1-3, 08r), which is a literal translation of the French: 'plongea son visage dans la toison orangée' (1951, 15). In the first typescript, however, Beckett changed the verb to '**buried** his face' (ET1, 08r). As this example shows, it is not just a question of staying close to the meaning of the original in the early stages of the translation, but rather of using English verbs that have a Romance origin.

Usually, the phenomenon occurs in the second typescript, such as when Molloy explains that the police constable was '**displeased** by my slowness' (ET1, 28r), which still uses a verb similar to the French: 'c'était ma lenteur qui lui déplaisait' (1951, 37). This was changed in the second typescript to '**angered** by my slowness' (ET2, 28r), slightly altering the meaning of the sentence as well. The phenomenon also affects adjectives, for example when Molloy states that 'for the ~~just~~ ^{righteous} the tumult of the world never stops' (ET2, 32r), which first followed the French adjective:'les justes' (1951, 42).

Sometimes there is no English equivalent to match the succintness of a French verb: 'J'aurais plaisir à la detailler' (1951, 21). To solve this problem, Beckett first paraphrases the sentence, using the French verb as an adjective in English – 'To **describe it in detail** would be a pleasure' (ET1, 14r) – before replacing the adjective with a less literal and also more idiomatic substitute: 'To describe it **at length**' (ET2, 14r).

This pattern of revision also affects certain phrases, which are first translated literally from the French before they are given a more natural form. 'Avais-je, sans le savoir, un protecteur en haut lieu ?', Molloy asks himself, which changed from '**a protector in high places**' (ET1, 25r) to '**a friend at court**' (ET2, 25r). Another example is Molloy's famous comment about the *Times Literary Supplement*: 'Les pets ne le déchiraient pas' (1951, 43), which was first translated literally before Beckett found a more eloquent way of putting things, perhaps better suited to the subject at hand: '~~Farts themselves~~ ^{Even farts} **did not** ^{made no impression} **tear** ^{on} it' (ET2, 33r).

A typical feature of longer phrases that are revised in the drafts is that they not only become less literal but also gradually shorter. A good example occurs in the passage where Molloy talks about his shortening legs: 'Mais quand il y a une qui se raccourcit, tandis que l'autre reste stationnaire, alors ça commence à être inquiétant' (1951, 117). While the opening phrase is slightly shortened in the manuscript fragment of the English *Molloy*, the rest is still quite close to the original and even uses a similar adjective: 'But when one shortens, **while the other remains stationary**, then **there is some cause for worry**' (EM, 77v). The sentence would be further revised to reach its final form in the first typescript: 'But when one shortens, **and the other not**, then **you begin to be worried**' (ET1, 90r). Another example occurs when Molloy retrieves his bicycle. In French, he states: 'Je finis par la trouver, ma bicyclette, appuy[é]e contre un buisson d'une grande mollesse qui en mangeait la moitié' (1951, 69), which is trimmed considerably in English: 'In the end I found it, ~~leaning against a bush that half swallowed it up, it was so yielding.~~ ^{half buried in a soft bush.}' (ET2, 54r).

Rarely, a phrase is not just translated more literally but also more elaborately at first, before a shorter, idiomatic and less literal solution is found. A good example would be the passage about Molloy's testicles: 'Et je leur cédais à tour de rôle, à ces tristes compères, pour leur permettre de comprendre leur erreur' (1951, 72), which was heavily revised in the second typescript: 'And ~~I let them have their way, this sorry couple, now one, now the other, so~~ ^{these inseparable fools I indulged turn about,} that they might understand their ~~error~~ ^{foolishness}' (ET2, 56r).

Though it happens less frequently, the reverse process also occurs. A substitution to make the English version less literal is reverted in the first typescript when *Molloy* imitates his mother, who takes him for his father: 'Dan, you remember the day I ~~rescued~~ ^{saved} the swallow' (ET1, 15r), which reinstates the verb that is used in the French version: 'le jour où j'ai sauvé l'hirondelle' (1951, 23). It also affects nouns, for example when Molloy exclaims that 'It's for the whole [of life] there seems to be no ~~remedy~~ ^{spell}'

(ET1, 29r), which is a more literal translation of the French 'grimoire' (1951, 34). Phrases, too, can be less literal in the first typescript of the translation than in the second typescript. When the police constable asks Molloy for his papers and he adds that he 'knew it **after a moment**' (ET1, 20r), this turn of phrase was changed to '**a moment later**' (ET2, 20r), resembling the French more closely: 'je le sus un instant plus tard' (1951, 28).

In rare cases, what on the surface of the published text appears to be a revision to make the English translation less literal, is in fact a return to a phrasing as it occurred in the French manuscript. It happens when Molloy ponders the reason for his release from prison:

> Avait-on ~~trouvé~~ réussi à trouver ma mère et ~~fait~~ à faire confirmer par elle, ou plus probablement par ~~l'un~~ les autres locataires, ~~au moins~~ une partie au moins de mes dires? (FN1, 60r)

> Avait-on **réussi à joindre** ma mère et à faire confirmer par elle, ou par les gens du quartier, une partie de mes dires ? (1951, 34)

> Had they **succeeded in reaching** my mother and obtaining from her, or from the neighbours, partial confirmation of my statements? (ET1, 25r)

> Had they **succeeded in finding** my mother and a°btaining from her, or from the neighbours, partial confirmation of my statements? (ET2, 25r)

Whereas 'finding' is a freer translation of 'joindre' than 'reaching', and thus appears to take more distance from the French, it is actually a literal translation of the first recorded variant in the original manuscript ('trouver').

Idiomatic English

Closely related to the category of literal translation is the tendency to insert more idiomatic terms in the later stages of the English drafts. In these cases, a word or phrase is not just replaced with a non-literal equivalent but also one that is more colloquial and specific or less neutral and general. Again, different classes of words are affected by this pattern, beginning with nouns. The 'digestif' (1951,157) that father Ambrose offers Moran becomes a '~~digestive~~ cordial' (ET2, 13r) and his son Jacques' 'pré-molaire' (1951, 160) is revised to a '~~premolar~~ bicuspid' (ET2, 15r) in the second typescript. In both cases, the first translation was a term that resembled the French closely, but such a word could not always be found in English. When Molloy says that his buttonhole was large enough to hold an entire 'bouquet' (1951, 18) of flowers, the literal and idiomatic 'bunch' (ET1, 11r) was later replaced with the even more idiomatic 'nosegay' (ET2, 11r).

Idiomatic revisions were made as late as the proofs, on which Jacques' 'receding' chest (ET2, 46r) – 'le buste en retrait' (1951, 201) – was changed to 'sunk' (1955, 178). An example of a verb is Moran's 'I ~~packed~~ shouldered my bags again' (ET2, 73r), which is more idiomatic and more accurate because it is closer to the French 'je chargeai à nouveau mes sacs' (1951, 237), frequently used in the expression 'charger quelque chose sur son épaule'. Longer phrases are also affected by the tendency towards more idiomatic English. 'Gaber's ~~prodigious exactitude in everything connected with his missions~~ corpse fidelity to the letter of his messages' (ET2, 29r) is not only less literal and considerably shorter than the French but also more idiomatic and fluent than the initial translation: 'l'exactitude prodigieuse de Gaber pour tout ce qui touchait à ses commissions' (1951, 178).

Sometimes idiomatic translations are reverted and lengthened, for example when Beckett translated the 'démarche' of B (1951, 17) first as a colloquial 'gait' (ET1, 10r), but then more circumloquaciously as a 'way of walking' (ET2, 10r).

Register

Closely related to the previous category are instances when a perfectly idiomatic word is replaced with a slightly more obscure or specialized one, causing a shift in register, such as 'the **blow** on the skull' that Molloy deals to the old man in the forest (ET1, 99r) – 'coup sur le crâne' (1951, 129) – which later becomes a '~~blow~~ ^dint^' (ET2, 99r), or the 'mouettes' (1951, 140) that Molloy hears at the seaside, first translated with the neutral '**Seagulls**' before being replaced with '**Mews**' (ET2, 107r). Similarly, when describing where his mother lived, he explains it is close by the 'abattoirs' (1951, 31), first translated literally as '**slaughterhouse**' (ET1, 22r) but then replaced with the more archaic '**shambles**' (ET2, 22r). This change is effectuated on a number of occasions, but the term 'slaughterhouse' is retained, with added hyphen, in the sentence: 'every butcher has his **slaughter·house** and the right to slaughter, according to his ~~needs~~ ^lights^' (ET2, 31r). Words related to animals are particularly vulnerable to this pattern, for example when Molloy describes the story of Lousse as '~~an udder~~ ^a dug^ at which I tug in vain' (ET2, 65r), which is a more specialized term than the French 'un pis sur lequel j'ai beau tirer' (1951, 84).

Part II of the translation shows the same penchant for slightly obscure or specialized words. Moran calls his son a '**dirty little ~~cheat~~ ^twister^**' (ET2, 77r) – 'Il trichait' (1951, 242) – for letting the air escape from the tire on purpose, stalling their progress on purpose, and he does not take place in the '**fore**' but in the '**van**' of the bicycle (ET2, 83r), in French 'en tête' (1951, 249).

Other substitutions in this category result in downright archaic terms, which Beckett sometimes introduced but then removed or rephrased again at a later stage. According to Molloy, Lousse 'favoured voluminous tempestuous ^shifts and^ petticoats ~~and stomachers~~ and other undergarments whose names I forget' (ET2, 67r). The term 'stomacher', a V-shaped piece of cloth worn by men and women over the chest and stomach in the 16th century, was a slightly anachronous translation of 'volants' (1951, 86), so that Beckett replaced it with the more accurate 'shift', an unwaisted dress or loose-fitting piece of undergarment. Two other examples occur when Molloy throws down his bicycle and lies down 'on the ground, on the ~~greensward~~ ^grass^' (ET2, 54r) – 'grass' being more neutral and in keeping with 'le gazon' (1951, 70) – or when he mentions Edith's futile attempts to interact with him, adding that 'further insistence ~~were nugatory~~ ^{was useless}' (ET2, 56r), which was markedly more formal at first than the French: 'ne servirait à rien' (1951, 72).

Slightly literary terms in French also stood the risk of being rendered more archaically in English, for example Molloy's claim that he saw the world 'in ~~a~~ a way inordinately formal, ~~while at the same time~~ ^{though I was far from} being ~~in no wise~~ an aesthete, or an artist' (ET2, 58r). The original wording is somewhat ironic, for although Molloy claims not to be an aesthete or an artist, he does use the slightly literary term 'moindrement' to make his point: 'sans pour cela être le moindrement esthète, ni artiste' (1951, 75). The final translation avoids this irony by using a more neutral term, while the cancelled alternative 'in no wise' would have given the claim an archaic sense rather than a poetic one, thus confirming Molloy's point.

Other examples of this category in the drafts of *Molloy* are not so much related to idiomatic use of language but simply lower or elevate the register. In the majority of cases, the tone is lowered, for example when Molloy states that A and B '**descended** into the same trough and in this trough finally met' (Sp1-3, 04r), which was changed to '**went down**' (ET1, 04r). The French term 'dévalèrent' (1951, 10) is not only more formal but also carries a slightly different meaning (to go down or descend rapidly). The same happens when Molloy admits that 'To say they **were acquainted**, no, nothing warrants it' (ET1, 04r), which was not changed until the second typescript, showing that the opening passage was revised gradually, in many different stages: 'To say they **knew each other**' (ET2, 04r). In this case the phrase is closer in tone to the original: 'ils se connaissaient' (1951, 10). Other parts of the novel also show the revision pattern, for example when Molloy speaks about the moon and adds: 'if it happens that I speak of the stars it's **inadvertently**' (ET1, 12r). Beckett's revision, '**by mistake**' (ET2, 12r), is again more in keeping with the French 'par mégarde' (1951, 19).

Less frequently, the register is upscaled in the drafts, as illustrated by the replacement of the colloquial '**vet**' by the more formal '**veterinary surgeon**' (ET2, 37r) to which Lousse was taking her dog Teddy before Molloy ran him over. The original 'vétérinaire' (1951, 47) is a rather neutral term, not particularly formal and especially not as informal as 'véto', the French equivalent of 'vet'.

Many examples of elevated register occur in passages about the nether regions of the body. Because the compound 'linge de corps et de maison' (1951, 71), in the context of Lousse's application of lavender bags, does not have a direct equivalent in English, the two terms had to be translated separately. The first choice was 'undies and house-linen' ET2, 56r) but, perhaps because the difference in register between the two terms was too great, it was revised to 'underclothing and house-linen' (ET2, 56r) in the same typescript. Beckett did not immediately find the right word for Molloy's climax when he relates how Edith put his 'so-called virile member' in the 'hole between her legs': 'until I ~~came~~ ᴸᵉᵗ ᶠˡʸ ᵈⁱˢᶜʰᵃʳᵍᵉᵈ' (ET2, 66r). Whereas he hesitated between registers in English, the French had the more formal expression 'jusqu'à ce que j'émisse' (1951, 85) in all surviving versions. In general, terms related to bodily functions are sensitive to revision in the drafts of the novel. When Molloy refers to the act of sexual intercourse as 'Un jeu de con' (1951, 85), punning on the female sex organ, Beckett first duplicates but then removes the connotation in English: 'A ~~balls of a~~ ᵐᵘᵍ'ˢ game in my opinion and tiring on top of that, in the long run' (ET2, 66r). Similarly, Beckett switches registers when Molloy explains the purpose of the paper he carries about. In French he is quite polite – 'quand je vais à la garde-robe' (1951, 28) – which was first translated explicitly before Beckett adopted a more medical term: 'when I ~~go to the toilet~~ ʰᵃᵛᵉ ᵃ ˢᵗᵒᵒˡ' (ET1, 20r).

Finally, some revisions of register involve Latinate phrases. When Moran tells the reader that he is not giving the conversation about the bicycle with his son 'in ~~extenso~~ ᶠᵘˡˡ' (ET2, 61r), the term used in French is anglicized. Conversely, on two occasions, Beckett considered translating 'liliacées' (1951, 159) as 'lilies' but eventually opted for the Latin term: 'liliaceae' (ET2, 14r).

Since there are examples that make the language of the novel both more and less formal, it seems fair to say that revisions try to find a balance between registers. As such, it is no surprise that most of these changes happen in the second typescript, when Part II had also been translated, which would have made it easier to supervise the novel as a whole.

Expressions and puns

Expressions are often hard to translate and Beckett, too, struggled to find English equivalents for French idioms on a number of occasions. Molloy's comment about accepting food from social workers, for example ('de quoi ne pas tourner de l'œil', 1951, 33), was changed from 'to ~~keep~~ ʰⁱⁿᵈᵉʳ you from ~~passing out~~ ˡᵒˢⁱⁿᵍ ᶜᵒⁿˢᶜⁱᵒᵘˢⁿᵉˢˢ' (ET1, 24r) into 'to hinder you from swooning'

(ET2, 24r) and, having run over Lousse's dog Teddy, he soon finds himself overtaken by a group of men and women 'preparing to ~~set about me~~ ^{tear me to pieces}' (ET2, 37r), which reveals Beckett's trouble to render the expression 'me mettre en hachis' (1951, 47) into English. Examples can also be found in Moran's part. Explaining that Verger Joly kept a list of the faithful, ticking off their presence as they received the host, Moran adds that Father Ambrose knew nothing about this practice and would have condemned it strongly: 'il aurait chassé le bedeau sur le champ s'il l'avait cru capable d'une telle outrecuidance' (1951, 148). The expression caused Beckett some trouble in English: 'he would have **sent the verger ~~packing~~** ^{flying about his business}' (ET2, 06r). While he usually attends the last mass, Moran admits he knows nothing about the other offices, 'où je ne mettais jamais les pieds' (1951, 148). In English he '**never went ~~near~~** ^{within a mile of} **them**' (ET2, 06r).

Some variants are craftier. On the search for his mother, Molloy wonders if he is in the right town, 'celle qui m'avait donné la nuit' (1951, 45). This is a typically Beckettian pun on the French saying 'donner le jour' (to give birth), which equates birth and death, as in the famous phrase from *A Piece of Monologue*: 'Birth was the death of him' (*KLT* 117). The first known attempt to render the expression into English was 'where I first saw the **light of night** ^{murk}' (ET1, 34r). The phrase adapts the common saying 'to see the light of day' and plays on the similarity of 'light' and 'night' to create a *chiaroscuro* effect – as Beckett did in the drafts of *Stirrings Still* (Van Hulle 2011, 83) – but then it shifted to darkness with the addition of 'murk'. In the next typescript however – a carbon copy of the first – Beckett saw a new opportunity for wordplay by reversing the *clair-obscur* contrast in the original English terms: '~~**light of night**~~ ^{murk of day}' (ET2, 34r). Beckett capitalizes on a similar kind of wordplay when Molloy mentions the blue gloom that guided his way through the darkness, but again after considerable hesitation: 'I don't like gloom to lighten, ~~**it's suspicious**~~. ~~there's something shady about it~~ there's something shady about it.' (ET2, 98r) In this case, the pun was not that explicit in the original French: 'Je n'aime pas que l'ombre s'atténue, c'est louche' (1951, 127).

Some additions of wordplay to the translation may have been intended as a form of compensation. One of the most central puns to Part I of the novel has to do with Molloy's quest for his mother ('mère'), which eventually takes him to the seaside ('mer'), possibly alluding to the notion that the sea is linked to the mother figure in Jungian psychology. The homophones 'mère'/'mer' proved impossible to recreate in English and there is no evidence in the drafts that Beckett and Bowles even tried. Yet when Molloy mentions the imperatives that have led him to the seaside – and also the forest – instead of his mother, he concludes: 'they never led me anywhere, but tore me from places where, if all was not well, all was no worse than anywhere else, and then went silent, leaving me ~~on the rocks~~ stranded' (ET2, 101r), a pun that was not present in the French: 'me laissant en perdition' (1951, 132).

Another creative, though less inspired, solution is arrived at in the context of Moran's stockings, which he only wears at night because they make him look silly. The term that Moran uses in French is 'chie-en-lit' (1951, 192), which can refer to a carnival mask or costume in particular, and disorder in general. Literally it means 'shit-in-bed', so that it resonates with both Moran's question to his son 'As-tu chié, mon enfant ?' (1951, 183) and the fact that his son still wets the bed. Unable to capture these connotations in English, Beckett nevertheless tried to come up with a worthy alternative. Perhaps because '**laughing stock**' punned too obviously on 'stocking', he eventually opted for '**looked a sight**' (ET2, 39r), though its double use of seeing is a meek alternative for the semantic richness of the original expression.

As the examples above illustrate, expressions are often exploited for wordplay, as is Molloy's follow-up comment to the truism that saying is inventing: 'Faux comme de juste' (1951, 46). The second typescript shows that Beckett struggled to render the phrase in English: 'Wrong, and rightly so. ~~very rightly~~ very rightly wrong.' (ET2, 35r) A few French expressions were simply too compact to match in English, like Gaber's 'Sacré Moran !' (1951, 254), for which Beckett tried out two alternatives: '~~There was~~ Ah Moran, he ~~never the like of Moran, he said.~~ said, what a man!' (ET2, 86r).

Several revision sites in the drafts of the English translation also posed difficulties in the original manuscript, for example when Moran feels suddenly hungry upon his return from the communion with Father Ambrose: '~~Si l'âme était rassasiée, le ventre ne l'était~~ L'âme ~~rassasiée~~ assouvie, j'avais une faim de tonnerre' (FN2, 142r), which was further revised to: 'L'âme assouvie j'avais le dent' (1951, 156). The English expression, also revised, was not as colourful: 'My soul appeased, **I was ~~starving~~** ravenous' (ET2, 12r).

Some expressions are translated so peculiarly that they become obscure in English. When Molloy says that he may later seek refuge in his mother's room, 'shame drunk, my prick in my rectum', it is because he has exhausted all other options – 'à bout d'expédients' (1951, 26) – which Beckett first translated as 'bet' (ET1, 18r), and later expanded as **'bet to the world'** (ET2, 18r).

Corrections

As is common for the genesis of any translation, the remaining drafts of the English *Molloy* are corrected in several places to achieve a better result, for example when a word has been wrongly translated, such as '**~~understanding~~** ᵗᵃᵏⁱⁿᵍ' for 'entreprise' (1951, 170) or father Ambrose's 'portable **~~pyre~~** ᵖʸˣ' (ET2, 12r) for his 'ciboire-valise' (1951, 156) – 'pyre' being non-interchangeable with 'pyx'. Molloy's statement that he sometimes 'forgot not only who I was, but that I was', in other words 'forgot to be' (1955, 65; *Mo* 48) – 'il m'arrivait d'oublier non seulement qui j'étais, mais que j'étais' (1951, 73) – was also corrected in the second typescript: 'not only who I was, but **~~what~~** ᵗʰᵃᵗ **I was**' (ET2, 57r). Prepositions are sometimes fixed, as in 'Nous n'allons pas dans le désert' (1951), which is revised to '**~~w~~**ᵂe are not going **~~to~~** ⁱⁿᵗᵒ the wilderness' (ET2, 15r), and occasional grammatical slips are adjusted, for example when Molloy states he was 'straining towards **those suprious deeps**, their lying promise of gravity and peace, from all my old poisons I struggled **towards it**' (ET1, 21r), which is changed to the plural on the second typescript '**towards them**' (ET2, 21r). Finally, words apparently dropped by mistake were added at a later stage, such as the cause of death for Moran's wife: 'he finds himself saddled with a wife long since deceased, ⁱⁿ ᶜʰⁱˡᵈ⁻ᵇᵉᵈ as likely as not' (ET2, 40r) – 'en couches' (1951, 193).

Some revisions are improvements rather than corrections, however, capturing the sense of the original more accurately. When Moran asks his son to put on his green suit, he corrects his father – revealing that Moran is colour-blind: 'But it's blue, **~~father~~** ᵖᵃᵖᵃ, he said' (ET2, 14r). Clearly, 'papa' is the right choice here, since Moran elsewhere states that his son has a deliberately annoying way of pronouncing the word. Also, when the stranger that Moran encounters in the forest bars his way, '**~~encouraged~~** ᵉᵐᵇᵒˡᵈᵉⁿᵉᵈ' by his limp, this is indeed a better translation of 'il s'enhardissait' (1951, 234). Finding 'le mot juste' was not always easy, for example when 'le veneur' (1951, 137), first translated as **'hunter'**, was then changed to **'huntsman'** (ET2, 105r). The difference is slight but, as opposed to a 'chasseur', a 'veneur' hunts with dogs ('chasse à courre'). In this sense, a 'huntsman' would be better suited, as the term designates both a 'hunter' and a hunting official in charge of the hounds. Similarly, the two men that Molloy describes at the start of the novel could not see each other because the undulating land caused the road to be in waves '**not deep, but deep enough, deep enough**' (ET1, 04r), which follows the French – 'peu profondes mais suffisament, suffisament' (1951, 10) – which is then changed to '**not high, but high enough, high enough**' (ET2, 04r), it being more correct to speak of waves as 'high' instead of 'profound'.

Translations sometimes have the tendency to undo or resolve ambiguities and some examples of this pattern are to be found in the drafts of *Molloy*. 'Regarder les filles' (1951, 154) is an excuse that Moran would have preferred his son to use for not going to church. The first recorded translation was 'To look at the **girls**' but then Beckett changed it to '**tarts**' (ET2, 10r), which more readily evokes prostitutes than the rather euphemistic French. In cases when a passage could be misread, and this was not Beckett's intention, the phrase was also disambiguated. Moran's comment 'I could ~~stand~~ ^{bear} no more' (ET2, 86r) could easily have been interpreted as referring to his immobility, but Beckett undid the confusion and brought the text back in line with the French: 'j'en avais assez' (1951, 253).

Conclusion

Beckett started writing *Molloy* on 2 May 1947. Only a month or two earlier, as John Bolin points out in *Beckett and the Modern Novel*, Beckett wrote the essay 'Peintres de l'Empêchement', notably the following passage that was also published in English as part of the catalogue of the Samuel M. Kootz Gallery in New York under the title 'The New Object': 'An endless unveiling, veil behind veil, *plane after plane* of imperfect transparencies, light and space themselves veils, an unveiling towards the unveilable, the nothing, the thing again' (Beckett 2011b, 880). Bolin interprets this passage in light of Beckett's 'interest in a form of internal duplication as a central motif and governing formal characteristic of the artwork' (Bolin 2012, 122; emphasis added). Bolin draws attention to the word 'plane', which recalls the terminology Beckett had first used in his discussion of the structure of André Gide's *Paludes* and *Les Faux-Monnayeurs* in his lectures at TCD in the early 1930s (TCD MIC 60, 33, 37). In these lectures, he advocated what he called the 'integrity of incoherence', which is why Racine (unlike Corneille or Balzac) was comparable to Gide. In his 1947 essay Beckett is talking about the paintings of Bram and Geer van Velde, but as Bolin suggests, he may also be talking about his own poetics at that moment, a poetics in which modernity is inseparable from the use of 'a self-reflexive form that depicts the process of unveiling that brought it into being' (Bolin 2012, 122).

This 'process of unveiling' is what we have examined in this book. Beckett's poetics had of course developed since his lectures at TCD, but the 'integrity of incoherence' was still a crucial notion. One could even argue that he applied it more radically than he had ever done before. No traces of a general plan or programme for the novel have surfaced. Apart from a general sense of working with a form of internal duplication, he allowed the writing to take shape as he went along. Not unlike Sterne's *Tristram Shandy*, Beckett distrusts 'system-builders' and allows his characters Molloy and Moran to indulge in long digressions. Even Moran, who seems to be more of a system-builder than Molloy, becomes more and more disoriented and commits a 'crime immotivé' (TCD MIC 60, 14) with a 'geste gratuit' (39) that cannot be explained or 'reduced to motive' (14), as Beckett called it in his lectures, according to Rachel Burrows's notes.

The form of internal duplication with 'planes' reflects the multiple drafts structure of the writing process, and in that sense presages the multiple drafts model of consciousness, suggested by Daniel C. Dennett (1991). The idea that consciousness is a constant process of revision also involves a form of 'narrative selfhood' that is applicable to Molloy and Moran. When Moran says 'Oh je pourrais vous raconter des histoires' (FN3, 84r) ['Oh the stories I could tell you' (1955, 188; *Mo* 143)] the published version adds 'si j'étais tranquille. Quelle tourbe dans ma tête, quelle galerie de crevés. Murphy, Watt, Yerk, Mercier et tant d'autres' (1951, 212) ['if I were easy. What a rabble in my head, what a gallery of moribunds. Murphy, Watt, Yerk, Mercier and all the others' (1955, 188; *Mo* 143)]. The addition of meta-comments in subsequent versions, which as we have seen is one of the tendencies in the genesis, accords with the use of a self-reflexive form that depicts the process of unveiling Beckett mentioned in his 1947 essay, just before he started writing his novel.

This process of unveiling also accords with the 'continuing incompletion' that characterizes autography, according to H. Porter Abbott, discussed in the Introduction. In the autograph manuscripts, we not only see the autographer at work, but we are also witness to the way autography works in terms of 'worldmaking' (Goodman 1978). The dialectics of composition and decomposition in the manuscript show how the crucial notion of 'I can't go on, I'll go on' is actually brought into practice. When Moran is talking to his son about the assignment to go to Carrick/Hole, he continues interrogating him: 'Pour quoi faire.' ['What for?'] ~~Pour acheter une bicyclette~~ ['To buy a bicycle'], his son replies. Beckett cancels this sentence and makes Moran say: 'Non, je ne peux pas continuer' (FN3, 94r) ['No, I can't' (1955, 196; *Mo* 149)] – prefiguring the closing line of *L'Innommable*. This 'I can't go on' moment is all the more striking in the autograph, because the sentence is actually struck through. But even though they cannot go on, both the author and his character/narrator go on nonetheless. And this structure of 'continuing incompletion' goes on in the epigenesis (the continuation of the genesis after publication), for instance in the translation: in the first paragraph, Molloy indicates that this will not be the last 'plane', that there will be another one after this: 'Cette fois-ci puis encore une autre je pense (FN1, 02r). And in the English translation (after several versions) this became: 'This time, then once more I think, then perhaps a last time' (ET1, 02r). It is clear that Beckett is not identical to Molloy, in a similar way as Molloy is not identical to Moran. This book is not a biographical reading. But what they do have in common is that they all write. In that sense, Dennett's notion of 'narrative selfhood' becomes more specifically 'writing selfhood'. And although this tendency to self-write or narrate a 'self' is clearly recognized by Beckett, he seems to be counteracting and criticizing this 'fundamental tactic of self-protection, self-control, and self-definition' (Dennett 1991, 418). In the process of writing, his characters seem to be undoing their tactically narrated selves. This is especially noticeable in Moran's report. His neatly composed world, dominated by Youdi, decomposes day by day in the course of the dated autograph. So, the writing is an attempt at undoing this self-narrated, seemingly coherent self to come closer to the integrity of incoherence in 'an unveiling towards the unveilable'. But Beckett is also aware that this is a process without end, an '*endless* unveiling'. For in spite of the attempted unveiling, every text weaves a new veil at the same time. The revealing is also a reveiling process, 'veil behind veil, plane after plane of imperfect transparencies', as the multiple versions of *Molloy* illustrate. These versions create what, in the first sentence of the autograph, is called a sense of the penultimate ('le sens de l'avant-dernier'), which then becomes a sense of 'the last but one but one' in the English version. So when the autograph opens with 'Cette fois-ci, puis encore une autre je pense [...] c'est ce sera fini' it is only appropriate that one of the first undoings is the present-tense 'c'est fini', substituted with the future-tense 'ce sera fini', thus prefiguring Clov's opening words in *Fin de partie*: 'Finished, it's finished, nearly finished, it must be nearly finished' (*E* 6).

Appendix

In this appendix, we offer an English translation of the long, omitted fragment concerning Ballyba's economy (following its paragraph structure). The translation is based on the top layer (excluding deletions but including additions) of the manuscript version. Variants between the manuscript and typescript versions of this passage are discussed in chapter 2.2.

Paragraph 86 (FN3, 65r-66r)

'What then was the source of Ballyba's riches? I'll tell you. The stool of its citizens. Since time immemorial. A few words on the subject. This is perhaps the last time I will have the opportunity to surrender myself to a passion for local particulars, for what gives each lot its unique flair, for what I call the folklore of the subsoil.'

Paragraph 87 (FN3, 66r-71r)

'Ballyba was completely surrounded by an agricultural zone about half a mile wide. Out there the rarest of greens neighboured on common root vegetables, such as the turnip and the potato, with indescribable luxuriance. Every year hundreds – what am I saying – hundreds of thousands of tons of superb vegetables of all kinds were carted off from Ballyba to national and foreign markets. How was this agreeable outcome achieved? Thanks to the citizens' excrements. Let me explain. Every person who, following the most recent census report, could be considered a resident of Ballyba, be it in the village or on the countryside, and starting from the age of two, owed the A.O. (Agricultural Organisation) a certain amount of fecal matter every year, to be delivered on a monthly basis. The [FN3, 67r] required quantities, established with law and equity by a committee devoted to that sole purpose, differed according to the age, the circumstances, the diet, the temperament, etc., of the contributor, and in case of sickness, or chronic deficiency, considerable disencumbrances could be consented, up to total exemption, upon the presentation of a medical certificate duly stamped by a second committee on round-the-clock availability to this end. As for travellers it mattered not whether they were absent for pleasure, for business, because of a pilgrimage, out of familial piety, or for whatever other reason, as the same obligation was indiscriminately imposed on them, namely that of having to compensate in cash what they owed to the A.O. in kind, everyone according to his purse of course, and a mercurial posted at the town hall at the beginning of every month revealed to the population what the value was for each category of this valuable commodity, which – in the good years – peaked at 12 or 15 cents per

[FN3, 68r] kilo. This was enough to dissuade the inhabitants of Ballyba from travel, and actually – apart from a few ano-erotics, seduced by the quiet seclusion of exile, and certain very well-to-do families – the residents of Ballyba stayed home. Certain officials, on the other hand, such as the mayor, the police sergeant, the teacher, the curator of the museum of sacred art, etc., and of course the officers of the A.O., could be absent without recompense for a period never exceeding 8 days, on the condition that they could justify their absence with a travel order. Travel orders, which were very difficult to obtain, were delivered by a curious character called the Odibil. Without party, without denomination, elected for life on the very day of his predecessor's demise, the Odibil enjoyed discretionary powers that were far-reaching, yet quite difficult to comprehend, for a foreigner. He did not seem to occupy himself with territorial matters per se, but he was the only one who could settle certain issues of primordial importance, such as deciding whether a departure from Ballyba was indispensable or whether it could be avoided. But situations in which people

[FN3, 69r] had to resort to his decisions, which were of course indisputable, were rare. And he mostly stayed in his beautiful house, with nothing on his hands, waiting for a case needing his judgment to present itself. Although princely, his fees were not excessive, if one considers the nature of the oath he had to swear before taking up office, and which obliged him to live chastely from then on (the occasional past infractions being of no consequence), to wear only clothes, underwear included, of an immaculate whiteness, and to never leave his house as one could not conceive that a duly-elected Odibil could be replaced, albeit it for only a short period of time, and one believed that only death could relieve him of his obligation to perform his duties, and whenever he was ill, and even in his death throes, people consulted him when required with the same confidence and the same submissive air as when he had been in perfect health. But I will have the chance to behold the Odibil of Ballyba from close-up (I figured as much upon leaving my home) so I will not add anything at this point

[FN3, 70r] except for the following few remarks. There are no applicants for the post of the Obidil,[176] but the entire population gathers on the large square in front of the house of whom death has just relieved, and there, in a frenzy of pain followed by joy and by means of I don't know what kind of collective instinct, without rhyme or reason, it designates its preferred successor, shouting his name. And, what is even more strange, he who is empowered with the position does not have the right to reject it, but without even saying goodbye to his wife and children, if he is married, or to his mistress, if he is not, he has to enter his new and splendid abode without delay, putting on the obligatory white underwear, socks, shirt, suit, shoes, tie (strictly mandatory), gloves, and hat, in order to appear on the balcony and present himself to the crowd. And on several occasions it has happened, according to well-placed witnesses, that he would stop smiling and waving to raise his head and let his gaze dwell upon the village, the vast vegetable fields and beyond, on the lean countryside which probably hid his

[FN3, 71r] house somewhere, and that his eyes welled with tears, for the first time perhaps since he had reached the age of reason, for it is necessary to have attained the age of reason (set at 23 years in Ballyba) to be able to be elected Odibil.[177] Enough on the Odibil – at least for the time being.'

Paragraph 88 (FN3, 71r-72r)

'But travel orders were not limited to public officials, military staff, and civic notables; members of the clergy, numerous in Ballyba, were entitled to them as well, in principle. But they practically never obtained any, so to speak. And that was not the only measure undertaken to discourage them from leaving Ballyba; for there were others, the most important of which being referred to as the residence bonus. Because the A.O., having ordered advanced studies on the influence of profession on the stools of the people, learned that the average man of God did not defecate in quite the same manner as the layman, and that the fecal matter in particular contained substances of incomparable fertility, above all with regard to lettuce. Which some people would not

176 Here, the manuscript suddenly starts talking about the 'Obidil' instead of the 'Odibil'.
177 This and the next occurrence of the name was 'Obidil' in the first layer of inscription, which was overwritten and replaced by 'Odibil'.

hesitate to attribute to the presence, in the bowl, of seminal elements – going wherever they could.

[FN3, 72r] A rather unscientific theory, no doubt, and[178] of little worth from the perspective of the one that regarded this merely as an effect of the sacrament, extending its habitual grace to the digestive tract.'

Paragraph 89 (FN3, 72r-73r)

'As for visitors and tourists, they were granted a three-day delay, after which they became tributary to the A.O. in the same way as the residents, obliging them to show compliance, in the form of a deposit slip, before leaving the territory. This was to answer to the case of those staying with private individuals, who did not make use of the public toilets that were directly linked up with the agricultural periphery through a radial system of cesspits, whose mechanism presented certain particulars worthy of admiration. We will come back to this topic anyway. As a result the expression 'Ballyba weekend' had come to be used in common parlance to refer to all periods of fragile immunity, and, by extension, all suspension of pain spoiled by the certainty that it would soon come back. People used to say, for example, of the convalescent whose relapse seemed imminent, Poor devil, it's only a Ballyba weekend. And the metaphysical poet Clark had gone as far as to compare the Ballyba weekend to the period of love that ranges from dating to mating, and people

[FN3, 73r] cited other verses by him, composed at the age of 75, where, in a surge of irresistible optimism, he made not only human life, but eternity itself benefit from that same comparison.'

Paragraph 90 (FN3, 73r-74r)

'The collection of excrements took place on the first and fifteenth of each month. That is to say, half the population started counting on the first, the other half on the fifteenth. This facilitated collecting the excrements

---

178   Here, the manuscript changes from blue ink to black ink. The date ('9.10.47') and place name ('PARIS') on the verso is written in the same black ink.

and putting it in silos. Enormous carts (also used for the transportation of vegetables) pulled by grey asses harnessed four by four, halted at every house in front of which the dustbins were aligned, shining like silver, each marked with a name. They stood there since the previous evening. People competed zealously to scrub and polish them. There was a fine on lack-lustre bins, more or less high depending on whether they were very lack-lustre, moderately lack-lustre or a bit lack-lustre. The disposal team carried out a preliminary verification, paid out money,

[FN3, 74r] loaded the dustbins onto the carts, replacing them with empty ones. A more scrupulous checkup took place at the warehouse. If everything was finished before noon, the afternoon could be spent at will. In the evening a ball would be held in the main square. Sometimes it would fall on a Sunday, which in that case was deferred to the next day.'

Paragraph 91 (FN3, 74r)

'Monthly shortcomings, be it in terms of quantity or quality, were not really fussed about, as long they weren't excessive. What mattered most was the annual output. A bad month could be made up for during the next months. At the end of the year the accounts were closed. Whoever found himself to be in deficit still, had to compensate for the deficit in cash, at the average rate of the previous year. Whoever found himself to have exceeded his required contribution received a certificate. These certificates were very much sought after. They were of different colours, depending on the extent of merit. The yellow diploma from the A.O. was highly desirable. It entailed considerable advantages. In particular it facilitated access to certain high offices.'

Paragraph 92 (FN3, 74r-76r)

'Keeping a small portion of one's excre- [FN3, 75r] ment for oneself, for one's own garden, whilst acquitting oneself entirely of one's impositions, was not within the power of people with a normal constitution. But certain odd characters did manage to do so, even beyond their personal needs, and could thus resell it to the deficient. There was a certain Colbert, famous throughout the entire country, who amassed a considerable fortune simply by eating and defecating. He was a little old codger of extreme gauntness. He lived alone. His cellars were full of fecal matter. People suspected him of adulterating it with bird shit. At his place one could get 5 kilos, 10 kilos at a time. He sold it at the official price. He did not care about the yellow diploma. Every year larger quantities were demanded from him, yet he always retained a surplus quantity. He could have been charged with monopolization, restrictive actions could have been undertaken against him, but civil upheavals were feared. Once, private vegetable gardens were almost forbidden. He named his clients. Not a single one possessed a vegetable garden. His argument, which proved worthless, won the day. The A.O. offered to buy all of his surplus. He refused. He was outraged and made no secret of it that the annual deficits

[FN3, 76r] were paid for at a rate that was three times lower than the official one. I only sell to the impoverished deficient people, he proclaimed; it is scandalous to exploit these people's light constipations. Eventually they could hold nothing against him. He sold at the official price, assented to loans without collateral, with nothing more than a signature, and was loved by all the poor. I repeat, the name of this extraordinary being was Colbert. One day they will make a statue of him. Seated, I hope. I heard tales about a poor woman from Bally, a scavenger I believe, who talked about him as if he had already been canonized. Saint Colbert, shit for us, she would shout, in her robust slang, every night, in her prayer.'

Paragraph 93 (FN3, 76r)

'I would've liked to devote a paragraph to the toilet facilities, both private and public, of Ballyba. They were curious, ingenious. But the desire seems to have left me. Perhaps it will come back. I hope so.'

Paragraph 94 (FN3, 76r-78r)

'What about public health, exposed continuously to this accumulation of organic matter? I don't know. All that belongs to the public sphere eludes me. It must have been like everywhere else, neither particularly good nor particularly bad. Had it been particularly bad it seems to me I would have known. A few cases of typhoid or cholera morbus from time to time probably. All those stories of refuse disposal, far away from the impure, were deliberately devised to stultify the people. When you

[FN3, 77r] are born in excrements and when you live your entire life in its proximity, you can adapt to it quite easily. The administrators of Ballyba understood this well. I have said that visitors were few in number. That is true. The presence of a foreigner in Ballyba was quite an event. You didn't go there for pleasure, that much is sure. People feared that robust reception of the excremental man. They preferred the sentimentality of the cesspit. Even I, lucid as I am, approached it with anxiety. I saw myself, as in a nightmare, pursuing Molloy through chunks of faeces. I called to my aid everything I had read on Ballyba, on its cultivation, its manuring system, its toilets, its inhabitants. Were there never any atrocious scenes in what I envisioned? No. If one may believe these stories, everything proceeded calmly and in orderly fashion, nothing about this gigantic mobilization of natural necessities was shocking. I continued to ask myself questions, and to answer them, I became quite fond of catechistic reasoning. What did I know for example, about Ballyba's odour? Nothing. It was never even mentioned! Wasn't that in itself enough to arouse suspicions? Who were the authors of those accounts? People from [FN3, 78r] Ballyba, mostly. Testimonials from foreigners did exist, however. I was familiar with just one. Briefe aus einem Scheissdorf by a balneotherapist named Kottmann. He was the inventor of the fecal bath as a treatment for mental illnesses and proposed to the A.O. to build reservoirs where the excrement could be stored to this end, before it was to be spread out. Nothing would be lost for the crops, he said, or so little. But they sent him away saying that the bodies of the bathers constituted a source of pollution. But it seemed to Kottmann that this was but a pretext and that the real motivations behind the refusal were entirely different. It was a scientific work but one that did not lack considerations of a more general nature, on the charm (Reiz) of Ballyba and the merits of its inhabitants. Nothing to justify my fears. As for impartial witnesses in the flesh, neither myself nor anyone else that I know of had ever encountered one.'

Works Cited

Works by Beckett

— Beckett, Samuel (1950), 'Two Fragments', in: *Transition Fifty* 6 (October): 103-5.

· (1951), *Molloy* (Paris: Les Éditions de Minuit).

· (1953a), 'Extract from *Molloy*', in: *Merlin* 2.2 (Autumn): 89-103.

· (1953b), *Molloy* (Paris: Les Éditions de Minuit).

· (1954a), 'Extract from *Molloy*', in: *New World Writing* 5 (Spring): 316-23.

· (1954b), 'Extract from *Molloy*', in: *The Paris Review* 5 (Spring): 124-35.

· (1955a), *Molloy* (Paris: Olympia Press).

· (1955b), *Molloy* (New York: Grove Press).

· (1958), *Nouvelles et Textes pour rien* (Paris: Les Éditions de Minuit).

· (1959a), *Molloy, Malone Dies, The Unnamable: A Trilogy* (Paris: Olympia Press).

· (1959b), *Molloy, Malone Dies, and The Unnamable: Three Novels by Samuel Beckett* (New York: Grove Press).

· (1959 [1960]), *Molloy / Malone Dies / The Unnamable* (London: John Calder).

· (1963), *Molloy / L'Expulsé* (Paris: Union générale d'éditions).

· (1965a), *Proust and Three Dialogues with Georges Duthuit* (London: John Calder).

· (1965b), *Three Novels by Samuel Beckett: Molloy / Malone Dies / The Unnamable* (New York: Grove Press).

· (1966a), *Molloy / Malone Dies / The Unnamable* (London: Calder and Boyars).

· (1966b), *Molloy* (London: Calder and Boyars).

· (1971a), *Molloy* (Paris: Les Éditions de Minuit).

· (1971b), *L'Innommable* (Paris: Les Éditions de Minuit).

· (1982), *Molloy* (Paris: Les Éditions de Minuit).

· (1984), *Disjecta: Miscellaneous Writings and a Dramatic Fragment*, ed. by Ruby Cohn (New York: Grove Press).

· (1992a), *Dream of Fair to Middling Women*, ed. by. Eoin O'Brien and Edith Fournier (Dublin: Black Cat Press).

· (1992b), *Krapp's Last Tape: The Theatrical Notebooks of Samuel Beckett, vol. 3*, ed. by James Knowlson (London: Faber and Faber).

· (1999a), *Beckett's 'Dream' Notebook*, ed. by John Pilling (Reading: BIF).

· (1999b), *En attendant Godot* (Paris: Les Éditions de Minuit).

· (2009a), *Endgame*, pref. by Rónán McDonald (London: Faber and Faber).

· (2009b), *Krapp's Last Tape and Other Shorter Plays*, pref. by S. E. Gontarski (London: Faber and Faber).

· (2009c), *Molloy*, ed. by Shane Weller (London: Faber and Faber).

- (2009d), *Murphy*, ed. by J.C.C. Mays (London: Faber and Faber).
- (2009e), *The Letters of Samuel Beckett, vol. I, 1929–1940*, ed. by George Craig, Martha Dow Fehsenfeld, Dan Gunn and Lois More Overbeck (Cambridge: Cambridge University Press).
- (2009f), *Watt*, ed. by C. J Ackerley (London: Faber and Faber).
- (2010a), *Fin de partie* (Paris: Les Éditions de Minuit)
- (2010b), *Malone Dies*, ed. by Peter Boxall (London: Faber and Faber).
- (2010c), *More Pricks than Kicks*, ed. by Cassandra Nelson (London: Faber and Faber).
- (2010d), *Texts for Nothing and Other Shorter Prose 1950–1976*, ed. by Mark Nixon (London: Faber and Faber).
- (2010e), *The Unnamable*, ed. by Steven Connor (London: Faber and Faber).
- (2010f), *Waiting for Godot*, pref. By Mary Bryden (London: Faber and Faber)
- (2011a), *The Letters of Samuel Beckett, vol. II, 1941–1956*, ed. by George Craig, Martha Dow Fehsenfeld, Dan Gunn and Lois More Overbeck (Cambridge: Cambridge University Press).
- (2011b), 'The New Object', in: *Modernism / modernity* 18.4 (November): 873-7.
- (2014), *The Letters of Samuel Beckett, vol. III, 1947–1965*, ed. by George Craig, Martha Dow Fehsenfeld, Dan Gunn and Lois More Overbeck (Cambridge: Cambridge University Press).
- (2016), *The Letters of Samuel Beckett, vol. IV, 1966–1989*, ed. by George Craig, Martha Dow Fehsenfeld, Dan Gunn and Lois More Overbeck (Cambridge: Cambridge University Press).

Other Works Cited or Consulted

— Ackerley, C. J., and S. E. Gontarski (2006), *The Faber Companion to Samuel Beckett* (London: Faber and Faber).
— Ackerley, C. J. (2015), 'Monadology: Samuel Beckett and Gottfried Wilhelm Leibniz', in: *Beckett / Philosophy*, ed. by Matthew Feldman and Karim Mamdani (Stuttgart: Ibidem Verlag), 185-210.
— Abbott, H. Porter (1973), *The Fiction of Samuel Beckett: Form and Effect* (Berkeley: University of California Press).
- (1984), *Diary Fiction: Writing as Action* (Ithaca and London: Cornell University Press).

· (1996), *Beckett Writing Beckett: The Author in the Autograph* (Ithaca and Londen: Cornell University Press).

— Atik, Anne (2001), *How It Was: A Memoir of Samuel Beckett* (London: Faber and Faber).

— Austen, Jane (2014), *Northanger Abbey*, ed. by Susan J. Wolfson (Cambridge, MA: The Belknap Press of Harvard University Press).

— Bair, Deirdre (1978), *Samuel Beckett: A Biography* (London: Vintage).

— Baker, Phil (1997), *Beckett and the Mythology of Psychoanalysis* (London / New York: Macmillan / St. Martin's).

— de Biasi, Pierre-Marc (1996), 'What is a Literary Draft? Toward a Functional Typology of Genetic Documentation', in: *Yale French Studies* 89: 26-58.

— Beplate, Justin (2011), 'Samuel Beckett, Olympia Press, and the Merlin Juveniles', in: *Publishing Samuel Beckett*, ed. by Mark Nixon (London: The British Library), 97-109.

— Bergson, Henri (1900), *Le rire: essai sur la signification du comique* (Paris: Presses universitaires de France)

— Bernini, Marco (2014), 'Gression, Regression, and Beyond: A Cognitive Reading of *The Unnamable*', in: *Samuel Beckett Today / Aujourd'hui* 26: 193-209.

— Boie, Bernhild, and Daniel Ferrer (1993), *Genèses du roman contemporain. Incipit et entrée en écriture* (Paris: CNRS Éditions).

— Bolin, John (2012), *Samuel Beckett and the Modern Novel* (Cambridge: Cambridge University Press).

— Bowles, Patrick (1962), 'Translator's Preface', in: Friedrich Dürrenmatt, *The Visit: A Tragi-Comedy*, trans. by Patrick Bowles (New York: Grove Press).

· (1990), Unpublished interview with Martha Dow Fehsenfeld.

· (1994), 'How to Fail: Notes on Talks with Samuel Beckett', in: *P.N. Review 96* 20.4 (March-April): 24-38.

— [Brunet, Pierre Gustave] (1884), *Curiosités théologiques par un bibliophile*, nouvelle edition (Paris: Garnier Frères).

— Calder, John (2014), *The Garden of Eros: The Story of the Paris Expatriates and the Post-War Literary Scene* (Surrey: Alma Books).

— Campbell, James (1996), 'Waiting for Beckett', in: *The Guardian* 18 Jan. 1996, 13.

· (2013), *Exiled in Paris: Richard Wright, James Baldwin, Samuel Beckett, and Others on the Left Bank* (Berkeley: University of California Press).

— Camus, Albert (1965), 'Le Mythe de Sisyphe: Essai sur l'absurde', in: *Essais*, ed. by R. Quillot and L. Faucon (Paris: Gallimard), 90-211.

— Conrad, Joseph (1990), *Heart of Darkness and Other Tales*, ed. by Cedric Watts (Oxford: Oxford University Press).
— Clark, Andy, and David J. Chalmers (1998), 'The Extended Mind', in: *Analysis* 58.1 (January): 7–19.
— Cohn, Ruby (2005), *A Beckett Canon* (Ann Arbor: The University of Michigan Press, [2001]).
— Cordingley, Anthony (2013), *Self-Translation: Brokering Originality in Hybrid Culture* (London: Bloomsbury).
— Dante, Alighieri (2002), *The Inferno*, trans. by Robert and Jean Hollander (New York: Random House / Anchor Books).
— Defoe, Daniel (1889), *The Earlier Life and the Chief Earlier Works of Daniel Defoe*, ed. by Henry Morley (London: Routledge).
— Dennett, Daniel C. (1991), *Consciousness Explained* (London: Penguin).
— Driver, Tom (2005), 'Interview with Beckett (1961): Tom Driver in "Columbia University Forum",' in: *Samuel Beckett: The Critical Heritage,* ed. by Lawrence Graver and Raymond Federman (London: Routledge), 241-7.
— Ferrer, Daniel, *Logiques du brouillon: modèles pour un critique génétique* (Paris: Seuil, 2011).
— Feldman, Matthew (2006), *Beckett's Books: A Cultural History of the Interwar Notes* (London: Continuum).
　· (2011), 'Samuel Beckett, Wilhelm Windelband and the Interwar "Philosophy Notes"', in *Modernism / modernity* 18.4 (November) 755-70.
　· (2014), 'Beckett's Trilogy on the Third Programme', in: *Samuel Beckett Today / Aujourd'hui* 26: 41-26.
— Fifield, Peter (2011), 'Introduction to Samuel Beckett, "The New Object"', in: *Modernism / modernity* 18.4 (November): 873-7.
— Fletcher, John (1967), *Samuel Beckett's Art* (London: Chatto & Windus).
— Fletcher, John, and Raymond Federman (1970), *Samuel Beckett: His Works and His Critics* (Berkeley: University of California Press).
— Freud, Sigmund (1967), *Jenseits des Lustprinzips* (Frankfurt am Main: Fischer).
— Frost, Everett, and Jane Maxwell (2006), 'Catalogue of the Samuel Beckett Manuscripts at Trinity College Dublin', in: *Samuel Beckett Today / Aujourd'hui* 16: 183-202.
— Gellhaus, Axel (2004), 'Marginalia: Paul Celan as Reader', in: *Reading Notes*, ed. by Dirk Van Hulle and Wim Van Mierlo (Amsterdam: Rodopi), 201-19.
— Genette, Gérard (1972), *Figures III* (Paris: Seuil).

— Geulincx, Arnold (2006), *Ethics: with Samuel Beckett's Notes*, ed. by Han van Ruler and Anthony Uhlmann, trans. by Martin Wilson (Amsterdam: Rodopi / Brill).

— Gide, André (1923), *Dostoïevsky: articles et causeries* (Paris: Plon).

— Gilmore, Thomas B. (1976), 'The Comedy of Swift's Scatological Poems', in: *PMLA* 91.1: 33-43.

— Girodias, Maurice (1990), *Une Journée sur la terre vol. II: Les Jardins d'Éros* (Paris: Éditions de la Différence).

— Goethe, Johann Wolfgang von (1923), *Goethes Faust*, ed. by Robert Petsch (Leipzig: Bibliographisches Institut).
   · (1999), *Die Leiden des jungen Werthers*, Studienausgabe, Paralleldruck der Fassungen von 1774 und 1787 (Stuttgart: Reclam).

— Gontarski, S. E. (2015), *Creative Involution: Bergson, Beckett, Deleuze* (Edinburgh: Edinburgh University Press).

— Gontarski, S. E., Martha Fehsenfeld, and Dougald McMillan (1989), 'Interview with Rachel Burrows', in: *Journal of Beckett Studies* 11: 6-15.

— Goodman, Nelson (1968), *Languages of Art: An Approach to a Theory of Symbols* (Indianapolis: Bobbs-Merrill).
   · (1978), *Ways of Worldmaking* (Hassocks: Harvester).

— Grutman, Rainier (2009), 'Self-Translation', in: *Routledge Encyclopedia of Translation Studies*, 2nd edition, ed. by Mona Baker and Gabriela Saldanha (London and New York: Routledge, [1998]), 257-60.
   · (2013), 'Beckett and Beyond: Putting Self-Translation in Perspective', in: *Orbis Litterarum* 68.3: 188-206.

— Hay, Louis (1984), 'Die dritte Dimension der Literatur', in: *Poetica* 16.3-4: 307-23.
   · (1986-7), 'La troisième dimension de la littérature', in: *Texte* 5/6: 313-28.

— Helfand, William H. (1991), *The Picture of Health: Images of Medicine and Pharmacy from the William H. Helfand Collection* (Philadelphia: University of Pennsylvania Press).

— Herman, David (2013), 'Narrative and Mind: Directions for Inquiry', in: *Stories and Minds: Cognitive Approaches to Literary Narrative*, ed. by Lars Bernaerts, Dirk De Geest, Luc Herman and Bart Vervaeck (Lincoln: University of Nebraska Press), 199-209.

— Hill, Leslie (1990), *Beckett's Fiction: In Different Words* (Cambridge: Cambridge University Press).

— Hone, Joseph M., and Mario M. Rossi (1934), *Swift: or, The Egotist* (London: Victor Gollancz).

— Juliet, Charles (1995), *Conversations with Samuel Beckett and Bram van Velde* (Leiden: Academic Press Leiden).
— Jones, Ernest (1923), *Papers on Psycho-Analysis* (London: Bailliere, Tindall & Cox).
— Joyce, James (1939), *Finnegans Wake* (London: Faber and Faber).
  · (1986), *Ulysses*. The corrected text, ed. by Hans Walter Gabler, with Wolfhard Steppe and Claus Melchior (New York: Vintage Books / Random House).
— Kamel, Nadia (2016), 'Un après-midi avec Samuel Beckett', in: *Samuel Beckett Today / Aujourd'hui* 27: 141-5.
— Kearney, Patrick J. (2007), *The Olympia Press*, ed. by Carroll Angus (Liverpool: Liverpool University Press).
— Keats, John (2001), *The Complete Poems of John Keats* (London: Wordsworth Editions).
— Kern, Edith (1959), 'Moran-Molloy: The Hero as Author', in: *Perspective* 11 (Autumn): 183-93.
— Knowlson, James (1997), *Damned to Fame: The Life of Samuel Beckett* (London: Bloomsbury, [1996]).
— Lake, Carlton (1984), *No Symbols Where None Intended* (Austin: Humanities Research Center, University of Texas at Austin).
— Le Juez, Brigitte (2008), *Beckett before Beckett* (London: Souvenir Press).
— Leopardi, Giacomo (2011), *Canti*, trans. by Jonathan Galassi (New York: Farrar, Strauss and Giroux).
— Lernout, Geert (2010), *Help My Unbelief: James Joyce and Religion* (London: Continuum).
— Levy, Eric P. (2007), *Trapped in Thought: A Study of the Beckettian Mentality* (Syracuse: Syracuse University Press).
— Lodge, David (2011), *The Art of Fiction* (London: Vintage Books, [1992]).
— Logue, Christopher (1999), *Prince Charming: A Memoir* (London, Faber and Faber).
— Maude, Ulrika (2015), 'Beckett, Body and Mind', in: *The New Cambridge Companion to Samuel Beckett*, ed. by Dirk Van Hulle (Cambridge: Cambridge University Press), 170-84.
— Mays, J. C. C. (1980), 'Review of *The Samuel Beckett Manuscripts: A Study*', in: *Journal of Beckett Studies* 6: http://www.english.fsu.edu/jobs/num06/Num6Mays.htm.
— Montaigne, Michel de (1965), *Essais I* (Paris: Gallimard Folio Classique).

— Mooney, Sinead (2011), *A Tongue Not Mine: Beckett and Translation* (Oxford: Oxford University Press).

— Morin, Emilie (2005), '"But to hell with all this fucking scenery": Ireland in Translation in Samuel Beckett's *Molloy, Malone meurt / Malone Dies*', in: *Global Ireland: Irish Literatures for the New Millennium*, ed. by Ondřej Pilný and Clare Wallace (Prague: Litteraria Pragensia), 222-34.

· (2009), *Samuel Beckett and the Problem of Irishness* (Basingstoke: Palgrave Macmillan).

— Murray Scott, Andrew (2012), *Alexander Trocchi: The Making of the Monster* (London: Kennedy and Boyd, [1991]).

— Neary, J. Peter, and Cormac Ó Gráda (1991), 'Protection, Economic War and Structural Change: The 1930s in Ireland', in: *Irish Historical Studies* 27.107: 250-66.

— Nixon, Mark (2011), *Samuel Beckett's German Diaries 1936–1937* (London: Continuum).

— O'Hara, J. D. (1992), 'Freud and the Narrative of "Moran"', in: *Journal of Beckett Studies* 2: 47-63.

— O'Neill, Christine (1996), *Too Fine a Point: A Stylistic Analysis of the Eumaeus Episode in James Joyce's* Ulysses (Trier: Wissenschaftlicher Verlag Trier).

— O'Reilly, Édouard Magessa (2006), '*Molloy*, Part II, Where the Shit Hits the Fan: Ballyba's Economy and the Worth of the World', in: *Genetic Joyce Studies* 6: n.p. (http://www. geneticjoycestudies.org/articles/GJS6/GJS6OReilly).

— Perloff, Marjorie (1981), *The Poetics of Indeterminacy* (Princeton: Princeton University Press).

— Petrarca, Francesco (1824), *Le Rime di Messer Francesco Petrarca*, vol. 1. (Milan: Nicolò Bettoni).

— Pilling John (2006), *A Samuel Beckett Chronology* (Basingstoke: Palgrave Macmillan).

· (2011), *Samuel Beckett's* More Pricks than Kicks*: In a Strait of Two Wills* (London: Continuum).

— Plimpton, George (1981), 'The Paris Review Sketchbook', in: *The Paris Review* 79: 308-420.

— Pothast, Ulrich (2008), *The Metaphysical Vision: Arthur Schopenhauer's Philosophy of Art and Life and Samuel Beckett's Own Way to Make Use of It* (New York: Peter Lang).

— Pountney, Rosemary (1998), *Theatre of Shadows: Samuel Beckett's Drama 1956-76. From* All That Fall *to* Footfalls *with Commentaries on the Latest Plays* (Gerrards Cross: Colin Smythe, [1988]).

— Prince, Gerald (1988), 'The Disnarrated', in: *Style* 22.1: 1-8.

— Proust, Marcel (1926), *À la recherche du temps perdu: Du Côté de chez Swann*, vol. 2 (Paris: Éditions de la Nouvelle Revue Française).

    · (1928), *À la recherche du temps perdu: Du Côté de chez Swann*, vol. 1 (Paris: Éditions de la Nouvelle Revue Française).

    · (1929), *À la recherche du temps perdu: A l'ombre des jeunes filles en fleurs*, vol. 3 (Paris: Éditions de la Nouvelle Revue Française).

— Rabinovitz, Rubin (1979), '*Molloy* and the Archetypal Traveller', in: *Journal of Beckett Studies* 5 (Autumn): 22-44.

— Richardson, Brian (2001), 'Denarration in Fiction: Erasing the Story in Beckett and Others', in: *Narrative* 9.2: 168-75.

    · (2006), *Unnatural Voices: Extreme Narration in Modern and Contemporary Fiction* (Columbus: Ohio State University Press).

— Rose, Marilyn Gaddis (2000), 'Beckett', in: *The Oxford Guide to Literature in English Translation*, ed. by Peter France (Oxford: Ofxord University Press): 294-6.

— Rosset, Barney (2016), *Dear Mr. Beckett: Letters from the Publisher. The Samuel Beckett File*, ed. by Lois Oppenheim (New York: Opus).

— Salisbury, Laura (2012), *Samuel Beckett: Laughing Matters, Comic Timing* (Edinburgh: Edinburgh University Press).

— Seaver, Richard (1952), 'Samuel Beckett: An Introduction', in: *Merlin*, 1.2 (Autumn): 73-9.

    · (1991), 'Introduction', in: *I can't go on, I'll go on: A Selection from Samuel Beckett's Work*, ed. by Richard Seaver (New York: Grove Press, [1976]), ix-xlv.

    · (2012), *The Tender Hour of Twilight. Paris in the '50s, New York in the '60s: A Memoir of Publishing's Golden Age*, ed. by Jeannette Seaver (New York: Farrar, Strauss and Giroux).

— Schopenhauer, Arthur (1969), *The World as Will and Representation*, 2 vols., trans. by E. F. J. Payne (New York: Dover Publications).

— Shenker, Israel (2005), 'Interview with Beckett (1956): Israel Shenker in "New York Times"', in: *Samuel Beckett: The Critical Heritage*, ed. by Lawrence Graver and Raymond Federman (London: Routledge), 160-3.

— Sorrell, Martin (2000), 'Rhyme's Wrongs: Dealing with Verlaine's Rhymes in English', in: *On Translating French Literature and Film II*, ed. by Myriam Salama-Carr (Amsterdam: Rodopi), 73-86.

— Spencer Jones, H. (1939), 'Is There Life in Other Worlds?', in: *Discovery* (New Series) 2.10 (January): 36-47.
— St. Jorre, John de (2009), *The Good Ship Venus: The Erotic Voyage of Maurice Girodias and the Olympia Press* (London: Faber and Faber, [1994]).
— Swift, Jonathan (1824), 'A Dialogue in Hibernian Style between A and B', in: *The Works of Jonathan Swift, vol. VIII*, ed. by Sir Walter Scott (Edinburgh: Ballantyne), 156-7.
— Tucker, David (2012), *Samuel Beckett and Arnold Geulincx: Tracing A Literary Fantasia* (London: Continuum).
— Uhlmann, Anthony (2006), *Samuel Beckett and the Philosophical Image* (Cambridge: Cambridge University Press).
— Van Hulle, Dirk (2006), 'Samuel Beckett's "Faust" Notes', in: *Samuel Beckett Today / Aujourd'hui* 16: 283-97.
  · (2011), *The Making of Samuel Beckett's* Stirrings Still / Soubresauts *and* Comment dire / what is the word (Brussels: University Press Antwerp).
  · (2014a), 'The Obidil and the Man of Glass: Denarration, Genesis and Cognition in: Beckett's *Molloy, Malone Dies* and *The Unnamable*', in: *Samuel Beckett Today / Aujourd'hui* 26: 25-40.
  · (2014b), *Modern Manuscripts: The Extended Mind and Creative Undoing* (London: Bloomsbury).
  · (2014c), 'Textual Scars: Beckett, Genetic Criticism and Textual Scholarship', in *The Edinburgh Companion to Samuel Beckett and the Arts*, ed. by S. E. Gontarski (Edinburgh: Edinburgh University Press), 306-19.
  · (2015), *The Making of Samuel Beckett's* Krapp's Last Tape / La Dernière Bande (Brussels and London: University Press Antwerp and Bloomsbury).
— Van Hulle, Dirk, and Mark Nixon (2013), *Samuel Beckett's Library* (Cambridge: Cambridge University Press).
— Van Hulle, Dirk, and Shane Weller (2014), *The Making of Samuel Beckett's* L'Innommable / The Unnamable (London and Brussels: Bloomsbury and University Press Antwerp).
— Verhulst, Pim, and Wout Dillen (2014), '"I can make nothing of it": Beckett's Collaboration with *Merlin* on the English *Molloy*', in: *Samuel Beckett Today / Aujourd'hui* 26: 107-20.
— Verlaine, Paul (1968), Œuvres poétiques complètes (Paris: Gallimard).
— Virgil (1999), *Eclogues, Georgics, Aeneid I-VI*, ed. by G. P. Goold, trans. by H. Rushton Fairclough (Cambridge and London: Harvard University Press).

— von der Vogelweide, Walther (1994), *Werke, Band 1: Spruchlyrik* (Stuttgart: Reclam).
— Weller, Shane (2011), 'Beckett's Last Chance: Les Éditions de Minuit', in: *Publishing Samuel Beckett*, ed. by Mark Nixon (London: British Library), 111-30.
— Wimbush, Andy (2015), 'The Pretty Quietist Pater: Samuel Beckett's *Molloy* and the Aesthetics of Quietism', in: *Literature and Theology* (Advance Access): 1-17.
— Winstanley, Adam (2014), '"Grâce aux excréments des citoyens": Beckett, Swift and the Coprophagic Economy of Ballyba', in: *Samuel Beckett Today / Aujoud'hui* 26: 91-105.
— Wordsworth, William (1936), *Poetical Works*, ed. by Thomas Hutchinson, rev. by Ernest de Selincourt (Oxford: Oxford University Press).
— Woolf, Virginia (2000), *Mrs Dalloway*, ed. by Elaine Showalter (London: Penguin).
— Zeller, Hans (1995), 'Record and Interpretation: Analysis and Documentation as Goal and Method of Editing', in: *Contemporary German Editorial Theory*, ed. by Hans Walter Gabler, George Bornstein and Gillian Borland Pierce. (Ann Arbor: The University of Michigan Press), 17-58.

Index